RELEASED

Service Quality

Issues in Organization and Management Series
Arthur P. Brief and Benjamin Schneider, *Editors*

Employee Ownership in America:
  The Equity Solution
Corey Rosen, Katherine J. Klein, and
  Karen M. Young

Generalizing from Laboratory to
  Field Settings
Research Findings from
  Industrial-Organizational Psychology,
  Organizational Behavior, and Human
  Resource Management
Edwin A. Locke, editor

Working Together to Get Things Done
Managing for Organizational Productivity
Dean Tjosvold

Self-Esteem at Work
Research, Theory, and Practice
Joel Brockner

Implementing Routine and Radical
  Innovations
A Comparative Study
Walter R. Nord and Sharon Tucker

The Outsiders
The Jews and Corporate America
Abraham Korman

Organizational Citizenship Behavior
The Good Soldier Syndrome
Dennis W. Organ

Facilitating Work Effectiveness
F. David Schoorman and
  Benjamin Schneider, editors

Futures of Organizations
Innovating to Adapt Strategy and
  Human Resources to Rapid
  Technological Change
Jerald Hage, editor

The Lessons of Experience
How Successful Executives Develop on
  the Job
Morgan W. McCall, Jr.,
  Michael A. Lombardo, and
  Ann M. Morrison

The Invisible Powers
The Language of Business
John Clancy

The Processes of Technological
  Innovation
Louis G. Tornatzky and
  Mitchell Fleischer

Pygmalion in Management
Productivity as a Self-Fulfilling Prophecy
Dov Eden

Service Management and Marketing
Managing the Moments of Truth in
  Service Competition
Christian Grönroos

Meanings of Occupational Work
A Collection of Essays
Arthur P. Brief and Walter R. Nord

Service Quality

Multidisciplinary and Multinational Perspectives

Edited by

Stephen W. Brown
Arizona State University

Evert Gummesson
University of Karlstad

Bo Edvardsson
University of Karlstad

BengtOve Gustavsson
University of Karlstad

This volume represents the cooperative efforts of the Service Research Center at the University of Karlstad (Sweden) and the First Interstate Center for Services Marketing at Arizona State University (United States).

Lexington Books

D.C. Heath and Company/Lexington, Massachusetts/Toronto

Library of Congress Cataloging-in-Publication Data

Service quality : multidisciplinary and multinational perspectives /
  edited by Stephen W. Brown . . . [et. al.].
    p.   cm.
   Includes index.
   ISBN 0-669-21152-4 (alk. paper)
   1. Service industries—Quality control—Congresses.   I. Brown,
Stephen Walter, 1943– .
HD9980.5.S4253   1991
658.5'62—dc20   90-38082
                                      CIP

Published simultaneously in Canada
Printed in the United States of America
International Standard Book Number: 0-669-21152-4
Library of Congress Catalog Card Number 90-38082

The paper used in this publication meets the minimum requirements of
American National Standard for Information Sciences—Permanence of
Paper for Printed Library Materials, ANSI Z39.48-1984. ∞ ™

Year and number of this printing:

91 92 10 9 8 7 6 5 4 3 2 1

Contents

Part III   How to Implement Service Quality   155

Foreword

Jan Carlzon
President, Scandinavian Airlines System (SAS)

I n order to develop a business successfully, managers should listen to the market and their own customer-contact staff, as well as researchers; theory and practice should go hand in hand. Therefore, I urge all executives in service companies—and also those in manufacturing companies, where services are growing in importance—to read this book carefully; reflect on the ideas, theories, models, and empirical results; and try them out in their companies.

This book is about service quality, and quality is a major factor for achieving commercial success. A quality culture that permeates the entire company constitutes the competitive edge in the present-day business world.

Service quality is a matter of knowing your customers, designing services to meet customers' needs, and finally managing the service production and delivery process to the customers' satisfaction. For SAS—Scandinavian Airlines System—and other Scandinavian companies, quality management is a key factor in strategic development. At SAS this means that we want to be the airline that the frequent business traveler prefers to all others. We want to provide quality services.

Nations have gradually begun to understand the vital importance of the service sector. In many countries up to 70 percent of all employees work in services. Net increases in the number of jobs in many economies stem mainly from service organizations, both private businesses and governmental bodies. The service sector accounts for 70 to 80 percent of all investment in information technology.

Although services have been growing in importance for decades, the interest in service quality is of recent origin. Researchers from our part of the world have made significant contributions. "The Nordic School of Services"—with Christian Grönroos, Evert Gummesson, and Richard Normann, among others—plays a central role in developing management thinking for service organizations.

To establish the state-of-the-art in research on service quality, an international symposium—Quality in Services (QUIS)—was held at the Service

Research Center (CTF), University of Karlstad, Sweden, in August 1988. SAS proudly accepted the invitation to become a sponsor of this event, which attracted leading researchers in the area of service quality. Their contributions are presented in this book. A unique aspect of this book is that the contributors come from many disciplines and from many countries. The book thus provides an overview of service quality research not to be found elsewhere.

Foreword

Benjamin Schneider
Series Editor, Lexington Books

Arthur P. Brief
Series Editor, Lexington Books

How do economists, political scientists, marketers, and industrial-organizational psychologists conceptualize service? What is the difference between delivering service in a chain of budget hotels in England and delivering home-care services to the elderly in Sweden? What is high-quality service and does the definition of high-quality service differ in different cultures?

Answers to these and many other questions are found in this book, the product of an international, multidisciplinary, conference on service quality held in Sweden in 1988. The conference was sponsored by the Service Research Center at the University of Karlstad (Sweden) in cooperation with the First Interstate Center for Services Marketing at Arizona State University (United States). Organizers of the conference persuaded a broad range of consultants, academics, and government leaders to contribute their insights into understanding what service is, how to assess service quality, and how to improve the delivery of service.

What emerges from this collection of papers from different perspectives is a montage of the wide variety of issues that constitute service quality. This is not surprising for those who have seriously studied either service or quality. Yet, having the issues so thoroughly discussed, as they are here, makes extremely clear the idea that service quality is not just a smile and a handshake. Unfortunately, the smile-and-a-handshake approach to service quality seems to be the one business people try first when attempting to improve service quality. This approach fails to produce results because it fails to consider the social, political, economic, psychological, and marketing issues surrounding the definition and perception of quality. It also fails because it places the burden of service quality on the deliverers of service rather than on the systems in which those deliverers function. The editors of this book have chosen their authors well—no one reading the chapters here can come away with anything less than that service quality is the responsibility of management. Management must create the systems by which quality can be delivered.

A most interesting feature of this collection is the multicultural perspective it presents on service quality. As our world becomes increasingly integrated, we will all need to understand the differences and similarities in the ways we think about many things, including service and service quality. Business people interested in moving into new multicultural markets will find clues and suggestions here for issues requiring attention if they are to be successful in these new markets. In addition, academics interested in the multicultural study of service production and delivery will find here many models and frameworks requiring elaboration and testing.

We are extremely pleased that the editors selected our series as an outlet for this book. The book makes a broad-based and interesting contribution to the growing study of service and quality, and, in that way, is a unique contribution to the literature.

Preface

Quality has become *the* 1990s byword of businesspeople, government officials, and business and economics scholars. Consumers, employees, management, and boards want quality. Most organizations claim to have it. In a special feature on quality improvement, the September 26, 1988, issue of *Fortune* magazine quoted Robert E. Allen, Chairman of the Board of AT&T, "Quality does all. It saves. It sells. It satisfies." While nearly everyone recognizes the pervasive impact of quality, at the same time, everyone seems to have difficulty grasping its many dimensions.

We do know that quality contributes to customer satisfaction, market strength, and profitability. Studies show that customers are often willing to pay higher prices for what they perceive to be higher quality. The Strategic Planning Institute has found that market share, return on investment, and asset turnover are all highly linked to the perceived quality of the company's goods and services. Through its well-known PIMS (Profit Impact of Market Strategy) program, the Institute has collected data on nearly three thousand strategic business units for periods of up to twelve years. This massive study concludes that in the long run, the most important single factor affecting a business unit's performance is the quality of its goods and services, relative to those of competitors.

Quality is especially difficult to define, describe, and measure in services. While quality and quality control measures have long existed for tangible goods, few such measures have traditionally existed for services. In essence, quality is determined by imprecise individual factors: perceptions, expectations and experiences of customers and providers, and, in some cases, additional parties such as public officials.

In addition to being elusive, quality means different things to different people. The growing importance of quality and the realization that its study requires the perspectives of a variety of academic disciplines led to a special symposium called Quality in Services in August 1988 at the University of Karlstad in Sweden.

xiv • *Service Quality*

The QUIS symposium was organized by the Service Research Center (CTF) at the University of Karlstad in cooperation with the First Interstate Center for Services Marketing at Arizona State University. Some discussion of this unique event is warranted because it served as the catalyst for the development of this book.

More than one hundred academics, business people, and government leaders participated in the symposium. The 25 people invited to present papers included some of the world's foremost authorities on service quality. Recognizing that this topic is not the exclusive domain of any one field or country, the symposium's chairs sought out and received participation from ten different countries and from scholars representing the disciplines of marketing, operations management, economics, psychology, political science, sociology, and linguistics. The multinational and multidisciplinary nature of the program participants proved to be the most valuable feature of the symposium. New vistas and insights were opened for the speakers and attendees as the scholars offered perspectives that were often novel.

The speakers were flown to Sweden from all over the globe courtesy of Scandinavian Airlines System (SAS), the major sponsor of the symposium. SAS has received international recognition in recent years for its customer orientation and service quality. Seventeen other corporate sponsors from Sweden also added support to the event.

The symposium was chaired by Evert Gummesson and co-chaired by Stephen W. Brown. Joined by Bo Edvardsson and BengtOve Gustavsson, the chairs concurred that the contributions from the QUIS symposium experience needed to be shared with a wider audience, which naturally led to the idea of developing a book representing a collection of the symposium's papers.

In producing this book, we wish to recognize and indicate appreciation to the authors of the papers, the other QUIS symposium attendees, the event's sponsors, the University of Karlstad, Arizona State University, our faculty collegues at our respective universities and our centers. In addition, a financial contribution towards the publication of this book has been received from the Swedish Council for Research in the Humanities and the Social Sciences.

We most importantly recognize the substantial contribution of Professor Michael Cooper of the University of Karlstad. In serving as the editorial consultant for the non-American papers, he polished much of the work and served as an inspiration to the editors with his diligence and performance. Serving in an appreciated editorial capacity for the American papers were Gretchen Rowe of Arizona State University and Goutam Challagalla, an MBA graduate of ASU and currently a doctoral student at the University of Texas at Austin. Ms. Rowe, in particular, added her special editorial capabilities to the entire manuscript as it neared final publication form. Also contributing in various ways were Pat Wira of the First Interstate

Center for Services Marketing and Donald Saunders, a Ph.D. candidate at ASU.

Special mention goes to Benjamin Schneider, a QUIS speaker and contributor to this volume, who also serves as a consulting editor for Lexington Books. His first-hand participation in the symposium experience enabled him to provide wise counsel to the editors and the publisher. Special appreciation is also extended to Robert D. Bovenschulte, Caroline McCarley, Karen E. Hansen, Lyri Merrill, Richard Tonachel, and the rest of the fine staff of Lexington Books.

Finally, we offer our deep and enduring thanks to our families for their love, encouragement, and understanding.

About the Research Centers

T his book and the symposium that preceded it represent the cooperative efforts of the four editors and the research centers with which they are associated. The centers are located in Sweden and the United States, and focus on management and marketing problems associated with the service sector of economies.

The Service Research Center (CTF) in Karlstad, Sweden, is the only one of its kind in Scandinavia to focus on management problems in the service sector. CTF's main activities are research and development, advanced management education, and network-building. Priority is given to the following areas:

the quality of services

public services

internationalization in service companies

services in manufacturing enterprises

The center's sponsors and clients include private companies and public authorities, large corporations and small enterprises. In direct cooperation with clients and with the participation of experts in research and education, the center offers courses and seminars. Its work is publicized by means of a Swedish newsletter.

The center is run by a board of directors with Dr. Bo Edvardsson as the executive director. It also has two research directors: Dr. Evert Gummesson, Professor of Service Management, and Dr. Benny Hjern, Professor of Political Science.

Its address is: Service Research Center
Box 9055
S-650 09 Karlstad
Sweden

The First Interstate Center for Services Marketing (FICSM) at Arizona State University is North America's leading university-based program for services marketing and management study and research. The FICSM's objectives are (1) to expand the frontiers of knowledge through research in services and (2) to enhance student and executive education in services based on a solid foundation of research. Some of the major topics being investigated include the following:

building the service relationship

professional and client perceptions of service quality

impact of physical surroundings and employee responses on consumer satisfaction

Results of many of the studies have been published in leading journals and are available as part of the center's working paper series.

In addition to encouraging student education, the FICSM offers a select number of executive education programs, most notable being the acclaimed Services Marketing Institute, cosponsored annually with the American Marketing Association and held on the ASU campus.

A board of advisers composed of distinguished executives and university leaders provides direction to the center. Firms participate through a charter membership program. FICSM includes Executive Director, Dr. Stephen W. Brown and the involvement of key faculty, Drs. Teresa A. Swartz and Lawrence A. Crosby; Services Marketing Institute Directors, Michael P. Mokwa and Mary Jo Bitner; and staff members Pat Wira and Gretchen Rowe. The Center also benefits from its close tie to the ASU Department of Marketing and the marketing faculty.

Its address is: First Interstate Center for Services Marketing
College of Business
Arizona State University
Tempe, AZ 85287-4106
U.S.A.

Service Quality

Part 1
What Is Service Quality?

Defining quality in services is especially difficult because of the intangible nature of the service offering. The definition of quality may vary from person to person and from situation to situation. In this section, service quality is examined from a variety of perspectives in an attempt to provide a frame of reference for further discussions on the topic. Issues from theory and practice are brought together to form an interesting and thought-provoking collage of service-quality considerations.

This section begins by addressing service quality from a theoretical perspective. Evert Gummesson's chapter provides an integrative perspective that merges *production*—do things right—and *marketing*—do the right things—orientations with interfunctional actions, which results in customer-perceived quality. Quality, productivity, and profits are interrelated, and Gummesson argues that when the customer notices a difference in quality, the ultimate effect will be seen in the corporate bottom line.

The critical time for service quality to be clearly defined is in the one-to-one interactions that occur between the consumer and the provider. Because most services are created and delivered simultaneously, these "moments of truth" must be managed well if customer-perceived quality is to be assured. Mary Jo Bitner's chapter traces the evolution of the service marketing mix, focusing on "moments of truth," or service encounters. The mix is presented as a useful tool for effectively managing or enhancing the quality of service encounters. Looking at services, Bitner augments the traditional four P's of marketing (product, price, place, and promotion) with the additional P's of physical evidence, participants, and process. She presents a model to evaluate the service encounter and provides a frame of reference for continued research.

Benny Hjern and Lennart Blomquist's chapter presents a compelling case for the difficulty in achieving service quality in complex settings. In the context of geriatric care, they describe the intricacies of organizing for service quality when the service is co-produced by service professionals and government agencies. They point out that defining customer needs and appropriate resource allocations are potential pitfalls in co-produced service settings.

Concluding this section is an economic perspective of service quality presented by Orio Giarini. While services are generally viewed as secondary to goods production, this chapter presents a carefully crafted argument for the economic value of service quality. Most costs result from the services necessary to produce and deliver the good or service. Giarini argues that service functions intervene in various levels of the production process, and the value of the service is a function of the level of performance provided.

1
Service Quality
A Holistic View

Evert Gummesson

Quality turns out to be extremely difficult to define in a few words, a trait it shares with many phenomena in business and social sciences. It is rather a matter of creating a deeper insight into the many dimensions that form a fuzzy entity that, through social consensus, is referred to as quality.

So much is currently happening with service quality—in many disciplines, in many countries, and in many languages—that no one can claim to present anything but a personal state-of-the-art snapshot, a photograph taken and developed on the spot. Language barriers prevent one from retrieving all existing sources, a reason the accounts are too often limited to references from the most widely spread English-speaking magazines and books. Written sources for important developments may be lacking, or they may be proprietary information hidden inside organizations.

Vantage Points

A *holistic perspective* rests on the following four propositions:

1. *Quality is an integrator in two respects: between production-orientation and marketing-orientation, and between interdepartmental activities in processes.*

    One could list a large number of definitions of quality (Garvin 1984), but two are of particular value. The first is primarily *technology-driven* and *production-oriented* definition: quality is *conformance to requirements* (Crosby 1984). It states that in order to achieve quality a company must establish requirement specifications, and once these are established the quality goal of the various functions of the firm is to comply strictly with these specifications. This is *quality management: Do things right!*

    A crucial question is: Whose requirements and whose specifications? The second definition states that quality is *fitness for use* (Juran

1982). This definition is primarily market-driven and customer-oriented as it puts customer utility and satisfaction in focus. It raises the question of what should be included in the specifications, *Do the right things!*

The two definitions can be united in the concept of *customer-perceived quality:* quality is in the eye of the customer. This is often considered to be a *subjective quality*, an erroneous conclusion; customer-perceived quality is a blend of objective facts and subjective judgments, of knowledge as well as of ignorance. Equally unfortunate is suppliers' notion that only they are able to produce *objective quality*, considering themselves experts and the customers amateurs. It is a dangerous notion—the provider turns into Big Brother and will not be sensitive to customer needs and wants. This can easily turn into "specsmanship," a bureaucratic and rigid adherence to technological specifications (specs) with limited interest in customer utility, in effect, nothing more than *vendor-perceived quality*.

The traditional doctor-patient relationship is an example of the unfortunate consequences of providers' distorted views: doctors consider themselves expert and their patients ignorant; doctors see themselves as curers, their patients as passive recipients. Actually, doctors' knowledge is quite limited even if they know facts about diseases that patients do not. Patients have knowledge about themselves and how they feel that doctors may have great difficulty in discovering. It is more realistic to accept that doctors treat patients both from a medical, objective point of view and from a subjective view that is influenced by experience, intuition, empathy, personal chemistry, and mood. Both behave objectively and subjectively, both are ignorant and knowledgeable in some kind of unidentified mix. A key concept is *interactive production* in which quality contributions come from the concerted efforts of customer and provider.

A prevalent reaction is that improved quality is expensive. For example, silver spoons are more costly to produce than plastic spoons and consumers will have to pay a higher price. This approach deters the development of quality. Instead quality is a matter of finding the *right quality*, the quality that fits a specific customer segment. The price becomes part of customers' perception of quality: they do not expect a Mercedes for the price of a small Japanese car. They may want the luxury car but are not blaming the small car for bad quality because of that.

Customer-perceived quality as the target for providers' efforts has already reached a high level of acceptance (more so in statements than in actual implementation, though). In order to achieve quality operations management must be united with marketing management, fitness for use with conformance to requirements. This leads to a rather dramatic conclusion that has not yet been properly brought to general attention: *Quality is the integrating concept between production-orientation and marketing-orientation, between technology and customer satisfaction.*

But this thinking concerns not only the *external* customer. In quality management the *internal* customer has been introduced: all employees should see themselves as customers of colleagues from whom they receive products, documents, messages, decisions, and so on. Ishikawa, one of the fathers of modern quality management, used the slogan "the next process is your customer" back in the 1950s "to resolve fierce hostility between workers from different production processes of a steel mill . . ." and "still uses it today in his lifelong effort to break through the barriers of sectionalism in business organizations" (Lu 1985, viii; Ishikawa 1985). Principles of process management have long been used in manufacturing; these principles are now being applied to administrative operations and internal services (Kane 1986). There is no doubt that the barriers between different specialists and functions severely hamper efficiency and quality; when processes become chains with missing or weak links, they become victims of "tribal warfare" (Neuhauser 1988). Thus a further conclusion could be drawn: *Quality can be used as an integrating concept between all activities and processes, thus replacing the less dynamic and often rigid "administrative routines."*

2. *All companies produce/sell both goods and services (although the ratio may be different between the two). Thus, in managing quality, companies must pay respect to both goods and service quality and the synergy effects between them.*

Service companies need two different types of products in their production of services. First, they need consumables. Second, they need to invest in goods in order to establish their service operation: buildings, machinery, and other equipment. For example, a manufacturer of computers has to consider goods quality in purchased components in its manufactured components, and in assembly. But he is also a provider of services, such as customized software, training and education of customers, delivery services, installation, and maintenance. The supplier of consumer goods, for example eggs, may provide services to the producers—the farmers—by collecting the eggs at the farms, and inspecting, packaging, and distributing them to wholesalers, retailers, restaurants, and so on. A hotel is traditionally classified as a service business, but in connection with its core service—overnight stays—it provides buildings, beds, food, and other products. In all these cases, the combined quality of goods and services has to be handled properly. Thus, all firms must understand and implement the essentials of goods quality as well as service quality.

3. *Quality of computer software is of crucial importance to both service companies and manufacturing companies.*

   Seventy to 80 percent of investment in information technology—computers and telecommunications—goes to service industries (Quinn, Jordan, and Paquette 1987, p. 56). An illustration of the significance of software quality for services is provided the very day this chapter is being written: the radio reports that a twenty-three-year-old student in the United States has managed, almost overnight, to install a virus in sixty thousand computers, paralyzing research institutions and damaging top secret military databases. Research and defense are just two service operations heavily dependent on software, both for data processing and for communications.

4. *Quality, productivity, and profits are triplets; separating one from the other creates an unhappy family.*

   The *PIMS—Profit Impact of Market Strategy*—studies on the covariation between quality and profits support the conclusion that quality pays: "There is no doubt that relative perceived quality and profitability are strongly related . . . business with a superior product/service offering clearly outperform those with inferior quality" (Buzzell and Gale 1987, p. 107).

   Quality affects all the variables that constitute the profit formula: *revenue, cost,* and *capital* investment. Quality improvements affect revenue through an *improved image, increased sales, economy of scale,* and *decreased price competition.* They affect cost through *diminished costs for rework, scrap, warranty,* and *product liability.* Finally, *work-in-progress* and *inventory* are reduced, and orders can be filled and invoiced earlier, leading to *faster payment.* Consequently, *capital is freed for alternative investment.* All this *improves productivity* and eventually the *bottom line.* Several of these effects concern service operations. Still further implications exist for services, a company selling machinery that requires services like installation and maintenance, for example. Installation costs go down, as do costs for maintenance and repair. This could be used as a selling argument. The result is a smaller service organization with lower costs for staff, service vans, telephone calls, and so on.

   The successful turn-around of SAS (Scandinavian Airlines System) in the early 1980s can be attributed to the fact that revenue, cost, and capital were balanced, with quality, productivity, and revenue as the focal point for action (Carlzon 1987).

   From these vantage points, which constitute a paradigm for approaching service quality, this chapter will deal with four types of quality: *goods quality, service quality, computer software quality*— all of crucial importance for success in service operations. Eventually, I would like to introduce the concept *holistic quality* as an extension of the concept total quality management (or *total quality control*) currently in use.

Goods Quality: The Grand Elder

There is no doubt that goods quality is the grand elder. This elder is nearly seventy years old if the use of the statistical control chart is marked as the birth of the modern, systematic approach to quality management. Yet the elder has not retired but is more vigorous than ever. In fact, two of the most influential international personalities in the field of quality, J. M. Juran and W. Edwards Deming, are both more than eighty-five years old and still going strong.

A selection of dishes from the goods quality smorgasbord follows. The selection is based on experience, as well as on insights spelled out by a number of authors. It should demonstrate the rich know-how available for service firms. The major written sources are Crosby (1979, 1984), Deming (1986) and his "interpreter" Scherkenbach (1986), Ishikawa (1982, 1985), Juran (1979, 1982, 1987), and Taguchi (1981). Many of these sources claim that their conclusions and recommendations work equally well for services. The concepts emanate, though, from a long manufacturing tradition rather than from the adolescent service management culture described in the next section. These insights can be applied to services *as long as one understands the specific characteristics of services and adjusts the use accordingly.*

Quality inspection has probably existed since time immemorial. In its simplest form, before the good is delivered the provider inspects it to make certain that it fulfills his requirements. Consumers make several inspections of goods; for example, when in a supermarket, they look at and touch a fruit. In industry the inspections may be extremely sophisticated, such as a factory using high-tech instruments to measure selected parameters of the performance of an engine.

The introduction of *quality control* is attributed to Walter A. Shewhart's use of the control chart and statistical process control (SPC) at Bell Telephone Laboratories during the 1920s (Shewhart 1931). Whereas quality inspection aims at *removing bad products before shipment or purchase*, quality control aims at *increasing the percentage of good products being manufactured.*

Continuing improvements has been implemented with great force by the Japanese since the 1950s. Its basic notion is that one must never rest in the effort to improve quality. By keeping an open mind to improvements, organizing feedback from customers, sales people, service people, and so on, and by making use of advances in technology, management techniques, and so forth, quality can be continuously improved.

Continuing improvements already suggest that quality work is *long term.* This does not mean that it necessarily takes a long period to achieve results; some come instantly but others, such as changing the quality culture, will take time.

QC Circles (Quality Control Circles), where everyone in an organization becomes engaged in quality, are successfully used by the Japanese as an instrument for ongoing improvements. Though the use of QC Circles in the Western world has often been a success, they have frequently failed as well, an example of the need for sensitivity in finding applications that fit different national and corporate cultures.

Prevention means that defects should be avoided at the source. It is an emphasis on *cause control* instead of *result control*. It recognizes that as soon as a mistake is allowed to enter a production process, poor quality starts to cost money: the costs of correction and of customer dissatisfaction. The slogan is: "Do it right the first time!"

Quality-by-design or *designed-in quality* means that quality should be designed in from conception. Goods are designed through the establishment of *specifications, blueprints, prototypes,* and *pilot series* of the new or revised good. When the design is completed and the good is being manufactured, not much can be done about it except grumbling about inefficient performance and the constant need for servicing. One essential aspect is to make the design *robust,* meaning that it should be relatively insensitive to likely variations in materials, components, and the environment of the factory, as well as that of the user (Taguchi 1981). Like quality control, designed-in quality is preventive; the design stage is the first stage where a company can "do it right." According to Deming (1986, p.315) 94 percent of all defects are designed into the system and will thus be continuously repeated, while the operator can only influence 6 percent.

Quality should be measured by *internal and external measures* preferably in quantitative terms: "What gets measured, gets done!" The focal point can be the internal process in the company, or the external processes, that is customer-related measures like attitudes toward a product. Both measures are extremely important, but the tradition for those involved in quality management is directed toward internal measures and conformance to specifications. The current focus on customer-perceived quality and fitness for use is reflected in a trend toward more market research. This trend shows, for example, in the application guidelines for the *United States National Quality Award* where as much as 30 percent of the points are gained in customer-related measurement (United States Department of Commerce and National Institute of Standards and Technology 1989).

The traditional strategy in industrial production is to allow a certain percentage of defective goods in a shipment to the customer. There are elaborate methods for measuring and controlling this *acceptable quality level.* The rationale behind not requiring perfection is that it would be too costly and a point exists at which the sum of the costs for goods quality and the cost incurred by customer dissatisfaction reaches a minimum. The *zero defects* strategy refutes this approach, claiming that it leads to sloppiness. Instead the question should be: "What can be done to move the cost minimum toward zero by improved systems, organization, product design, production control, inspection methods, more motivated personnel, investment in better equipment, and so on?" Thus redesigning the service production system until it approaches zero defects. All the same, defects will occur, but *defects should not be allowed to remain in the system and to be repeated.*

Benchmarking is best known for being used by Xerox worldwide in its long-term quality improvement program. Benchmarking reflects the fact that target-setting methods have largely failed, stimulating the *mediocre* instead of the *best:*

> The benefits of using benchmarking are that functions are forced to investigate external industry best practices and incorporate those practices into their operations. This leads to profitable, high-asset utilization businesses that meet customer needs and have a competitive advantage (Camp 1989, p. 62).

Quality is not the sole concern of quality professionals or a quality department; it is the concern of every individual in an organization. *Everyone contributes to quality.* This is emphasized in the *4 Q contribution model* (Gummesson 1987), which states that final quality has its source in everyone's work and that there are four major qualities, the 4 Qs, to which the personnel can contribute: *design quality, production quality, delivery quality,* and *relational quality.*

Management Commitment is often referred to as the single most important factor for success but all too often lip service reigns. A commonplace situation is top management kicking off a major quality improvement program, then delegating quality to a vice president of quality, or worse, two tiers further down the pyramid, to a quality staff manager with extremely limited access to the CEO.

Concluding Comments on Techniques, Methods, and Programs.

Extensive know-how is available from quality work in the manufacturing sector. Only a selection has been listed; other techniques are in general use, such as *statistical process control, SPC* (for continuous follow-up of quality and removal of causes of unquality), Ishikawa's *fishbone analysis* (to identify causes of unquality). Juran's *pareto analysis* (identifying the "vital few and the trivial many"), and programs such as *Deming's 14 point program*. Each company has to make or develop its own selection of techniques. For example, in *Excellence—The IBM Way*, Harrington (1988, p.7) listed the following as instrumental in creating IBM quality: *design review, design evaluation, in-process inspection, failure analysis, process qualification, supplier surveys, field and in-process reporting, customer surveys, operator training, acceptable quality levels based on customer requirements, basic beliefs by management that excellence is a way of life,* and *standard quality practices.* These items can be further broken down into a series of techniques, for example, how to make different kinds of customer surveys.

The relevance of the quality smorgasbord to services will be reviewed later in relation to holistic quality.

Service Quality: The Adolescent

Service quality is an adolescent, a teenager, attempting to break into the adult world but who is still in an unstable condition and not quite ready.

Research in services started to grow in the late 1970s in several parts of the world but altogether only a handful people were involved. Researchers, consultants, and practitioners from Northern Europe were among the pioneers, and *The Nordic School of Services* became a designation for contributions mainly from Sweden and Finland (Grönroos and Gummesson 1985). Individual researchers and organizations in France, the United Kingdom, and the United States were also in the forefront.

The real trendsetter among service firms in Northern Europe was SAS, the international airline owned by the governments and private industry of Sweden, Denmark, and Norway (Carlzon, 1987). In Northern Europe, service management and the development of service companies and public authorities have grown into a movement.

Through this work, quality has gradually come to be seen as the most important issue. This conclusion is supported by a recent study carried out among executives in 128 major European corporations. Of eighteen key strategic marketing issues, the number one priority for the 1990s was: "Coping with the increasing importance of product quality and greater service content" (Larreché, Powell, and Ebeling 1987, p. 22).

Service quality stands out for several reasons:

- Service industries lag behind in systematic quality efforts.
- There is considerable customer dissatisfaction with service quality.
- Manufacturing firms need to differentiate their goods from those of competitors, and added services provide such opportunities.
- The public sector, which was originally meant to serve the citizen, has

lost its mission to a large extent. It has grown steadily, burdening taxpayers, at the same time being accused of high costs, inefficiency, and low quality. Efforts to get it back on its original course are being made in various ways, among them deregulation and privatization.

In an attempt to classify the approaches to service quality, the following four categories have been chosen: *dimensions of service quality, gap analysis, the design approach,* and *the direct application of quality know-how from goods to services.* These categories will be briefly presented.

Dimensions of Service Quality

One approach to quality is to list those characteristics essential in assessing the quality of a service. In one model, customer-perceived service quality is viewed as the result of two generic types of quality: *technical* (or *output*) quality and *functional* (or *process*) quality (Grönroos 1984; Lehtinen 1985). The first determinant corresponds to traditional quality control in manufacturing: it is a matter of properly producing the core benefit of the service. One example is surgery, which should be of lasting value: the patient should survive, not suffer side effects, not be forced to live uncomfortably (e.g., because of a visible scar), and not have to repeat the operation unnecessarily. The second, which is a novel dimension, is the way the service is delivered; it is the process in which the customer is a participant and co-producer. In the case of surgery, the patient may experience the event as pleasant (or at least less unpleasant) depending on the hospital environment, the sympathy of doctors and nurses, the behavior of fellow patients, and so on.

Parasuraman, Zeithaml, and Berry (1985) identified ten determinants of service quality that may relate to any service: *reliability, responsiveness, competence, access, courtesy, communication, credibility, security, understanding/ knowing the customer,* and *tangibles.* Later these were boiled down to five: *tangibles, reliability, responsiveness, assurance,* and *empathy* (Parasuraman, Zeithaml, and Berry 1988). Grönroos (1988) has suggested six criteria, five of which coincide with those previously listed, whereas the sixth adds an essential dimension—*recovery.* This has the same effect as the *junk yard strategy,* which is used to supplement the *zero defects strategy:* "The junk yard refers to the pile of bad products and services which are delivered to customers and which cause dissatisfaction. There should be a clear strategy to remove the junk and make the customers happy" (Gummesson 1988).

The significance of these quality characteristics can vary considerably between types of services and individual buyers. For example, bank customers are likely to find security a prime determinant although security would mean little to consumers of a shoeshine service.

Gap Analysis

It is trivial to state that people perceive reality differently: a vendor believes he is delivering the proper quality while the customer thinks otherwise. There are, then, *perception gaps*. However trivial the conclusion, in managing organizations and customer relations, various gaps interfere with quality.

Parasuraman, Zeithaml, and Berry (1985) have identified five gaps:

1. consumer expectation—management perception gap
2. management perception—service quality specification gap
3. service quality specifications—service delivery gap
4. service delivery—external communications gap
5. expected service—perceived service gap

The basic idea is that when these gaps exist, quality is at stake. The strategy should be to narrow and eventually close the gaps. Thus, the right quality, the perfect fit, is achieved.

Another gap model, referred to as *consistency analysis*, is proposed by Edvardsson and Gustavsson (1989). It is a diagnostic model identifying inconsistencies, gaps, on two scales: (1) between *ideas and goals* at one end and *implementation and actual results* at the other; (2) between the *formal and official* at one end and the *informal and subjectively experienced* at the other. These scales combine into a four-cell matrix and constitute the basis for auditing a service organizations's quality and productivity.

Design Approach

In this approach the constituent parts of the service are identified. They are the design of the service, its specification, and how the items of the specification are connected; the approach corresponds to the blueprint used in manufacturing.

Shostack's *blueprinting* (1984, 1987) is a method by which the service production and delivery process is described, including chains of activities, the use of facilitating goods and equipment, and time and cost effects. The same advantages can be gained from blueprinting the service as from blueprinting an engine. It makes it possible to overview the offering and all its interrelated parts and look at it from various angles: strategy, production, purchasing, quality, productivity, organization, and so on. It is also a prerequisite for making employees comprehend the service delivery process and their own contribution to the quality of the service. Applications of blueprinting are reported by Kingman-Brundage (1988) and George and Gibson (1990).

In a model by Dale and Wooler (1990)—*Strategy and Organization for Service (SOS)*—parts, activities, events, and so on constituting the service are identified, assessed, and structured. The work is carried out in a project group by eliciting group members' experience and judgment, and structuring the information by means of a computer program. The output is a type of blueprint that identifies the parts of the service, their significance for quality and profits, and their present performance. From this, an action program to improve the service can be established.

Gummesson (1978) identified eight generic components that constitute the core of professional service:

1. *specialist know-how*
2. *the individual professional*
3. *other resources and attributes*
4. *the diagnosis and formulation of the problem and the goal of a specific assignment*
5. *the way to operate the assignment*
6. *the solution to the problem*
7. *the implementation of the solution*
8. *the result of the implemented solution*

These components can be combined into different designs for the professional service.

Direct Application of Quality Know-how from Goods to Services

The approaches previously mentioned are based on the unique features of services and the theories of service management and marketing that developed during the late 1970s and the 1980s. They recognize that services are different in nature from products and therefore require novel approaches to quality. The application of know-how from manufacturing is highly pertinent in relation to number two above, which stated that service companies are dependent on goods for their operations. It also seems to have been the most common way to approach service quality in general. It is a dangerous approach, though, if the "soul" of services is not properly understood. Rosander (1985, p. 4) has warned against the dangers of imitating factory practices:

> There is a strong tendency to apply quality control techniques to service operations without careful analysis of the quality aspects and requirements of the latter . . . the customer . . . may be ignored because all the empha-

sis is placed on the internal operations of the company . . . on techniques such as systems analysis, cost-benefit analysis, statistical methods, and the like.

There have probably been discussions for decades on the problems of service quality and how quality management from the product sector can be applied to services. One such example was presented in an article by a Mariott director (Hostage 1975). He discussed quality in hotels and restaurants, stressing the development of people as crucial for quality by quoting founder J. Willard Mariott's motto: "It takes happy employees to make happy customers." The article noted one important aspect of services: the role of the employee interacting with customers adds new dimensions to quality control. When that difference and others have not been understood, the straightforward application of quality know-how from the goods sector to services has sometimes led to catastrophic results. In many countries it showed during the 1960s and 1970s when huge schools and hospitals were built on the notion that human beings are the same as mechanical components. Consequently, educational and health services were "manufactured" to take advantage of large-scale economies and specialization. In other service industries, status declined and services were not considered efficient unless they could be automated. Quality was forgotten and quantity became king.

One successful transfer of know-how from manufacturing to services is the self-service store and the supermarket. The assembly line principle was turned to retailing: the customers move along the assembly line—the shelves—and instead of waiting in a line, do the assembly. In some ways this has increased service quality, at the same time lowering costs. However, intoxicated by the belief in industrial efficiency, its designers went too far: the concept proved to work less well for certain types of fresh food such as bread, meat, fish, cheese and for delicatessen. Realizing this, and after some resistance, manual service was partially reintroduced in these areas.

With these expressed warnings in mind, the contributions from goods quality should be investigated and adjusted for possible use in service operations.

Computer Software Quality:
The Juvenile Delinquent

One type of quality that clearly unites goods and services is the *quality of computer software*. In service quality modeling so far, no particular emphasis has been placed on software quality although computers are of prime importance in service operations. Data processing and telecommunications constitute a significant part of many services, such as air travel, banking, and professional services.

But why label software quality a juvenile delinquent? It is a metaphor to emphasize a phenomenon that causes trouble to others, lacks roots and is unstable, often will not cooperate, and exhibits behavior that is a riddle to those not belonging to the tribe of programmers.

One might argue that software quality is no more important than the quality of human resources, the quality of computer hardware, buildings, airplanes, or other components needed to produce services. However, software quality needs to be spotlighted for several reasons. First, most of the interest in service quality is directed toward human resources and less toward the intricacies of nonhuman information processing. Second, computer hardware, buildings, vehicles, and so forth are the target of product quality management. Third, services are extremely vulnerable to computer whims and caprices: down time, bugs, security problems, viruses. Fourth, as a result of information technology, investment in service industries has increased enormously. Fifth, software quality has its own unique features such as the debugging of a program. Sixth, programming is a highly specialized profession. Finally, the quality management of software is of recent origin and the rapid development of electronics, creating new computer generations at a fast pace, has not left the quality of computer software to mature disturbed.

What are the unique characteristics of quality management of computer software? To quote Dunn and Ullman (1982, p.71):

> Computer software is produced by well-defined disciplines, presumably executed by bright, clear-eyed men and women . . . computer programs are inherently precise and contain no mechanical or electrical parts that can degrade in performance. What could possibly go wrong? . . . Unfortunately, just about everything.

Everyone probably has some personal experience with software problems. The problems are caused by a number of circumstances (Dunn and Ullman, p. 78):

- One hundred percent testing is impossible because of program complexity. Thus, programs are often put into use with latent "bugs" that may surface unpredictably.
- Programs do not take into account all aspects of the operational environment.
- Software maintenance is difficult because of incomplete documentation, complex program flow, and poor modularity.

- If the computer is replaced, the transport of a program to the new computer may prove hazardous.
- Loss of configuration control occurs when the program is put into actual use.

As an addendum to this list, a communication gap exists between computer specialists and those who understand the management of a specific service. They belong to different tribes, their jargon is different, and they see the world from different vantage points. Computer specialists tend to ignore or not fully grasp the significance of the "moments of truth" and how customer interaction and customer-perceived quality affect a business; managers may not be able to define demands on a program as their knowledge is partly "tacit knowledge," lacking concepts and terms for communication. This, of course, leads to a plea for more explicit service design, taking advantage of the emerging design techniques.

The unique nature of software makes the techniques used to manage goods and service quality less applicable. Originating in the 1960s, a specific tradition of software quality management is being developed that provides methods and techniques such as *measurement of complexity* and *error history analysis*.

As computer software is so crucial for many services, service quality is heavily influenced by its software. Computer programming often constitutes a major portion of the service design, rapid information processing being the core of the services. Thus, quality development in the information technology industry is a prerequisite for the successful service operations of its customers.

Holistic Quality: The Baby

Holistic quality is a newborn baby who observes, touches, smells, tastes, trying to form a worldview. The baby expresses itself in cries and laughs, but lacks words and concepts for communication. Much is expected of this infant when it grows up; may it assume leadership in the quality battlefield.

The general interest in quality management in the service sector started sixty years later than in the goods sector; software quality is still young and unstable. From a services perspective, however, the time should be ripe to integrate thinking from all quality areas because, within service management and marketing, unique concepts and models are contributing to a new service theory; services no longer risk being tyrannized by manufacturing-oriented quality management.

So far, research and literature have concentrated on either goods, services, or software and have perhaps mentioned the others in passing; they do not explicitly integrate the thinking from all three areas. Also those engaged in goods quality have often not seen service quality as particularly significant and unique, treating it as a stepchild. The recent models of service quality that have been widely publicized are also limited in scope.

Only a limited number of texts treat the combination of goods and service quality. In an article from 1985, King pointed out differences in quality control between services and goods. Voss et al. (1985) used their knowledge from manufacturing to analyze service production and quality issues; the same approach is reflected in Johnston (1988). One attempt at integration has been made by Gummesson and Grönroos (1987), who combined two models of quality, one based on the study of services, the other on manufacturing. Langeard (1987) used the concept ISGO, "Integrated Services and Goods Offering."

Goods quality, service quality, and computer software quality each have generic traits that make them different to deal with. All three have a different history. At the same time, all appear in every company, whether it is called a manufacturing company or a service company and whether it belongs to the private or the public sector. Computer software is important to all of them. Administrative routines that could be turned into internal services exist in all companies. In order to achieve a superior end result, every company has to master all these types of quality.

Reviewing the Goods Quality Smorgasbord

Apart from realizing that service operations are also dependent on the quality of the tangible product, approaches, techniques, and experiences from manufacturing may contribute to excellence in services. The smorgasbord of quality dishes from manufacturing presented earlier in this chapter will be briefly reviewed in relation to service quality. This review cannot be as distinct as the world-renowned *Michelin Guide*, in which the quality of restaurants is assessed and each restaurant is assigned a number of stars. Unfortunately, a less precise evaluation must be used.

It may be more difficult to perform *inspection* on a service as one might need to consume the service at least once before knowing whether it has the proper quality. Moreover, service delivery is characterized by a high degree of variability, while the variability of mass-produced goods of a certain brand is low. Thus, the next time the same organization delivers a service, one may experience its quality as very different. The idea behind *quality control* is to increase the percentage of error-free products before they reach the customer. Who could actually object to such a strategy? However, the distinction between inspection and quality control becomes less obvious as services are co-produced to some degree by the customer, who may also consume them, at least partly, during the very production and delivery process. *Continuing improvements* are certainly essential for services. If a stage of superior quality has once been reached, it may quickly deteriorate if it is not continuously maintained and adjusted to new conditions. Improving and maintaining quality becomes a *long-term* commitment.

Many service firms in the Western world report successful application of *QC Circles* or variations on the circle concept; a much publicized example is *The Paul Revere Insurance Companies* (Townsend 1986). Of course, *prevention* must also be a key quality strategy in service firms since the cost of correcting errors increases the further from the source the errors are detected. *Designed-in quality* is the springboard to prevention: a clear outline of the service, a blueprint, and a robust design minimize sensitivity to variations in the behavior of staff, time of day, type of customer, and so on. Service development and design could learn from the systematic procedures used in the goods sector.

People often think it is more difficult to *measure* quality of services than the quality of goods. It is not more difficult but it is different, and measuring approaches have yet to be worked out. Those involved will have to learn to measure the correct and important quality factors: beware of superficial measures that are chosen because they are easily accessible and can be easily quantified! The *zero defects* approach is just as valid for services. It is a state of mind, never settling for second best, the same idea as reflected in *benchmarking:* Quality is *everyone's* concern. This approach is even more obvious in services where so many employees are involved in direct customer interaction. *Management commitment* is general and applicable to any type of organization.

This review reveals that the quality smorgasbord served by manufacturing offers a tempting array of opportunities to be consumed by service organizations. However, beware of indigestion if the dishes are swallowed too quickly and without consideration; no simple yes or no answer exists to whether approaches, techniques, and methods successfully used in manufacturing are directly applicable to services. It is rather a matter of giving each a fair trial while at the same time being sensitive to the service production process and its peculiarities.

Adding the L-factor

One aspect of service quality as presented in the literature is missing, which I would like included in holistic quality. It can be characterized by the following words: *love, compassion, empathy, sense of humor, tacit knowledge, knowledge by acquaintance, insights.* Call it the *love factor* or simply the *L-factor.* Dass's and Goreman's book *How Can I Help?* (1985) described this lost dimension of service quality. The book is about voluntary action although its basic message would also be applicable to commercial services to some degree and to public and governmental services to a large degree. What the ratio of family and other voluntary services is may not easily lend itself to statistics, but the public sector in industrialized countries varies between 7 percent (Japan) and 33 percent (Sweden) of the total employment, with the United States in the middle of these extremes (Swedish Coalition of Service Industries, 1987). The L-factor is of particular significance for quality in care services like hospitals, children's day-care centers, social security services, and so on, but also, for example, in education. Everyone probably knows intuitively what it is. The fact that it is not included in goods quality is partly understandable—mechanical components do not need love (as far as people believe)—but it is more alarming that it has not yet been explicitly included in models of service quality.

From Total Quality Management
to Holistic Quality Management

Are the terms *total quality control, total quality management,* and now *holistic quality* only gimmicks to make old knowledge stand out as new? No. *Total*

Table 1–1
Characteristics of Four Types of Quality

Goods Quality: The Grand Elder

Systematic quality efforts started in manufacturing in the 1920s; often misused when applied to services; can contribute to services for two reasons: (1) service operations need products (consumables, investment goods), (2) the long tradition has developed powerful tools that may be adjusted to services.

Service Quality: The Adolescent

New approaches developed since the late 1970s; based on the unique features of services; strong interest among researchers and practitioners; service quality heavily criticized; still a long way to go.

Computer Software Quality: The Juvenile Delinquent

Crucial for service organizations; quality control not mature; unique quality problems that need unique quality management methods

Holistic Quality: The Baby

Holistic quality recognizes
• that all organizations produce and sell both goods and services but in varying proportions and that the customer is buying utility and need satisfaction, not goods or services as such (there are exceptions: certain products or services have a symbolic or personal value in themselves).

• that service operations are heavily dependent on information technology and thus software quality is crucial for service quality.

• that the three types of quality are different in nature and have unique features that have to be considered.

• the need to approach quality also from a deeper, humanistic perspective with the L-factor, "love" in its widest sense, as the key.

quality management is a term created to emphasize the need for a complete approach to quality, not just quality efforts in the factory or purchasing department. *Holistic quality* is taking it one step further.

In table 1–1 the four types of quality and their characteristics are summarized.

Conclusion

Conclusions on service quality are summed up in the concept of holistic quality. One thing must be added, though: *implementation*. Peter Drucker once said that the problem with good ideas is that they quickly deteriorate into hard work. The implementation of new concepts, the experience gained through the implementation, feedback, and revision, all done in real settings and in various types of service organizations, are necessary to prove the validity of the new quality thinking. The acid test, however, is when customers notice a difference and when this difference favorably affects the bottom line. Simultaneously, and in dialogue with practitioners, researchers should continue developing concepts, models, methods, and so on in service quality. The holistic approach is still in its infancy.

References

Buzzell, Robert D., and Bradley T. Gale. (1987). *The PIMS Principles*. New York: The Free Press.

Camp, Robert C. (1989) "Benchmarking: The Search for Best Practices that Lead to Superior Performance." *Quality Progress*, January, 62–68.

Carlzon, Jan. (1987). *Moments of Truth*. Cambridge, MA: Ballinger.

Crosby, Phillip B. (1979). *Quality is Free*. New York: McGraw-Hill.

———. (1984). *Quality without Tears*. New York: New American Library.

Dale, Alan, and Stuart Wooler. (1991). "Strategy and Organization for Service: A Process and Content Model." In S. W. Brown et al. (eds.), *Service Quality: Multidisciplinary and Multinational Perspectives*. Lexington, MA: Lexington Books.

Dass, Ram, and Paul Gorman. (1985). *How Can I Help?* London: Rider.

Deming, W. Edwards. (1986). *Out of the Crisis*. Cambridge, MA: Massachusetts Institute of Technology.

Dunn, Robert, and Richard Ullman. (1982). *Quality Assurance for Computer Software*. New York: McGraw-Hill.

Edvardsson, Bo, and BengtOve Gustavsson. (1991). "Quality in Services and Quality in Service Organizations." In S. W. Brown et al. (eds.), *Service Quality: Multidisciplinary and Multinational Perspectives*. Lexington, MA: Lexington Books.

Garvin, David A. (1984). "What Does 'Product Quality' Really Mean?" *Sloan Management Review*.

George, William R., and Barbara E. Gibson. (1991). "Blueprinting: A Tool for Managing Quality in Service." In S. W. Brown et al (eds.), *Quality in Services: Multidisciplinary and Multinational Perspectives.* Lexington, MA: Lexington Books.

Godfrey, Blanton A. (1986). "The History and Evolution of Quality Control at AT&T." *AT&T Technical Journal,* Vol. 65, Issue 2, (March–April).

Grönroos, Christian. (1984). "A Service Quality Model and Its Marketing Implications." *European Journal of Marketing,* Vol. 18, No. 4.

———. (1988). "Service Quality: The Six Criteria of Good Perceived Service Quality." *Review of Business,* St. John's University, Vol. 9, No. 3 (Winter).

Grönroos, Christian, and Evert Gummesson. (1985). *Service Marketing—Nordic School Perspectives.* Stockholm: University of Stockholm, Department of Business Administration, Research Report, R 1985:2.

Gummesson, Evert. (1978). "Toward a Theory of Professional Service Marketing." *Industrial Marketing Management,* No. 7.

———. (1987). *Quality—The Ericsson Approach.* Stockholm: Ericsson.

———. (1988). "Service Quality and Product Quality Combined." *Review of Business,* St. John's University, Vol. 9, No. 3 (Winter).

Gummesson, Evert, and Christian Grönroos. (1987). "Quality of Services—Lessons from the Product Sector." In Carol Surprenant, *Add Value to Your Service.* Chicago: American Marketing Association.

Harrington, James H. (1988). *Excellence—The IBM Way.* Milwaukee: ASQC Press.

Hostage, G. M. (1975). "Quality control in service businesses." *Harvard Business Review,* July–August.

Ishikawa, Karou. (1982). *Guide to Quality Control.* Tokyo: Asian Productivity Organisation.

———. (1985). *What is Total Quality Control? The Japanese Way.* Englewood Cliffs, NJ: Prentice-Hall.

Johnston, Robert, ed. (1988). *The Management of Service Operations.* Proceedings of the 3d Annual International Conference of the Operations Management Association. Warwick, UK: University of Warwick.

Juran, J. M. (1982). *Upper Management and Quality.* New York: Juran Institute.

———. (1987). *On Quality Leadership.* Wilton, CT: Juran Institute.

Juran, J. M., F. M. Gryna, and R. S. Bingham, eds. (1979). *Quality Control Handbook.* New York: McGraw-Hill.

Kane, Edward J. (1986). "IBM's Quality Focus on the Business Process." *Quality Progress,* April, 24–32.

King, Carol A. (1985). "Service Quality Assurance Is Different." *Quality Progress,* June.

Kingman-Brundage, Jane. (1988). "The ABCs of Service Blueprinting." Paper presented at the American Marketing Association's 7th Annual Services Marketing Conference, Arlington, VA, October.

Langeard, Eric. (1987). *Integrated Services and Goods Offering in New Service Strategies.* Aix-en-Provence, France: IAE, Université de Droit, d'Economie et des Sciences d'Aix-Marseille, May.

Larreché, Jean-Claude, William W. Powell, and Hardy Deutz Ebeling. (1987). *Key Strategic Marketing Issues for the 1990s.* Fontainebleau, France: INSEAD.

Lehtinen, Jarmo R. (1985). "Improving Service Quality by Analyzing the Service

Production Process." In C. Grönroos and E. Gemmesson (eds.), *Service Marketing—Nordic School Perspectives.* Stockholm, Sweden: University of Stockholm, Department of Business Administration, Research Report R 1985:2.

Lu, David J. (1985). "Translator's Introduction." In K. Ishikawa *What Is Total Quality Control? The Japanese Way.* Englewood Cliffs, NJ: Prentice-Hall.

Neuhauser, Peg C. (1988). *Tribal Warfare in Organizations.* Cambridge, MA: Ballinger.

Parasuraman, A., V. A. Zeithaml, and L. L. Berry. (1985). "A Conceptual Model of Service Quality and Its Implications for Future Research." *Journal of Marketing,* Vol. 49 (Fall).

———. (1988). "SERVQUAL: Multiple-Item Scale for Measuring Consumer Perceptions of Service Quality." *Journal of Retailing,* Vol. 64, No. 1 (Spring).

Quinn, James Brian, J. Baruch Jordan, and Penny Cushman Paquette. (1987). "Technology in Services." *Scientific American,* Vol. 257, No. 6 (December).

Rosander, A. C. (1985). *Application of Quality Control in the Service Industries.* New York: Marcel Dekker/ASQC Quality Press.

Scherkenbach, William W. (1986). *The Deming Route to Quality and Productivity.* Washington, DC: CEEPress, George Washington University.

Shewhart, Walter A. (1931). *Economic Control of Quality of Manufactured Product.* New York: Van Nostrand.

Shostack, Lynn G. (1984). "Designing Services that Deliver." *Harvard Business Review,* January–February, 133–39.

———. (1987). "Service Positioning through Structural Change." *Journal of Marketing,* 51 (January) 34–43.

Swedish Coalition of Service Industries. (1987). *Statistics of the Service Sector.* Stockholm, Sweden.

Taguchi, Genichi. (1981) *Design and Design of Experiments.* Tokyo: Japanese Standards Association.

Townsend, Patrick. (1986). *Commit to Quality.* New York: Wiley.

United States Department of Commerce and National Institute of Standards and Technology. (1989). *Application Guidelines—Malcolm Baldridge National Quality Award.* Gaithersburg, MD.

Voss, C., C. Armistead, B. Johnston, and B. Morris. (1985). *Operations Management in Service Industries and the Public Sector.* Chichester, UK: Wiley.

2

The Evolution of the Services Marketing Mix and Its Relationship to Service Quality

Mary Jo Bitner

W ithin the field of marketing, service quality is frequently defined as the consumer's judgement about a firm's overall excellence or superiority, similar in many ways to the consumer's
general attitude toward the firm (Parasuraman, Zeithaml, and Berry 1988;
Zeithaml 1987; Bitner 1988). Customers' perceptions of service quality are
based on a complex set of variables including their own direct experiences
and relationships with the firm or others like it, information they have
read, seen, or heard about the firm, and what they know about others'
experiences and relationships with the firm. These elements have been
captured in proposed models of service quality (e.g., Grönroos 1988; Parasuraman, Zeithaml, and Berry 1985). In addition, customer perceptions of
service quality are also influenced indirectly by much broader managerial
issues such as organizational structure, philosophy, and corporate culture
(Schneider 1986; Bowen and Schneider 1988; Grönroos 1984; Lovelock
1988; Heskett 1987; Zeithaml, Berry, and Parasuraman 1988). For example,
a strong internal service culture is likely to lead to higher quality in service
delivery, which in turn will lead to higher perceived service quality from
the customer's point of view.

Although recognizing the extremely complex nature of service quality,
this chapter focuses narrowly on managing service encounters, the discrete
interactions between customers and service firms sometimes referred to as
"moments of truth." How customers evaluate these individual encounters is
one important ingredient in their overall perceptions of service quality. In
many cases, a lasting or even lifelong relationship with a customer or client
may depend on the customer having experienced numerous instances of
satisfaction in repeated service encounters with the firm. Thus, skillful
management and control of individual encounters becomes a primary concern to firms wanting to improve service quality and build long-lasting
customer relationships. This chapter proposes that the services marketing
mix represents a useful, effective, and simple tool for managing and enhancing the quality of service encounters.

The Marketing Mix

Definition

The marketing mix is one of the most widely accepted concepts in the discipline of marketing (McCarthy 1960; Bartels 1983; Shapiro 1985). The marketing has been defined as the controllable variables the company puts together to satisfy target markets and achieve the firm's cbjectives (McCarthy and Perreault 1987; Kotler 1988). By this definition, the marketing mix includes any and all elements that may potentially satisfy the consumer and over which the firm has some level of control. Underlying the marketing mix definition is the unspoken (and sometimes forgotten) assumption that satisfied customers are potential repeat customers who may eventually enter into lasting relationships with the firm. By ensuring satisfaction and quality in every encounter, the firm has taken one essential step toward retaining the customer.

Traditionally, the marketing mix has included four broad categories of variables known as the 4 P's: product, price, place, and promotion (McCarthy 1960). The 4 P's are widely used as an organizing concept both in planning corporate marketing strategies and formulating implementation plans to achieve specified marketing objectives (Shapiro 1985). The marketing mix concept emphasizes and reflects the tactical and managerial aspects of marketing as opposed to the broader social, organizational, competitive, and economic issues also of concern to the discipline (Hunt 1983; Bartels 1983; Alderson 1957; Bagozzi 1975).

The Services Marketing Mix

A number of writers have suggested that the particular elements in the marketing mix will vary or should be expanded beyond the 4 P's depending on the context in which they are being used (e.g., Kotler and Bloom 1984; Shapiro 1985; Booms and Bitner 1981: Renaghan 1981. In 1981, Booms and Bitner proposed the idea of an expanded marketing mix for general use by service organizations. The expanded mix includes all of the traditional mix elements as well as three new ones as defined below:

The Services Marketing Mix

Product
Price
Place
Promotion

Physical evidence   The environment in which the service is assembled and where the firm and customer interact; and any tangible

	commodities that facilitate performance or communication of the service.
Participants	All human actors who play a part in service delivery and thus influence the buyer's perceptions; namely, the firm's personnel and other customers in the service environment.
Process	The actual procedures, mechanisms, and flow of activities by which the service is operationalized and delivered.

Over the years, the expanded mix has received considerable attention as a services marketing framework used by corporations in their strategic planning and marketing implementation, as a framework for developing courses in services marketing (see Hansen 1987), in textbooks on services marketing (e.g., Cowell 1984), and as a framework for research (e.g., Bitner 1988; Grove, Fisk, and Bitner 1989). In all cases the framework has been used because it offers a simple organizing mechanism by which to address issues of expressed concern in service organizations. The following reviews how and why the expanded marketing mix for services evolved and develops some of the initial ideas further.

The services marketing mix developed out of a recognition of the differences between services and goods (e.g., Shostack 1977; Grönroos 1984; Berry 1980; Zeithaml, Parasuraman, and Berry 1985; Langeard et al. 1981). Because customers are frequently in the service firm's "factory," interacting directly with its personnel and other customers, and observing (and sometimes even interacting with) its operational systems, it was concluded that service firm managers have (under their control) considerably more variables that may communicate with and satisfy target markets. Because of services' intangibility, customers are frequently looking to such cues as decor, design, employee appearance, newness of equipment, and apparent systems for information about the service prior to purchase (e.g., Berry and Clark 1986; and Bitner 1982).

The expanded mix also evolved as a partial solution to some of the unique challenges faced by service firm managers (Knisely 1979; Zeithaml, Parasuraman, and Berry 1985). Extensive interviews with service firm managers and marketers confirmed what others had also observed: that many of the most pressing problems revolved around issues of quality control and dealing with customer interaction in the service delivery process (Booms and Bitner 1981). The expanded mix explicitly recognizes the role of service firm personnel and customers in the service delivery process by highlighting the marketing role played by both.

The new mix variables will influence customers *whether or not* their marketing impact is appreciated and managed. Thus, in order to draw attention to them as variables of equal (and sometimes even greater) importance than traditional mix elements, the services marketing mix gave each of the new variables its own place. This was not meant to imply that the new variables are independent of the traditional mix elements, but rather that they are of expressed importance to service firm managers and therefore deserving of focused attention in services marketing planning.

Criticism of the Marketing Mix

Some writers have critized the general value of the marketing mix by suggesting that it artificially limits the scope of marketing management by implying that marketing decisions can be neatly fit into the four boxes labeled by the traditional 4 P's (e.g., Grönroos 1989). *If* the marketing mix were the sole focus of marketing management, it would indeed be much too limiting. However, it is clear from a review of marketing texts, journals, and the content of marketing conferences and symposia that the concerns of marketing managers and academics extended far beyond the marketing mix (e.g., Hunt 1983; Webster 1981). Indeed, topics such as relationship marketing (Dwyer, Schurr, and Oh 1987; Crosby and Stephens 1987), issues related to quality and value in product/service performance (e.g., Zeithaml 1988; Zeithaml, Berry, and Parasuraman 1988), and the interaction of marketing with other functional areas (e.g., Ruekert and Walker 1987) are a few of the broad topics receiving increasing attention in marketing. Thus, while the marketing mix will continue to be useful and important to marketing managers, it is not, nor has it ever been, the sole tool or framework used within the discipline.

In addition to this general criticism of the marketing mix, the specific concept of an expanded mix for services has also been criticized. Buttle (1986) suggested that the new elements of the mix may apply equally well to goods-producing companies, and that in any case the new elements could be subsumed within the 4 P's, making a specialized "services marketing mix" unnecessary. Following on the first part of the critique, Buttle asked whether or not we might be "beginning to reach a stage where we can accept that the 7P's of Booms and Bitner are appropriate for both goods and services" (p. 12). While it may be true that the new elements apply to many goods producing firms, we are far from the stage (in the United States at least) of accepting a broadened marketing mix across all industries. Given the importance of the new elements in the delivery of many services, and the apparent usefulness of the framework, it seems appropriate to retain the notion of the services marketing mix. The second part of the criticism suggests that the new elements could conceptually be encompassed within the traditional mix. While this may be true, separating them draws attention to variables that have received little attention in marketing and that are of expressed, critical importance to many service firm managers. Thus, including physical evidence, participants, and process as separate items highlights their importance and marketing impact in services.

Their independence from other mix elements is not the issue; in fact, all elements of the marketing mix are and should be interdependent.

The Services Marketing Mix and Service Quality

Evolution of the Services Marketing Mix Concept

Applying the expanded services mix concept in consulting situations, management education, and university courses over several years made it apparent that the concept was useful and had great intuitive appeal to both students and managers. As researchers and academics we asked ourselves: Why is the expanded mix so relevant to people, and, from a more theoretical perspective, what underlying factors within service businesses were being influenced by the expanded mix elements? Our understanding of marketing and consumer behavior led us to theorize that the mix elements (particularly the new ones) might be critical to determining customer satisfaction and perceptions of quality. In a roundabout way then, we were saying that if service firm managers and students of services marketing see the expanded marketing mix as highly relevant to their concerns, then the expanded marketing mix must be important to their key objectives. Because key objectives are the attainment of customer satisfaction, service quality, and long-term customer retention, then perhaps management of the expanded marketing mix is directly related to these objectives.

The focus then turned to understanding theories of customer satisfaction and to conceptualizing the role of marketing mix variables in determining satisfaction and service quality. The model of service encounter evaluation incorporating marketing mix effects shown in figure 2–1 was the outcome of an extensive literature search and synthesis that spanned a variety of theory bases from consumer behavior to environmental psychology to social psychology. The model relies on consumer satisfaction theories developed in the consumer behavior literature (e.g., Churchill and Surprenant 1982; Swan 1983; Oliver 1980; Oliver and DeSarbo 1988) and attribution theory as it has evolved in the social psychology literature (e.g., Weiner 1980, 1985a, 1985b; Folkes 1988). The model also illustrates a hypothesized relationship between service encounter satisfaction and perceived service quality based on ideas expressed in services marketing literature (Parasuraman, Zeithaml, and Berry 1988; Zeithaml 1987).

A brief description of the model is followed by a specific illustration of how the new mix elements might operate in a real consumption situation. (For a more detailed discussion of the model and its theoretical underpinnings see Bitner (1988).)

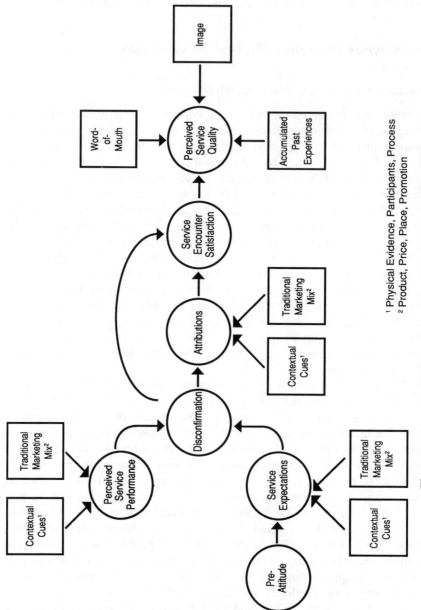

Figure 2–1. A Model of Service Encounter Evaluation.

[1] Physical Evidence, Participants, Process
[2] Product, Price, Place, Promotion

A Model of Service Encounter Evaluation

The first portion of the model suggests that a general preattitude toward the service may exist prior to the formation of expectations regarding a particular encounter (Swan 1983; Oliver 1980). This general preattitude will influence the consumer's expectations regarding the outcome of a particular service encounter, as shown in the model. Given the inherent variability in service outcomes, the preattitude and expectations will not necessarily be identical. For example, a consumer's general preattitude toward a given service provider may be extremely positive, but expectations regarding the outcome in a particular instance may be low depending on circumstances.

The second stage of the process suggests that the customer's immediate reaction in the service encounter experience depends on a comparison of prior expectations and perceived performance. When expectations match performance, confirmation occurs. However, when the magnitude of the discrepancy between expectations and performance is large enough, disconfirmation will occur. Negative disconfirmation occurs when expectations exceed perceived performance, while positive disconfirmation occurs when perceived performance exceeds expectations. To this point, the framework is consistent with models tested in the consumer literature (Churchill and Surprenant 1982).

Previous conceptualizations, however, have shown disconfirmation leading directly to dissatisfaction or satisfaction. The model suggests that causal attributions for disconfirmation will mediate customer satisfaction. In other words, before customers determine their level of dissatisfaction or satisfaction, they will diagnose the causes of disconfirmation and, depending on the perceived nature of the causes, they may modify their level of dissatisfaction or satisfaction and subsequent behaviors. Thus, the component labeled *attributions* is added to the consumer satisfaction paradigm. Support for adding attributions to the model is drawn from the attributon and consumer behavior literatures. Social psychologists have shown that people are likely to seek causes for events that are unexpected and/or negative (Weiner 1985a). The nature, of the attributions made has been shown to influence both affective and behavioral responses (Krishnan and Valle 1979; Folkes 1984, 1988; Folkes, Koletsky, and Graham 1987; Weiner 1980, 1985b; Bitner 1988). To be more specific, when the consumer believes the causes for negative disconfirmation to reside in the firm (i.e., the firm rather than the customer, caused the problem), to be within the control of the firm (i.e., the disconfirmation could have been prevented), and due to a nontemporary cause (i.e., it is likely to occur again), the consumer will be more dissatisfied than when the opposite conditions hold. The final portion of the model shows service encounter satisfaction influencing perceived service quality. Here, perceived service quality is viewed as equivalent to a general postpurchase attitude (Parasuraman, Zeithaml, and Berry 1988; Zeithaml 1987). As shown in the model, other variables beyond satisfaction with the individual encounter will also influence perceived service quality (i.e., word-of-mouth; perceived image; accumulated past experiences).

The Services Marketing and Service Encounter Evaluation

The model of service encounter evaluation includes those variables within the control of the firm that might influence components of the model. Elements of the traditional marketing mix will clearly influence satisfaction with services just as they influence satisfaction with goods. The traditional marketing mix is shown in the model; however, the influence of the traditional mix elements will not be discussed in detail because there is adequate discussion of their influence throughout marketing literature. Instead, the following focuses on the influence of the new marketing elements proposed in the expanded mix (Booms and Bitner 1981). In figure 2–1, the construct "contextual cues" encompasses the three new elements: physical evidence, participants, and process. Contextual cues are shown as entering the service encounter satisfaction process by directly influencing three components of satisfaction: expectations, perceived performance, and attributions. Each of these effects will be discussed below through use of a specific example.

Applying the Model

Effects of Contextual Cues on Expectations

Because services are intangible and usually cannot be experimented with prior to purchase, customers look for tangible evidence of what they are about to experience in a given service encounter (Shostack 1977; Berry and Clark 1986; Langeard et al. 1981; Zeithaml 1981). Even when a consumer has had considerable past experience with a service provider, variations and contextual cues will affect the consumers expectations of the immediate service encounter.

A concrete example illustrates the relationships. Suppose a traveler arrives about dinner time in a town where he or she has never been before. The traveler is directed by the concierge at the hotel to a nearby street where the traveler can find a number of restaurants of various types and prices. The traveler wanders along the street peering into restaurant windows. Through one window the traveler views tables set with white cloths, vases of red roses, waiters wearing tuxedoes, and elegantly dressed patrons. A little further down the street, the traveler hears modern jazz music coming from another restaurant. The clientele appear rather young and dressed very casually, as are the waiters and waitresses. On the next corner the traveler can see a brightly lit establishment with counter service and a neon menu board. A family with small children is heading for the door.

In all of these examples, the traveler uses cues associated with the physical evidence of the restaurant (its personnel, patrons, signage, and so on) and its operational characteristics to assess and categorize the restaurant, thus allowing him or her to form certain expectations regarding the nature of the service encounter that would be experienced in each establishment. Even if this were not the traveler's first visit to the area and he or she had in fact eaten at one of the above restaurants several times, contextual cues could affect his or her expectations of the particular experience that evening. For example, if he or she saw a crowd waiting outside the jazz restaurant, it might be assumed that the restaurant was overly busy that night and that the traveler might not have the same relaxed experience he or she had had on past occasions.

Effects of Contextual Cues on Perceived Performance

Continuing the above example, suppose the traveler chooses to dine at the casual-appearing restaurant with the jazz music. Having made the choice, and having certain expectations regarding the service encounter he or she is about to experience, the traveler proceeds to evaluate the actual service performance. Again, the traveler will be influenced by traditional marketing mix elements as well as contextual cues. Elements of physical evidence such as noise level, odors, temperature, colors, textures, comfort of seating, and menu appearance will all influence perceptions of the service encounter. For example, suppose the music is too loud or the temperature is too hot. Research in environmental psychology suggests that such variations in atmosphere can affect perceptions of the experience (Griffitt 1970; Maslow and Mantz 1956; Biggers and Pryor 1982).

Similarly, the attitudes and behaviors of service participants will also influence perceptions of actual performance in the service encounter. In the current example, the attitudes and actions of the host and waitpersons as well as their outward appearance (Solomon 1985) will affect the traveler's overall evaluation. In addition, the traveler may also be influenced by the experiences of other customers in the restaurant and their verbal and non-verbal behaviors. For example, suppose the traveler is seated next to a large party of young people who drink too much, talk and laugh too loudly, and generally interfere with his or her enjoyment of the music and atmosphere. These negative behaviors may very well influence the traveler's perceptions of service encounter performance even though the behaviors of the young people are clearly not associated with the traveler's own meal or his or her own interactions with service personnel.

Effects of Contextual Cues on Attributions

Finally, contextual cues may also influence satisfaction in the service encounter through their effects on attributions for service disconfirmation as shown in figure 2–1. As discussed, attribution theory suggests that when outcomes are *not as expected*, people have a tendency to search for reasons. Their assessment of the "why" will influence final evaluation of the outcome.

To illustrate, the restaurant example used previously to show the effects of contexual cues on expectations will be carried further. Suppose that the traveler's expectations are not met because he or she cannot fully enjoy the experience due to the interference of the large party seated near by. In such a case, *why* he or she was seated at that particular table will no doubt influence the traveler's overall evaluation. Suppose the restaurant was filled to capacity and the host had kindly searched out this one available small table to accommodate the traveler. The host had little control or choice in where to seat the traveler and in fact had been very accommodating. Attribution theory (Weiner 1985a; Folkes 1984, 1988) would predict that in this case, the negative effects of the large party on overall evaluations would be mitigated since the host had little control over where the traveler could be seated. On the other hand, suppose a number of larger tables had been available on the other side of the restaurant, but the host indicated that he wanted to save those tables for parties of two or more, so the only available choice was the small table next to the roudy group. In this case, the host had control over where to seat the traveler and still chose the undesirable small table. Attribution theory predicts that, under these circumstances, the traveler is more likely to be disgruntled and allow his or her perceptions of the entire experience to be negatively influenced by where he or she was seated.

Research Based on the Model

A program of research has developed around the services marketing mix and the model of service encounter evaluation previously discussed. The research has been of two types: empirical tests of model relationships and exploratory work to increase understanding of the effects of the new mix elements.

Research to Test Model Relationships

An experiment was conducted testing a portion of the service encounter model to assess hypthesized effects of attributions on satisfaction and to determine whether variations in contextual cues could indeed influence customers' attributions in a service failure context (Bitner 1988). Results of the scenario-based experiment (conducted in a travel agency context) showed that travelers' attributions in a service failure situation were more forgiving when the failure was experienced in an organized travel agency versus a disorganized one) and when they were offered externally oriented explanations and offers to compensate for the failure. In turn, the nature of the travelers' attributions influenced their overall satisfaction with the travel agency encounter. When they believed the failure was within the control of the travel agent and when they believed a similar failure was likely to occur in the future, subjects were more dissatisfied with the encounter than when the opposite conditions existed. These results suggest that attributions can indeed influence dissatisfaction or satisfaction and that management of contextual cues can change attributions, particularly in service failure situations. Future research will continue developing the model through replication of the experimental results in other settings and testing of other relationships inplied by the model.

Substantive Research on Extended Mix Elements

Qualitative research using the critical incident method has been conducted to explore the nature of contact employee (or "participant") behaviors in both satisfactory and dissatisfactory service encounters (Bitner, Booms, and Tetreault 1988). One study examined service encounters in three industries: hotels, restaurants, and airlines. Approximately seven hundred incidents collected from customers in these industries were categorized to gain insights into the underlying causes of satisfaction and dissatisfaction. Results suggested three broad categories of behaviors that can be used to classify both satisfactory and dissatisfactory incidents in the three industries: employee response to service delivery system failures; employee response to customer needs and requests; and unprompted and unsolicited employee actions. Twelve subcategories were enumerated within the three broad categories. The study provided insights into the effects of specific employee actions and introduced a new method in the study of service encounters.

Future research will continue to explore the influence of participants and physical evidence as marketing mix variables. A tremendous gap in knowledge exists about these new mix variables in terms of their marketing impact. New methods for testing the impact of participants and physical evidence are also needed. For example, research was conducted as a preliminary step in developing a measure of service environment ("physical evidence") meaning (Ward, Bitner, and Gossett 1989) that would allow service firm managers to assess customers' perceptions of the meaning of various cues in the firm's environment.

Conclusion

This chapter traces the evolution of the services marketing mix and its usefulness as an organizing tool for managing customer satisfaction in service encounters. Over the years, the expanded mix proved to be practically useful in marketing applications and as a framework for services marketing education. Later, its theoretical relationship to customer satisfaction and service quality was proposed in a model based on a literature synthesis incorporating theories from consumer behavior, services marketing, and social psychology. The model and the mix itself now provide a frame of reference for continuing research involving tests of theory, exploration of mix elements, and the development of appropriate methods for studying service encounter variables.

References

Alderson, Wroe. (1957). *Marketing Behavior and Executive Action*. Homewood, Ill: Irwin.

Bagozzi, Richard P. (1975). "Marketing As Exchange." *Journal of Marketing*, 39 (October), 32–39.

Bartels, Robert. (1983). *The Development of Marketing Thought*. Columbus, OH: Grid Publishing.

Berry, Leonard L. (1980). "Services Marketing is Different." *Business*, May–June, 24–28.

Berry, Leonard L., and Terry Clark. (1986). "Four Ways to Make Services More Tangible." *Business*, October–Decenber, 53–54.

Biggers, Thompson, and Bert Pryor (1982). "Attitude Change: A Function of the Emotion-Eliciting Qualities of Environment." *Personality and Social Psychology Bulletin*, Vol. 8, No. 1 (March), 94–99.

Bitner, Mary Jo. (1988). "Evaluating Service Encounters: The Effects of Physical Surroundings and Employee Responses." Working Paper No. 7, Tempe, Arizona: The First Interstate Center for Services Marketing, Arizona State University.

Bitner, Mary Jo, Bernard H. Booms, and Mary Stanfield Tetreault. (1988). "The Service Encounter: Diagnosing Favorable and Unfavorable Incidents." Working Paper No. 12, Tempe Arizona: The First Interstate Center for Services Marketing, Arizona State University.

Booms, Bernard H., and Mary J. Bitner. (1981). "Marketing Strategies and Organization Structures for Service Firms." In *Marketing of Services*, James H. Donnelly and William R. George (eds), Chicago: American Marketing Association, 47–52.

———. (1982). "Marketing Services by Managing the Environment." *The Cornell Hotel and Restaurant Administration Quarterly*, Vol. 23, No.1 (May), 35–39.

Bowen, David E., and Benjamin Schneider. (1988). "Services Marketing and Management: Implications for Organizational Behavior." In *Research in Organiza-*

tional Behavior, B. M. Staw and L. L. Cummings (eds), Volume 10, Greenwich, CN: JAI Press.

Buttle, Francis. (1986). "Unserviceable Concepts in Service Marketing." *The Quarterly Review of Marketing,* Spring, 8–14.

Churchill, Gilbert A., and Carol Surprenant. (1982). "An Investigation into the Determinants of Customer Satisfaction." *Journal of Marketing Research,* 19 (November), 491–504.

Cowell, D. (1984). *The Marketing of Services,* London: Heinemann.

Crosby, Lawrence A., and Nancy J. Stephens. (1987). "Effects of Relationship Marketing on Satisfaction, Retention and Prices in the Life Insurance Industry." *Journal of Marketing Research,* 24 (November), 404–411.

Dwyer, F. Robert, Paul H. Schurr, and Sejo Oh. (1987). "Developing Buyer-Seller Relationships." *Journal of Marketing,* 51, 2 (April), 11–27.

Folkes, Valerie S. (1984). "Consumer Reactions to Product Failure: An Attributional Approach." *Journal of Consumer Research,* Vol. 10, No. 4 (March), 398–409.

———. (1988). "Recent Attribution Research in Consumer Behavior: A Review and New Directions." *Journal of Consumer Research,* Vol. 14, No. 4 (March), 548–65.

Folkes, Valerie S., Susan Koletsky, and John Graham. (1987). "A Field Study of Causal Inferences and Consumer Reaction: The View from the Airport." *Journal of Consumer Research,* Vol. 13, No. 4 (March), 534–539.

Griffitt, William. (1970). "Environmental Effects on Interpersonal Affective Behavior: Ambient Effective Temperature and Attraction." *Journal of Personality and Social Psychology,* Vol. 15, No. 3, 240–244.

Grönroos, Christian. (1984). "A Service Quality Model and Its Marketing Implications." *European Journal of Marketing,* Vol. 18, No. 4, 36–44.

———. (1988). "Service Quality: The Six Criteria of Good Perceived Service Quality." *Review of Business,* 9 (3), 10–13.

———. (1989). "Fundamental Research Issues in Services Marketing." In *Designing a Winning Service Strategy,* Mary Jo Bitner and Lawrence A. Crosby (eds), Chicago: American Marketing Association, 9–10.

Grove, Stephen J., Raymond P. Fisk, and Mary Jo Bitner. (1989). "Dramatizing the Service Encounter: A Managerial Approach." Unpublished working paper, Oklahoma State University.

Hansen, Nancy. (1987). "A Collection of Course Syllabi on Services Marketing." Chicago: American Marketing Association.

Heskett, James L. (1987). "Lessons in the Service Sector." *Harvard Business Review,* March–April, 118–126.

Hunt, Shelby. (1983). "General Theories and the Fundamental Explananda of Marketing." *Journal of Marketing,* 47 (4), 9–17.

Knisely, Gary. (1979). Series of interviews appearing in the January 15, February 19, March 19, end May 14, 1979, issued of *Advertising Age.*

Kotler, Phillip. (1988). *Marketing Management,* Sixth Edition, Englewood Cliffs, NJ: Prentice-Hall.

Kotler, Phillip, and Paul N. Bloom. (1984). *Marketing Professional Services.* Englewood Cliffs, NJ: Prentice-Hall.

Krishnan, S., and Valerie A. Valle. (1979). "Dissatisfaction Attributions and Consumer Complaint Behavior." William Wilkie (ed), *Advances in Consumer Research*, Vol. 6, Provo VT: Association for Consumer Research, 445–449.

Langeard, Eric, John E. G. Bateson, Christopher Lovelock, and Pierre Eigler. (1981). *Services Marketing: New Insights from Consumers and Managers*, Report No. 81-104, Cambridge, MA: Marketing Science Institute.

Lovelock, Christopher. (1988). *Managing Services: Marketing, Operations and Human Resources*, Englewood Cliffs, NJ: Prentice-Hall.

Maslow, A. L. and N. L. Mintz. (1956). "Effects of Esthetic Surroundings." *Journal of Psychology*, Vol. 41, 247–54.

McCarthy, E. (1960). *Basic Marketing: A Managerial Approach*. Homewood, IL: Irwin.

McCarthy, E. Jerome, and William D. Perreault, Jr. (1987). *Basic Marketing*, 9th Edition. Homewood, IL: Richard D. Irwin.

Mintz, Norbett L. (1956). "Effects of Esthetic Surroundings II: Prolonged and Repeated Experience in a "Beautiful' and an 'Ugly' Room." *The Journal of Psychology*, 41, 459–66.

Oliver, Richard L. (1980). "A Cognitive Model of the Antecedents and Consequences of Satisfaction Decisions." *Journal of Marketing Research*, 17 (November), 460–69.

Oliver, Richard L., and Wayne S. DeSarbo. (1988). "Response Determinants in Satisfaction Judgments." *Journal of Consumer Research*, Vol. 14, No. 4 (March), 495–507.

Parasuraman, A., Valarie A. Zeithaml, and Leonard L. Berry. (1985). "A Conceptual Model of Service Quality and Its Implications for Further Research." *Journal of Marketing*, Vol. 49, No. 4 (Fall), 41–50.

———. (1988). "SERVQUAL: A Multiple-Item Scale for Measuring Consumer Perceptions of Service Quality." *Journal of Retailing*, Vol. 64, No. 1, 12–40.

Renaghan, Leo M. (1981). "A New Marketing Mix." *The Cornell Hotel and Restaurant Administration Quarterly*, 22 (2), 30–35.

Ruekert, Robert W., and Orville C. Walker, Jr. (1987). "Marketing's Interaction with Other Functional Units: A Conceptual Framework and Empirical Evidence." *Journal of Marketing*, 51, 1 (January), 1–19.

Schneider, Benjamin. (1986). "Notes on Climate and Culture." In M. Venkatesan, Diane M. Schmalensee, and Claudia Marshall (eds), *Creativity in Services Marketing*, Chicago: American Marketing Association, 63–67.

Shapiro, Benson P. (1985). "Rejuvenating the Marketing Mix." *Harvard Business Review*, September–October, 28–34.

Shostack, G. Lynn. (1977). "Breaking Free From Product Marketing." *Journal of Marketing*, 41 (April), 73–80.

Solomon, Michael R. (1985). "Packaging the Service Provider." *The Services Industries Journal*, July, 64–71.

Swan, John. (1983). "Consumer Satisfaction Research and Theory: Current Status and Future Directions." In Ralph L. Day and H. Keith Hunt (eds), *International Fare in Consumer Satisfaction and Complaining Behavior*, Bloomington, Indiana: School of Business, IN: University, 124–29.

Ward, James C., Mary Jo Bitner, and Dan Gossett. (1989). "SEEM: A Measure of

Service Environment Meaning." In Mary Jo Bitner and Lawrence A. Crosby (eds), *Designing a Service Strategy*, Chicago, IL: American Marketing Association, 34—39.

Webster, Frederick E., Jr. (1981). "Top Management's Concerns about Marketing: Issues for the 1980's." *Journal of Marketing*, 45 (3), 9–16.

Weiner, Bernard. (1980). "A Cognitive (Attribution) -Emotion-Action Model of Motivated Behavior: An Analysis of Judgments of Help-Giving." *Journal of Personality and Social Psychology*, Vol. 39, No. 2, 186–200.

———. (1985a). "'Spontaneous' Causal Thinking." *Psychological Bulletin*, 97, No. 1, 74–84.

———. (1985b). "An Attributional Theory of Achievement Motivation and Emotion." *Psychological Review*, Vol. 92, No. 4, 548–573.

Zeithaml, Valarie. (1981). "How Consumer Evaluation Processes Differ Between Goods and Services." In J.H. Donnelly and Wm. R. George (eds), *Marketing of Services*, Chicago: American Marketing Association, 186–90.

———. (1987). *Defining and Relating Prices, Perceived Quality, and Perceived Value*, Report No. 87–101, Cambridge, MA: Marketing Science Institute.

———. (1988). "Consumer Perceptions of Price, Quality, and Value: A Means-End Model and Synthesis of Evidence." *Journal of Marketing*, 52 (3), 2–22.

Zeithaml, V. Leonard L. Berry, and A. Parasuraman. (1988). "Communication and Control Processes in the Delivery of Service Quality." *Journal of Marketing*, Vol. 52, No. 2 (April), 35–48.

Zeithaml, V., A. Parasuraman, and Leonard L. Berry. (1985). "Problems and Strategies in Services Marketing." *Journal of Marketing*, Vol. 49, No. 2 (Spring), 33–46.

3
Managing Quality in Home-Care Services

Benny Hjern
Lennart Blomquist

Introduction

More than in many Western societies, the expansion of welfare state services in Sweden could be reconceptualized as the municipal welfare expansion. As employers and main providers of services, Swedish municipalities have had to master the intricacies of rapid public sector growth based on a deliberate state policy of charging local government with major social policy responsibilities. The staffing and managing of service organizations has preoccupied local politics and administration for quite some time now.

The political and administrative basis for a return to a more decentralized model of social welfare provision started in the 1960s with reapportionment of the Swedish local government structure. Of approximately 1,000 to some extent small and impoverished municipalities, 280 wealthier ones were formed. During the 1970s and 1980s, vast changes occurred in local service organizations and in the field of social services in particular. Before the reapportionment, just some 50 percent of Swedish municipalities had more than one full-time professional employee in social services. Today, even small municipalities with a population less than fifteen thousand, employ more than one hundred.

In this chapter the capability of local governments to organize and manage service quality in the field of social services will be addressed. It is all too easy to forget—and in fact, most Swedes and many researchers have probably already forgotten that the large-scale, formal organization of local social services is a rather new phenomenon in Sweden. A private firm growing in a controlled fashion from one to one hundred employees in twenty years would represent a considerable success. In fact, data seem to support the fact that the size bracket between fifty and one hundred employees is crucial for firms in several branches. Management that orga-

The paper partly draws on material collected and analyzed by B. A. Per Viklund, Umeå University, Sweden. The authors are responsible for errors or omissions.

nizes control techniques adequately in that bracket helps firms grow further. Most firms approaching some two hundred employees seem marked as moribund, the more so the older they are at the time.[1] The public service organizations under study have reached these age levels and size brackets in which the viability of the "system" is challenged.

This chapter will first discuss characteristics of service quality management in young local public organizations that have recently grown rapidly. Second, the service problem selected for study—municipal home-care of the elderly—also provides case material for assessing conditions of quality management in settings of intergovernmental, or interorganizational, co-production of services.

Individuals in the client group of the elderly are potential consumers of home-care services from two subnational governments, municipalities, and county councils. Swedish municipalities are charged with a broad mandate for the welfare of their citizens, the county councils mainly with health care services. Both municipalities and county councils are political entities in their own right, with separate elections, albeit on the same day every third year. But representatives in their elected bodies belong to the same local party organizations and consequently should be in a position to define policy for the client group across administrative lines of jurisdiction. In conclusion, therefore, the paper also raises questions concerning conditions of "political" management.

Some contextual information pertaining to the clients and the formal organization of home-care services is provided in two subsequent sections. In the main sections of the chapter findings from field research in seven Swedish municipalities (and seven county councils) are presented. The results are evaluated in a concluding section.

Clients of the Home-Care Services

Municipal home-care is a service for several different groups: the elderly, the handicapped, the mentally retarded, and persons with long-term health care needs, for example. The largest group, however, is the elderly, seventy-five or more years of age.

For several reasons, municipal home-care is a relevant focus for studying the management of service production and quality in Sweden. In 1985, total public expenditure (gross) for the service amounted to at least SEK four billion, or 0.5 percent of GNP. Over the past twenty years this share has increased continuously. As elsewhere, developments in the field give cause for serious concern about how Swedish home-care services should be financed and staffed in the public domain in the future (Hjern 1988).

Figure 3–1 shows that there will be a decrease in the number of individuals in the sixteen- to twenty-four-year-old age group until the year

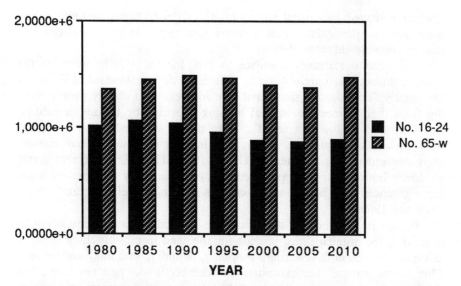

Figure 3–1. **Forecast of the number of individuals in two age categories.**

2005 whereas the number of people aged sixty-five or more will increase until 1990. Thereafter a gradual decrease will occur until 2010 when the trend will once more be reversed.

In terms of clients, then, the service will expand. In the coming decades the number of older people (seventy-five years of age and over), a group that is already overwhelmingly dominant in the service, will increase even further in Sweden. And as a result of pension reforms in the 1960s, individuals in the group will increasingly be in a position to afford to stay in their homes longer than before, if they choose to do so (Montin 1983).

Municipal home-care is not only a service challenge but also an area of research interest for many reasons. The elderly are already an important consumer group, and have been transformed more and more from a group that, politically, has not voiced its demands very actively into an organized pressure group. Many of their concerns, of course, are at the heart of Swedish welfare state ideology and cannot easily be neglected in the election strategies of political parties. At the same time, it is everywhere acknowledged that the quality of service, justly demanded by the elderly, will challenge the innovative organization capacities of political parties and municipal managers in the near future.

Presently some 50 percent of home-care services in Sweden are provided within families. The other half are almost entirely produced by public organizations, mainly by personnel from the municipalities and, to some extent, from the county councils, with guidelines from and grant systems managed by central state authorities. In addition, separate guidelines and, in particular, grant systems also apply to municipalities and county councils (Montin 1988).

The general statutory mandate to care for the elderly refers to the municipalities, which are obliged to maintain a decent standard of living for the elderly. Traditionally municipal care has relied on elderly people moving from their homes into special housing provided by the municipalities. But from the 1950s, as a result of care policy and costs, state programs with the aim of helping the elderly stay in their own homes have increasingly demanded political attention (Hjern 1976). Home improvement grants to elderly house owners are provided, but predominantly programs of housing allowances have helped senior citizens remain in their flats and houses since the 1960s.

Staying in their homes, the elderly are entitled to services equivalent to those that the municipalities provide for the aged in multidwelling housing facilities, for example catering, shopping, laundry, cleaning, and so on. This "home service" has expanded considerably in the past ten years, but the first steps were taken in the 1940s. Recent developments in Swedish care ideology have placed greater demands on the organization of these services.

The negative aspects of institutionalized care—in hospitals as well as in homes for seniors—were documented and accepted politically early in the 1980s. The trend toward deinstitutionalization started to blur the boundary between municipal home care and county council health care. The thrust of the new policy is to provide as much home health care as possible, allowing the elderly to stay in their homes for as long as they wish and medical indications allow. This, of course, means that more qualified home-care services are required, not only in a medical but also in a general sense. In addition, it means that an organizational division of labor—including budgetary responsibilities—must be negotiated between county councils and municipalities.

The need to develop new criteria for the division of labor between county councils and municipalities springs mainly from the "blurring" of the line between health care and home-care inherent in the national policy of having the elderly stay at home rather than move into institutions. But it is also a consequence of a statutory set-up that stipulates on the one hand the overall aim for county councils is to provide citizens with "good care" (including primary health care) and on the other hand (for the municipalities) the overall aim is to maintain a decent standard of living for the elderly.

For large groups of citizens, the borderline between a state of ill health, requiring "good care" or primary health care by the county council, and the state of decent standards of living, calling for municipal care, is easily defined, but not so for the elderly whose decent standard of living is often directly dependent on spells of good health care, increasingly in their own homes. This situation provides scope for antagonistic conceptions and definitions by those involved. Municipal officials tend, for example, to define senility (senile dementia) as an illness to be treated in a hospital. County council professionals define it as part of normal aging, requiring no hospitalization.

For the group of elderly people entitled to home-care services it is not readily apparent why some tasks in the service can only be provided by county-council staff or municipal staff. The two providers themselves are aware of cost inefficiencies within the current system when the same client is visited, within hours, by personnel from each organization—each traveling far but not together. Apart from cost efficiency arguments, quality of service—from the client's viewpoint—will most likely decrease with the increasing number of personnel involved. One overall aim of caring services—in Sweden as elsewhere—is to reduce the number of persons treating each client in order to attain higher service quality. But if the development of home-care services from 1980 to 1985 is considered, an increase in costs of approximately $100 million, is evident while the number receiving help has decreased by about 35,000 (Montin 1987a, 1988).

As the number of elderly people living outside institutions increases, the "market" for public home-care services has to become more differentiated, and municipal services will have to take on "new" functions. The differentiation is necessary because more individualistic demands need to be considered and, concurrently, it will prove necessary to include more health care proper in the services. In practice these developments are already well under way in Sweden. However, the organizational and management structures to "control" developments—across different subnational government jurisdictions—are not yet well established.

County and Local Government Organization

Municipal home care has become the alternative to providing for the social welfare needs of the elderly in institutions. A precondition for implementing this "new" Swedish care ideology of deinstitutionalization is that professionals in county councils and municipalities coordinate their activities. A redefinition of tasks between county councils and municipalities is now being established, as indicated by negotiations concerning where costs occur in the provision of home-care services and how the two layers of government should clear their financial relationships in the field.

Such negotiations proved the more necessary because the county councils, without contracted municipal prearrangements but with formal backing in state policy, soon started to dehospitalize and release from institutions substantial numbers of socially handicapped persons, who were, in principle, eligible for home-care services. The main determinant for this policy, of course, is the availability of adequate housing for those released. And housing is the responsibility of Swedish municipalities, a rather costly responsibility.

The lines of responsibility between county councils and municipalities, in terms of the elderly, are not only or foremost a legal or budgetary problem. They also create confusion at the frontline of service delivery, where personnel may start playing the game: Is this my client or yours? County council and municipal professionals have different training and career patterns. With regard to the elderly, the organization and incentive structures for home-care services are, therefore, mixed. Several layers of government need to define consistent management strategies to coordinate their functions with respect to the same group of clients for the quality of service to be raised. A brief introduction to the formal organization of Swedish subnational government is necessary before the arrangements of specific functions are described.

Some general indications were previously cited regarding the challenges created for established organizational and management structures by the enlarged role of municipal home-care. One of the most significant problems concerns the need to redefine tasks and budget responsibilities for primary health and home-care services. County councils and municipalities are both democratically elected governments, county councils with (mainly) regional jurisdiction and the municipalities with local. The former are almost exclusively engaged in health care tasks and the latter in the full range of social and other types of services. Some of the services are state mandated. But subnational governments almost completely control the organization and staffing of services, buttressed by their right of taxation. (In fact, the internationally high taxation in Sweden pertains more to the flat income tax rates of subnational than to the proportional ones of national government.)

Formally, relationships between the state and subnational government depend on which of three statutory categories a public service belongs to: general powers as defined by the Local Government Act, specific powers as defined by special legislation, and/or powers defined in particular enabling acts. The service field studied mainly belongs to the first and third categories.

National as well as subnational elections in Sweden are held on the same day every third year. Municipal and county councils are elected directly by voters. The councils, in turn, elect members of the county or municipal executive committee and various specialized committees. They also appoint chairpersons of the committees. Members of committees are selected on a party proportional basis. Leaders and senior representatives of the local parties are elected to the executive committee and other prestigious, specialized committees of subnational government. It used to be common that party representatives fulfilled functions both in county and municipal bodies. As a result of professionalization and an increased work load, this is becoming more and more unusual. Home-care for the elderly is the responsibility of municipal social welfare committees. In the county councils, services in the field are part of primary health care, which includes various utilities in different parts of Sweden; hence, the formal organization differs.

Municipal social welfare committees prepare both policy and administrative issues for decision in the council of the powers of these committees are considerable; in all municipalities professional managers in the social welfare administration retain significant control in policy and budgetary matters.

Home-care in all municipalities is managed by a home-care inspector, directly under the head of the social welfare administration. He or she is in charge of several home-care assistants, how many depends on the size (both as regards population and geographical area) of the municipality. (In the research sites the number varies between four and twelve.) The assistants manage the services in a home-care district with a team of attendants who visit the elderly. The municipal home-care districts generally overlap with the districts served by a nurse in the county council's organization of primary health care.

County councils define the details of primary health services differently. Care is provided by health care centers, district nurse offices, nursing homes, and so on. Professionals from these health units visit or receive elderly patients. Home-care services are provided mainly by teams of nursing assistants supervised by a district nurse. These teams interact with the home-care attendants of the municipalities.

Two basic organization models for the management of primary heath services exist. During the 1980s, a minority of Swedish county councils set up politically elected primary health committees directly under the executive committee of the council and responsible for primary health only. The degree to which county councils have decentralized administrative functions from the central office to the primary health committees differs, but a few have undertaken far-reaching decentralization reforms. The jurisdiction of a primary health committee corresponds to the geographical area of a municipality in the county. Hence, this model of organization, in principle, makes it easier for local political leaders and managers to coordinate county council and municipal home-care services for a group of elderly citizens.

Such coordination is not made easier by the second type of organization that county councils use for managing primary health services. A majority of Swedish county councils organize local health care districts across several municipalities. Management functions for primary as well as hospital care are delegated to the directorates of these districts from the central executive committee and administration of the county. The directorates can have lay boards with members nominated by the political parties, but central executive committees retain control of political management functions.

The field research to be reported pertains to seven municipalities in seven Swedish counties. These were selected, so differing formal organizational features of municipal and county council home-care service were represented in the study. The design is not meant to "control" in any rigid sense for such characteristics. The focus of the field research is on how the various actors involved in home-care services organize their work, not if they organize according to one formal organization model or another. Across municipalities, however, if common properties in the organization of work tasks are discerned, despite differences in formal organization structures, it seems possible to generalize these as characteristic of service provision per se.

The Organization of Home-Care Tasks

The study is designed to analyze, from the perspective of elderly people in need of home-care services in Swedish municipalities, the organizational structures, strategies, and resources employed to attain service quality. It is less concerned with the outcomes as these relate to national guidelines than with the questions: Who organizes? and With what ideas and how? These serve to illuminate the tasks of (1) defining needs, (2) making priorities, and (3) mobilizing resources for (4) evaluating home-care services.

During the field work, semistructured interviewing was used to establish the networks of persons (if any) engaged in the four tasks, starting with personnel, the municipal home-care attendants, who working closest to the elderly in need of services (for methods, cf. Hjern and Porter 1981 and Hull and Hjern 1988). The four tasks have a long history in organization theory. They need to be performed and linked if systematic services provision is to be attained.

An overview of the findings is presented in figure 3–2. In the figure the tasks used to structure field interviewing are given vertically, and classes of actors engaged in them are presented horizontally. (The order has no meaning in hierarchic/organizational terms. The arrangement is made solely for purposes of presentation.)

Need Definition

In a few of the home-care districts studied, the local manager, for example the home-care assistant, professes to have more than impressionistic notions

Task

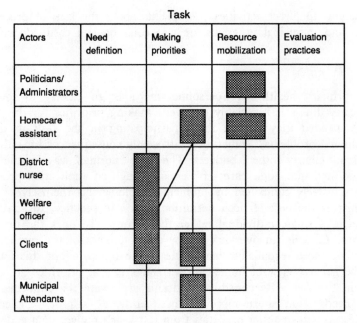

Actors	Need definition	Making priorities	Resource mobilization	Evaluation practices
Politicians/ Administrators			▓	
Homecare assistant		▓	▓	
District nurse		▓		
Welfare officer				
Clients		▓		
Municipal Attendants		▓		

Figure 3–2. The organizing of homecare at the district level.

of the actual need profiles of the district. For the municipal personnel, need definition cannot really be distinguished from the task of making priorities about the extent of services an individual eligible for home-care needs. An answer to the question, How large is the group of potentially eligible persons?, cannot, in general, be provided by municipal home-care managers.

As indicated in figure 3–2, individuals in need of home-care services are defined for and not by those engaged in the municipalities, notably by personnel from county council health-care units but also by the elderly themselves or their families. The first category meets potential home-care clients in two ways: in the primary health services and as the elderly are released from hospital treatment. Health-care personnel use crude indicators (share of district population, seventy years of age or over, etc.) to assess needs for services. These are combined with specific rules-of-thumb and provide little relevant information for municipal home-care planners at any rate.

In the material are examples of how personnel from the primary health and municipal home-care services together have made inventories of and visited the elderly population in a district, but resources for such work are not easily mobilized in the age of budget cuts. In general, then, those engaged in need definition for municipal home care use very little quantitative information- to direct activities. Complaints about the lack of precision in statutes and municipal programs are also common and easily documented.

Making Priorities

When primary health care personnel help, assign elderly to municipal home-care, illness is invariably involved. Making priorities for the kind of services needed may engage those participating in the task in difficult "definitional problems," sometimes with costly consequences for either municipal and county council budgets. The more "normal" way for the elderly to be defined into home-care services is through an application procedure, more exclusively controlled by municipal professionals themselves. In any case, just as the task of need definition refers, in practice, to activities in relation to a single individual rather than groups, so does the making of priorities. Lacking an overview of the characteristics of the population to be served, those responsible have little choice but to adopt this focus.

The general view of home-care managers is that priorities are hard to make in the field. Responsible politicians are aware that information on actual needs is in short supply. Consequently, as will be detailed, they muddle through, making priorities from last year's budget data and reports on the work load of front personnel. Top administrators find that politicians are aware of the broad questions involved but are reluctant to make definite priorities, recently with respect to home-care versus institutionalized care. Hence, in practice, priorities are made by the personnel closest to the clients. Because professionals with different training and career patterns are involved, criteria are not easily reconstructed. They depend on the strength of the claims that municipal and county council professionals bring to negotiations about individual cases.

Two different organizational contexts influence the way different claims are traded off. When county councils organize primary health as part of local, multipurpose directorates, usually comprising a geographical area of several municipalities, the context slants negotiations even further from parity for the municipal representative. Functioning working groups of both the municipal home-care service and county council primary health-care units are harder to organize, and it is more common that district nurses make priorities about who should receive home-care services, without consulting municipal personnel. Nurses claim priorities are made on medical grounds. These, of course, are hard for municipal managers to question, especially when a client has already been referred to them.

Organizational structures for trading off claims from different professionals are somewhat less slanted against municipal interests, provided management of the county councils primary health services is decentralized to local committees with a jurisdiction corresponding to just one municipality.

Groups for local home-care planning, with representatives from both local governments, are easier to establish. In the districts researched these invariably had more members with medical training; that is, representing county councils rather than municipalities. And the municipal representatives find it hard to argue against medical criteria.

At the center of discussion in the groups of home-care planning is how senile elderly people (cases of senile dementia) should be treated. Are they ill or are their spells of confusion formal and states that home-care services can manage? Members of the groups are fully aware of the budget consequences these local decisions may have for their principals, but authoritative and precise instructions are lacking.

Discussions in the home-care planning groups are also influenced by the fact that hospital and institution beds are in short supply generally. Within health care proper more restrictive criteria than before are employed for admission to a bed. This, of course, has consequences for home-care services. Patients with "worse diagnoses" have claims on beds in short supply in institutions, and some diagnoses, earlier hospitalized, will have to be referred, to home-care. Consequently, eligibility criteria for home-care services change, if resources for the services are not increased accordingly.

An explanation of the connection between how priorities are made locally on the one hand, and how (personnel) resources are defined centrally in municipalities on the other is crucial for defining essential management features in the field of home-care services. Presently, resources for services in home-care districts are mobilized on the basis of information pertaining to the work loads of attendants (and last year's budget). The indicators of work load, however, relate more to how municipal attendants and home-care assistants define individuals, referrals, or applicants into priority groupings and less to the needs of clients in a district (of which information is very patchy).

The older person admitted for home-care service is placed in one of three groups, indicating the extent of help needed. The grouping is essential for scheduling the work load of home-care attendants. In group one, normal cleaning, shopping, and services are sporadically provided; in group two, services are planned regularly up to twice a week; and in group three, services are provided more than twice a week or as often as needed. The work hours spent with an elderly person on each occasion are not necessarily longer in group three than in group one. Referrals from county council units are frequently placed in groups two and three, and the services provided more often include health care.

The amount of time to be spent and the services to be provided in an encounter with an older person are defined mainly by means of visits by the home-care assistants, sometimes together with the district nurse and/or attendants. From district to district, the priorities made greatly influence the level of resources required, but these have little bearing on the actual need for home-care services in a district. Hence, while each individual person may be correctly assessed as far as the need of home-care is concerned, without credible estimates of need in the district's elderly people, overall municipal priorities may lead to extremely inefficient and costly resource mobilization.

Resource Mobilization

By far the most important resource for home-care services is personnel, especially attendants. And in most municipalities this personnel category is a bottle-neck factor in the services. Attendants work in a low status job with relatively few openings into other careers. The actual need for services is largely unknown in the municipalities (and clients are not massively claiming their "rights" to create a marketlike definition of demand). Given that resources in districts—mainly the number of attendants—are held constant and have little bearing on actual needs, four different situations, characteristic of inefficient resource allocation, may ensue if managers continue to neglect the need to develop instruments for better need definition:

1. If the number of attendants is too low, then the work load in the districts is too high, and district personnel may respond by downgrading clients from one priority grouping to a lower one and/or reducing the work hours spent in each client encounter.

2. If the number of attendants is too low, then the work load in the districts is too high, and personnel may also respond by developing strategies to render it more difficult for eligible clients to become accepted into the population being served in the district.

3. If the number of attendants is too high, then the work load in the districts is too low, and district personnel may respond by upgrading clients from one priority grouping to a higher one and/or increasing the work hours spent in each client encounter.

4. If the number of attendants is too high, the work load is too low, and personnel may also respond by developing outreach strategies to find eligible elderly people among the district's needy population.

Like home-care managers, we have little information to define an ideal situation in the districts researched. Because no consistent strategies for outreach activities have been observed, situation four is unlikely to prevail, however. In some municipalities it was observed that one home-care district lent an attendant to another, a possible indication that a situation approaching situation number three above existed. But again, without adequate information on actual needs in the districts, the situation cannot realistically be assessed.

The most likely situation that exists in the districts approximates definitions one and two. Neither is easily verified empirically because only longitudinal data would settle the issue, not available at the present time. Situation two is more unlikely than one, however. As described earlier, many elderly people are defined into home-care by county council professionals on medical grounds and municipal managers find it hard to counter priorities based on medical arguments.

For want of adequate information about actual needs, resource mobilization in the municipalities is generally carried out in discussions on work loads in the districts, mainly by a group of top administrators and responsible politicians as part of the yearly budget planning procedure. Until recently, not even the homecare assistants were systematically heard to provide firsthand knowledge of the situation in their districts before resource allocations were decided. Regular discussions with the officials responsible for county council budgets are still atypical, despite the fact that need definition and the making of priorities are strongly influenced by personnel from county council units.

This is the more surprising because in several of the local settings studied, the politicians involved are members of the leading group of the same political party, and supposedly, a party line with regard to the home-care of elderly exists. It would seem that politicians identify more with the political institution than with the party they represent, sometimes it would seem with detrimental effects for the elderly in need of home-care services.

Home-care services depend on systematic intergovernmental cooperation at several levels of responsibility. With regard to resource mobilization, several lines may be pursued to explain the low level of cooperation at higher management layers of county councils and municipalities. In the end, cutback management strategies will turn out to be the common denominator.

For reasons relating to the professional understanding of medical groups, the status of primary health strategies is still under debate in the Swedish public health sector. Until recently they enjoyed the status of development field, exempted from major, political cutback requirements. This is no longer the case. Due to budget problems, mainly created by developments in institutional care, primary health has also come under cutback pressure in county councils. But not only there.

For the elderly, the cost of institutionalized care has also skyrocketed in municipal budgets, and for this group in particular, an organization designed to produce a high local quality of home-care services is the key to controlling costs. The formation of such local organizations will depend on incentives and control strategies jointly developed by county councils and municipalities. Discussions on strategies are hampered by the (natural) interest of each principal to have the other finance its share—at least.

Two pieces of information are vital for defining these budget shares: (1) a fairly precise picture of the number and characteristics of the group to be served and (2) from the point of view of the clients, an updated outline of the local division of labor between the organizational units providing the services. For the home-care districts studied, responsible managers lacked both.

Evaluation Practices

Only a few of those responsible for home-care services at different layers of government claimed to be engaged in the evaluation of results. The lack of initiatives to make systematic inventories of the elderly in the districts is a conspicuous result of the study. This omission on the part of responsible managers is partly explained by the fact that the definition of additional needs may increase the total costs for the services. In a cutback situation those who are administratively or politically accountable for budgets are provided with disincentives for energetic "need detection," and initiatives "from below" to start intensive outreach activities are not encouraged.

At this point it should be stressed, however, that assistants, attendants, and nurses in the districts generally make a thorough assessment of individuals referred to or applying for home-care services. Annual reports on their work is the main information, besides budgetary data, top managers rely on to plan the future volume and allocation of the resources required. Without additional reliable data to calibrate reports, however, managers of home-care services have to apply rather crude instruments in defining control strategies and incentives. They also—politicians as well as top administrators—profess to feel quite uncertain about how to evaluate local work reports.

The lack of instruments for systematic evaluation is a common feature across a range of Swedish social service fields at present (cf. Blomquist 1988; Bostedt 1988; Hjern 1988; Lövqvist 1988; Montin, 1987). The decentralization of tasks, sometimes in a controlled but frequently in an informal fashion, characterizes Swedish public administration in the 1980s. But management structures are not yet very well adapted to the fact that decentralization entails a much more prominent role for evaluation than is the case in centralized organizations. In terms of the conception used in this chapter, that reliable need definition and evaluation activities are keys to managing the decentralized organization of tasks, the more developed need definition and evaluation activities are, the less central management has to interfere with the way local managements make priorities and distribute resources.

A large number of interviewees could be cited who ask for better need definition and evaluation criteria in home-care services, mainly by others and especially from politicians and top managers. This, of course, implies that centralized organization thinking prevails throughout the service. The first steps toward a systemic management of the service would then have to include incentives for locally responsible personnel to engage in activities to evaluate themselves to find criteria that define when they themselves provide good services. Obviously, in a situation where managers have difficulty defining useful criteria for need definition and evaluation, the personnel more directly involved in encounters with the elderly are essential for establishing legitimate norms. An incentive strategy to secure this basic involvement of key personnel was not mentioned in any of the municipalities/county councils studied.

Managing Co-produced Service Quality

The argument of this chapter concerns strategies to improve quality in a public service area that constitutes an increasingly important financial and political challenge. The organization of the service is young due to the continuous growth in personnel in the past twenty years. The consumers are largely "silent" but are generally acknowledged to be entitled to improved service quality. The service is provided within an intergovernmental setting of two principals, county councils and municipalities.

A main finding of this chapter is that the management of the tasks and incentive structures of the service lacks consistency in several respects. Home-care services share this characteristic with several other Swedish social services at the present time. The overall explanation is that managers have not adopted the instruments needed to control and provide incentives for the decentralized organization of tasks. In the case of home-care services these omissions are compounded by the fact that the challenges of decentralization have to be met concurrently within two subnational governments.

In relation to management, a conspicuous finding is the absence of incentives to encourage personnel in local service units to help in defining the need population and the evaluation criteria for service production in home-care districts. Strategies to organize such incentives are blocked by several factors. The ones stressed in this chapter are related to uncertainties about how the financing of the services should be shared between municipalities and county councils. Before justifiable shares are defined, energetic outreach activities by any one party to find more eligible elderly people could affect the costs of the other in ways hard to anticipate.

Home-care services for the elderly are costly, but not as costly as care in institutions. The latter has led to financial crises in county councils especially, crises that municipalities in a county hesitate to help resolve before financial contracts between them and the county council have been negotiated. Municipalities also find institutional care too costly and plan to reduce such care as much as possible. But the group of elderly people receiving home-care frequently engages professionals from both types of subnational governments. So a connection exists between strategies for finding more eligible elderly people and financing cutbacks for the institutionalized services of county councils and municipalities. It is the more grave because in most parts of Sweden, institutional care is both costly and in short supply.

Despite the uncertainties of co-production, it is argued in this chapter that strategies to resolve the blocks created in the home-care service will have to approach the question of need definition straight on. To justify the financial shares of the subnational governments involved, two informational items need be detailed: (1) a precise picture of the number and characteristics of the group to be served and (2) from the point of view of clients, updated outline of the local division of labor between the organizational units that provide the services. Both are necessary to improve the basis for cost-sharing in the home-care field.

So far, no major contribution to this strategy for resolving blocks has been forthcoming in practice. Executive powers in the field rest with political leaders. In the past they have tended to identify with the interest of either county councils or municipalities. Leaders from the same political party, supposedly with a policy to attain the highest quality of service for the elderly, negotiate from the view of, "their" government rather than from the view of the needs of the elderly, which requires professional, intergovernmental co-production. Hence, proceedings in the field of home-care services are still more accurately characterized as administrative politics than as political management. The latter will probably also need to be buttressed if quality is to be improved in home-care services.

Note

1. Empirically, of course, the exact relationships between the age, size and efficiency of control techniques of firms are difficult to disentangle. This discussion uses results from a study of manufacturing firms with less than two hundred employees; cf. Hull and Hjern (1988 pp. 66–67).

References

Blomquist, L. (1988). *Frikommunförsöken och samverkan mellan hemtjänst och primär-værd. (Reduced State Control of Municipalities and Cooperation between Home-Care Services and Primary Health Care)*. Working paper, Centre for Services Research. Karlstad, Sweden: University of Karlstad.

Bostedt, G. (1988). "Political Institutionalization at Local Level in Sweden—The Case of Municipal Occupational Safety and Health." Paper presented at ECPR, Rimini, April 5–10. Umeæ, Sweden: Umeæ University.

Hjern, B. (1976). *Statsbidragen som styrmetod (State Subsidies as a Control Mechanism)*. Stockholm, Sweden: Gleerup.

———. (1988). *Glesbygdsstödet* Umeæ *(Support for Marginal Areas)*. Umeæ, Sweden: Umeæ University.

Hjern, B., and D.O. Porter. (1981). "Implementation structures: A New Unit of Administrative Analysis." *Realizing Social Science Knowledge*, pp. 265–277. Wien/Würzburg: Physiea-Verlag.

Hull, C., and B. Hjern. (1988). *Helping Small Firms Grow*. London: Croom Helm.

Lövqvist, S. (1988). *Resursfördelning efter behov—politik i skolan (Resource Allocation According to Needs—Politics in School)*. Umeæ, Sweden: Umeæ University, Department of Social Sciences.

———. (1988a). Lokal anpassning. Organisation av barnomsorg och hemtjänst i nio kommuner. *(Local Adaptation: The Organization of Child Care and Home Care in Nine Municipalities)*. Örebro, Sweden: University of Örebro.

SCB (National Statistics Office of Sweden). (1983). *Sveriges framtida befolkning (Sweden's Population in the Future)*. Information i prognosfrægor (Forecasting Information), no. 2. Stockholm, Sweden; SCB.

———. (1988a). *Hælsan i Sverige (Health in Sweden)*. Stockholm, Sweden: SCB.

———. (1988b). *Statistisk ærsbok (Statistical Abstract of Sweden)*. Stockholm, Sweden: SCB.

SOU (Swedish Goverment Official Reports). (1987). *Äldicomsorg i utveckling (The Development of Elderly Care)*. Report no. 21. Stockholm, Sweden: SOU

4
Notes on the Concept of Service Quality and Economic Value

Orio Giarini

From the Value of Material Products in the Industrial Economy to the Value of Performance of Systems in the Service Economy

The traditional industrial society can be described as a situation in which the privileged and by far the most important way to produce wealth and welfare is through the manufacturing process, whereby raw materials are transformed into final usable products sold on the market.

In this situation, the main preoccupation is to produce goods; services, although sometimes recognized as important, are nonetheless secondary. In other words, services are not as important as and generally not essential to production.

John Stuart Mill (1968) stated explicitly that the economic process was aimed exclusively at producing "utilities fixed and embodied in outward *objects*." In other words, even if material objects eventually had a destination and a practical use value, there was no need to consider that the process of utilization of these material objects needed any disembodied or outside economic activity. It is therefore with good conscience that the industrial revolution concentrated on the production of material goods as the essential process to further the wealth of nations.

But if all sectors of contemporary economic activity are now examined, it is easy to see that services of any sort represent the essential part of production and delivery system of goods and services. A fundamental fact to be considered is that for each product bought, be it an automobile or a carpet, the pure cost of production or of manufacturing is seldom higher than 20 to 30 percent of the final price of these products. More than 70 or 80 percent is represented by the cost of making the complex service and delivery system work, which means that service functions have become the object of the greatest concern and investment even within the most traditional industrial companies.

It must therefore be clear that the service economy is not in opposition to the industrial economy, but represents a more advanced stage of development in economic history.

In the same way, at the beginning of the Industrial Revolution, agricultural production was not eliminated; on the contrary, it remained a fundamental economic activity. But through industrialization, directly or indirectly, agriculture has become more efficient. Now both the agriculture and manufacturing industry have to rely more and more on the development of services to ameliorate their economic performance in production and distribution.

The service functions, which intervene at several levels in the production and use of wealth, can be broadly classified into five categories:

1. Services performed long before any production begins, such as research and development. Only after 1930 did this function become a specific, professional one deserving separate budget accounting. In some high technology sectors, this preproduction service function can represent more than 50 percent of the total cost of a full production series. Services functions such as investment programs and marketing research studies also often intervene before a production process of any sort has started.

2. Concentration and specialization of production have required a greater and greater emphasis on service functions like planning, maintenance, storage, quality control, and safety measures.

3. Distribution is already per se essentially a service function of great complexity and is obviously essential for the efficient organization of systems making products and services available.

4. A unique characteristic of the service economy is the growth of service functions related to the utilization of any sort of products during their period of useful life. Users are called on more and more to invest in their education in order to transform the potential value of any product or service into something of practical use. Users often become part of the production system ("prosumers"), in order to make things work and yield their potential value.

5. Services now come into play more frequently to manage both the waste and pollution produced at all levels of the manufacturing process, as well as at the end of the useful life span of products (when they become wastes themselves).

During the Industrial Revolution, the transformation process from raw materials to the final product was the key feature of the economic system. Today, the larger part of economic resources is absorbed by functions parallel to this process on the right and on the left of figure 4–1. On the

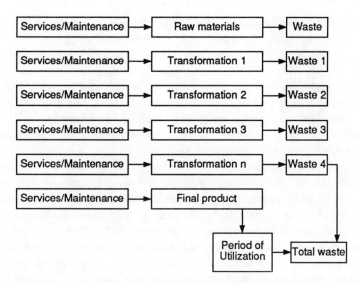

Figure 4–1. The complexification of the economic system.

one side, an increasing number of services are needed before and during production: research, development, investment planning, storage and distribution systems, maintenance and repair, security measures and insurance, market research, and so on. On the other side, costs for the disposal of the waste accumulated during production and after the utilization of products are clearly growing. Some critics of the service economy maintain that products are still the essential part after all and that without products services would not even exist. In the same way two hundred years ago, critics of the Industrial Revolution maintained that agricultural production was the real priority in the economic system and that without the produce of land, industrialization could only be considered secondary. This debate is clearly trivial and irrelevant.

It is obvious that the agriculture and manufacturing industries are essential and cannot simply be forgotten. However, any sort of product today that does not rely on the functioning of services is simply not in a condition to be used or even produced. Products of any sort can only exist economically through the service system.

Therefore, a key difference between the industrial economy and the service economy is that the first essentially values products that exist materially and that are exchanged, whereas the service economy values more the performance and real utilization (in a given time period) of products (material or not) integrated in a system. During the classical economic revolution the value of products could be identified essentially with the costs involved in producing them. The notion of value in the service economy is shifting toward evaluating costs incurred with references to obtaining results in utilization.

The first approach considers the value of a washing machine per se. The second evaluates the actual performance of the washing machine, taking into consideration not only its cost of production, but also other costs (learning time of the people using the machine, maintenance and repair costs, etc.). The applicability of the two approaches in most cases depends on the technological complexity of the products: in the case of simple products and tools, the assessment of the value can be limited to the tool or the product per se. No one buying a hammer would think it necessary to take courses to learn how to use it. In the case of a computer, however, the cost of learning how to use it tends to surpass the purchase cost of the machine, especially if the costs of all the necessary software are added.

Similarly, people buying tools such as dishes or even a bicycle will not consider signing a maintenance contract. With the purchase of electronic typewriters, photocopying machines, or even television sets, however, maintenance contracts—even for individual consumers—are becoming common. In the service economy, the *functioning* of a tool is being purchased (thus including costs of maintenance and repair): people are more and more buying functioning "systems," not just products.

The real change toward the service economy stems precisely from the fact that services are becoming indispensable if products and services are to fulfill basic needs. Services are no longer simply a secondary sector. They are moving into the focus of economic action, where they have become *indispensable production tools* to satisfy basic needs and increase the wealth of nations.

Reconsidering the notion of economic value provided by John Stuart Mill, in the modern service economy, the value of the material objects cannot be considered as limited to their mere existence anymore. The utilization of all material objects more and more requires the functioning of services. Services have become, contrary to the Industrial Revolution, real production factors, indispensable for the creating wealth for nations on the same level as material production itself. In quantitative terms, the allocation of resources to services is greater than to agricultural and manufacturing processes together.

The evolution of the insurance industry in the 1970s and 1980s is a typical example of the relevance of the service economy concept. Until 1980 everyone, including people in the insurance industry, accepted that insurance policies covering life risks or material damages were a typical secondary product in the traditional economic sense and that they could only expand once basic needs were satisfied by material production. However, during the ten years following 1973, when the growth of GNP in the world dropped from an average of 6 percent to less than 3 percent per year, the overall sales of policies grew at 5 percent per year. If insurance consumption were of secondary importance, the slowdown in other activities and in manufacturing in particular would have produced more than a proportional reduction in insurance sales, according to Engels' law.

In fact, Engels' law reproduces the traditional industrial economics paradigm in which services are a secondary type of economic good and can only be consumed after basic needs are satisfied through so-called essential economic activities (agricultural products and industrial manufactured goods). Even allowing that this law is valid in some specific cases, cases in which some types of consumption (including industrial products) only arise after a certain level of wealth, it completely misrepresents the function of services that are essential to make even the most basic goods available today. For example, many situations of poverty and even hunger in the world are due more to the poor functioning of services than to the mere existence of agriculture products and manufactured goods per se.

The explanation for continuous growth of insurance activities, even in periods of declining overall growth, lies precisely in the nature of the modern production system, which depends on services as key tools to guarantee its proper functioning. At an extremely advanced technological level of production, in which risks and vulnerabilities are highly concentrated and represent an essential managerial challenge, insurance has become—increasingly so in the last decades—a fundamental precondition for investment. Similarly, at a more general level, social security, health and life insurance have by now achieved the status of a primary need in most industrialized countries.

The very process of technology development in the modern economy has led to an increasingly complex system, where logistics, organization, and information have become fundamental issues.

Considering the economy as a service economy also allows better appreciation of contributions make by contemporary technology: the latest technological advances have had their greatest impact on systems concerned with the communication and organization of information, exactly what is needed to better manage the development of present day economies. All this is quite different from the direction technology had taken during the Industrial Revolution, when all that mattered was how to improve the stages of production transforming raw materials into finished goods.

Quality and Performance

If it is accepted that economic value in a service economy is determined by the performance of a system, the idea that quality is fully integrated in the notion of performance itself can be proposed. Good quality performance has better value than lesser quality performance. The two notions of quality and performance are, in fact, identical. What is lacking is a system of measurement of economic value that can actually and effectively quantify the variations in wealth production generated by all types of economic systems.

In practice, a poor quality performance has a lesser economic value, and a performance that is extremely deficient can produce negative or destructive results, called "deducted values" (Giarini and Louberge 1978).

Also, the more modern economies become high technology service economies, the more quantity and quality tend to become interdependent. Even high technological mass production must incorporate qualitative aspects simply to function economically. For the more advanced systems and technologies, the notion of gaining in quantity at the expense of quality (performance) makes less and less sense.

It should be stressed that quality refers to how a system performs in relation to stated objectives.

In some cases, the necessity of having the right type of quality and performance exists. For instance, some products must be destroyed after use. The cost of destruction must not increase disproportionately because the quality of the product during use has been reinforced to the extent of becoming a *negative* quality when the product itself passes from utilization destruction, recycling, or reconditioning. This is a problem of optimizing duration or the life cycle of products (Börlin and Stahel 1987).

Quality and the Measure of Productivity in the Service Economy: Integrating Monetarized and Nonmonetarized Indicators

The problem of measuring the productivity of services clearly reveals that an economy essentially based on service functions can no longer rely on the traditional productivity measures developed for the industrial economy. Many scholars have exploited as much as possible traditional ways of measuring services output with some modest results.[1]

The key issue is defining what the product is, what an output of a service activity is as compared with an industrial activity.

In both cases, it is relatively easy to quantify the cost of the production factors and the inputs. In the case of the industrial economy, the product is identified by a material object sold on the market. Normally, productivity means the capacity of production factors to produce more and more units of these material products in a given time period. In the case of services, a performance is key, and therefore the traditional measurement of productivity leads in most of cases to erroneous conclusions.

The methodological difficulty is that traditional economic theory is based on the assumption of a price equilibrium between supply and demand. Therefore, with a logical bypass, the cost of production is easily equated with the value of demand. As a result, the measurement of the value and productivity of services is often based on production value factors. In this way, a public administration that doubled its employees or their salaries with no additional performance would be considered as having doubled its value in terms of gross national product. In the same way, an inefficient administration, poorly paid, as is the case in one European Community country, has been considered as having an above average productivity because its costs relative to those of other national public administrations are lower, and they are all supposed to perform the same functions. Once again, no measurement of the *real performance or quality* of the services produced is taken into account and integrated into the traditional economic evaluation.

The extension of service functions in modern economies will increasingly oblige economists and all those involved with economic issues to decide (1) *either* to maintain their evaluation on the basis of the traditional accounting of value added as proposed by classic and neoclassic industrial economics, which will constantly diminish the relevance and significance of such measurements; *or* (2) find practical, as well as theoretical ways, to integrate measurements of services performances, or measurements of the *quality* of outputs (which is the same), in order to reestablish a significant and useful means of measuring the real wealth produced by the economic system.

This implies that the measurement of the costs and productivity of health-related activity is not done in terms of the value-added produced, but in terms of the level of health achieved for a given population and/or a given individual. Once more, these quality indicators must be integrated into a system of evaluation including, of course, the traditional measurement of added value. Whatever the objections concerning the difficulty of this task and the problems of integrating monetarized and nonmonetarized indicators, these objections cannot change the nature of the problem to be solved. It is up to modern economic thinking to face this challenge.

At a time when 70 percent of the working population in the advanced economies (and more than 50 percent in the rest of the world) perform service functions, it is high time to seriously redefine the type of wealth they produce in real terms and how these activities can be realistically quantified. In other words, how can the quality of the performance be measured in economic terms that finds an updated answer to the old question of identifying "the wealth of nations."

All these considerations lead one to look closer at the problem of integrating monetary and nonmonetary economic values (Giarini 1982). The

Industrial Revolution has solved this dichotomy by considering nonmonetary values to be outside the economic realm.

In fact, the substitution of a nonmonetary activity by a monetarized activity, even though entailing certain specific sacrifices, has, in practice, been considered desirable. The productivity of the monetarized sector will more than compensate in the long term and often also in the short term for any loss in the traditional, essentially nonmonetarized sector. The Industrial Revolution itself has been organized around the process of monetarization of a larger and larger part of human wealth-producing activities. In classic economic theory, the debate on use value implicitly admitted that economic, material welfare may also be produced by the traditional, nonmonetarized sector, so that material welfare (TW) can be defined in general as:

$$TW = V_{NM} + V_M \quad (V = \text{value}$$
$$NM = \text{nonmonetarized}$$
$$M = \text{monetarized})$$

But in practice, nonmonetarized values were finally kept outside the dominant economic model because essentially, if not priced, they were either outside the exchange system or outside the world of scarcity.

A relatively high degree of nonmonetarized values has however persisted, even in the most industrialized nations, for example, nonremunerated work (housewives, benevolent activities), nonremunerated goods and services (unpolluted air and water).

What should be emphasized here is that insofar as V_{NM} is the truly dynamic part of the process in adding to TW (where V_{NM} is particularly static and/or irrelevant), the economist could and did normally assume that $TW = V_M$.

However, V_{NM} is not independent of V_M; V_M in fact reduces the field of the NM economy and/or transforms it.

As stated, it is normally assumed that any loss in the NM sector will be more than offset by the $M-$ substitutive activity. In terms of value, gain in V_M will be greater than any loss in V_{NM}.

But it is only under such conditions that TW will in fact increase. The difficulty in analyzing such an equation is due not only to the problem implicit in evaluating nonmonetary activities, but also to the concept of value in traditional economic theory, when this is equated with welfare.

If the notion of value is limited to the monetarized production process, it implies that any production that only considers price boundaries is producing welfare. This can happen, as has been seen, when the advantages of industrialization are overwhelming, indisputable, and do not suffer from the diminishing returns of technology. If the value is based, as proposed, on its utilization, it becomes a matter of common sense to identify welfare with the total net contribution of the nonmonetarized and the monetarized economic system to the satisfaction of material needs.

In other words, the basic paradigm—the concept of value—of traditional economics (be it the Smithian or demand-based concept), represents an obstacle to assessing the true net contribution to welfare by nonmonetarized economic activity.

The following points may clarify this:

A closer look at any production process reveals that, among the production factors, many inputs are not monetary or not monetarized: the cost of air for a company producing nitrogen through the liquefied air process is nil, as are the large quantities of river water used by a paper or and aluminum mill.

If this air or water is highly polluted, costs will be incurred in returning these "free" raw materials to their initial purity—the problem is intensified in that most advances in technology may not be able to avoid pollution emission and may even tend to aggravate the total environmental control problem.

Consequently, in the initial industrialization phase, the industrial system will have many essential production inputs free of charge. Subsequently they will have to be paid for: this transfer into the monetarized system does not indicate that a process is increasing total welfare, but simply that it is first increasing the total costs for producing welfare.

This may also be illustrated at the level of the individual with a similar example: swimming in a nonpolluted sea or lake free of charge is an element of welfare. The invention of the automobile led to an increase in total welfare by adding to the choice of places to go swimming, an obvious increase in total welfare (based on the services available from the nonmonetarized economy and from the monetarized one). In a third phase, the same industrial system that makes the production of automobiles possible leads to the pollution of seas and lakes. Diminishing welfare (utilization value) results: the costs entailed in reestablishing the utilization value of water will be "catching up" costs and not costs added to total welfare (or utilization value). Encountered here, once again, is the concept of value deducted.

Starting from the traditional notion of value, it can be said that, in current economic accounting, a certain number of production phases (and a number of products) are not produced to increase added value, but to restore utilization values previously destroyed. They now have to be recycled or reintegrated at some cost in order to permit the economic machine to run. If the rise in national income in recent years is increasingly due to the development of the antipollution industry (detection systems, chemical products, incinerators, compacting machines for domestic use, etc.), this production does not add to the initial level of welfare, but it is being used more to fight the negative effects of industrial expansion.

The resultant added value is *not* a measure of added welfare: it represents the cost of previous consumption that now has to be paid to restore utilization possibilities. It is, in fact, a deducted value. The indicator of GNP as a sum of added values is, in fact, diverging more from an indicator of welfare; rather, it is increasingly clear that it is only an indicator of cost. If, in the golden era of the Industrial Revolution, it could also be assumed to be an indicator of material/economic welfare, it is because in a period of no actual diminishing returns of technology almost all the production costs become net real wealth. Now, an ever-greater portion of those costs represents a negative feedback loop effect on the overall trend of the total monetarized cost indicator, the GNP.

It is at the moment when increasing resources must be used to restore the utilization values destroyed that performance measures to identify wealth are needed, whereas traditional added value is becoming less relevant.

Quality and Uncertainty: The Management of Risk

The notion of system has become essential in the service economy. Systems produce positive results or economic value (equal to the real "quality" increase of wealth) when the function properly.

Systems operation (or functioning) requires the consideration of real time and the dynamics of real life. And whenever real time is considered, the degree of uncertainty and probability that conditions any human action becomes a central issue.

In contrast, the economics of the Industrial Revolution could rely on the fiction of a perfect equilibrium theory (outside real time and duration) based on the assumption of certainty.

The importance of utilization in the service economy has another consequence in terms of the appreciation of economic value. Utilization is a process that takes place over a period of time. The duration of the utilization periods of products and services therefore becomes an important element to assess to optimize economic activity. Cost/benefit analysis has to be conducted with reference to different possible periods of utilization, and the cost of waste after use must be integrated in the features of products at the planning stage. The optimization of duration and also of durability is, de facto, taken more into consideration when products are marketed and sold through leasing systems, for instance. In these cases, what is sold and bought is the product's utilization including all costs linked to make it function throughout its life span.

Any system working to obtain some future results is, by definition, in a situation of uncertainty, even if different situations are characterized by different degrees of risk, uncertainty, or even indetermination.[2] But risk and uncertainty are not a matter of choice; they are simply part of the human condition and activity.

Rationality is therefore not so much a problem of avoiding risk and eliminating uncertainty but of reducing them to acceptable levels in given situations.

Furthermore, the very systemic nature of the modern economy and the increasing complexity of technological developments require a deeper and deeper economic understanding and control of the increasing vulnerability of these systems.

Unfortunately, the notion of vulnerability is generally misunderstood. To say that vulnerability increases parallel to the increase in the quality and performance of modern technology might seem paradoxical. In fact, the higher level of performance of most technological advances relies on a reduction of the margins of error that a system can tolerate without breakdown. Accidents and management mistakes still happen, even if less frequently, but their effects now have more costly systemic consequences.

Opening a car door in motion does not necessarily lead to a catastrophe. In the case of a modern airplane, it will. This shows that systems functioning and vulnerability control become a key economic function in which the contributions of economics and engineers must be integrated. Similarly, problems of social security and savings for the individuals have to take into account vulnerability management at a personal level.

Vulnerability is also relevant to productivity. In fact, the notion and measurement of productivity is an important issue for the service economy. Clearly, if economic value depends on the proper functioning of a system, productivity cannot simply be linked to the quantity of inputs compared to the quantity of measurable outputs, but rather to the *quality of performance*. Hence, vulnerability is a factor conditioning real productivity in the industrial economy, a quality in which specific indicators of "results" have to be integrated with price indicators.

In any case, the question of measuring quality in economic terms is becoming a major issue in itself, an obvious additional indication of the emergence of the service economy.[3]

Risk has become increasingly concentrated at levels in which the vulnerability is such that the overall uncertainty of the economic process increases.

How many managements twenty years ago dreamed of the decision possibility experiences today? Consumers are also reluctant to become consumers of "risk." The unique situation in the field of product liability and malpractice in the United States, although amplified by a specific legal environment, is beginning to affect other parts of the world. A typical trend of demand in the service economy, the consumer is more conscious that tools and products exist for given purposes and even experts are only of value when the results of their "utilization" are positive. The fact that their utilization might give negative results is refuted and gives rise to requests for compensation (Shavell 1979; Geneva Papers 1987). Product liability is a great issue in the United States where litigation has led in some cases to extremely high and even excessive compensation. Chemical and pharmaceutical companies have a special problem (9) in this area (Hailey 1985).

Doctors, lawyers, and other experts are sued for malpractice and must compensate clients if found guilty (Jackson and Powell 1982). At the European level, the Directive on Product Liability (1985) resulted from ten years of discussions and preparations to manage the expanding phenomenon of the public's increasing perception that producers of economic wealth are liable for delivering a "product" that yields negative results. Once again, in the contemporary economy, "performance" with economic value is what counts rather than the simple "existence" of a product or service.

The problem of environmental hazards, which is often linked to the transportation and storage of dangerous materials, is part of the same type of risks and vulnerabilities that modern society must face (Kunreuther 1986).

Nothing is more explicitly relevant than the explosion of liabilities in the modern advanced economic world to indicate the profound changes of "demand" in the contemporary service economy. This phenomenon is easy to identify in practice and has already led many economists to consider it in conjunction with the development of legal issues.[4]

Here again, the theoretical objection that measuring quality is difficult is overrun by reality. If the quality or performance of a system is what matters, all theoretical efforts have only one aim: to provide a comprehensive and coherent analysis of what present economic reality entails.

Notes

1. See, for instance, the excellent study by Bernard Ascher and Obi Whichard, "Improving Services Trade Data," in O. Giarini (ed.), *The Emerging Service Economy*, Oxford: Pergamon Press, 1987, 255–82, as well as the article by Philippe Trogan, "Les statistiques de production sur les services marchands et la mesure de la productivité," in O. Giarini and J. R. Roulet (eds.), *L'Europe face à la nouvelle économie des services*. Paris: PUF, 1988, 95–112.

2. The following definitions are adopted in this chapter: risk represents a probable occurrence or event of a subjective (following a decision to act or not to act) or an objective nature (independent of one's decision) influencing a given system at different levels of magnitude; uncertainty measures the degree of confi-

dence one can have in a given probability; indetermination refers to systems or situations that cannot be defined.

3. See, for instance, the chapter, "Quality, Productivity and Strategy," in R. Normann, *Service Management*, New York: John Wiley & Sons, 1984; see also the chapter, "Services and Productivity," in D. Riddle, *Service-Led Growth*, New York: Praeger Special Studies, 1986; and the chapter, "Measurement of Output and Productivity in the Service Sector," by John Kendrick, in R. Inman, *Managing the Service Economy*, New York: Cambridge University Press, 1985.

4. One of the signs of the growing interest in this area is provided by the Law and Economics Association in Europe, created just a few years ago, which brings together academic representatives from both the legal and economic disciplines.

References

Börlin, M., and W. Stahel. (1987) *Stratégie économique de la durabilité*. Zurich: Swiss Bank Corporation.

The European Community, *Directive on Product Liability*, 1985.

Geneva Papers on Risk and Insurance (1987). *Liability Insurance and Safety Regulation*, no. 43, April (special issue).

The following considerations are taken from Giarini, O. (1982). *Dialogue on Wealth and Welfare—A Report to the Club of Rome*. Oxford: Pergamon Press.

Giarini O., and H. Louberge. (1978). *The Diminishing Returns of Technology*. Oxford: Pergamon Press.

Hailey, Arthur. (1985). *Strong Medicine*. London: Pan Books.

Jackson, R., and J. Powell. (1982). *Professional Negligence*. London: Sweet & Maxwell.

Kunreuther, H. (ed.). (1986). *Transportation, Storage and Disposal of Hazardous Materials*. Papers from a conference at I.I.A.S.A., Laxenburg (Vienna), Wharton School, University of Pennsylvania, Philadelphia.

Mill, John Stuart. (1968). *Principles of Political Economy*. London: Routledge and Kegan Paul.

Shavell, S. (1979). *Accidents, Liabilities and Insurance*. Harvard Institute of Economic Research, Discussion Paper no. 685.

Part II
How to Develop
Service Quality

This section examines methods and issues related to the development of service quality. Designing a quality offering is not simple in that it requires analysis of the service from both the provider and consumer perspectives. How each element of the service is designed to assure quality may be different for various functional and consumer stakeholders. The chapters in this section address these development issues as well as factors that may affect customer perceptions of service quality.

An important technique used in the development and analysis of service offerings is blueprinting. William George and Barbara Gibson's chapter provides an overview of blueprinting and an example of its use in the design of a new service. The authors demonstrate that blueprinting offers insights into service quality, provides a means to control the service delivery, and facilitates the management of quality in services.

Martin Senior and Gary Akehurst's chapter highlights the importance of service delivery to the consumer's perception of quality. Using budget hotels as an illustration, the authors make the case that low-cost, basic services are not an excuse for mismanaging the service encounter. Rather, a reliable delivery combined with a corporate quality culture are the distinguishing characteristics of good, low-cost services.

The development and delivery of a service are the result of many actions. As discussed in Friedhart Hegner's chapter, chains of actions are global guidelines transcending functional areas, organizations, and people in clarifying customer wants. The author describes the meaning of chains of actions and shows how service quality may be achieved in the delivery system through building chains of means-end relationships.

Increasingly, service marketers are realizing the importance of tangible aspects of the service offering. Jean-Paul Flipo's chapter develops a list of criteria for classifying tangible factors and then discusses the strategic implications of these factors for industrial services. He concludes that the ultimate goal of tangible elements is to assist suppliers in managing customer expectations.

Often the consumer or observer sees only a snapshot of the service production and delivery processes. Jarmo Lehtinen's chapter examines the service production process across several different cultures to aid in understanding service delivery styles. He finds that the production process, service style, and quality are all quite distinct among Oriental, European, American, and Soviet cultures. The chapter concludes with managerial implications for service delivery processes.

This section concludes with the development of a service quality map offered as an approach to studying and developing service quality. David Collier's chapter is based on the premise that information about quality is available from both operations and marketing perspectives. Marketing information focuses on customer perceptions, and operations information is concerned with the technical quality of the service offering. Collier addresses the managerial issues of coordinating and evaluating the offering using these two sets of quality information.

5
Blueprinting
A Tool for Managing Quality in Service

William R. George
Barbara E. Gibson

Introduction

This chapter analyzes the service blueprinting process as a means of managing service quality. A service blueprint is a tool used to depict and analyze all the processes involved in providing a service. The research presented in this chapter suggests that use of the blueprinting process to manage service quality may include designing new services, evaluating existing services and restructuring them as needed, and controlling service delivery. Determining the line(s) of visibility and failpoints is a logical starting point for managing service quality. An example of the blueprinting process is given to illustrate its significant role in ensuring quality in services.

Recognition of the importance of service quality for both goods and services has grown tremendously the past ten years. Proponents who support the importance of service quality in the goods sector include Leonard and Sasser (1982), Takeuchi and Quelch (1983), and Garvin (1983). In the service sector significant attention to the importance of service quality has also grown.

Quality in Services

The Marketing Science Institute has funded research in the area of service quality (Parasuraman, Zeithaml, and Berry 1985, 1988; Zeithaml, Berry, and Parasuraman 1988). This work suggests that differences between expected service and perceived service (gap 5) may be a focal point for quality in services problems (cf Grönroos 1984; Lewis and Booms 1983).

The Nordic School of Services Marketing provides another perspective

The contributions to this study by Carol Beale and Wendy Hosick, Richmond Metropolitan Blood Service's Strategic Research Program, and by Annette Gow, graduate assistant, College of Commerce and Finance, Villanova University, are gratefully acknowledged.

on service quality models (Grönroos 1980, 1984, 1985, 1986; Lehtinen 1985). Grönroos believes that the experienced service is a function of two dimensions: *technical quality—what* the customer gets as a result of the buyer-seller interactions—and functional quality—*how* the customer gets it. According to the Grönroos model these two quality dimensions determine the corporate image, which in turn influences the consumer's perceived service quality. This perceived quality is an outcome of the consumer's evaluation of the perceived service as compared with the expected service.

In a thoughtful critique of the Grönroos theory of service quality, Shostack (Bernhardt and Shostack 1983) finds the theory deficient in three areas. First, she believes that two dimensions of technical and functional quality do not fully describe all elements of a service. Second, she takes exception to the priority of functional over technical quality. Shostack believes that the final problem with the theory is its overwhelming bias toward services rendered by people.

Measurement and Control of Quality in Services. Measuring and controlling quality remains a topic of great interest, especially in services, in which quality may be even more challenging than in goods. King (1985) provides an insightful, nonquantitative assessment of the special factors to be considered. She observes that most services result from an entire series of functions performed in sequence. This means that "measurements should be identified for each of the critical functions in the sequence— those affecting the end result as experienced by the customer" (p. 16). She recommends the presence of the customer in the production process be considered when developing the service quality control system: "The quality assurance system must include standards for functions that direct and control the customer's interactions with the service delivery system" (p.16).

Blueprinting Services

Shostack in a series of articles (1981, 1984a, 1984b, 1985, 1987) has convincingly argued for using a service blueprint as a tool for depicting and analyzing all she processes involved in delivering services to the consumer. Her primary focus with blueprinting has been on the design and positioning functions of services marketing. She has also encouraged its use as a quality mechanism without, however, devoting any detailed attention to this aspect of blueprinting.

Lines of visibility and failpoints are two components of service blueprinting especially relevant to quality. The *line of visibility* separates those processes that are visible to the consumer from those that are not. Several articles include details about this component (Shostack 1984a, 1985). The percentage of the blueprint above the line of visibility varies according to each service, but often, the majority of the blueprint is below the line of visibility. Shostack likens what lies above the line of visibility to the tip of an iceberg. She believes that particular attention must be paid to the processes below the line even though customers are often totally unaware of them. These processes *are* the service and can cause success or failure in the portion of the blueprint visible to customers. She notes, however, that attention to the portions of the blueprint above the line cannot be ignored. Such processes provide the only tangible evidence a consumer uses to verify the effectiveness of the service. Therefore, all processes below the line as well as all visible aspects of the service, that is, tangible clues, must be carefully designed to maximize the desired effect on the consumer.

Failpoints identify those processes of the service most likely to "go wrong" and function other than intended, thereby adversely affecting an aspect of service quality (Shostack 1984b). Although a blueprint will usually include only those failpoints most likely to cause execution, quality, or consistency problems, it allows the service manager to evaluate all points for potential problems. Once the blueprint has been developed, failpoints can be determined by statistical monitoring or by hypothesis and testing methods (Shostack 1985). Failpoints can be internal and invisible to the customer or visible to the customer, that is, below or above the line of visibility. Failpoints allow a proactive management approach to quality in services.

Research Design

Research Problem and Questions

This exploratory chapter is qualitative in nature, undertaken to gain new insights into managing quality in services. It describes the testing of the service blueprinting process within a health-care environment. A blueprint of the major service of a health-care organization is the test subject. The research questions under investigation include: 1) Does blueprinting provide insights about service quality issues? 2) Does blueprinting provide a means of managing quality in services? and 3) Does blueprinting provide a means of controlling service quality delivery? The conclusion addresses these questions.

Research Setting

Richmond Metropolitan Blood Service (RMBS) is a not-for-profit regional blood center established in 1974 to collect blood from volunteers and supply it to fourteen area hospitals. By the end of twelve months the blood center had a staff of thirty-five to provide five services: recruit donors; collect 15,644 units of blood; test it for hepatitis and syphilis; process it into components; and distribute the components to hospitals. At that time the service staff collected blood at the main center and at one mobile drive at a different location each day.

During the ensuing thirteen years the blood service has tripled its staff and expanded into nine new blood programs and services. In addition to changes brought about by this expansion, the main service line has undergone significant changes with the emergence of acquired immunodeficiency syndrome (AIDS).

Today the blood service collects approximately fifty thousand units of blood at four donor centers and five mobile drives each week day. It provides highly sophisticated products and services around the clock for traumas and transplants as well as for more routine procedures. The need to control and standardize the ever-increasing service offerings while providing excellent customer service, often in a climate of fear and mistrust, is evident.

Research Methodology

The Grönroos model of service quality was chosen as the framework for testing the research questions about blueprinting as a tool for managing quality in service. This model was chosen for several reasons. The research setting involves services rendered by people and is very "people intensive." The two dimensions of technical and functional quality are parsimonious and appear to encompass adequately the service process studied.

The Study: Blueprinting of a Health Care Service

The blood service's first experience with blueprinting was in its investigation of diversification opportunities. The Strategic Research Program, RMBS's research and development group, used blueprinting to model services under consideration. In the course of its investigations the group evaluated genetics testing, air and ground transportation, a clear pharmacy, and other services. From this experience in using blueprinting in evaluating proposed new services came the hypothesis that, with some modification, the mechanism could be extremely helpful in understanding and managing current services.

Mobile Collections Blueprint

More than 70 percent of total collections per year are produced by the mobile blood drives. Yet, of all the operations in a blood center, the mobile blood drive is where the most failpoints are likely to occur. There are far more variables to manage here than at a fixed site. For example, the blood service is dependent on the sponsoring group to recruit and schedule the donors, to provide a room with adequate facilities, and to modify its usual operations to permit its employees or members to donate blood. The blood collection team must create a positive environment for blood donation in an unfamiliar (and sometimes unsupportive) setting. Under these circumstances, standardization of service delivery, a complex activity under the best of conditions (King 1984), becomes even more difficult as more variables are added to the process.

In the case of a mobile drive, two primary customers must be served: the sponsoring group and the donor. A third customer, the potential blood recipient, is also present because each customer may need blood products and services at some time in the future. Thus, all customers' perceptions about quality help create the blood recipient's expectations through both direct and indirect experience. As King (1985) has observed, the standards for quality service levels may vary according to each group's different criteria when making the evaluation. For example, the president of a corporate sponsor group may function as all three customer types—sponsor, donor, blood recipient. In this instance the evaluation may vary according to which role the customer has assumed. Consequently, expectations may not only vary according to customer group, but also may overlap as customer groups overlap. For the sake of clarity in the blueprinting process for mobile collections, the assumption that everyone is a potential blood recipient was made. (The patient is considered a primary customer for blood services in special cases such as autologous [self] donations and outpatient transfusions.)

Two customer groups necessitate two lines of visibility. The additional line of visibility is a departure from Shostack's work. Two lines enhance the analytical power of the blueprinting process for complex service delivery systems. Donors experience only those activities above the primary line of visibility. The secondary line of visibility includes activities experienced by the donors as well as those activities experienced only by the sponsoring group. The analysis here is simplified and enhanced by the additional line of visibility distinguishing between the two customer groups. For example, the development of monitoring approaches and communication avenues can now be more focused for each group.

Blood services' staff have always known that the mobile blood drive was extremely complex. The blueprint makes this point far more persuasively than a procedure manual or other narrative description. While a blueprint reinforces the complexity of a service delivery system, it also introduces clarity and cohesiveness into the analysis process. Seeing the infrastructure of a system that may have evolved over years with additions being made out of necessity, perhaps with little regard for the system as a whole, can be illuminating. It can change forever how people in organizations think about their operations. The blueprint facilitates a system-wide perspective of the entire service process, allowing greater understanding of institutional quality. Such overall quality can best be analyzed by starting with the blueprint's failpoints.

The initial blueprinting step for managing quality was the identification of the most common failpoints. These were identified using several methods. Anecdotal information provided the initial list of failpoints. Previous donor surveys about the level of satisfaction with the process surfaced some failpoints. Interviews with staff, sponsoring group representatives, and donors garnered the most useful information, however. In addition, the blueprinting process revealed other failpoints for this service delivery process.

Shostack suggests that "little of the service is actually visible to the customer" (1985, p. 7). The mobile collections blueprint, however, tells a somewhat different story. Of the twenty-eight failpoints specified, nineteen were above the primary line of visibility and three were above the secondary line. That blood collection activities are people intensive and involve direct personal encounter may explain why more of the actual service is above the primary line of visibility. The blueprint of Mobile Collections Service Delivery (figure 5–1) depicts the twenty-eight failpoints related to the service encounter. Special training sessions for staff have been conducted to help them understand how to avoid such failures and how to handle them if they occur.

Table 5–1 indicates the significance of each failpoint as it relates to quality. Each failpoint was rated independently by two people based on the criteria of "more important/less important," the degree of "technical/functional quality," and its position on the blueprint. Several patterns emerged once these ratings were completed.

First, those failpoints determined to be "more important" involved direct interaction with the customer, that is, above the primary line of visibility. Second, two-thirds of the failpoints were strongly related to functional quality. Indeed, all the "more important" failpoints, except one, were characterized by strong functional quality. This finding is critical to service delivery because functional quality is least often addressed in operations manuals and is least likely to be monitored routinely.

All activities shown below the secondary line of visibility focus primarily on technical quality, while those above involve aspects of both technical and functional quality. The authors believe that for health care services both of these qualities are equally important. Blueprinting of the mobile collections service process provides additional support for that belief. By using the blueprint, for example, the training program for those who draw blood can focus on each quality dimensions, as well as on interactions between technical and functional quality for each service activity.

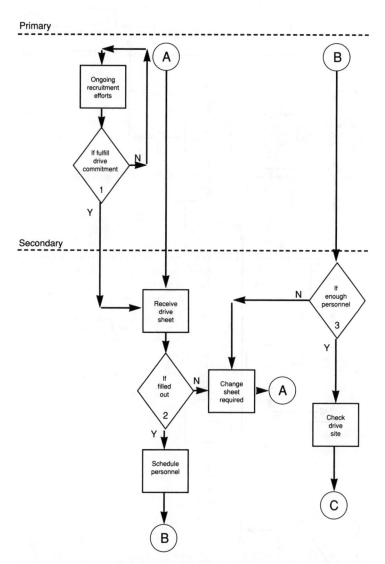

Figure 5–1. Mobile collection service delivery blueprint.

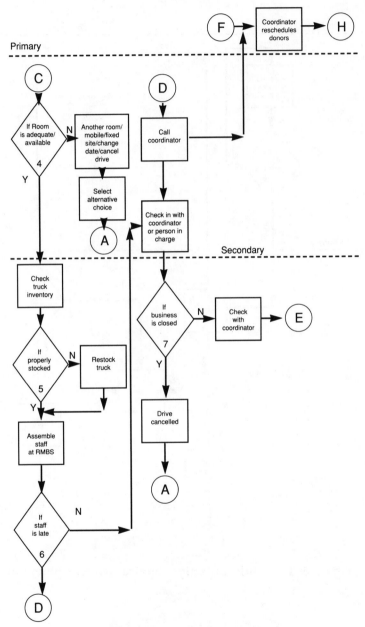

Figure 5–1. (continued)

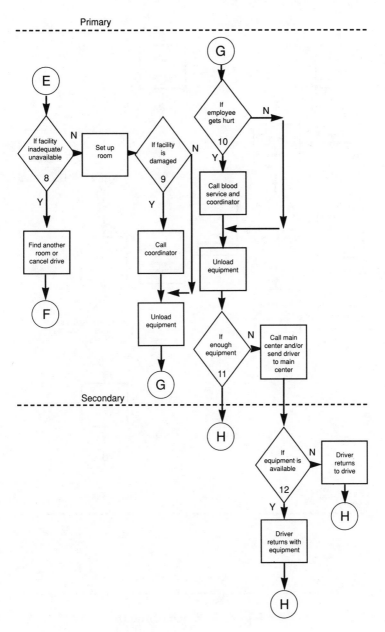

Figure 5–1. (continued)

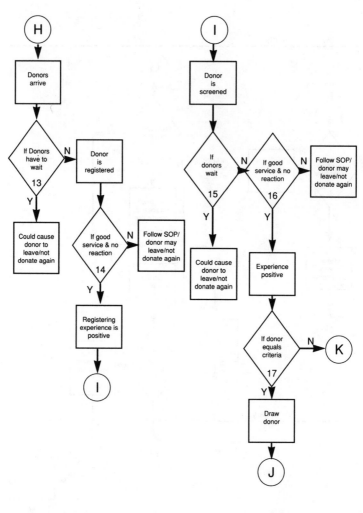

Primary

Secondary

Figure 5–1. (continued)

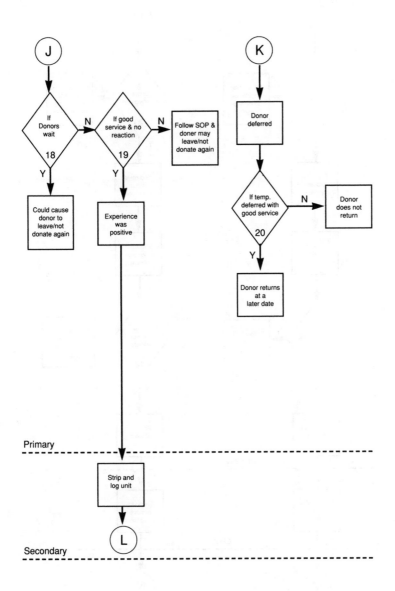

Figure 5–1. (continued)

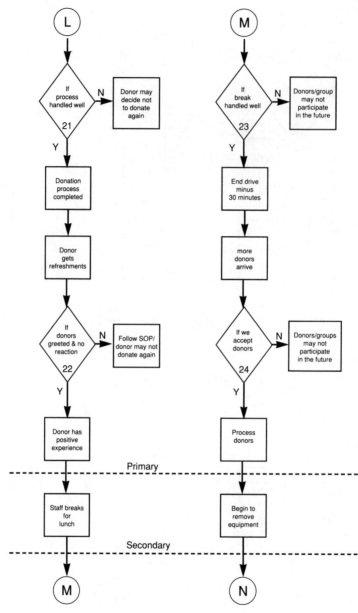

Figure 5–1. (continued)

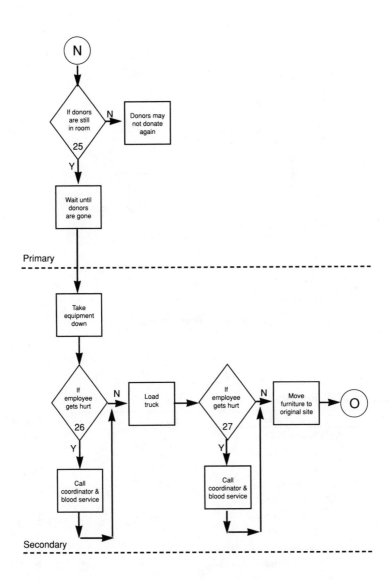

Figure 5–1. (continued)

Primary
- -

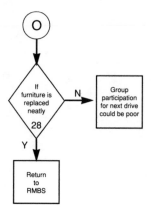

Secondary
- -

Figure 5–1. (continued)

Table 5–1
Evaluation of Failpoints

Failpoint	Line Position	Rating*	Quality Dimension**
1	Below Primary	2	tF
2	Below Secondary	2	Tf
3	Below Secondary	1	TF
4	Below Primary	2	F
5	Below Secondary	2	T
6	Below Secondary	1	F
7	Below Secondary	2	T
8	Below Primary	2	F
9	Below Primary	2	F
10	Below Primary	2	T
11	Below Primary	2	T
12	Below Secondary	2	T
13	Above Primary	1	F
14	Above Primary	1	tF
15	Above Primary	1	F
16	Above Primary	1	tF

Table 5–1 (continued)

Failpoint	Line Position	Rating*	Quality Dimension**
17	Above Primary	1	T
18	Above Primary	1	F
19	Above Primary	1	tF
20	Above Primary	1	TF
21	Above Primary	1	TF
22	Above Primary	1	tF
23	Above Primary	1	F
24	Above Primary	1	F
25	Above Primary	1	F
26	Below Primary	2	T
27	Below Primary	2	T
28	Below Primary	2	F

Key:
* 1: More Important
  2: Less Important
** T: Technical Quality
   F: Functional Quality
   t: Some Technical Quality
   f: Some Functional Quality

Conclusion: Using Blueprinting to Manage Quality in Services

This conclusion is written with the assumption that it can be generalized beyond the current research setting to most people intensive services. It is based on a current service as discussed above as well as on a proposed diversification service.

The Grönroos model of perceived service quality (1986, p. 3), includes the two key dimensions of technical and functional quality. Figure 5–2 suggests that blueprinting can be viewed as a supporting mechanism within the framework created by technical quality, functional quality, and corporate image. This adaptation of Grönroos's diagram of perceived service quality shows the central position blueprinting can play in manipulating the quality dimensions to achieve the desired levels of quality in service. For example, because functional quality is often not as easily managed and controlled, managers must document activities involving considerable functional quality, develop training programs to address these activities, and control them through ongoing monitoring systems. Thus, service managers using blueprinting have a potent tool for designing, implementing, monitoring, and controlling service quality as an integral component of the core offerings of their firms.

Perceived Service Quality

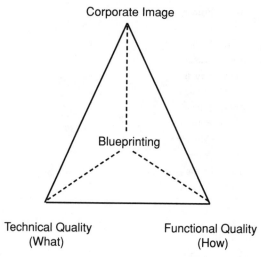

Figure 5–2. Blueprinting quality in service.

An underlying theme of service quality is that "quality evaluations are not made solely on the outcome of a service; they also involve evaluations of the process of service delivery" (Parasuraman, Zeithaml, and Berry 1985, p. 42). Blueprinting is a tool to evaluate the process of service delivery. It is comprehensive to all services and can provide a common framework for evaluating different kinds of services within a diversified service firm.

Blueprinting helps to pinpoint where each dimension of service quality appears in the process by documenting the series of activities that make up the service. The service becomes tangible and employees have a picture of the service process that includes key quality determinants. It becomes a model to guide them in their work. For example, employees can achieve a higher level of competence and can have more positive interactions with customers because the blueprint makes the service and its quality components easier to understand. The blueprint becomes a tool to control perceived service quality by showing how technical and functional quality are integrated within the whole service system.

No longer is the service delivery system considered a series of discrete events. It can now be visualized as an interconnecting whole in which both the visible aspects of the service and activities behind the scenes influence institutional quality across divisional boundaries. Because of this all employees can better understand why they must become "part-time marketers" (Gummesson 1987) and how their work within the service process contributes to overall institutional quality.

Blueprinting can be used to model the actual versus the desired qualities of the service delivery system. For example, a marginal service can be modified based on blueprint analysis. The manager now has a control mechanism to assist with the introduction of the revised service.

In summary, blueprinting is a management tool with applications for quality control in many functional areas of the service firm. For example, it facilitates the orientation and training of employees. As a marketing research input, it can provide guidelines for monitoring customer satisfaction with each step of the process and enable managers to modify the system based on customer expectations.

Based on this research it can be concluded that blueprinting does facilitate the management of quality in services. Within this research setting all the proposed research questions can be answered in the affirmative. It is likely that those affirmative answers can be generalized across many service environments.

Directions for Future Research

Additional research is suggested with two different purposes. First, further testing should be conducted to determine if the service blueprinting process for managing quality in services can be generalized for use in all service situations. New tests could include: 1) other types of service organizations in addition to the health care environment; 2) other services that are not people intensive; and 3) other service quality models—for example, the SERVQUAL model. The current study provides a starting point for this further testing of the service blueprinting process.

A second purpose of future research is to determine more precisely the tactical role blueprinting can play in managing service quality. That is, can blueprinting contribute to more effective and efficient daily operations of the service firm? The functional management areas of control and monitoring appear particularly fruitful. A number of examples illustrate the possible service blueprinting applications to be tested: 1) establishing service quality objectives—the more important failpoints may provide a useful frame of reference; 2) establishing a manual of standard operating procedures to assure expected quality for each failpoint—this may be especially important for achieving desired functional quality that has received less managerial specification than technical quality; 3) establishing internal monitoring systems to be used on a routine basis—perhaps a software package of questions about each of the more important failpoints could track daily operations; and 4) establishing external monitoring systems to measure changes in customer expectations—these changes may give new meaning to current failpoints or create new ones. These two research thrusts will provide a broader base for understanding blueprinting as a tool for managing quality in services.

References

Bernhardt, Kenneth L., and G. Lynn Shostack. (1983). "Comments on Christian Grönroos" *Strategic Management and Marketing in the Service Sector.*" Report No. 83–1045, Cambridge, MA: Marketing Science Institute, 1–13.

Garvin, David A. (1983). "Quality on the Line," *Harvard Business Review* September–October, 65–75.

Grönroos, Christian. (1980). "An Applied Service Marketing Theory," Swedish School of Economics and Business Administration, working paper.

———. (1984). "A Service Quality Model and Its Marketing Implications," *European Journal of Marketing*, Vol. 18, No. 4, 36–44.

———. (1985). "Service Oriented Strategies in Industrial Marketing," Swedish School of Economics and Business Administration, working paper.

———. (1986). "Developing Service Quality: Some Managerial Implications," Helsinki, Finland: Swedish School of Economics, working paper.

Gummesson, Evert. (1987). "The New Marketing—Developing Long-term Interactive Relationships." *Long Range Planning*, Vol. 20 (114), 10–20.

King, Carol A. (1984). "Service-Oriented Quality Control," *The Cornell H.R.A. Quarterly*, November, 92–98.

———. (1985). "Service Quality Is Different." *Quality Progress*, June, 14–18.

Lehtinen, Jarmo R. (1985). "Improving Service Quality by Analyzing the Service Production Process." In Christian Grönroos and Evert Gummesson, (eds.), *Service Marketing—Nordic School Perspective*, University of Stockholm, 110–119.

Leonard, Frank S., and W. Earl Sasser. (1982). "The Incline of Quality." *Harvard Business Review*, September–October, 163–171.

Lewis, Robert C., and Bernard H. Booms. (1983). "The Marketing Aspects of Service Quality." In L. Berry, G. Shostack, and G. Upah, (eds.), *Emerging Perspectives on Services Marketing*, Chicago: American Marketing Association, 99–107.

Parasuraman, A., Valerie A. Zeithaml and Leonard L. Berry. (1985). "A Conceptual Model of Service Quality and Its Implication for Future Research." *Journal of Marketing*, 49 (Fall), 41–50.

———. (1987). "SERVQUAL: A Multiple-Item Scale for Measuring Consumer Perceptions of Service Quality." College Station, TX: Texas A & M University, working paper.

Shostack, G. Lynn. (1981). "How to Design A Service." In J. Donnelly and W. George (eds.), *Marketing of Services*, Chicago: American Marketing Association, 221–29.

———. (1984a). "Designing Services That Deliver," *Harvard Business Review* January–February, 133–139.

———. (1984b). "Service Design in the Operating Environment." In William R.

George and Claudia E. Marshall (eds.), *Developing New Services*, Chicago: American Marketing Association, 27–43.

———. (1985). "Planning the Service Encounter." In J. Czepiel, M. Solomon, and C. Suprenant (eds.), *The Service Encounter*, Lexington, MA: Lexington Books, 1–23.

———. (1987). "Service Positioning through Structural Change." *Journal of Marketing*, 51 January, 34–43.

Thompson, Phillip, Glenn DeSouza, and Bradley T. Gale. (1985). "The Strategic Management of Service Quality," *Quality Progress* June, 20–25.

Takeuchi, Hirotaka, and John A. Quelch. (1983). "Quality is More Than Making a Good Product." *Harvard Business Review* July–August, 139–45.

Zeithaml, Valerie A., Leonard L. Berry, and A. Parasuraman. (1988). "Communication and Control Processes in the Delivery of Service Quality." *Journal of Marketing*, 52 (April), 35–48.

6

The Development of Budget/Economy Hotels in the United Kingdom
The Consumers' Perception of Quality

Martin Senior
Gary Akehurst

The economy or budget hotel concept started in the United States during the 1960s and in France and other parts of Europe during the 1970s. The first United Kingdom budget or low-cost hotel was introduced in 1985. The concept is fast becoming established as a major sector of the U.K. hotel industry. Increased competition in the industry has forced companies to adopt hotel segmentation strategies by developing a range of accommodation units to suit disparate market segments. The larger companies are now developing portfolios containing a range of accommodation units from budget through to deluxe to meet specific customer needs.

The development of budget hotels was a natural choice for companies wanting a presence in every segment of the U.K. market. The industry has polarized in recent years with considerable upgrading in the middle and upper range of hotels and stagnation at the lower levels. This left a gap in the market for good standard accommodation offering few unnecessary frills at reasonable prices, that is, offering perceived value for money. These hotels with few facilities and limited services appear to have been developed on price and location considerations alone though. Because they are all similar in style, their long-term survival in this increasingly competitive market may depend more on understanding some of the less obvious consumer choice variables rather than just price and location. This raises interesting questions about consumer perceptions of quality.

Introduction

Recently, some of the larger hotel and catering companies in the United Kingdom have exhibited a growing interest in developing new chains of low-cost and low-tariff accommodation units, commonly referred to as *budget hotels*. This development stems from the success of the emerging budget chains in Europe, notably France's well-organized range of economy hotel chains, and in the United States where the economy hotel and motel concept was developed (and where oversupply and keen competition has resulted in reduced profits) (Pannell Kerr Forster 1986).

Most developments in U.S. economy hotels have been associated with the transportation system, spurred on perhaps by the American love of cars, and consequently the increase in traveling by road (Walsh-Heron 1988). Many of the units being developed in the United Kingdom are also located on or near major road networks, enabling a traveler to locate accommodation easily without straying too far from a planned route. In particular, these units may appeal to motorists looking for reasonably priced accommodation en route to a further destination, by business people who do not wish to enter a town and city, or by those people who are, or consider themselves, financially unable to afford to stay in a city-center hotel.

The budget hotel has been designed to offer basic overnight facilities to the passing traveler without offering extensive secondary facilities such as restaurants and swimming pools. Core services are therefore kept to a minimum, and peripheral services are also minimized or virtually eliminated. Because the hotels offer only basic facilities and are built on inexpensive land, the room traffics can be considerably less than that charged in comparable full-service hotels (Walsh-Heron 1988; Schneider and Feiler 1987). The budget hotel developments in the United Kingdom are now having a major impact on the structure of the British hotel industry. Several companies are now developing chains of budget hotels as an extension or addition to their existing hotels or catering portfolio, marking their presence within a wider range of markets and in effect spreading some of the risk as far as some companies are concerned. Due to increased competition in both the international and domestic economy and the undoubted increase in profitability it brings, hotel companies are now segmenting and targeting markets more specifically, generally by identifying consumer types and designing hotel products to suit each segment of the population. Many recent developments include all-suite hotels, dual-brand hotels, executive floors, time-share, and budget accommodation. The large companies are now attempting to offer a complete portfolio of products ranging from budget hotels, for the price-sensitive customer, to deluxe hotels for those with discretionary incomes.

The Budget Hotel Concept

It is difficult to find a single name or generic term that aptly describes the new type of low-tariff accommodation units presently being developed in the United Kingdom, but the term *budget hotel,* not liked by the British operators because it may convey the image of a down-market establishment, has been used quite extensively by the British (and U.S. media). The British operating companies have had a tendency to call them *lodges, inns,* or *motor hotels* as opposed to hotels or motels. In the United States they are commonly referred to as economy or limited-service hotels/motels. Rather confusingly the French companies entering the U.K. market are simply calling their units *hotels.* Research is showing that the British consumer is reasonably clear as to what a lodge offers but is unsure as to what a budget hotel represents.

The concept of the budget hotel is an interesting one for both re-searcher and service business person. Customers often judge quality of a service in relation to its price; in addition, quality of service is related to customer expectations. Here is a service concept or package that promises the following:

low prices relative to other accommodation providers

a tightly specified service package with certain core physical items and services (a bed, shower/bathroom, and toiletries in a room of certain size)

a minimum of peripheral services such that the customer will under-take certain aspects of the operation themselves, such as carrying their luggage to their room

reduced contact with service personnel compared to other types of hotel accommodation

food and beverage facilities may be severely restricted or even non-existent

maintenance of certain features of the service package regardless of the physical location of a group's budget hotel unit.

However, a high degree of uncertainty exists among potential customers as to what a budget hotel *actually* offers. Indeed, hotel operators themselves are divided as to what is contained within such a labeled package. In itself *low prices* is a relative term and highly subjective or individualistic; it is a shifting term within a frame of reference difficult for the consumer to truly identify. What is considered high in price in this time period may not be so considered in another time period when real disposable income may have considerably increased. A tendency for the low prices of today to increase over time and for budget hotels to add more peripheral services (increasing prices further) so that the budget hotel may no longer be distinguishable (if it ever was) from other hotels is understandable. A general hypothesis being tested by research is that the budget hotel concept is part of the strategic positioning of hotel companies, who have identified market segments in which price sensitivity (value for money) is a major consideration, developing strong brand names and images based on well-specified service packages. Research is showing that at least in Britain the consumer is relatively brand-indifferent or indeed brand-ignorant. This has far-reaching implications for operators, but the consumer may well become brand-conscious over time. These service packages need to be consistently delivered and replicated time and again in the face of high customer expectations of value for money (Grönroos 1983; Normann 1984). The provision of information to the potential customer and actual customer is absolutely essential so that the gap between expected service and experienced service is minimized or reversed.

Ignoring the issue of finding a substitute name for the term *budget hotel*, the concept can be explicitly expressed as a core product with a restricted service for a low tariff; that is, the hotel actually offers: (1) a tightly specified package of core physical items; (2) a minimum of peripheral services; and (3) low prices relative to competitors.

However, because many of these early units have been developed with minimal or nonexistent catering facilities, the hotel guest is often required to obtain refreshments from an adjoining operation; usually this is an established free-standing restaurant designed primarily to appeal to the passing motorist. A lodge or hotel user will more than likely require some form of refreshment during an overnight stay. In realization of this, most budget hotel operators are essentially offering a package. The total budget hotel offering may be, therefore, defined as a package offering a core product with restricted services for a low tariff, including limited ancillary (or peripheral) services such as food and beverage facilities that may be severely restricted to a small integral catering operation or the use of an existing free-standing outlet. Three other factors appear to be common to the majority of hotels being developed: (1) many are strategically located for the passing traveler (beside a major highway and where land is less expensive); (2) most are newly built, often using fast low-cost modularconstruction techniques. This enables companies to achieve a wide geographical presence at reasonable cost; and (3) practically all are being developed with distinctive brand-names that promise to maintain certain features of the service package regardless of the physical location of the unit.

All these factors contribute to keeping the tariff low. The distinctive brand names attempt to reassure the consumer that a reliable, consistently produced product and service will be provided throughout the chain at any location at a low tariff without compromising quality.

The Growth of the Budget/Economy Hotel

Low-tariff accommodation in the United Kingdom has traditionally been provided by small independent operators, typically family-run guest houses and hotels, while larger companies have concentrated on providing accommodation in the middle and higher tariff ranges. Many traditional guest houses and hotels are able to provide personal service but often with an unpredictable range of facilities and services. To some extent this has led to a loss of their previous popularity (Legate 1985). Several factors have contributed to this loss of business: changing leisure patterns; increased foreign travel; greater media coverage of holidays abroad; and the general rise in the standard of living. These and other factors have made the consumer more discerning in the selection of overnight accommodation and more demanding of value-for-money products that unfortunately cannot always be met by the present hotel stock in the United Kingdom.

Some of the larger hotel and catering companies have seen an opportunity to exploit this unsatisfied yet increasingly sophisticated demand, extending their portfolios to the lower price levels of the accommodation sector by developing their own brands of budget/economy hotels. These new hotels may displace some of the traditional guest houses and small hotels that specifically cater to the traveler on the move, while at the same time stimulate demand among previous nonusers of hotel accommodation. The tariff structure they are offering is often lower than traditional full-service accommodation establishments, and most of the companies are intending to offer modern facilities and a consistent product and service throughout their particular chain.

The development of budget chains in the United Kingdom started in late 1985 with the opening of the first Little Chef Lodge at Barton-under-Needwood and the Ibis Hotel (part of the Accor group) at Heathrow airport. Little Chef restaurants are part of the Trusthouse Forte (THF) group, which is planning a large chain of budget-style accommodation units throughout the country over the next few years. Several other companies have also shown a keen interest in developing and establishing a chain of budget/economy hotels throughout the United Kingdom. These include the Granada Company, the Rank Organisation, Whitbread, Tattinger Champagne, and Arcade. Other U.K.-, French-, and U.S.-based companies are now at various stages of buying land and building their first units in Britain.

The predictions of the growth of the budget/economy hotel in the United Kingdom suggest growth similar to that in the United States and France. Between 1985 and 1988 some eighty units had opened. By 1995 there could be as many as five hundred budget hotels operating with twenty-five thousand bedrooms; this could represent an addition of 5 percent to the present bedroom stock in the United Kingdom (Slattery and Roper 1986). This rate of growth will present a considerable challenge to traditional suppliers of accommodation. Today's competitive lodging market compels hoteliers to know exactly how well their properties are meeting guests' needs (Trice and Layman 1984). Some companies operating the new budget hotels have been reporting high levels of occupancy, which might suggest high levels of consumer satisfaction or a considerably undersupplied market.

Because the budget hotel is a relatively new concept in the United Kingdom, it is difficult to anticipate how competitive this sector will become over the next few years, but some indications may come from the experiences in the United States. During the 1970s, the early years of the economy hotel sector in the United States, high occupancy levels were reported. This led to more suppliers entering the sector, which in turn eventually led to an oversupply of economy bedrooms (Leonard 1987). This oversupply led to increased competition, and together with an economic recession lower occupancies and slimmer profits being reported (Daniele 1986). Some companies fought back by reducing tariffs to remain competitive, while others competed by adding more facilities and services to the existing service product, raising the tariffs accordingly. This put many economy hotels into a situation in which they would then compete head on with the full-service accommodation sector.

The U.S. economy hotel sector is still experiencing considerable activity because economy hotels are considered to be more profitable than fullservice hotels. Few sites remain for developing budget hotels, and new entries into the sector will have to seek less favorable locations, perhaps in inner-city areas where land costs may be much higher. Several larger companies are now repositioning themselves and establishing their niches in the marketplace while many of the smaller companies and operations are disappearing through mergers, acquisitions, and even liquidations. It has been suggested that as the economy hotel market matures, brands offering differentiated products will remain more competitive than those relying merely on inexpensive rates.

The pattern experienced in the United States may not occur in the United Kingdom, but the projected expansion programs of the budget-style companies suggests that considerable competition could occur in particular locations. This could result in the consumer having more choice and therefore becoming more discriminating in the selection of overnight accommodation. Consumer choice then becomes an important issue for surviving in a competitive environment, and apart from location, price appears to be the major attraction for using a budget hotel. Eventually, if and when the consumer becomes more knowledgeable of budget hotels, competition may then occur among the budgets themselves.

Differentiation

Companies wishing to survive and prosper in a competitive budget/economy hotel sector must meet the needs of the consumer better than the competition does. Berry (1988) correctly points to service as a competitive, differentiating device—using service to be different, to earn customer loyalty, and to enhance productivity. Enhancing the service elements could lower costs in the long term, but herein lies a problem for the budget hotel operator. Adding service to the core product may differentiate the product from competitors, provided the consumer is able to recognize (and appreciate) such differences and has actually experienced the product of competitors. At this time relatively few consumers in Britain have experienced different budget hotel services; generally, consumers have little past experience to refer to, reflected in widespread consumer brand-indifference. Over time, of course, this may change.

Identifying customers' needs more accurately must then become a priority. This can be achieved through effective market research. It has been shown, however, that the hospitality industry often fails to identify the vital elements of consumer choice and, indeed, considerable ignorance still surrounds the purchasing of hotel services. Consumers of hotel services are often unsure of their own motives and are unable to express perceptions accurately through quantitative research techniques (Lewis 1984). Research has shown that many service organizations develop their own perceptions of what their customers want; managers and staff may not agree among themselves as to what the customer wants, which often differs from what the customer actually does want (Nightingale 1984). Many organizations rely on intuition when planning strategies, or when they do use market research they tend to rely on past purchasing behavior and demographic consumer data that provides historical data but may not be a reliable predictor of future behavior.

Therefore, a key to a successful marketing strategy is developing products and promotional stimuli that consumers perceive most relevant to their individual needs. Clearly the consumer of a particular service is seeking to satisfy a set of needs or wants, and while the service is being provided, the consumer will form a judgment about how well it satisfies those needs and measures up to expectations. Because individuals have different characteristics, beliefs, attitudes, and accumulated experiences, the same stimulus will often be perceived and evaluated differently by two individuals, leading to different behavior. However, all products and services will ultimately be expected to exceed a minimum threshold; for example, hotels would be expected to provide a clean bedroom. If a budget hotel exceeds a customer's expectations, there is every chance of repeat business. It is possible that being perceived by a consumer as better than the competition is perhaps more advantageous than actually being better (Trice and Layman 1984).

Most services research to date has perhaps concentrated on consumer perceptions and satisfactions, focusing especially on specific transaction service encounters in which consumers make a subjective assessment of the encounter between themselves and the service provider (both organization and contact personnel). This leads to a consideration of role performances by the encounter participants (Surprenant and Solomon 1987; Solomon 1985; Solomon et al. 1985). Other writers have taken a broader view of this encounter or moment of truth as a time period in which a consumer is interacting with all service elements (tangible, intangible, front and back room) as part consumer and part producer. In the process they react to contextual clues provided by the physical environment, contact personnel, and other customers (Bitner 1988; Shostack 1985). To emphasize this wider perspective Booms and Bitner (1981) have expanded the basic marketing mix (of product, price, place, and promotion) to include "physical evidence" (the environment in which the service takes place), "participants" (including contact personnel and other customers) "process" (the service delivery processes/flows). Bitner correctly suggests a close relationship between the satisfaction derived from each service encounter and perceived service quality. The distinction is made, however, between single transaction satisfaction and cumulative satisfactions derived from past service encounters with the company and its competitors. Perceived service quality is the consumer's judgment or assessment of a business influenced by the accumulated experience of previous encounters. Clearly this is an important consideration for budget hotel operators.

Because many budget hotels in the United Kingdom are being developed along similar lines with similar tariffs, the consumer may initially have difficulty in differentiating among brands. As consumers become more experienced in using budget hotels, they may become more aware and experienced in perceiving the true differences between competing brands and may even become brand-loyal. Location will always be important in hotel selection but choosing between two budget hotels in the same location may require the consumer to identify less obvious differences before making a final selection. Because of the apparent simplicity of the concept, differentiating one budget hotel from another is not at first obvious. Differentiation may occur through either improving a product or extending it. Differentiating the core product (of basic overnight facilities) by adding to it (for example, restaurants, bars, or leisure facilities) or improving the standard (by for example, using higher quality materials) may necessitate raising tariffs to a level unacceptable to the target market (the price-sensitive customer prepared to accept fewer facilities at lower prices). Improving the service will almost certainly require altering operating, training,

and recruitment procedures and policies so that a trade-off between enhancing or extending service and increasing costs occurs. Therefore, a fine
line exists between differentiating a budget hotel from its competitors and
keeping tariffs as low as possible to remain profitably in the budget sector.

Given this analysis, the most attractive option for operators, without
altering the core product or restricted services, would be to improve the
service through changing or enhancing operating, training, or recruitment
procedures. The strategy of differentiation through service quality could
provide a budget hotel organization with a distinctive competitive advantage
yet still maintain services and facilities in a restricted form; this preserves
the product in its original conceptual form for the target market. Reconcil-
ing the concept of the budget hotel and the concept of service quality
provides an interesting challenge for hospitality managers.

Most budget hotels being developed in the United Kingdom have followed a similar pattern to the United States in terms of adding to and
differentiating the basic product by the provision of ancillary services,
especially restaurant facilities. The units are often located close to free-
standing restaurants that are often company-owned but operating almost
independently from the hotel unit. Many of the catering facilities have in
fact been designed for passing motorists and not for hotel users. Research
indicates that hotel users may not necessarily feel psychologically comfortable using free-standing motorist facilities—facilities that have not always
had a good reputation for service quality. Research has shown that if the
core product and the restricted services are not the principal differentiating
features between brands, then ancillary offerings will almost certainly be
important attributes in brand selection. A consumer experiencing poor
restaurant facilities would almost certainly be detracted from using further
facilities associated with a brand name or package. Budget hotel differentiation comes therefore from providing a superior service, one that separates
itself from the competition and yet remains limited. If management and
staff remain ignorant of service quality, they may already be unwittingly
providing a differentiated product by simply providing a particularly poor
service. Understanding the consumer's perception of a service and understanding the nature of service quality becomes crucial in defending or
increasing market share in a competitive climate.

Service Quality and Service Quality Strategy

One of the most common complaints and compliments of hospitality products concerns quality of service (Martin 1986). The service function in a
budget hotel is by definition limited and, therefore, may not be considered
especially important. However, it is easy to provide poor or indifferent

service, and even a short contact time with a service provider may leave a lasting impression on the consumer's perception of a product. Quality is difficult to define and a complex concept, but if the service function of a product is sufficiently meeting a customer's needs, then it is delivering a quality service. Quality as both a concept and business philosophy suggests, however, that striving to go beyond providing merely a satisfactory service is necessary for business survival, provided that costs are contained of course.

Although service quality may be an elusive concept, the practical significance of striving for quality for hotel operators is beyond doubt. Chase and Bowen (1988) suggest that relevant research offers three alternative conceptualizations of (1) attribute theory, in which service quality reflects the service delivery system attributes; the major assumption here is that management has considerable *control* over these factors; (2) customer satisfaction theory, which examines service quality through the perceptions and experiences of the consumer (the work of Parasuraman, Zeithaml, and Berry (1985) in identifying and measuring gaps impeding the delivery of services is of particular interest here); (3) interaction theory, in which service quality arises through the satisfaction of both employee and customer needs (Klaus 1985). Other distinctions focus on process/functional quality (how the customer gets it) and outcome/technical quality (what the customer gets) (Grönroos 1984) or interactive quality (between encounter participants), physical quality (tangibles), and corporate quality (the image of the firm) (Lehtinen 1985).

Quality is partly determined then by the expectations and perceptions of the customer, and because each individual perceives stimuli differently, quality will be different for each customer. The American Hotel & Motel Association has shown that hospitality managers do not agree on a clear definition of quality, but after much consideration the Association has agreed that "Quality is the consistent delivery of individual standards" (Collins 1984, p. 56). Clearly this is taking a supplier approach. King (1984, p.32) has mentioned that quality can only be determined by customers from their personal experiences, because they experience the transaction. Nightingale (1984, p. 41) has said that "quality lies in the eyes of the beholder."

Quality is then a word used by an individual to describe whether his or her perception of a product or service has reached a satisfactory level of excellence (quality). If consumers believe a product/service will provide certain benefits at a satisfactory level time and again, they may rapidly decide that the product/service has reached a particular threshold of excellence and thus be deemed a quality product. To set quality standards in an organization, it is necessary in part to set criteria at a level that reaches or preferably exceeds the target market's threshold of excellence. Organizations find it easier to measure product-related criteria than service-related criteria since tangibility and measures of acceptance/nonacceptance can be clearly specified for products. Because services are intangible, unique performances by contact personnel interacting with customers and because individuals have unique perceptions, criteria for service standards are more difficult to specify, articulate, and control. It is not, however, impossible. To overcome problems of measuring service quality, it is necessary to establish what is and is not acceptable to the customer in broad terms (partly by market research) and to ensure that these specifications are communicated to each and every member of the organization. Management can ensure that all employees understand exactly what the customer wants within organizational constraints (Berry 1988). In this way an organizational infrastructure is built that allows each employee, individually or collectively, to work toward a common goal of providing customers with what they want. Thereby, a quality service is provided.

A quality strategy for services is not a rigid rule book with strict mechanistic procedures; it is a philosophy or culture, one that recognizes satisfied customers mean repeat purchases and favorable word-of-mouth recommendations. Continued prosperity for the organizations and employees is the result. Such a philosophy is based on effective organizational communications: allowing customers to communicate likes/dislikes through various channels such as contact personnel; interaction with unit managers; market research; and vital feedback provided to all employees, enabling them to work together in the same direction.

The role of senior management in any organization, including those in the budget hotel sector, is to satisfy the customer by providing a *consistently reliable* quality service or product. This can be effectively achieved only by developing and engendering a service quality culture, an essentially shared philosophy, one that cannot work unless personnel understand the principles behind it and are encouraged to practice it. It may also be considered as a commitment to *continual improvement*, a point stressed by Berry (1988).

Conclusion

Many budget hotels in the United Kingdom are being developed along similar lines. Each company is offering a consistent core product and restricted service throughout its particular chain. However, each company offers only a slightly differentiated product, service, and tariff structure, which suggests that consumers may initially have difficulty in perceiving differences among competitors. Research indicates that consumers may initially use the ancillary services (e.g., the restaurant facilities) as surrogate measures for assessing quality among hotels, suggesting that such points of high visibility are potential fail points even if the core product (the bedroom) is perceived by the customer to be satisfactory. In such circumstances, promotion of a brand name offering a differentiated, superior product and service becomes particularly important. As the budget hotel sector matures, the consumer will become more experienced and knowledgeable in using and choosing among various brands. The consumer is then likely to seek out those units that offer the best value in terms of perceived quality; the development of repeat business will depend critically, however, on the satisfactory delivery of ancillary or peripheral services. While it may be virtually impossible to radically alter the physical budget/economy hotel concept, nevertheless, improving the quality of the service function, the delivery of the product, and the service interaction will become the distinctive competitive advantage for a brand name.

The unanswered question at this time is whether budget hotels are nothing more than a transitory phenomenon as hotel companies seek to position themselves in an intensely competitive market with diversified hotel portfolios based on brand names and careful market segmentation. Commercial survival in a competitive environment does not have to rely on the U.S. economy hotel experience of cutting tariffs or significantly upgrading facilities, but in truth should rely more on the ability to develop and maintain a service-quality culture throughout the organization and provide the customer with a quality (albeit limited) service. All persons in the organization need to understand the features of quality in the eyes of the consumer and develop a quality culture, one that allows a rapid and consistent diffusion of a shared philosophy, through the products and services to the customer. This culture will underpin the credibility of a brand name, differentiating itself as being consistently superior to others in the marketplace.

In summary, what has the current research identified so far? First, the terms *budget* or *low cost* are *relative* terms, perceptions of which (whether by customer or supplier) change over time in various subtle ways; no fixed reference point exists.

Second, use of the terms *budget* or *low cost* raises questions of low price–minimum quality thresholds, that is below a certain price for accommodation (which will be different for different consumers) quality perceptions may be affected or adverse reactions received regardless of service levels.

Third, quality is itself a difficult concept, but with a changing and relative concept such as the budget hotel, it becomes even more complex. What constitutes budget accommodation and the quality of that accommodation is a subjective matter. Not only will the stock or population of this type of accommodation be changing over time, consumer expectations and perceptions of this type of accommodation will shift over time. The core product of accommodation may well prove satisfactory for the consumer, but evidence suggests that overall perceptions of quality may be adversely affected by failings (however small or large) in the ancillary service provision. In short, where are the quality parameters?

Fourth, adding to core services various peripheral services such as restaurant facilities, bars, and so on, will add to price so that over time a budget hotel could become virtually indistinguishable from other hotels. But does this matter? Low price and severely limited services may virtually be the only distinguishing marks of a budget hotel, but managements are beginning to realize, that the true distinguishing marks are the consistent and reliable delivery of a credible product underpinned by a corporate quality culture.

Fifth, as the selling emphasis is on low price, any exceeding of customer expectations once the service is experienced is likely to lead to feelings of well-being and perceived improved quality. This must be one recipe for success.

Sixth, as the budget hotel concept has a high element of tangibles and less human service provision elements, quality of the service package may be controlled more closely, producing a consistent replicable product that reduces consumer uncertainties.

The authors are particularly conscious that budget hotels as a concept are but one part of changing corporate strategies for market positioning, and form a part of a diversification of hotel group portfolios in an attempt to meet apparently unsatisfied market demand (based on price sensitivity). The lasting feature may well be the establishment of certain brand images around the lodge or inn name.

It must be remembered that lodging properties in the future must become not only customer oriented but also competitor oriented. With the projected expansion of budget hotels in the United Kingdom it is likely that intense competition could occur in particular locations. This would ultimately result in the consumer having more choice among competing hotels and could result in some units not achieving the desired occupancy level, thus becoming financially unviable.

The shakeout that occurred in the United States hospitality industry and economy hotel sector in the late 1970s and early 1980s has resulted in changes in corporate policies. Because labor costs will always be high and are still rising in the United States, improved operations and new approaches to management are being employed that will contain costs so a competitive edge can be retained (Leonard 1987; Scheider and Feiler 1987). More importantly, thorough consumer research, considered the key to success in the future, is being employed.

Firms known to measure customer satisfaction are usually market leaders (Jarvis and Mayo 1986). To maintain a competitive edge in a competitive environment, the budget hotel operators will have to identify consumer needs, perceptions, and expectations more accurately. Customer perceptions and expectations are not static though; they are always changing in response to needs and experiences. The consumer's perspective of quality is ultimately subjective and is not always rational. Therefore, products and services that will satisfy these subjective and evolving expectations must be provided.

Because perceptions play a critical role in consumer choice, suppliers will need to constantly monitor consumer perceptions and differentiate their product in the consumer's eyes, thus continuing to provide a unique service of ongoing value to the consumer. Adding additional facilities and services to the basic budget hotel may make it less competitive because of the necessity to raise prices. But by ensuring that service equals or transcends involving consumer expectations, price levels, always important among substitute service products, may become less of an issue in product choice if significant differences in the perception of quality exist among competing brands.

References

Barrington, M. N., and M. D. Olsen. (1987). "Concept of Service in the Hospitality Industry." *International Journal of Hospitality Management* Vol. 6, No. 3, 131–138.

Berry, L. L. (1988). "Delivering Excellent Service in Retailing." *Arthur Anderson & Co Retailing Issues Letter*, Vol. 1, No. 4 (April).

Bitner, M. J. (1988). "A Model of Service Encounter Evaluation and Marketing Mix Effects." Quality in Services Symposium, University of Karlstad, Sweden.

Booms, B. H., and M. J., Bitner. (1981). "Marketing Strategies and Organisation Structures for Service Firms." In J. H. Donnelley and W. R. George (eds.), *Marketing of Services*. Chicago: American Marketing Association.

Chase, R. B., and D. E. Bowen. (1988). "Service Quality and the Service Delivery System: A Diagnostic Framework." Quality in Services Symposium, University of Karlstad, Sweden.

Collins, R. F. (1984). "What the American Hotel and Motel Association Learned from Its Quest for Quality." In Robert C. Lewis et al. (eds.), *The Practice of Hospitality Management II*. New York: AVI Publishing, 55–59.

Daniele, D. W. (1986). "Economy Hotels in the USA." *Travel & Tourism Analyst*, June, 13–25.

Grönroos, C. (1982). "Strategic Management and Marketing in the Service Sector." Swedish School of Economics and Business Administration.

———. (1983). "Strategic Management and Marketing in the Service Sector." Bromley: Chartwell-Bratt.

———. (1984). "A Service Quality Model and Its Marketing Implications." *European Journal of Marketing*. Vol. 18, No. 4.

Jarvis, L. P., and E. J. Mayo. (1986). "Winning the Market-Share Game." *Cornell Hotel and Restaurant Administration Quarterly*, November, 73–79.

King, A. C. (1984). "A New Look at Quality Assurance—The Quest for Quality."

In Robert C. Lewis et al. (eds.), *The Practice of Hospitality Management II*. New York: AVI Publishing, 27–35.

Klaus, P. (1985). "Quality Epiphenomenon: The Conceptual Understanding of Quality in Face-to-Face Service Encounters." In J. A. Czepiel, M. R. Solomon, and C. F. Suprenant (eds.), *The Service Encounter*. Lexington, MA: Lexington Books.

Legate, P. (1985). "UK Holidays, Fall and Rise." *HCIMA Reference Book 1985/ 1986*. London: Sterling, 81–82.

Lehtinen, J. R. (1985). "Improving Service Quality by Analyzing the Service Production Process." In C. Grönroos and E. Gummesson (eds.), *Service Marketing—Nordic School Perspective*. University of Stockholm.

Lehtinen, V., and J. R. Lehtinen. (1982). "Service Quality: A Study of Quality Dimensions." Helsinki Service Management Institute, working paper.

Leonard, S. F. (1987). "Hotel Chains in the USA." *Travel & Tourism Analyst*, October, 43–46.

Lewis, R. C. (1984). "The Basis of Hotel Selection." *Cornell Hotel and Restaurant Administration Quarterly*. May, 54–69.

Martin, W. B. (1986). "Defining What Quality Service Is for You." *Cornell Hotel and Restaurant Administration Quarterly*. February, 32–38.

Nightingale, M. (1984). "Defining Quality for a Quality Assurance Programme." In Robert C. Lewis et al. (eds.), *The Practice of Hospitality Management II*, New York: AVI Publishing, 37–53.

Normann, R. (1984). "Service Management." *Strategy and Leadership in Service Businesses*. Chichester: J. Wiley.

Pannell Kerr Forster (1986). *Trends in the Hotel Industry—1986 International Edition*. London: Pannell Kerr Forster, 46–54.

Shostack, G. L. (1985). "Planning the Service Encounter" In J. A. Czepial, M. R. Soloman, and C. F. Surprenant (eds.), *The Service Encounter*. Lexington, MA: Lexington Books.

Slattery, P., and A. Roper. (1986). *UK Hotel Groups 1986/87*. Eastbourne: Cassell, xiii–xvii 1–3.

Soloman, M. R. (1985). "Packaging the Service Provider." *Service Industries Journal*, Vol. 5, No. 1.

Soloman, M. R., C. F. Suprenant, L. Czepiel, and E. G. Gutman. (1985). "A Role Theory Perspective on Dyadic Interactions: The Service Encounter." *Journal of Marketing*, Vol. 49, No. 1.

Surprenant, C. F., and M. R. Soloman. (1987). "Predictability and Personalization in the Service Encounter." *Journal of Marketing*, Vol. 51, No. 2.

Trice, A. D., and W. H. Layman. (1984). "Improving Guest Surveys." *The Cornell Hotel and Restaurant Administration Quarterly*, November, 10–13.

Voss, C., C. Armistead, B. Johnston, and B. Morris. (1985). "Operations Management in Service Industries." Chichester: J. Wiley.

Walsh-Heron, J. (1988). "Motels—No Longer at the Crossroads." *Leisure Management*, March, 73–74.

Zeithaml, V. A., et al. (1985). "A Conceptual Model of Service Quality and Its Implications for Future Research." *Journal of Marketing*, Vol. 49.

Zeithaml, V. A., et al. (1985). "Problems and Strategies in Services Marketing." *Journal of Marketing*, Vol. 49, (Spring), 36–45.

7

The Design of Chains of Actions
A Prerequisite for the Development and Design of Service Strategies and Managerial Processes

Friedhart Hegner

Introduction

The personal experience hidden behind the reflections is that the practitioners responsible for the development and design of a particular type of service urgently need some kind of an image; that is, a leading idea that works as a global guideline for people who belong to different professions, departments, organizations, and so on. The image used in this chapter is the chain of actions, the chain of progression from the articulation of wants to the development of means for want satisfaction (e.g., services) and, from there, to the use of these means. In designing services and service organizations this global image has to be broken into pieces: two or more specific chains of actions, each of them combining particular networks of actions to be coordinated, services to be delivered, clients or customers to be served, and technology (sets of technical, organizational, and human resources) to be used.

The Mix of Social Science Paradigms: An Outline of Criteria for the Assessment of Service Quality

In the process of designing services and delivery systems many practitioners, in West Germany (FRG) start by looking for scientific paradigms that can be used as an initial guideline. Practitioners need manageable and easy-to-use paradigms. Therefore, the scientific consultant has to "translate" empirical and theoretical findings, that is, transform complex sets of findings into manageable units or "cognitive maps." The term *paradigm* (Kuhn [1962] 1970) is applied to the following four sets of concepts and empirical findings, which have been rediscovered in the FRG to assess the quality of services and delivery systems.

Paradigm A: The distinction between public and private services and service delivery systems

Since the middle of the 1970s interest has grown in the development of new public-private relationships in social and health policy (Hegner 1979; Badura 1980; Dahme and Hegner 1982; Kaufman 1986). It has been argued that the designing and implementation of service delivery systems have to take into consideration four arenas or sectors: (1) the public sector (government organizations and activities on the national, regional, and local levels); (2) the parapublic sector (self-governed, old-age pension and health-insurance organizations financed by public subsidies as well as contributions from members); (3) the private sector of for-profit organizations (e.g., private asylums and hospitals, the pharmaceutical industry, established medical professions); (4) the private sector of nonprofit organizations (e.g., charities run by the churches or well-established welfare associations; self-help and mutual-aid groups).

The analytical distinction between the sectors is based partly on modes of funding and financing (e.g., taxes, contributions, donations, payments, and profits), partly on the kinds of rules and regulations (e.g., public and private law), and partly on the characteristics of the organizations involved (e.g., bureaucratic versus professional, formal versus informal). The latter aspect is more familiar to sociologists whereas the problems of financing and regulation belong to the domains of economists, lawyers, and political scientists (Kaufmann 1986).

The so-called public-private mix can be defined as a conglomerate of actors and actions bound to specific modes of funding and financing (mobilization of resources), particular kinds of rules and regulations (legitimization of actions), and specific forms for the coordination of actors and actions. This conglomerate of actors and actions is said to be responsible for the production and delivery of a large variety of services in cash, kind, and people processing (Hood 1986).

The distinction between public and private services or service delivery systems is too vague and too far from everyday reality. Therefore, it cannot adequately work as a criterion for assessing the quality of services. Perhaps it is even misleading to use this distinction for the formulation of strategy visions and operating strategies.

Paradigm B: The responsiveness of service delivery systems to clients' needs as a prerequisite for the well-being of the public served

This paradigm was developed by G. F. W. Hegel in his "Rechts-philosophie" ([1821] 1970) and by Robert von Mohl in his article "Ueber Buerokratie" ([1846] 1962). Both stated that the well-being and satisfaction of citizens is dependent not only on the quantity and quality of the services offered but also on the characteristics of service delivery in direct contact with clients (management of encounters).

In the FRG, empirical research done in the 1970s revealed that the feeling of well-being did not increase parallel to the expansion of social services (Grunow and Hegner 1978; Grunow, Hegner, and Kaufmann 1978; Grunow, Hegner, and Schmidt 1980). In this context, representatives of the social sciences preached the following credo (cf. Grunow and Hegner 1978b): To increase the objective *and* subjective well-being of public served it is necessary to (1) give better sociopsychological training to employees in contact with the clients; (2) shape organizational and interorganizational factors so personnel can coordinate benefits in cash and in kind with personal services; and (3) adapt the process of service delivery to the specific social problems of different target populations, that is, particular groups of clients with specific material and nonmaterial wants.

Paradigm C: The relevance of the social setting for the impact of health care delivery

This paradigm was developed in the nineteenth century by physicians like Rudolf Virchow (1848, 1849), advocating improvement of public health services. At that time, epidemiological studies revealed that not only the emergence of diseases but also the chances of getting rid of them were dependent on the social setting of the patients (e.g., whether one belonged to the lower or middle classes; whether one lived in a large city or in the countryside).

In the FRG, this paradigm had a great revival in the late 1960s and early 1970s (von Ferber 1967; Bradura 1978; von Ferber and von Ferber 1983). Empirical research done during the past fifteen years revealed that the chance of being affected by or getting rid of certain diseases depends not only on the quantity and quality of professional medical care but also on the social support given by relatives, friends, and neighbors. Against this background, representatives of social medicine, social psychiatry, and medical sociology put stress on (1) preventive medical and social care taking into account flaws in the social setting and (2) the necessity of strengthening social support needed by the sick and handicapped (Bradura 1978; von Ferber and von Ferber 1983).

Paradigm D: The activation of individual self-help and social self-help arrangements

The historical basis of the modern self-help movement can be found in the nineteenth century, when discussions on the relationship between state activities and private charities paralleled the emergence of modern forms of social and health policy (Pankoke 1970).

Empirical research as well as sociological theorizing in the 1970s made it evident that the specialization of medicine and the division of work between medical care and social services have negative consequences for certain groups of clients (von Ferber and von Ferber 1983). Particularly, the mentally ill, chronically ill, and handicapped suffer from deficiencies in the given status of service delivery systems. Due to the long-term effects of their ill-health and to the coincidence of physical, psychic, social, and economic impairments, or handicaps, they are in need of permanent and well-coordinated services.

Since the status of public and private service delivery systems does not sufficiently provide this type of benefit, representatives of social medicine, social psychiatry, and medical sociology have emphasized the supplementary functions of individual self-help, mutual aid, and social self-help arrangements (Kickbusch and Trojan 1981; von Ferber 1983). This "proclamation" can also be seen as a consequence of the growing antibureaucratism and antiprofessionalism (Hegner 1979). Here, contemporary social scientists are fighting the products and consequences of former scientific findings and claims. The rediscovery of an extremely old paradigm (solidaric self-support as a fundamental means of subsistence) is beginning to replace a newer one (the overall responsibility of the state and market for the provision of specific goods and services).

It is the mix of the four paradigms that is characteristic of the discussions of the 1980s. This mix is mainly due to the changing nature of social and health problems as well as changing definitions of problems.

The Mix of Social Problems and Individual Wants: A Starting Point for the Development of Service Strategies

A differentiation is made between two types of problems and the ways they are processed: the improvement of living conditions and the reduction of social inequality. The first can be conceived as a set of economic problems, the second as a set of social problems (Polanyi 1944). "Improvement of living conditions" (economic problem) implies some insufficiency in the goods and services that are perceived as means of want satisfaction. "Reduction of social inequality" (social problem) implies that some people are insufficiently included in, or are not sufficiently participating in, the provision for the means of material or nonmaterial want satisfaction.

These notions are based on the assumption that a discrepancy exists between (1) observable economic and social deficiencies, and (2) defined standard of quality living conditions and desired social equality (Merton 1971). The coincidence of economic and social discrepancies forms the fundamental problem in social and health policy (Heimann [1929] 1980); Robson 1976). Due to this coincidence, social services is characterized by a large spectrum of problem mixtures.

There are not only problem mixtures, but each social and economic problem represents a mixture of individual wants, that is, needs, demands, and claims (Hegner 1980). The want mixtures require mixtures of means for satisfying wants, sets of tangible and intangible means. Nonmaterial wants cannot be as easily standardized as material wants, both being mixed and linked to *individual* (personal) emotions, expectations, and situational definitions. Therefore, only a small proportion of intangible means and nonmaterial wants can be adequately provided for and dealt with by transaction processes that are governed by the logic of formal rational action (Hegner 1980). The same proves true for the provision of tangible goods and goods-centered services *if* want satisfaction can only be reached by adaptation to the particularities of individual cases (Scitovsky 1976).

It is the sensibility of a growing number of practitioners that (1) the interdependence of economic *and* social problems and (b) the coincidence of material *and* nonmaterial wants has induced the search for new service delivery systems. This leads to a mix of organizational and professional forms of service provision. To find the adequate mix requires a better understanding of the logic of different forms of social organization.

The Mix of Forms of Social Organization: An Approach to the Design of Service Delivery Systems and Operating Strategies

Some problems can be solved by individual actors without the help of others. These problems are left aside, here. Other problems can be processed only by the cooperation of actors, by the coordination of actions *and* actors within organized social systems. At least two basic modes of social organization exist: informally organized collectivities and formal organizations. Both have to be considered in the process of designing delivery systems and operating strategies.

The processing of problems and wants in *informally organized collectivities* (e.g., self-help groups, family households) requires only the coordination of individual actors. The willingness and the abilities of the individual members are the most important resources of the social system. The willingness of the individual members depends mainly on feelings of sympathy and personal loyalty as well as on social norms that stabilize reciprocity and solidarity. This puts limits on the complexity of the chains of means-end relationships and on the capacity of problem processing (Hegner 1986); Kaufman 1986).

Due to these limits, a more complex type of coordination is needed. Its basic principle is called formalization, the abstraction from the feelings and motives of individual actors as well as the establishment of social norms to stabilize the obedience to abstract professional, legal, and technical standards (Luhmann 1964). Formal organizations like public agencies, big firms, and well-established charities consist of social subsystems (e.g., departments). There is a need not only for the coordination of individual actors but also the coordination of collective actors (Blau and Scott [1962] 1969). The same proves true for relationships between formal organizations or corporate actors, that is, interorganization networks (cf. Hanf and Scharpf, 1978; Hull and Hjern 1983). In both cases, formal rules of coordination form the basis of a more detailed division of labor and a more complex network of actions. Consequently, the capacity of problem processing can be increased.

This may induce a misunderstanding. It could be assumed that formal organizations are capable of solving *more* problems than informally organized collectivities. This assumption only proves true (1) with regard to the provision of standardized means of want satisfaction for a great number of people and (2) with regard to processes of problem-solving which require long chains of means-end relationships (Hegner 1978). It does not necessarily prove true with regard to personal services and those tangible goods that lead to want satisfaction—only if they are adapted to the particularities of individual cases (Hegner 1979; Luhmann 1981). These problems can be handled better by social systems that are not primarily based on formal rules.

To summarize: Formally organized service delivery systems that dispose of abstract intermediary means like money and legal entitlements cannot be seen as a panacea for problem solving. Additional to, or substituting for, formal organization is the need for cooperation based on altruism, loyalty, reciprocity, and solidarity (Ouchi 1980). It can take place within formal organizations (e.g., in small work groups) or outside them (e.g., in self-help groups). Within the process of designing service delivery systems, the two modes of coordinating actions must be combined with regard for the economic and social problems to be processed. The quality of the service depends on the way informally organized collectivities and formal organizations, are combined.

The Mix of Institutional Arrangements: An Approach to the Design of Strategy Visions

Informally organized collectivities and formal organizations are embedded in a larger societal context based on a mix of institutional arrangements (Hegner 1986). The concept of *arrangements* indicates a need not only for the coordination of actors and actions (i.e., social organization), but also for the coordination of actors and material objects (material means of want satisfaction like instruments, technical equipment, goods, and money). The concept of *institution* indicates that arrangements are not only grounded on spontaneous agreements among actors, but also on predefined social rules (norms). They pattern the process of economic transactions (supplying people with the means of want satisfaction) as well as the status-relations among the actors allocating social positions, roles, and prestige).

Four aspects must be considered in designing and analyzing institutional arrangements:

1. the mode of transaction (reciprocal, redistributive, price-determined)

2. the balancing of benefits and costs or obligations within the collectivities (long-term versus short-term; informally expected versus formally, or abstractly, stated)

3. the status-relations among the actors (social symmetry versus social asymmetry)

4. the kinds of prevailing common experiences to which all members of a collectivity are exposed (common risks: obligations and rules; competitive actions of others)

Considering these aspects, three types of institutional arrangements can be distinguished: solidaric reciprocity, hierarchic, redistribution, and price-determined market exchange (Hegner 1986). They work as guidelines for strategy visions within the process of designing service delivery systems (see table 7–1).

Solidarity and reciprocity are often said to form the structural and psychosocial basis of nonprofit associations like charities, self-help, and mutual-aid groups (von Brentano 1980; Gross 1982). Hierarchic redistribution should *not* be equated with bureaucratic service delivery and professional dominance over clients. Bureaucratic and professional principles of social organization are nothing but instruments for the coordination of actions and actors within systems of hierarchic redistribution (Kruesselberg 1986). This proves true for private insurance companies as well as for charities and public agencies. Given the necessity of accommodating a large variety of wants and means, purely hierarchic coordination becomes too cumbersome (Luhmann 1981). There is a growing need for either the specification and differentiation of rules and control mechanisms, leading to intransparency and the enlargement of the allocative center, or for very generalized rules, leaving room for discretion and arbitrariness (Hegner 1978). These hierarchy failures can be counteracted by institutionalizing a minimum of solidarity or of price-determined exchange.

The coordination of actions and actors by solidarity, hierarchy, or market exchange can be found on all levels of social system formation (small groups, formal organization, interorganizational networks, societies). For

Table 7–1
Types of Institutional Arrangements

	Solidaric Reciprocity	Hierarchic Redistribution	Market Exchange
Individual Level	Feeling of common risk sharing	Sense of common duty or obligation	Belief in the common positive effects of competition
Personal Systems	Sympathy for other persons	Respect toward role incumbents	Interest in the goods of others
	Loyalty to other persons	Loyalty to position holders	Loyalty to abstract rules of equivalence
	Altruism/ Cooperativeness	Conformism/Rule obedience	Selfishness/Orientation to individual advantages
Interindividual Level	Reciprocal transaction	Redistributive transaction	Price-regulated transaction
Social Systems	Long-term balance of benefits and duties	Legalized (at least, legitimated) short-term imbalance of benefits and obligations combined with the announcement of a long-term balance	Formally stated or factual short-term equivalence of values/goods given and received
-Microsocial Level (small groups) -Mesosocial Level (forma organizations)	De facto or proclaimed social symmetry of participants	De facto social asymmetry of participants	Abstract, or formal, social symmetry of participants (the aspect of symmetry is reduced to specific and ephemeric transactions)
-Macrosocial Level (societal subsystems, societies)	Exposure of all members of a social system to common risks	Exposure of all members of a social system to common obligation and rules	Exposure of participants to the competitive actions of other participants

example, no modern economy based on price-determined exchange is working without hierarchically organized private firms and without the national planning of some resources within a system of hierarchic redistribution (Hull and Hjern 1983; Kruesselberg 1986). At the same time, no modern welfare state based on hierarchic redistribution is working without a minimum of collectivities that mobilized actions and actors with the help of solidaric reciprocity (Ouchi 1980).

Nevertheless, as was previously pointed out, specific structural prerequisites for coordination at the different levels of social system formation exists. They imply either the dominance by one of the three coordination mechanisms or a balanced mix of different types. The challenge to people responsible for designing service delivery systems is to find an adequate fit between the problem to be solved by the provision of services, the organizational forms at hand, and the institutional arrangements given. The testing and realization of these combinations form part of the process of developing service delivery systems.

The Development of Service Delivery Systems: Building up the Adequate Chain of Means-End Relationships

Every service delivery system can be seen as a chain of progression from the provision of means to the satisfaction of wants (Walker 1985). The chain of actions linking means to ends and ends to means can be short or long. There can be few or many intermediate steps and actions, which may form simple or complex networks of transactions (Parsons [1937] 1968). Some material or nonmaterial means (e.g., clothing, nursing) contribute directly to the satisfaction of wants (final consumption). In contrast, others contribute indirectly. They can be conceived as intermediary means (e.g., cloth, nurse training) that have to be processed or transformed to render possible final want satisfaction. The differentiation between final and intermediary means is paralleled by a diversification and refinement of wants, requiring complex sets of means (Quinn and Gagnon 1986). The complexity of the chains of means-end (want) relationships is symbolized by the variety of intermediary means needed to facilitate processes of exchange among the actors in the provision and consumption of goods and services.

Two types of intermediary means deserve special attention in modern welfare societies: money and legal entitlements (Luhmann 1981). Both render possible long and complex chains of means-end relationships that require calculative rationality, individual discipline, systematic planning, formal organization, and standardized evaluations. A third type of intermediary means has become of great importance during recent decades: technical equipment, or technology (e.g., diagnostic, surgical, and recovery equipment in medical services; flexibly designed computer systems in insurance companies and financial services).

Money, legal entitlements, and technical equipment form important components in the chains of means-end relationships in both the market economy and the welfare state. But they cannot form the final link in the provision of means to satisfy wants. They only facilitate the preparation and transaction of goods and services, especially of those goods and services that can be standardized and calculated. With regard to the provision of intangible goods (e.g., personal services) and of those tangible goods that lead to want satisfaction only if they are adapted to the particular situation of the needy, additional transaction processes are needed before final consumption can take place. The coordination of these final transaction processes is often carried out outside price-determined markets and hierarchic redistribution (e.g., in private households, self-help groups, consumer associations).

It is assumed that formally organized collective actors and interorganizational networks play a dominant part in the provision of those want satisfaction means (1) that can be standardized and calculated and (2) that require long, or complex, chains of means-end relationships (Luhmann 1981). With the help of organizational departmentalization, they may even succeed in providing standardized *and* nonstandardized means of want satisfaction at the same time. For example, within insurance companies or welfare agencies, there may be specific departments for the delivery of standardized benefits in cash and in kind that are paralleled by departments for the delivery of personal services (Fauri 1978; Hegner 1979). And within departments for the delivery of standardized benefits, there may be specific subdivisions for managing the encounters with clients or customers in a less standardized way.

Despite departmentalization, formal organizations often do not succeed in adapting the delivery of intangible goods (e.g., personal services) to the particular problems and wants of clients. This failure is due partly to legal constraints and budgetary restrictions, partly to inflexible technical equipment, and partly to the dynamics of bureaucratization and professionalization (Grunow and Hegner 1980a).

Can informally organized collectivities of clients or consumers, based on solidaric reciprocity, fill the service gap left open by formal organizations? Because of the specific sociopsychic and structural prerequisites for their working (Hegner 1986), it is assumed that today they primarily form complements to formal organizations. That is, they can be seen as complements to public agencies and private firms that form part of hierarchic redistribution and market exchange.

Informally organized collectivities (e.g., self-help and mutual-aid groups, associations of consumers, flexible work groups within formal organizations) currently only succeed in providing for want satisfaction under three circumstances (Hegner 1985): (1) if they focus on the provision of means that can be produced, distributed, and consumed within short and simple chains of progression (e.g., coping with everyday problems, do-it-yourself, self-service); (2) if they play a dominant part in the final stages of those long chains of provision based on the use of money, legal entitlements, and large-scale equipment; for example, groups of people who engage in the final equipping of lodgings, youth centers, or clubs for the elderly; and (3) if the coordination of actions based on altruism, reciprocity, or solidarity may be of use with regard to the provision of personal or human services; for example, self-help groups of (former) patients who need more than the medicaments, surgical skill, and technical perfection provided by a formally organized private or public hospital.

The examples given make it clear that informally organized collectivities side with, or rely on, goods and services delivered by formal organizations. That is, they only form part of a long chain of means-want relationships.

Breaking into Pieces Uniformly Structured Chains of Actions: The Fundamental Prerequisite for the Design and Development of Service Delivery Systems

The functioning of provision processes based on solidaric cooperation currently depends on breaking into pieces long and uniformly structured chains of means-end(want) relationships. With regard to the design and development of service delivery systems, that means (1) the particular steps within the progression from the articulation of needs to the provision of means (Hegner 1980) must be analyzed in terms of their respective closeness to different modes of the coordination of actions (forms of organization, institutional arrangements); (2) it has to be established whether the modes of coordination used up until now fit the particular economic and psychological problems that have to be processed step by step within the chain of progression; and finally (3) a decision has to be made whether to use either one type of social organization and institutional arrangement for the whole chain of progression or different types for the various steps in the chain.

The emergence of long chains of actions has been a characteristic of the modern state and society (Elias [1936] 1976). At the same time, the lengthening of chains of actions has been a prerequisite for the working of hierarchic redistribution and market exchange (Kaufmann 1986). Consequently, the number of specific systems for the provision of goods and services has grown. Most systems are specialized on a limited set of goods and services and most provision processes are based on a specific chain of uniformly structured actions. A most interesting task in designing service delivery systems today is to break long and uniformly structured chains of progression into partly autonomous working units (with regard to industry see Piore and Sabel 1984: chapters 2–3; with regard to business services, see Quinn and Gagnon 1986).

The segmentation, or differentiation, of uniformly structured chains, then, renders it possible to design and implement new patterns for the *combination* of different forms of social organization and institutional arrangements. It is the mix of coordination mechanisms that forms the most difficult task in designing and implementing service delivery systems.

References

Badura B. (1978). "Volksmedizin und Gesundheitsvorsorge." *WSI-Mitteilungen*, Vol.31, No. 4, 542–48.

———. (1980). "Self-help Groups as an Alternative to Bureaucratic Regulation and Professional Dominance in the Human Services." In D. Grunow, and F. Hegner (eds.), *Welfare or Bureaucracy?* Cambridge, MA: Oelgeschlager, Gunn & Hain, 199–212.

Blau, P. M., and W. R. Scott. (1969). *Formal Organizations.* London: Routledge & Kegan (first published 1962).

Brentano, D., von. (1980). "Die Bedeutung der Solidarität in Genossenschaften und bei Genossenschaftlichen Gründung svorgängen." *Archiv für öffentliche und Freigemeinnützige Unternehmen*, Vol. 12, 11–31.

Dahme H. J., and F. Hegner. (1982). "Wie Autonom ist der Autonome Sektor?" *Zeitschrift für Soziologie*, Vol. 11, 28–48.

Elias, N. (1976). *Der Proze der Zivillisation*, 2 Vols., Frankfurt: Suhrkamp (first published 1936).

Fauri, D. P. (1978). "Public Service as a Service to Clients." *American Behavioral Scientist*, Vol. 21, 859–69.

Ferber, Chr., von. (1967). *Sozialpolitik in der Wohlstandsgesellschaft.* Hamburg: Wegner.

———. (1983). "Laienpotential, Patientenaktivierung und Gesundheitsselbsthilfe." In Chr. von Ferber and B. Badura, (eds.), *Laienpotential, Patientenaktivierung und Gesundheitsselbsthilfe.* München/Wien: Oldenbourg, 265–93.

Ferber, Chr., von, and L. von Ferber. (1983). *Der Kranke Mensch in der Gesellschaft.* Reinbek: Rowohlt.

Gross, P. (1982). "Der Wohlfahrtsstaat und die Bedeutung der Selbsthilfebewegung." *Soziale Welt* 33(1982), 26–48.

Grunow, D., and F. Hegner. (1978a). *Die Gewährung Wirtschaftlicher und Persönlicher Sozialhilfe.* Bielefeld: Kleine.

———, eds. (1978b). *Welfare or Bureaucracy?* Cambridge, MA: Oelgeschläger, Gunn & Hain.

Grunow, D., F. Hegner, and F. X. Kaufmann. (1978). *Steuerzahler und Finanzamt.* Frankfurt: Campus.

Grunow, D., F. Hegner, and H. E. Schmidt. (1980). *Psychiatrische Versorgung durch Kommunale Gesundheitsämter.* Bielefeld: Kleine.

Hanf, K., and F. W. Scharpf, eds. (1978). *Interorganizational Policy Making.* London: Sage.

Hegel, G. W. F. (1970). "Grundlinien der Philosophie des Rechts." *Werke in Zwanzig Bänden, Theorie Werkausgabe.* Frankfurt: Suhrkamp 1970, Vol. 7, (first published 1821).

Hegner, F. (1978). *Das Bürokratische Dilemma.* Frankfurt: Campus.

———. (1979). *Bürgernähe, Sozialbürgerrolle und Soziale Aktion*, Bielefeld: Kleine.

———. (1980). "Can Micro-interaction Work as a Social Mechanism to Bridge the Gap between Service Organizations and the Public Served?" In D. Grunow and F. Hegner (eds.) *Welfare or Bureaucracy?* Cambridge, MA: Oelgeschlager, Gunn & Hain, 143–61.

————. (1985). "Offentliche Förderung von Selbsthilfe und Selbstorganisation." In K. D. Keim and L. A. Vaskovics (eds.), *Wege zur Sozialplanung.* Opladen: Westdeutscher Verlag, 156–81.

————. (1986). "Solidarity and Hierarchy: Institutional Arrangements for the Coordination of Actions." In F. X. Kaufmann, G. Majone, and V. Ostrom (eds.), *Guidance, Control, and Evaluation in the Public Sector.* Berlin/New York: de Gruyter, 407–29.

Heimann, E. (1980). *Soziale Theorie des Kapitalismus.* Frankfurt: Suhrkamp (first published 1929).

Hood, Chr. (1986). "The Hidden Public Sector: The 'Quangocratization' of the World?" In *Guidance, Control and Performance Evaluation in the Public Sector.* F. X. Kaufmann, G. Majone, and V. Ostrom (eds.), Berlin/New York: de Gruyter, 183–207.

Hull, Chr., and B. Hjern. (1983). "Policy Analysis in Mixed Economy," *Policy and Politics,* Vol. 11, 295–312.

Kaufmann, F. X. (1986). " 'Introduction' and 'The Relationship between Guidance, Control, and Evaluation'." In F. X. Kaufmann, G. Majone, and V. Ostrom (eds.), *Guidance, Control, and Evaluation in the Public Sector.* Berlin/New York: de Gruyter, 3–24 and 211–228.

Kickbusch, I., and A. Trojan, eds. (1981). *Gemeinsam sind Wir stärker. Selbsthilfegruppen und Gesundheit.* Frankfurt: Fischer.

Kruesselberg, H. G. (1986). "Markets and Hierarchies." In F. X. Kaufmann, G. Majone, and V. Ostrom (eds.), *Guidance, Control, and Evaluation in the Public Sector.* Berlin/New York: de Gruyter, 349–86.

Kuhn, Th., S. (1970). *The Structure of Scientific Revolutions.* Chicago: University of Chicago Press (first published 1962).

Luhmann, N. (1964). *Funktionen und Folgen Formaler Organisation,* Berlin: Duncker & Humblot.

————. (1981). *Politische Theorie im Wohlfarhrtsstaat.* München: Olzog.

Merton, R. K. (1971). "Social Problems and Sociological Theory." In R. K. Merton and R. N. Nisbet (eds.), *Contemporary Social Problems.* 3d ed. New York: Harcourt, 697–737.

Mohl, R., von. (1962). "Über Bürokratie." In R. von Mohl, (ed.), *Staatsrecht, Völkerrecht und Politik,* Vol. II/1. Tübingen: Mohr, 99–130 (first published 1846).

Ouchi, W. G. (1980). "Markets, Bureaucracies, and Clans," *Administrative Science Quarterly,* Vol. 25, 129–41.

Pankoke, E. (1970). *Sociale Bewegung—Sociale Frage—Sociale Politik. Grundfragen der Deutschen Socialwissenschaft.* Stuttgart: Klett-Cotta.

Parsons, T. (1968). *The Structure of Social Action,* 2 Vols. New York: The Free Press (first published 1937).

Piore, M. J., and Ch. F. Sabel. (1984). *The Second Industrial Divide.* New York: Basic Books.

Polanyi, K. (1944). *The Great Transformation.* New York: Van Nostrand.

Quinn, J. B., and Chr. E. Gagnon. (1986). "Will Services Follow Manufacturing into Decline?" *Harvard Business Review,* Vol. 64 (November–December), 95–103.

Robson, W. A. (1976). *Welfare State and Welfare Society.* London: Allen & Unwin.

Scitovsky, T. (1976). *The Joyless Economy.* Oxford: Oxford University Press.

Simon, H. A. (1965). *Administrative Behavior.* New York: MacMillan (first published 1945).

Virchow, R. (1848/1849). "Die Öffentliche Gesundheitspflege" (first published 1848), "Die Volkskrankheiten" (first published 1849). In H. U. Deppe and M. Regus (eds.), *Medizin, Gesellschaft, Geschichte.* Frankfurt: Suhrkamp 1985, 171–185.

Walker, R. A. (1985). "Is There a Service Economy? The Changing Capitalist Division of Labour." *Science & Society*, Vol. 49, 42–83.

8
On the Strategic Implications of Tangible Elements in the Marketing of Industrial Services

Jean-Paul Flipo

Introduction

Most researchers of services management highlight two major factors differentiating the marketing of services from the marketing of material goods: their intangibility and the part played by personnel in contact with clients. There is no point here in listing the many authors who have analyzed these two main differences. However, take note that the nature, importance, and particular role of intangible factors in the success of marketing services still remain open for discussion (Flipo 1988). On the other hand, some authors are working on the other aspect of marketing services: namely, tangible factors inevitably connected with any trade offer (Bitner 1985). However, Bitner and others (Arnold 1985) are concerned only with the immediate environment of the service delivery: the point of sale that, when dealing with services offered to the general public (distribution, banking, hotel business, etc.) is absolutely essential for contact with customers.

Most authors in this approach include in the concept of environment intangible factors such as atmosphere, quality of human relations, and so on. (Baker 1986).

This chapter deals only with a category of services for which specific points of sale rarely exist, that is, industrial services—services provided to organizations. In fact, the commercial contact and often the service delivery take place somewhere other than on the supplier's premises, usually on the customer's premises. The aim of this chapter is to draw a preliminary list of the nature, range, and varying importance of these tangible factors, which at first glance may be considered as minor for the marketing success of industrial services. It is an exploratory study consisting of a survey of ten firms, each with its own specialty, providing services for companies:

data processing services

advertising agency

private security services

industrial cleaning

temporary work

management consultancy

hygiene services (e.g., pest control)

consultancy services for exporters in a bank

goods transportation

aesthetic creations on industrial and urban buildings

The methodology consisted of in-depth interviews with top managers (general or marketing) in these different firms to find out how they viewed the tangible factors in the service offering, within a perspective of service quality.

The chapter is made up of two parts: first, a proposition of various classification criteria useful for the marketing of these services; second, the implications of these criteria from a strategic point of view. Bear in mind that no general scientific conclusion can be drawn from a simple exploratory approach. This chapter, therefore, has a more modest purpose; it only aims at pointing the way toward conclusions by suggesting possible ways of analyzing the problem.

Indeed, numerous authors have already stressed the impact of tangible elements on the perceived quality of services (Parasuraman, Zeithaml, and Berry 1985; Booms and Bitner 1982), which will be discussed in the second part, as considered from service providers' viewpoint.

Useful Criteria for the Classification of Tangible Factors

First, it is necessary to define the scope of inquiry from the conceptual point of view.

Tangible elements are defined as everything that has material reality, everything that is touchable and visible, and sometimes tastable. Therefore, other realities should be excluded, aspects such as the service performance itself, psychological elements (atmosphere, communication, etc.), or signs perceptible by other senses: odor, music. One may actually consider that, for a firm providing services to other firms, trade contacts are extremely limited: they consist of the visit made by a salesperson who first sells the service and then supervises the trade relationship. Meanwhile, other members of the contact personnel are only seen as "producers of the service"— for example, a truck driver in a transport company. Another and wider view considers every staff member in a service company responsible for the relationship with customers, and that, to a certain extent, all points of contact between the supplier and his or her customer contribute to the future success or failure of the commercial relationship (including all people involved in the purchase center, even external stake holders, such as the customer's customer).

Recent inquiries about criteria for assessing the quality of services (Parasuraman, Zeithaml, and Berry 1985) have shown that only the wider view of this problem is realistic.

An initial list of all these material elements shows they are numerous; in the companies chosen for this sample, it is possible to pick out thirty different material elements with which customers may have tactile or visual contact.

What the word *environment* includes is well-known: the front, the decor, the furniture, the functional layout of the place, written information, and every other facility that makes the service encounter possible and pleasant.

Necessary Equipment for the Service Delivery

No service can be provided without provision for a minimum of tangible factors. The most obvious of these is the means of communicating the result of the operation to the customer, for example, an intervention report by a management consultant. From this point of view, the least tangible service among the companies sampled was *temporary work*. Apart from the temporary worker, the only tangible elements of the service for the customer were the order form and the bill.

On the other hand, for some businesses the material elements of production are both extremely large and always fully relevant to the quality of the service provided: for example, the progressive mechanization in industrial cleaning, the need for computers in data processing services, the highly sophisticated electronic equipment used in closed-circuit camera surveillance services, and so on.

An exception occurs when the tangible elements attached to the performance itself are not a *means of production* but the result of it. Two of the companies selected confirm this: the advertising agency because the launching of a campaign is the result of the service ordered by the customer (posters, magazine advertisements, television commercials, etc.); and the company offering aesthetic creations to the properties of its customers (frescoes, for example, or colors adapted to the image the customer wants his or her firm to have). It is evident that these two suppliers work toward communicating their own service quality by material means.

Contact Personnel's Material Equipment

The aim of the personnel in contact with customers—a major component in service companies—is to satisfy the particular wishes of purchasers and meet their expectations. Consequently, the factors of service quality they deal with are mainly intangible: the quality of the communication, the atmosphere, the adapted behavior selected to match the service perceived and the service expected. But it is easy to forget that the staff also convey material factors that have a direct bearing on intangible elements. The first of these is their outward appearance, particularly important in such occupations as receptionists, models in specialized agencies, as well as in occupations requiring a high level of interaction with customers, such as a company consultant or advertising agency account manager. Moreover, some physical appearances, such as that of a security guard, must give a feeling of safety although others, such as that of an artist innovating in the field of communication, may surprise. So customers expect some particular appearance from personnel.

Personnel dress is another tangible factor belonging in this category. The clothes should fit well and be at least one of the factors in increasing the customer's confidence. For such an unknown and rather peculiar activity as industrial hygiene, the fact that the staff wear a uniform (and use spectacular equipment) is an important tangible factor. Temporary work agencies encourage their temporary staff to wear uniforms, which meets opposition above all from the administrative staff.

In this third category are the objects used by contact personnel and sometimes left for the customer. In the transport company investigated, a promotion pamphlet was designed for salespeople to clarify the range of services offered. This document has been designed, so it can be left for the customer as a catalog if the relationship between customer and supplier should develop later. Other media, such as audio or videotapes or telematic screens, can be used as well, as long as the supplier makes sure the customer has the appropriate equipment in which to use them. If not, he or she may provide it. (Such is the case of the transport company that uses this system to convey information concerning the goods delivered. In this context, this element would belong to the second category, that of the equipment needed for the provision of the service.) Also found in the third category is a last type of tangible factor: free gifts. They are widely offered by suppliers who do not have as much service equipment. In the sample, these are found in the temporary work agency and the consultancy services for exporters in a bank. The latter, for example, tries to put forward the idea that exporting firms are part of an elite and the prestigious gifts reinforce this.

Other Useful Criteria for the Classification
of Tangible Elements

The criteria discussed in this section will lend a better appreciation of the influence of each tangible element on the quality of service provided—

quality expected or quality perceived. In this exploratory approach a list of the criteria that have been mentioned during the investigation made within the companies in the sample is presented.

The Classification of Tangible Factors According to Their Order of Frequency of Exposure. To take two opposite examples: the nil frequency for a customer who never visits his supplier and so cannot judge the level of equipment of the service versus the very high frequency for a customer who requires the help of a management consultant and may be in daily contact with the supplier at the time of the operation.

Useful Communication Targets Affected by Tangible Elements. So far marketing logic has been used mainly in relation to clientele, but it is well known that in services contact personnel are themselves a target of the highest strategic importance where marketing is concerned (Flipo 1986). An example is the case of temporary work agencies that had difficulty in persuading staff to wear uniforms when working in their customers' offices. Uniforms are more readily accepted in transport companies.

Other communication targets are prospective buyers, people who influence the purchasing process, the general public, the employment market, and so on. Mobile elements are in contact with the largest and most varied number of targets and have the highest rate of repetition. It is estimated, for example, that a truck doing 55,000 miles a year creates several million visual contacts with the general public during that period.

Classification Based on the Ability to Express the Quality of the Service. The "value of accreditation"—the standard of quality of service as well as the supplier's ability to honor promises undoubtedly has such an impact in two specific ways: when the quality of the tangible factor is real proof of the quality of service; and when it is an indication of this quality as a new experience and there are no other indicators. An example of the first might be a security service company that works mainly at night while the customer is away (an essential occurrence); then, the material elements left by the nightwatchman show that the service was performed. The level of precision in the reports is relevant to the quality of service and will show whether the supplier has achieved his or her objectives or not. Companies responsible for urban aesthetics, like advertising agencies, show the quality of their service through their work or the campaigns they design. These works are among the best ways to promote themselves because they have a strong visual impact on many people.

An example of the second case (tangible clue): a pest control operation, for example, in an airplane, can be accomplished with impressive equipment. Possible hazards and the impatience of the customer are such that it may lead him or her to make the mistake of believing that the duration time of the operation will be short. This equipment is therefore just a clue to the service quality, and not proof.

Strategic Implications for Service Quality Management

Every service, industrial services included, needs at least one material means to be performed. Thus, the marketing criteria to choose equipment must be decided on, after the financial and technical criteria are taken into account. An example of this strategic problem is the choice of an office site for a management consultancy agency. The managers moved from a famous business area into a town in the working class suburbs to reduce rent costs. They did not realize that this would have a negative impact on the company's image and credibility.

In this section the following three aspects are studied: how to measure the strategic importance of tangible factors as compared with intangible ones: what making a service tangible means, and when and how this is to be achieved; finally, what are the problems involved in the implementation of a precise policy in this matter.

Assessing the Strategic Importance of Tangible Evidence in the Supplying of Industrial Services in Comparison with Intangible Elements

As services are by nature intangible (they are actions/processes), adding tangible elements to them cannot provide a total guarantee of quality, unlike technical features, which show the quality of material goods. No one can deny the influence of these tangible elements on the quality of the service supplied. They impact both aspects of service—the "expected service" (tangible clues) and the "perceived service"—because material equipment and facilities produce a basic level of performance and reliability. According to the specialists interviewed, these seem to be the important factors of tangible evidence in the perceived quality of the service.

The Nature of the Service, Especially Its Level of Mechanization. A most interesting classification of services activities, made by Dan Thomas (1978), is based on the level of mechanization in the service. Maximum mechanization was found in fully automatic services (cash points, car wash, etc.), yet it was minimal in services principally employing people and demanding a high level of skill from contact personnel (e.g., research services, consultancy). For reasons of mere performance efficiency, when dealing with highly mechanized or computerized services, tangible factors of production are all the more important. No matter how qualified a computer service company is in its specialty, if the computer being used breaks down, it cannot serve its customer.

The Supplier's Position When Faced with Competition. The strategic growth of service companies is built mainly on intangible elements: the overall ability of the personnel, the attitude, the overall atmosphere of performance, and the company image, which is the result of hundreds or thousands of daily contacts (Normann 1984). Thus, a highly competitive position is actually significant of strong, positive intangible factors, company image especially.

In this situation, tangible factors such as contact personnel's attire or the decor of the premises become less important. The creation of the expected service depends only in a secondary way on these supply elements. On the contrary, if the company is not well-known, if contact with customers is mediocre, if it is not possible to appreciate the ability of the staff in advance, the only way for the supplier to attract customers is to pay particular attention to tangible elements. Noteworthy is Levitt's famous example of a tradesperson who specialized in house-roof thermal insulation (Levitt 1980). Unfortunately, the author does not indicate which of the two suppliers is really the best or the more attractive (in physical and behavioral appearance). Surrogates can never totally replace the service reality.

Buyer's Behavior. The risks buyers foresee when looking for a service supplier stem from many factors attached to both supply and demand. As for supply, these factors include the overall image of the profession as a whole (good or bad), the intensity of the competition, the existence of trade standards, and so on. As for demand, the main factor is the importance attached to the service by the consumer or company and their motive for purchasing it.

Assuming that the greater the risk buyers perceive, the smaller the role tangible elements will play in the creation of service expectations (as compared with intangible ones). This is even more true of tangible factors that are not factors of service production but only indications of quality of service (decor, business documents, etc.).

As a result, purchasing processes within the firms are long and complex. The riskier the purchase, the longer and more complex the process, precisely in order to get behind the suppliers' appearance, to examine their intangible attributes better.

Finally, one must discuss the impact of purchase conditions on the strategic importance of tangible factors. Their importance is to help customers quickly estimate the level of service expectation. If there is an emergency and no intangible factors (in particular, the image), it is only the material elements of the supply that will influence the customer's choice. This rarely happens in services for companies, except sometimes for transport services or pest-control services, where time may be of fundamental importance.

How to "Tangibilize" a Service and Why It Is Necessary

It is obvious why services that use large equipment, such as industrial cleaning, computer processing consultancy, or urban aesthetics services, have to be tangible. The service itself is tangibilized as far as the means and/or results are concerned. For services relying almost entirely on human contact, such as consultancy or temporary work, the reason is not so obvious. To tangibilize means of creating material reality—to make ideas, concepts, arguments, images—perceptible to sight and/or touch, is not absolutely essential for the technical delivery of the service. It is an act of will.

Therefore, the question is not merely to choose a type of material tool to meet production needs; sketches and drawings are indeed necessary for artistic services (Friedman and Friebert 1986) and are therefore not relevant here. Nor is the point to make an intangible factor perceptible through another intangible factor, such as oral communication (Van Doren and Relle 1987).

The benefits of tangible evidence are obvious as long as they are seen as a vehicle for communication. Three different types of benefit exist:

1. Tangible elements, though not absolutely essential, help illustrate the difference between two suppliers. Tangibles show how professional the supplier is since their presence involves coding supplier/customer relationships; how serious he or she is because they may imply formal engagements; how willing he or she is to provide a good service and establish good and continuous relations with his or her customers. Tangibilization as an act of will is essential to show consideration to customers.

2. Because tangible elements are functional, practical, and real communication tools, they save time and improve production. A well-designed promotional brochure might replace the sales visit. A published set of questions and answers can help customers think clearly and formulate more precise requirements for consultancy companies so that services can be perfectly customized.

3. These tangible factors have a real impact as a medium for communicating the marketing positioning of a supplier. Thus, it is correct to assume that all the tangible factors previously pointed out have a real impact, either stronger or weaker as the situation varies. Many services

to the general public, such as hotel or restaurant chains, have been aware of this for a long time, but, as far as industrial services are concerned, major improvements are required.

The desire to make a service tangible can be achieved through many different actions. In other words, the scope for strategic action is extremely wide. The aim is to have a fully coherent range of tangible factors, each bringing forward the concepts differently, and reinforcing them at the same time.

The ultimate aim is make the purchaser feel as safe as when he or she buys material goods. To create this feeling, the marketer in industrial services must organize the contact between customers and positive tangible clues, for example, by inviting them to visit the company's premises or offices.

Operational Limits and Problems

The basic substance of services and their marketing peculiarities make it obvious that no attempt to provide a supply coherent in all aspects can ever lead to perfect consistency. Variety is an intrinsic element and lies in the individuality of each person—the suppliers and customers—in situations and in the inability of human beings to provide exact replicas of service every time. The material components of the service delivery are not more totally reliable even if failures do not occur as frequently as for individuals.

However, the inability to achieve consistency is not only a negative factor; it is also an opportunity for creative individuals to improve the level of performance. It is even indispensable for service companies whose function is precisely that of being creative. Could one ever imagine an advertising agency duplicating its campaign? On the other hand, it still can, and even has to, duplicate formal communication procedures to manage its relationship with customers.

The problem of consistency concerns mainly network service companies wishing to base strategic growth not only on the number of agencies or outlets but also on a coherent image and positioning being expressed through the service. Many service companies already have their book of standards. A hotel chain, for example, has standards for the architecture inside and outside, its description, decor, staff uniform, restaurant plates and dishes, bedroom and common room furniture, sanitary equipment, administration records and so on. However, in this case, it is part of the service concept to give identical performances. This is what customers actually look for so that they can follow the same habits and can feel at home anywhere in the world. The main intention of this service is that all elements of the equipment should support this plan or objective.

This is not true of companies providing services to other companies.

Only long after they were created have most of them understood how beneficial this idea of consistency could be from a marketing point of view. However, obstacles to the practical application of this desire for consistency abound.

Companies must be convinced of the impact of tangible elements on customers and of the need for similarity. Operational grades of the service, in particular, must be made aware of tangibles. (This would be even more difficult in a company that resulted from the amalgamation of several companies or a takeover by a parent company.) This is a marketing effort inside a company that requires a considerable amount of effort and determination from its executives.

Financial backing is needed to set up and standardize agencies or outlets. Often this requires high budget allowances which are only released gradually. This means it usually takes many years before a network is up to standard, and standards may have changed in the meantime.

Regular maintenance of particularly visible equipment, such as buildings or mobile equipment, or staff uniforms (if the staff actually wear the uniform is required).

Conclusion

The aim of this chapter has been to suggest a primary approach to strategic thinking about the tangible elements of a service offering, especially for the industrial services category.

It is understandable that only a few researchers have tackled the problem because services are intangible by nature (an action or a process), and their commercial success depends on other intangible elements (the service and company image, the client's expected service, the overall atmosphere of the service, etc.). Those who have dealt mainly with one category of services—those provided for the public—because the contact with the suppliers and their premises is more direct.

The author has tried to show how important the marketing of tangible factors is in industrial services as well although customers rarely visit suppliers of such services. First suggested were various systems of classification that might help clarify marketing thought. It was then shown how it is possible to use them from a strategic point of view. The main purpose of this analysis is to enable suppliers to contribute to expected service in customers' minds. Thus, standards of performance would correspond to supplier's commitments and customers would evaluate the quality of the service delivered to be good enough for them to remain loyal to suppliers. Because of the large number and variety of services for companies, no precise advice can be given in this chapter. However, the central idea to bear in mind is that the material elements of service supply must be regarded as one of the elements of the marketing mix. The strong point of tangibles is they are more easily manageable than the intangible and can naturally be more easily standardized, owing to their material nature.

It would be necessary, in a perspective of future research, to measure the perception of tangible evidence by customers to make useful comparisons with those perceived by managers.

One of the most relevant techniques would be to undertake experiments consisting of measuring the differential impact of several sets of tangible elements; this technique is regularly employed for advertisements and has been already used for larger sets of visual elements like landscapes (Schroeder 1982).

However, the impact of visual or tactile objects is largely unconscious, with mainly secondary or tertiary symbolic meanings of the signs emitted.

References

Arnold, Christopher. (1985). "The Service Environment: An Architect Perspective." In M. Venkatesan, Diane M. Schmalensee, and Claudia Marshall (eds.), *Creativity in Services Marketing: What's New, What Works, What's Developing*. San Francisco: American Marketing Association, 94–98.

Baker, Julie. (1986). "The Role of the Environment in Consumer Services: The Consumer Perspective." In John A. Czepiel, Carole A. Congram, and Jim Shanahan (eds.), *The Services Challenge: Integrating for Competitive Advantage* Boston: American Marketing Association, 79–84.

Bitner, Mary J. (1985). "Consumer Responses to the Physical Environment in Services Settings." In M. Venkatesan, Diane M. Schmalensee, and Claudia Marshall (eds.), *Creativity in Services Marketing: What's New, What Works, What's Developing*, San Francisco: American Marketing Association, 89–93.

Booms, B. H., and M. J. Bitner. (1982). "Marketing Services by Managing the Environment." *Cornell Hotel and Restaurant Administration Quarterly*, 23 (May), 35–39.

Flipo, J. P. (1986). "Service Firms: Interdependence of External and Internal Marketing Strategies." *European Journal of Marketing*, 5–14.

———. (1988). "On the Intangibility of Services." *Service Industries Journal*, Vol. 8, No. 3 (July), 286–98.

Friedman, Margaret L., and Debra Friebert. (1986). "Marketing Interior Design Services." *Journal of Professional Services*, Vol. 2, No. 1/2 (Fall/Winter), 147–56.

Levitt, Theodore. (1980). "Marketing Intangible Products and Product Intangibles." *Harvard Business Review*, May–June, 94–102.

Normann, Richard. (1984). *Service Management: Strategy and Leadership in Service Businesses*. New York: J. Wiley & Sons.

Parasuraman A., Valarie A. Zeithaml, and Leonard L. Berry. (1985). "A Conceptual Model of Service Quality and Its Implications for Future Research." *Journal of Marketing*, Vol. 49 (Fall), 41–50.

Schroeder, Herbert W. (1982). "Managing the Esthetics of Outdoor Recreation Sites: Some Analogies with Problems in Retailing." *Journal of Retailing*, Vol. 58, No. 1 (Spring), 22–33.

Thomas, Dan R. E. (1978). "Strategy Is Different in Service Businesses." *Harvard Business Review*, July–August, 158–65.

Van Doren, Doris C., and Paul B. Relle. (1987). "Confronting Intangibility: A Practical Approach." *Journal of Professional Services*, Vol. 2, No. 3 (Spring) 31–39.

9

Service Quality: Multidisciplinary and Multinational Perspectives
An Experimental Study of Service Production Processes in Different Cultures

Jarmo R. Lehtinen

Summary of the Definitions of Concepts

The concepts used in this chapter are briefly described here although the most important ones will be further discussed. More penetrating definitions can be found in earlier studies by service quality researchers.

The service production process (SPP) consists of three sets of resources: customer resources, contact resources, and physical resources. In most cases contact resources are the contact persons, the employees of the service provider. This chapter focuses on the interaction between customers and contact resources during the SPP.

Participation refers to the activity of taking part in and putting effort into the SPP. Both customers and contact persons participate in the SPP.

Participation style refers to the manner in which participation takes place. The backgrounds of participants influence their participation styles.

Service style is analogous to participation style but is performed by the contact persons.

Interactive quality is judged by the customer according to how his or her expectations are met during the SPP, and especially how his or her participation style is understood by the contact persons, and how contact persons adapt their service styles accordingly.

In this chapter *customer service* is synonymous with interactive quality, which relates to the interaction between the customer and the contact person.

The study for this chapter has been carried out in the following geographical regions:

Europe (Scandinavia, Central Europe, and the Mediterranean countries)
North America

Far-East Asia (including Japan and India)

Soviet Union (European part)

The basic method used was observation and participation, a method hermeneutical and clinical in nature. In practice, this means that the results help to further understanding and are not to be understood in a positivistic way.

This type of explorative study provides sufficient information for designing studies to measure more exactly differences in various service styles.

Differences in Economic Conditions

Before trying to understand how services are produced and what service quality means in different regions, it is important to understand how the economies of the areas differ. Two dimensions are used to illustrate differences. This two-dimension approach is fairly limited but is sufficient in this case. The dimensions are (1) deficit/surplus economy and (2) market/socialist economy.

It is of great importance whether there is a deficit or surplus of services and goods to be marketed. In a deficit economy practically everything produced can be sold easily, so it is not important to have sales promotion integrated in a service production process.

In a surplus economy more services are produced than there are consumers to consume them. Therefore, it is important to promote services and to attract new consumers.

In a market economy the enterprises have to market their own services in the market. They are not centrally controlled, except by the basic framework of legislation and rules, although the service sector has been one of the most regulated sectors of the economy in many countries. The performance of organizations is evaluated by a profit concept.

In a socialist economy all organizations producing services are controlled by highly centralized hierarchical structures. Generally little scope exists for organizations to act in accordance with the customers' particular situations. Marketing of services does not exist as a concept. These dimensions are illustrated in figure 9–1.

This means, for example, that in the United States services are produced in a surplus market economy whereas in some underdeveloped countries, like South-East Asian countries, they are produced in a deficit economy—but, at the same time, in a market economy. Finally, in socialist countries, in this example the Soviet Union, services are produced in a socialist deficit economy.

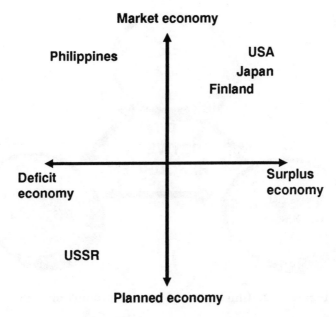

Figure 9–1. Illustration of the economic environment.

Definition of Service Styles and Participation Styles

The service production process has three elements: the customer, the contact resources, and the physical resources. To be able to operate, management of the service organization must find a fit or compatibility among the elements so that the service production process may function properly. This process is illustrated in figure 9–2.

The service style as well as the participation style concern both the customer and the contact resources. Participation style depends on the life-path and life-style of the customer; it is also situation specific and, to some extent, varies from time to time.

The interaction system thus produced also defines one quality dimension: interactive service quality. Two other dimensions are physical quality and institutional quality.

Because a certain service is produced jointly by the customer and the service provider in a service production process, it is easy to understand that interactive service quality is a result of the compatibility between the customer's participation style and the service style of the provider. Quality is interpreted by a customer in accordance with his or her expectations and how these are met during the service production process. If compatibility

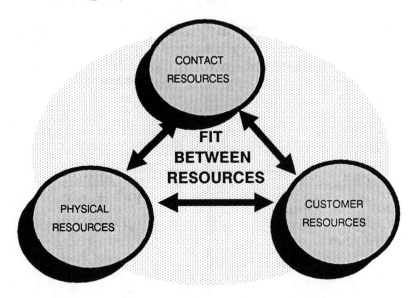

Figure 9–2. Illustration of service production process.

between the participation style and the service style expected by the customer exists, sufficient interactive service quality is produced.

This is shown in figure 9–3.

Definition of Customer Service Style Dimensions

Observations would suggest that different dimensions may be elaborated to describe different service styles. These dimensions are found in the service production process and may perhaps be divided into subdimensions; they can also be measured by defining suitable variables.

The dimensions used to describe customer service style in this chapter are as follows:

Empathetic/nonempathetic dimension: the degree of empathy shown by the service provider in his or her approach to the customer.

Efficient/nonefficient dimension: the efficiency of the service production process as seen from the customer's viewpoint.

Remote/close dimension: how customers experience the contact resources.

Attentive/nonattentive dimension: the speed with which contact persons react to the customer's needs.

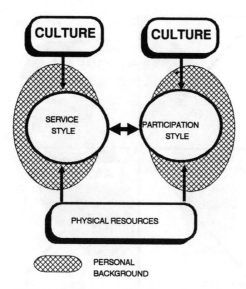

Figure 9–3. Fit between service style and participation style.

To illustrate the way these dimensions can shape the service styles in the different regions studied, see figure 9–4.

These dimensions enable us to describe the three basic (customer) service styles that exist in the regions studied.

The Oriental Service Style

The nature of the Oriental service style is empathetic but remote. For example, most taxi drivers in Tokyo wear white gloves during working hours. They do not talk to their customers but are very attentive and have even found a technical solution for opening the door for their customers automatically.

In Japan tour guides take extremely good care of their groups to prevent their getting into difficulties, but guides do not try to establish close contact with customers. They too wear uniforms and gloves, distinguishing them from tourists.

The American Service Style

The American service style can be described as extremely close and friendly; contact persons try to be attentive and friendly toward customers.

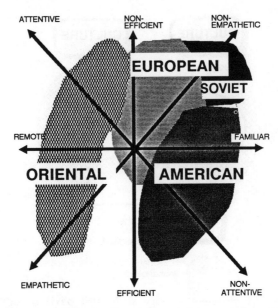

Figure 9–4. Illustration of customer service styles.

An illustration is a waitress who comes up to the customer and says, "Hi, I'm Judy, I'm your waitress today. What can I do for you?" She will address her customer in the same manner throughout the entire service production process. Efficiency is important because, working in a surplus market economy, she gets paid by results.

The European Service Style

The European style of service can be divided into various substyles because Europe is not integrated culturally. The service style in Scandinavia may differ considerably from that in the Mediterranean. In general, the European service style is not as efficient as the American and not as attentive as the South-East Asian style. It is also apparent that, north to south, attentiveness increases. In the Nordic countries remoteness is more clearly present.

The Soviet Service Style

In a sense, the Soviet service style may be seen as a substyle of the European service style. It is produced in a deficit economy in which the control system has a powerful effect on the service style. In practice, this means that the Soviet service style is exceedingly nonattentive, remote, and inefficient. There are, however, major differences within the Soviet Union, since many different subcultures exist and the Soviet Union lacks cultural integration. For instance, the service style in Estonia is closer to that in central Europe.

An illustration would be a small cafeteria with many empty tables that did not admit customers. The reason? Lack of personnel, and because the quotas for those working at the movement were filled, no customers were admitted since this would mean extra work for employees. As one of the older waiters said, "We don't need to admit any more people than we have to in order to fill our quotas; in any case, we don't get paid more."

In deficit economies, both in underdeveloped countries and in the Soviet Union, fairly large menus exist but only one or two dishes are served in practice.

Managerial Implications

The implications of understanding customer service styles are manifold. Here are just a few examples of managerial implications:

1. In order to be profitable in different countries companies must understand culture-based service styles. The service company has to adapt, to a certain extent, to the local service style. In some cases, however, it is important for companies to utilize successful standardized procedures, even in diverse cultures. McDonald's has proven to be extremely successful in this regard.

   The training and education of employees must be based on cultural values in order to be successful.

2. When doing business and forced to use services, organizations need to understand the differences in service styles globally.

For purely personal reasons, it is beneficial to understand differences in customer service styles in different cultures, to create expectations that can be met during the service production process.

References

Albrecht, K., and R. Zemke. (1985). *Service America!* Homewood: Dow Jones-Irwin.

Barney, Jay B. (1986). "Organizational Culture: Can It Be a Source of Sustained Competitive Advantage?" *Academy of Management Review*, Vol. 11.

Bateson, John E. G., Pierre Eiglier, Eric Langeard, and Christopher H. Lovelock. (1978). *Testing a Conceptual Framework for Consumer Service Marketing*. Cambridge, MA: Marketing Science Institute.

Berry, Leonard J. (1985). "Key Ideas in the Practice of Services Marketing." *American Banker*, Vol. 150.

Bitner, Mary J. (1986). "Consumer Responses to the Physical Environment in Service Settings." In *Creativity in Services Marketing: What's New, What Works, What's Developing*, M. Venkateson, Diane M. Schmalensee, and Claudia Marshall, editors. Chicago: American Marketing Association.

Bowen, David E. (1986). "Managing customers as Human Resources in Service Organizations." Vol. 25 *Human Resource Management*.

Burgelman, Robert A. (1984). "Managing the Internal Corporate Venturing Process." *Sloan Management Review*. Vol. 25.

Deal, T. E., and A. A. Kennedy. (1982). *Corporate Culture*. Reading, MA: Addison-Wesley.

Dwyer, F. R., P. H. Schurr, and S. Oh. (1987). "Developing Buyer-Seller Relationships." *Journal of Marketing*, Vol. 51.

Gardner, M. P. (1985). "Creating a Corporate Culture for the Eighties." *Business Horizons*, Vol. 28, No. 1

Hostage, G. M. (July/August 1975). "Quality Control in Service Businesses." *Harvard Business Review*, Vol. no. .

Mills, P. K., and J. H. Morris. (1986). "Clients as 'Partial' Employees of Service Organizations: Role Development in Client Participation." *Academy of Management Review*, Vol 11.

Reynierse, James H. (1986). "Measuring Corporate Culture." *The Bankers Magazine*, Vol 169.

Rosander, A. C. 1985. *Applications of Quality Control in the Service Industries*. Milwaukee, WI: ASQC Quality Press.

10

Evaluating Marketing and Operations Service Quality Information
A Preliminary Report

David A. Collier

Introduction

"Our internal operational measures of service quality are quite good," noted a senior division manager of a large bank, "yet the customer perceives service quality as poor based on marketing's recent customer survey. So, what's going on here? Can anyone at this meeting explain this mismatch between these two different sources of service quality information?"

Service firm managers repeat this conversation daily when attempting to integrate, coordinate, and use these two diverse sets of service quality information. Why is service quality so important? First, a recent American Banker's Survey (1986) found that consumers rank good service first when talking about what satisfies them most about financial institutions. Second, this information helps managers make decisions that will assure good service. Typical decisions that affect service quality include service facility design and layout, job and process design, training, service package management (Collier 1987a), employee incentive and performance evaluation schemes, advertising strategies and plans, pricing and target market strategies, and strategic direction definitions and competitive priorities.

Management often tends to evaluate service quality performance from an operations perspective simply because operations data is under their control and more readily available. External (to the service-providing organization) sources of service quality information most often fall under the domain of marketing.

Accordingly, the functional department mentality tends to complicate and inhibit the integration of these two service quality databases. These situations argue for a "service management" approach to defining, measuring, controlling, using, and managing service quality information. Mechanisms such as establishing a customer service committee to design comparable marketing- and operations-based service quality criteria, having marketing and operations managers report to a common top-level manager, and reorganizing around the service management concept could be utilized.

This chapter addresses management problems associated with coordinating, evaluating, and using these two sets of service quality information to imporove management decision making. This chapter begins by briefly reviewing how service quality can be defined. Then several preliminary levels of data analyses are explored using specific services and data from U.S. credit card providers. The idea of a service quality map is introduced. The chapter ends by briefly discussing possible uses of service quality maps and the future directions of this ongoing research.

Defining Service Quality

The issue of defining service quality has been discussed by many authors in previous articles and books (Collier 1987a, 1987c, 1989a, 1989b). Table 10–1 taken from Collier (1987a) summarizes some of these ideas on service quality.

This chapter assumes that effective indicators of service quality can be defined, measured, and regularly collected. The first management challenge is to accurately define the attributes that comprise the service package (i.e., a specific service or group of related services). The second challenge is to measure each attribute (Collier 1987a). Typical service quality attributes include accuracy, volume and activity, convenience, time-oriented responsiveness, reliability, professionalism and competence, friendliness and customer empathy, atmosphere and aesthetics, security and safety, productivity and efficiency, overall market and economic performance indicators, technology, and price/value/cost relationships.

A third challenge for management is to define these service quality measures in comparable ways for both the marketing (external) and operations (internal) measurement systems. In practice, most marketing and operations service quality collection and evaluation efforts are administered on an independent basis with few cooperative efforts.

Service Quality Data Collection Efforts

A total of six major U.S. corporations were contacted (Collier 1987b) about participating in this study. After much discussion and review, two companies had various degrees of service quality operations-based data per service package but little or no comparable marketing-based data. In one case, the company was simply behind the industry in collecting and evaluating service quality information. The other company dealt with the customer

Table 10–1
Defining Customer Service and Quality Levels

Excellent customer service and quality levels (CS&QLs) means consistently meeting customer expectations (external service standards and cost) and service delivery system performance criteria (internal service standards, cost, and revenue).

Excellent customer service and quality levels are achieved by the consistent delivery to the customer of a clearly defined service package specified by many internal and external standards of performance.

- *Excellent* means achieving performance standards 100 percent of the time.

- *Customer* is the next entity (person/department/firm) that receives, pays for, or experiences the output of the service (or manufacturing) delivery system. The customer includes entities within as well as outside your primary organizational identity.

- *Service* is any primary or complementary activity that does not directly produce a physical product—that is, the nongoods part of the transaction between buyer (customer) and seller (provider).

- *Quality* is the distinctive tangible and intangible properties of a product and/or service that is perceived by the customer as being better than the competition.

- *Levels* implies that a measurement system is in place to quantify, monitor, and evaluate CS&QLs.

- *Consistent* means daily conformance (low or no variability) to all standards of performance.

- *Delivery* means getting the right service in the right way to the right customer at the right time. The service delivery system provides the service.

- *Service* package is a clearly defined set of tangible and intangible attributes the customer recognizes, pays for, uses, and/or experiences. The package can be a service or group of services.

- *Specified* means by management.

- *Internal* standards of performance focus on in-house or backroom operating and marketing criteria that are hidden or decoupled from the customer. Measurement can be more objective against numerical specifications.

- *External* standards of performance focus on out-in-the-field or frontroom operating and marketing criteria that the customer expects/perceives while using or experiencing the product and/or service. Measurement is usually more dependent on human judgment.

Source: D.A. Collier, "The Customer Service and Quality Challenge." *The Service Industries Journal*, Vol. 7, No. 1 (January 1987), 79. Reproduced by permission.

through intermediaries (brokers, agents, etc.) and collected service quality feedback only once a year from these employees and to a much lesser extent from their customers. A third company declined to participate in the study due to the proprietary nature of the service quality data.

The three remaining companies did cooperate and participate in the study. However, one company relied almost completely on operation-based data to monitor service quality performance. Their data may be used in future studies but not in this chapter. For the remaining two companies, a total of twelve service packages were studied. These services ranged from retail banking to trust management services.

The credit card divisions of the final two companies provided the best set of operations- and marketing-based service quality data. Hence, the focus of this chapter is on measuring and evaluating service quality information for major bank/credit card providers.

Service Quality Data Analysis Methods and Insights

Traditional approaches to evaluate service quality data include fishbone diagrams, statistical process control, value of a loyal customer, acceptance sampling, inspection and maintenance plans, quality circles, managing by wandering around, Pareto analysis, quality audits, cost of quality, and so on. These ideas, techniques, and methods originated in goods-producing industries. Much attention has been focused on transferring these existing approaches from goods-producing to service-providing industries. In most cases, service industries have benefited from using these methods to help define, monitor, and control service quality.

Several attributes of a service-providing organization dictate a more tailored approach to defining, monitoring, and controlling service quality, however. These attributes (Collier 1985, 1989b) include the following: the service package possesses tangible (goods content) and intangible (service-content) attributes; the service often is the process; the customer often experiences the service while in the service-providing factory; the delivery of the service involves the simultaneous execution of marketing and operations tasks; customers judge the service process at least as much as the service outcome; the service itself is noninventoriable; and actual service quality is in reality perceived service quality. These characteristics of the service delivery system require that the marketing (external) and operations (internal) service quality databases be more closely integrated.

Three important attributes of ideal service quality data for this study follow. First, the service quality performance questions (and criteria) from the marketing surveys must match the operations service quality performance statistics. If many criteria are related to a latent variable then confirmatory factor analysis (Long 1987) can be used to define this relationship. Second, the service quality measures from the marketing and operations functions must be applied during the same planning horizon and time periods. Third, the number of observations must be large enough to result in statistically valid estimates of model parameters depending on the multivariate data analysis technique used.

The data used in this chapter come extremely close to meeting these three demanding requirements. For example, comparable customer survey questions and scores could be matched with operations performance statistics. Also, the operations (internal) service quality performance data was reported monthly while the customer survey data was administered quarterly. Thus, the quarterly customer survey score was used for each of the three months during the quarter. Finally, data was available for years 1985 to 1987 resulting in thirty-six observations per criterion. Also, the quarterly customer survey was administered such that "lagging" any of the variables was not required.

Three levels of data analysis are explored in this chapter. They are (1) descriptive statistics such as means, maximums and minimums, and correlations; (2) two way criteria linkages such as graphs and simple regressions; and (3) traditional multivariate data analysis such as multiple regression and path analysis.

Preliminary Data Analysis Results

The managerial objectives of the service quality data analysis techniques used in this chapter are to (1) encourage managers to define service quality for each service provided with comparable service quality data from the marketing and operations functions of an organization, (2) formalize numerically how well or poorly the marketing (external) and operations (internal) service quality data match up; and (3) add new service quality data analysis techniques and concepts to the repertoire of traditional service quality tools and methods.

A diagram of key credit card processing and customer evaluation relationships are shown in figure 10–1. First, note that the customer survey evaluated "the perception of service quality" on seven major performance areas (denoted with an m subscript). These seven major performance areas reflect the overall customer's evaluation of the credit card processing centers' service quality performance. Likewise, the operations function used many statistics to internally evaluate how well they were performing with regard to service quality performance (denoted with an o subscript).

To demonstrate the value of simple descriptive statistics and two-way linkage data analysis techniques, we shall focus first on "on-line availability." (See L_o and L_m in figure 10–1) Similar types of analyses were done for all key criteria.

Relationships between the Customer's Perception versus
Actual "On-Line Credit Card System Inquiry Availability"

One important measure of service quality for an organization that processes credit cards is "on-line availability." Customers either call the credit card processing center to inquire about the status of various accounts, or retail/

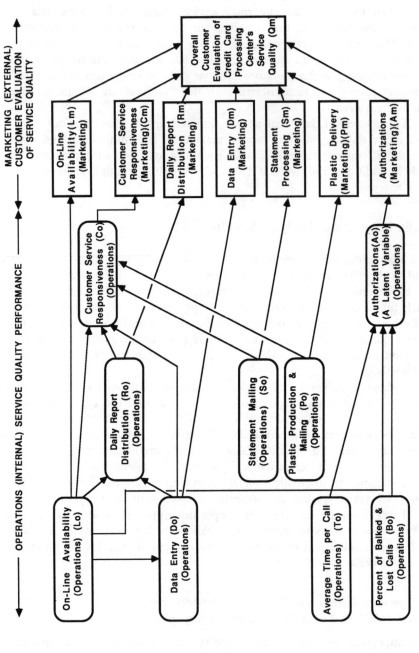

Figure 10–1. Marketing and Operations service quality relationships.

corporate customers have direct lines to the center's computer for immediate electronic inquiry. In both cases, on-line system availability is critical to providing excellent service.

The operations area measured on-line availability as the percent of total prime-time hours the system was available for customer use and inquiries. Likewise, the customer service department administered a customer survey each quarter that contained a similar question concerning on-line availability measured on a 0 to 100 point scale.

Descriptive statistics about on-line availability are summarized as follows:

On-Line Availability	Minimum (%)	Maximum (%)	Mean (%)	Standard Deviation (%)
Operations/Internal (L_o)	96.4	99.7	98.6	0.95
Marketing/External (L_m)	60	97	84.4	10.5

Correlation Coefficient Between Marketing (L_m) and Operations (L_o) Data $= 0.715$.

For example, when this service was measured as "excellent" by the operations function with a 99.7 percent rating, the customer also perceived the excellent service and responded with its highest average rating of 97 points. Moreover, the customer's reaction to lesser degrees of service was immediate and followed closely the operations-based statistics as captured by the positive 0.715 correlation factor. Even these simple statistics take much of the human intrepretation of the data out of evaluating service quality data from two such diverse sources.

Simple graphs of these data (not shown) highlight month-by-month performance, outliners, and frequency information. Other two-way criteria data analysis approaches include simple regression equations as documented by equations 1, 2, and 7 in table 10–2. The variables (D_o, L_o, L_m, etc.) shown in table 10–2 are briefly defined in figure 10–1. Please note that subscripts *o* and *m* mean *operations-* or *marketing-based* variables, respectively.

Intuitively, managers knew that on-line availability was the most important service quality performance measure. The network in figure 10–1 graphically shows on-line availability's importance and "several paths of influence." Thus, the data analysis quantitively related the customer's perception of on-line availability to actual internal (operational) measurements of on-line availability.

Relationships among Service Quality Customer
Survey Data

As multiple regression equations 5 and 6 document in table 10–2, overall customer evaluation of the processing center's performance (Q_m)

Table 10–2
Example Marketing and Operations Service Quality Regression Models

Relationships among Service Quality Operations Performance Measures

(1) D_o = -386.5 + $4.82\ L_o$ *R-Sq. = 32.2 % and L_o t-value = 4.2.

(2) C_o = -388.8 + $4.80\ L_o$ R-Sq. = 35.3 % and L_o t-value = 4.5.

(3) R_o = 61.5 + $0.32\ D_o$ R-Sq. = 11.8 % and D_o t-value = 2.4.

(4) C_o = 27.8 + $0.64\ D_o$ R-Sq. = 42.9 % and D_o t-value = 5.2.

Relationships among Service Quality Marketing Customer Survey Data

(5) Q_m = 32.8 + $0.091\ L_m$ + $0.093\ C_m$ + $0.236\ A_m$ + $0.054\ D_m$ + $0.08\ S_m$
       (t-value = 5.4)   (2.7)   (5.3)   (3.3)   (2.5)
       + $0.082\ P_m$ R-Square = 96.6 %

(6) Q_m = 54.3 + $0.057\ L_m$ + $0.176\ C_m$ + $0.165\ A_m$ R-Sq. = 95.0%.
       (t-value = 3.2)   (7.6)   (5.5)

Relationships between Marketing and Operations Service Quality Data

(7) L_m = -695.9 + $7.92\ L_o$ R-Sq. = 49.7 % and L_o t-value = 5.97.

(8) A_m = 115.5 $-$ $1.26\ T_o$ R-Sq. = 69.1 % and T_o t-value = -8.9.

(9) C_m = 703.3 + $7.38\ L_o$ + $0.837\ P_o$ $-$ $0.256\ S_o$ R-Sq. = 61.6%
       (t-value = 6.2)   (3.2)   (-2.6)

(10) Qm = -86.6 + $1.53\ L_o$ + $0.295\ C_o$ R-Square = 78.9 %
        (t-value = 4.03)   (6.1)

* R-Square statistic is adjusted R-Square.

can be reasonably explained by these models. The independent and dependent variables of equations 5 and 6 are based on marketing survey data only, but these equations provide insight into the relative importance of the seven major components of Q_m. Also, this analysis shows that customers were consistent in their overall evaluation of service quality.

Management was surprised that three key areas as described by equation 6 explained 95 percent of the variance in Q_m. This knowledge forced them to reevaluate their current policy of "equal emphasis on all areas and criteria."

Relationships between Marketing and Operations Service Quality Data

Simple linear regression models that tie operation's performance to the customer's perception and independent evaluation of service quality are shown by equations 7, 8, 9, and 10 in table 10–2. In each of these equations, the independent variables are operations performance statistics, and the dependent variable is the customer's perception of service quality.

Path Analysis

Unfortunately, simple one-to-one relationships between isolated variables are the exception. Complex causal relationships between marketing- and operations-based variables, errors in variables, and errors in equations characterized real service quality relationships. Hence, the power of covariance structure models (Joreskog and Sorborn 1986) was originally planned for the data collected in this chapter. However, as MacCallum (1986) documents, a sample size of thirty-six observations is too small for a complex LISREL model, analysis, and specification search.

Consequently, simple recursive path analyses on subsystems of figure 10–1 network were performed. For example, one recursive path model defined by variables L_o, D_o, R_o, S_o, P_o, C_o, and C_m in figure 10–1 is shown in figure 10–2. The four structural equations that characterize the relationships of figure 10–2 are documented by equations 1 to 4 as follows:

$$Y_1 = \qquad\qquad + Y_{11}X_1 \qquad\qquad\qquad\qquad + \zeta_1 \quad (1)$$

$$Y_2 = \beta_{21}Y_1 + \qquad + Y_{21}X_1 \qquad\qquad\qquad\qquad + \zeta_2 \quad (2)$$

$$Y_3 = \beta_{31}Y_1 + \beta_{32}Y_2 + Y_{31}X_1 + Y_{32}X_2 + Y_{33}X_3 + \zeta_3 \quad (3)$$

$$Y_4 = \qquad\qquad \beta_{43}Y_3 + \qquad\qquad\qquad\qquad\qquad\qquad + \zeta_4 \quad (4)$$

The LISREL parameter estimates for the path analysis model in figure 10–2 and equations 1 to 4 are shown in table 10–3. Other alternative models, parameter estimates, and statistical details are documented elsewhere (Collier 1988a). In this chapter, the ideas and techniques encompassing a service quality map are defined.

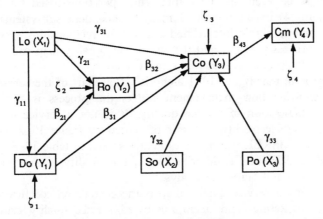

Figure 10–2. Path analysis model of equations 1 to 4 and Table 3

Source: "The Service Quality Map," David A. Collier, (under Review by Academic Journal), August, 1988, p. 16. Reproduced with permission.

Table 10–3
LISREL Parameter Estimates for Management's Model Depicted in Figure 10–4 of Customer Service Responsiveness

Model Parameter	Model 1
β_{21}	0.161
β_{31}	0.376
β_{32}	0.006
β_{43}	0.832
γ_{11}	0.585
γ_{21}	0.373
γ_{31}	0.381
γ_{32}	−0.301
γ_{33}	0.264
ζ_1	0.658
ζ_2	0.765
ζ_3	0.371
ζ_4	0.309

Source: David A. Collier, "The Service Quality Map," August, 1988, 18. Reproduced by permission.

Briefly, a service quality map exhibits the following characteristics: (1) it combines the insights of flowcharting the service delivery process with the power and parameter estimates of multivariate data analysis techniques, (2) it recognizes that "the process is often the service" for many service-providing organizations; (3) it defines (and connects) quantitatively the relationships between the marketing- and operations-based service quality information; (4) it can consist of many independent subsystems and relationships or one highly interrelated network of relationships; (5) it is company and process specific; and (6) one service quality map can be a subset of a more comprehensive service quality map.

Please note that figure 10–1 alone is a flowchart of the service delivery process, showing how management thinks the process is related to the customer's perception of service quality. It is not a service quality map. However, a service quality map is represented by figure 10–2, equations 1 to 4, and the LISREL parameter estimates shown in table 10–3. Of course, for causal models such as described here, the validity of the model should be based on sound statistical analyses.

The simplest service quality map is the correlation coefficient between a specific marketing- and operations-based service quality criterion. For example, the correlation coefficient of +0.715 between on-line availability as measured by marketing (L_m in figures 10–1 and 10–2) and operations

(L_0 in figures 10–1 and 10–2) meets all the requirements of a service quality map.

How to use the path analysis model and associated LISREL parameter estimates is the subject of articles by Collier (1988b, 1989b). For example, the following what-if questions are possible when using the ideas and techniques encompassing service quality maps.

Where in the operations process can the most improvement (benefit) be obtained with respect to perceived service quality for the least cost?

What will happen to the customer's evaluation of service quality if operation's performance on criterion X deteriorates by one-half of one percent?

Where in the service delivery process is overachievement of service quality unnecessary?

Can a manager's performance appraisal be tied into the performance of downstream departments?

Can the customer survey design be improved based on the insights gained from service quality maps?

What standards of service quality performance make the most sense?

What is the relative importance of key operational activities from the customer's viewpoint?

These example what-if questions provide some idea of the potential power of service quality maps. Research and field work on how managers can use service quality maps to gain a competitive advantage in the marketplace is continuing.

Future Research

Much has been learned from these preliminary studies. The general objectives of this ongoing research are to develop helpful managerial paradigms and guidelines about designing and managing a marketing- and operations-based service quality evaluation system and to determine what data analysis techniques are best to support this management effort. The service quality map, even in its simplest form of a correlation coefficient between marketing and operations criterion, is a step toward accomplishing these objectives.

References

Collier, D. A. (1985). *Service Management: The Automation of Services*. Englewood Cliffs, NJ: Prentice-Hall, 1–15.

———. (1987a). "The Customer Service and Quality Challenge." *The Service Industries Journal*, 7 (1)(January), 77–90. Reprinted in *Managing Service Quality— An IFS Executive Briefing*, Graham Clark, Ed., Kempston, England: IFS Ltd., 1990.

———. (1987b). This study is supported by a research fellowship from the Fishman-Davidson Center for the Study of the Service Sector at the Wharton School of the University of Pennsylvania, June 1987, to June 1988.

———. (1987). *Service Management: Operating Decisions*. Englewood Cliffs, NJ: Prentice-Hall, 43–47.

———. (1988a). "The Service Quality Map." August.

———. (1988b). "The Use of Service Quality Maps." *Quality Progress*.

———. (1989a). "Process Moments of Trust: Analysis and Strategy" *The Service Industries Journal*, 9 (2)(April).

———. (1989b). "Managing Service Quality." In D. E. Bowen, R. B. Chase, and T. G. Cummings (eds.), *Service Management Effectiveness*. San Francisco: Jossey-Bass.

Collier, David A., (1990). "Telephone Repair Service Performance," *Proceedings of the Quality in Services II (QUIS II) International Conference*, GTE Executive Development Center, Norwalk, Connecticut, July 8–11.

Collier, David A., (1990). "Measuring and Managing Service Quality," Chapter 10 (pp. 234–265) in *Service Management Effectiveness*. Eds., D. E. Bowen, R. D. Chase, and T. G. Cummings, Jossey-Bass Publishers, Inc.

Collier, D. A. (in press). "A Service Quality Process Map for Credit Card Processing." *Decision Sciences*, (forthcoming, tentative publication date is the Spring, 1991 issue).

———. (1986). "How Consumer America Views the Changing Financial Services Industry." *American Banker 1986 Survey* (1986). New York, 6.

Joreskog, Karl G., and Deg Sorborn. (1986). *LISREL IV* fourth edition, Mooseville, IN: Scientific Software.

Long, J. Scott. (1987). *Confirmatory Factor Analysis*. Beverly Hills: Sage Publications.

MacCallum, Robert. (1986). "Specification Searches in Covariance Structure Modeling." *Psychological Bulletin*, Vol. 100, No. 1, 107–20.

Part III
How to Implement
Service Quality

Implementing service quality involves matching customer desires with provider capabilities. In this section, a closer examination of the customer/provider dyad is undertaken to develop an understanding of the elements required to implement good service quality. Topics examined include organizing for service delivery, the role of customers in the delivery process, and how to select effective contact personnel. Taken together, a more complete guide to implementing quality service is presented.

To begin this section, Richard Chase and David Bowen's chapter provides a framework that examines service quality issues across different components of the delivery system. A framework is presented to aid in identifying issues that must be managed to improve service quality. The framework is a diagnostic tool for analyzing the effectiveness of the service delivery system.

The Robert Johnston and David Lyth chapter discusses the implementation of service quality as an integration of customer expectations and operational capbilities. Implications of the mismatch between customer satisfaction and the design, control, and implementation of service quality are presented. The chapter concludes with the development of a customer satisfaction model that incorporates operations variables considered necessary to improve the communication of service quality elements to operations personnel.

Alan Dale and Stuart Wooler next present a systemic model of organizational elements for constructing a sound service strategy. The discussion includes working group efforts at identifying service elements that make a difference in the strategy, how these groups are interrelated, and which are most likely to provide the greatest return. An example of a total service organization, as well as its subsidiary components, is provided.

Issues of customer empowerment within a public service are discussed in a chapter by Richard Saltmann and Casten von Otter. They contend that the empowerment of consumers is a vital requirement to improve the decision-making balance between consumers and providers within public human services. The authors maintain that the idea of civil democracy is not limited to a useful political or normative policy model but is functional in economic terms as well. Although this may be ideal, modern welfare states such as Sweden have been hesitant to allow individuals effective influence on their residence-related institutions such as health care, education, and child care. The chapter argues that the definition of welfare democracy states needs to be broadened to address issues of empowerment.

A major requirement for quality service delivery is selecting effective service personnel. Benjamin Schneider and Daniel Schechter's chapter offers a service orientation selection process as an organizational variable contributing to service effectiveness. Important selection considerations noted are the service inclination and competence of employees. The authors conclude that companies can take positive steps toward service excellence by paying attention to details in areas such as personnel selection.

This section concludes with a chapter highlightng the programmatic research of Teresa Swartz and Stephen Brown on professional service quality. Given that a major part of a professional service offering is the expertise of the contact person and recognizing that this expertise is difficult for consumers to evaluate, the authors contend that professional-client relationships are uique service experiences requiring special evaluation considerations. The chapter summarizes an on going research stream addressing both client and provider perspectives on service quality and satisfaction. Some of the difficulties in researching professional service quality are also noted.

11
Service Quality and the Service Delivery System
A Diagnostic Framework

Richard B. Chase
David E. Bowen

R ecent works on service have stressed that the delivery of service quality requires a system-wide effort. Examples of this include a new services text entitled *Managing Services Marketing, Operations, and Human Resources* (Lovelock 1988); a framework for integrating operations and human resource management in the service sector (Chase and Bowen 1988); an application of the Katz and Kahn (1978) subsystems model to assess the service organization's climate for service (Schneider and Bowen 1985); another text stressing the importance of having a functionally integrated "strategic service vision" (Heskett 1986); and the importance of having a marketing orientation dispersed throughout all functions of the organization (Grönroos and Gummesson 1985).

This chapter presents an integrated treatment of service quality issues across the different components of the delivery system by reviewing the items that constitute the authors' Service System Effectiveness questionnaire (see appendix 11–A). This is a preliminary diagnostic instrument intended to assess the performance of the service delivery system relative to the components of the framework depicted in figure 11–1: (1) *Technology*— the process technology; physical facility; and the extent of routinization, reliability, and consistency of the transformation process; (2) *Systems*— primarily production control systems; procedures for routing inputs to the transformation process, particularly the customers themselves; and (3) *People*—human resource management issues such as the selection and training of employees. Also included is the management of customer attitudes and behaviors, consistent with a view of customers as potential "partial employees" of the service organization (Bowen 1986; Mills 1986).

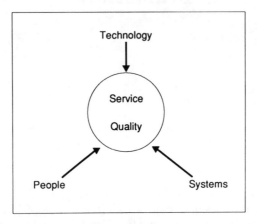

Figure 11–1. Service quality and the service delivery system.

These three service delivery system components operationalize the service firm's strategy, that is, decisions about the composition of the goods/ service bundle (Sasser, Olsen, and Wyckoff 1978), the specification of service levels, and pricing. Moreover, the attributes of these components determine the quality of service the system delivers.

The Service System Effectiveness Questionnaire: A Review of Service Quality Issues

Although several works on service quality have stressed the systems view (as mentioned), few offer an integrated systems measurement tool for enacting that view or assessing the effectiveness of its implementation. The two most visible service measures in the field are themselves limited in this regard. The subsystem dimensions in Schneider's climate for service work (Schneider, Parkington, and Buxton 1980; Schneider and Bowen 1985) do not include the production subsystem specifically, or much of an operations management flavor more generally. The most widely cited instrument for measuring service quality, SERVQUAL (Parasuraman, Zeithaml, and Berry

1986), did not assume a systems perspective in its conceptualization. The focus is primarily on customer perceptions of the intangibles associated with experiencing the service encounter. Recently, its developers have reported finding only a weak relationship between customer ratings of the individual dimensions of service quality and customer ratings of service quality overall (Parasuraman, Zeithaml, and Berry (1986). This may be attributed to the measure not accounting for the broader systems issues that affect service quality.

First, the particular perspective on service quality that guides the authors' diagnostic framework is identified. The twenty-eight items of the questionnaire are reviewed as system issues affecting service quality. All items in the questionnaire represent issues raised in the emerging scholarly literature on service quality. The items are reviewed for two purposes: to provide both service managers and academics with an integrated, system-wide diagnostic framework for identifying issues that need to be managed effectively for service quality to result; and to provide a detailed introduction to a survey instrument that can be administered to empirically assess the effectiveness of the service delivery system in managing these issues.

Service Quality

The combined work of academics and practitioners offers three alternative conceptualizations of service quality as expressed in the attribute theory, the customer satisfaction theory, and the interaction theory.

The attribute theory assumes that service quality primarily reflects the attributes of the service delivery system. It essentially applies the product quality framework to services (e.g., Deming 1986). An attribute theory perspective on service quality assumes that management has substantial control over the inputs defining these attributes and that these attributes are associated with service quality.

A customer satisfaction theory approach treats service quality as a perceptual phenomenon identified through the eyes of the customer. The meaning, definition, and evaluation of quality exist in the consumer's mind. Ultimate quality is the difference between service quality expectations and the perceptions of reality (e.g., Parasuraman, Zeithaml, and Berry 1986). This theory shifts focus from the production and output of the service to the customer. Whereas the attribute theory places primary importance on the technical aspects of production, the customer satisfaction theory places primary importance on customer perceptions.

The interaction theory approach to service quality has been presented by Klaus (1985), who defines service quality as a "shared experience of gain" by all participants in the service encounter. The experiences of the customer are interrelated with the experiences of the contact employee.

Service quality emerges through the mutual need satisfaction of both employees and customers.

The diagnostic framework presented here is based on an attribute theory approach to service quality. Specifically, it details those attributes of service delivery that service literature indicates are important determinants of service quality.

Description of Questionnaire Items

Planning of the Service Encounter

The service encounter is a period of time during which the customer interacts directly with the service system and its employees. Because service encounters are a main source of information for consumers in evaluating service quality and service differentiation, controlling and enhancing the service encounter is a critical task for service managers (Shostack 1985). Useful guidelines for planning the service encounter can be found in Shostack's "designing service blueprints," which maps the system requirements for supporting quality service encounters. Relatedly, Haywood-Farmer (1985) advocated that service managers design process flowcharts indicating the proper sequencing of service activities pre- and postencounter. Several management and marketing perspectives on the service encounter are offered by Czepiel, Solomon, and Surprenant (1985). Planning the service encounter requires attention to the "psychological subleties of the customer-service interface" (Chase 1985). The service encounter represents the essence of the service firm's strategy because it links the point of delivery options and corporate policy (Northcraft and Chase 1985).

Back-Office/Front-Office Coordination

The service delivery system is composed of both front-office and back-office operations (Chase and Tansik 1983). Front-office operations are conducted in the presence of the customer and must cope with the input uncertainty of customer contact and participation; back-office operations can realize the full potential of system rationality and efficiency possible when operations are sealed off from customer disturbances. The front office dominates some services (personal services) and the back office dominates others (distribution centers), but many services are mixtures of front-office customer contact and back-office work (branch offices).

Effective service delivery requires the coordination of front- and back-office operations. This is difficult, given that the two operations unfold in divergent environments, leading to their requiring different goals and operating objectives. Coordination of these mixed service systems requires multiple and heterogeneous boundary spanning tasks *within* the organization (Chase and Tansik 1983). Back-office support of front-office activities crosses numerous intraorganizational boundaries and creates the need for informational or material handling tasks. These tasks need to be coordinated via varying degrees of routinization and ad hoc agendas, as well as the technical and interpersonal skills of boundary-spanning personnel.

Another mechanism for the coordination of front- and back-office operations—and across back-office operations themselves—is suggested by the "customer-supplier philosophy" recently adopted by quality-conscious manufacturers. This refers to the notion that everyone in the organization is both a customer and supplier to a person or function up- or downstream. Perhaps the most noteworthy exponent of the approach is Xerox, which features this as the centerpiece of its "Leadership Through Quality" program. Obviously, the customer-supplier relationship is a service concept; however, it seems that manufacturers have made more use of it throughout the organization than have service firms. Apparently, the reason is that manufacturing firms think in terms of hand-offs—R & D handing off a new product to manufacturing engineering, manufacturing engineering to production, and so on. Services, on the other hand, because they work with mainly intangible products, seem less inclined to view internal linkages in such a structured way although Townsend (1986) offers the Paul Revere Insurance Company as a service example embodying the customer-supplier relationship.

Reliability of Service

This refers to whether the output of the service technology provides what it is supposed to provide—does it meet (or exceed) customer expectations? Some behavioral anchors of reliability include accuracy in billing; properly maintained records; and timely service, for example, airline flights leaving on schedule (Parasuraman, Zeithaml, and Berry (1985).

Consistency of Service

This refers to the absence of variation in the output of the service technology. Consistency implies that the customer gets the same treatment, the same level of service, time and again. McDonald's is probably the best example; no matter where in the world one eats a McDonald's burger, it will always be the same. Haywood-Farmer (1985) underscores the importance of consistency by noting that although people may judge a theme park's entertainment to be of lower quality than a play at a "high-class" theater, theme parks may well produce higher quality service because they are reproducible and finely tuned to meet customer demands for cleanliness, variety, wholesomeness, fun, fantasy, excitement, and so on, without surprises. He maintains that the service delivery system needs to be formalized to ensure that each customer interaction has little or no variation. Extensive procedure manuals, checklists, and mystery shoppers can all be used to ensure uniformity in delivery—for example, the forms filled out properly, the room made up correctly, a cheery "good morning" with a smile, and so on.

Finally, relative to maintaining both consistency and reliability, two recent developments in manufacturing may be useful in services, "statistical process control (SPC)" and "Taguchi methods."

SPC refers to a host of techniques designed to support the philosophy that high quality comes from achieving a perfectly functioning process rather than from after-the-fact inspection. The basic tools of the approach include Pareto analysis to distinguish between major and minor problems within the process; fishbone diagrams to identify causes of below-standard quality; and control charts to monitor process output and to signal when adjustments to the process should be made. Many SPC tools, if not the entire approach, are becoming widely used in services for problem-solving with quality circles. Townsend (1986), for example, describes how such tools are combined with value analysis in Paul Revere Insurance Company's "Quality Has Value" program. Oakland (1986) describes how they are applied "in several large international banks" using what he terms a "Self-Audit Program." Wyckoff (1985) describes their application to the Rusty Pelican restaurant chain and Midway Airlines.

Taguchi methods are a set of statistical methodologies developed by Genichi Taguchi currently sweeping the manufacturing world. A form of what is termed "off-line" quality control methods, it consists of quality and cost control activities conducted at the product and process design stages to improve manufacturability and reliability (Kackar 1985). The underlying philosophy of Taguchi methods is that the product should be designed to cope with process variability rather than the other way around, which is the traditional philosophy. A key feature of the approach is defining quality costs of defects as a continuous function rather than by whether a product is inside or outside statistical control limits. The traditional zero defects interpretation of being within control limits ignores the fact that any deviation from a quality target may have a cost impact on the producer. For example, in manufacturing a car door and its frame, both parts may be produced within their individual specification limits, yet the door may not fit perfectly when closed. The loss to the car manufacturer by not producing a perfect fit may be seen in rework before the car leaves the plant or customer dissatisfaction with a door that rattles. Relative to services, most managers are concerned with how much a service varies from its intended process, not solely with whether the service is good or poor. The Taguchi approach (which uses design of experiments and statistical clustering methods) could be of great value in formally specifying the shape of cost curves that arise from deviations from the desired service ideal.

Effective Use of Technology

This is an important factor in service consistency. The labor intensity typical of many service delivery systems makes it difficult to limit the variability in output and to exercise quality control. To resolve this, Levitt (1972, 1976) advocates a production line approach to service and the industrialization of services, in which service managers apply a manufacturing approach by substituting technology and systems for people. The prime example of this design philosophy is McDonald's hamburgers. In the context of the present model, this item raises the issue of whether the technology or the people component is dominant within the service delivery system. Overall, service technologies at one extreme consist of predominantly manual service provision (e.g., barbering); at the other extreme is predominantly machine-service provision (e.g., vending machines). In between are partial substitutions of technology for labor.

Right Degree of Standardization

This refers to how much flexibility the system is intended to display in serving the customer. À la Levitt, a central component in McDonald's strategy has been the limited menu, the relative standardization of both product line and operating tasks. As a result, productivity gains (hence cost advantages), as well as better quality control, have been achievable. It is not only in fast-food operations that this trend toward relative standardization is seen. The trend is even apparent in the more traditional professional services, as shown by specialized legal clinics, dentist offices in department stores, and the use of paraprofessionals with extremely standardized task assignments.

The effectiveness of a delivery system that offers only standardized output will depend on the service ideal as defined by customers with whom it does—or can—do business. "Service ideal" refers to the general expectations customers use to define the quality of service they receive (Schneider and Bowen 1985; Shamir, 1980). If customers prefer customization, to "have it their way" à la Burger King, they will define standardization as low service quality, possibly even if standardization offers price advantages. Indeed, a key issue here is whether customers will pay higher prices for customization over standardization. Blois (1983) summarizes some related issues concerning standardization/customization within service firms, including the potential of the operating system of offer cost-effective variations and the need for service firms to offer "signals" to customers that indicate the system's tolerance for variations.

Facility—Location, Adequacy, and Atmosphere

Physical facilities are the one tangible dimension, along with nine more intangible dimensions (e.g. courtesy, credibility) that define service quality from the customer's viewpoint (Parasuraman Zeithaml, and Berry 1985). The physical properties and atmosphere of the service facility is one of three operating characteristics in a service environment, the other two being the service concept (i.e., facilitating good, explicit intangibles, and implicit intangibles) and consumer-perceived service levels (Sasser, Olsen, and Wyckoff 1978).

The attributes of facilities relevant to service quality are too numerous to detail, but two are highlighted here: the operating implications of multi-location service delivery systems and the atmosphere encountered by the customer within each facility. The first, the need for services to be produced, delivered, and consumed in proximity to the customer can create a need for a service organization to use multiple locations/service delivery systems. The result is a decentralization of the service production process to the local level and a reduction in the opportunity for developing economies of scale (Thomas 1978). As a result, location decisions are often critical, and multiple locations can serve as a barrier to entry. One example is the car rental business, in which a large number of airport locations is extremely important.

The climate for service within each location is strongly related to both customers' and employees' perceptions of service quality (Schneider, Parkington, and Buxton 1980; Schneider and Bowen 1985). Climate for service refers to the summary perceptions individuals have of the practices and procedures of the service delivery system. For example, does the climate convey an overall impression of warmth and responsiveness or one of aloofness and an emphasis on the needs of the system rather than the customers? The climate for service research in branch banks indicates that everything from employee dress and behavior to the appearance of deposit slips and office machinery influences customer perceptions of the climate for service and service quality. The implication is that service managers need to manage all evidence visible to the customer to enhance service quality.

Logical, Consistent Business Hours

As Chase (1985) notes, it is a rare customer who boycotts a service organization because it is open too many hours, but plenty pass up a service firm that is not open when needed. Many banks and specialty-service businesses, in particular, frequently change their hours with little notice given to the customer. Parenthetically, Von's Supermarkets and Kinko's Copiers are now widely publicizing twenty-four-hour availability as a main feature of their service package. It is not necessary that all service firms maintain extended hours, only that all service firms keep reasonable and predictable hours.

Handling of Nonroutine Demands

Nonroutine customer demands are to be expected in any service delivery system, and the system must have at least minimal capability for dealing with them. Even systems characterized by routine tasks (e.g., ticket seller, cafeteria worker) can be subject to nonroutine demands (Chase and Tansik 1983). Resolving nonroutine demands without excessive disruption of the otherwise efficient system is the key. The basic matching logic is that each service (e.g., bank deposits or closing a home mortgage) is matched to the minimally qualified service resource (e.g., automated teller machines [ATM], bank teller, branch manager), and customers are then channeled to the efficiency-maximizing delivery mode (Northcraft and Chase 1985). However, this system must also have clear procedures for how a less-qualified service resource, for example, a bank teller, rechannels a customer with a nonroutine demand to a more qualified service resource, for example, a branch manager.

Handling of Emergency Situations

Similarly, the system must be able to handle emergency situations. A means for doing so, in addition to rechanneling, is to explicitly empower frontline customer contact personnel to resolve the situation—and to approach supervisory personnel only afterward. Some firms (e.g., SAS) are implementing this approach.

Provisions for Customer Privacy During the Service Encounter

Architects who advocate open offices within service firms apparently have never had to request a loan, argue over a bill, or otherwise divulge their innermost financial secrets in public (Chase 1985). The disruptive consequences of such open offices are illustrated in a situation described in Gitlow and Gitlow (1982), *The Deming Guide to Quality and Competitive Position*. One of the authors worked in a social service agency that provided family counseling services. A client satisfaction questionnaire revealed that families felt they could not talk about their "real" problems. No suitable explanation could be found until a social work intern confessed he did not share problems with his supervisor either. The office walls were about six feet high, so everyone could hear what was said.

Provisions for the Privacy of Records

A related issue is the need to ensure the privacy of customer records. Parasuraman, Zeithaml, and Berry (1985) identify "security" as a dimension of service quality that involves the customer feeling free from danger, risk, or doubt. An element of this is a sense of financial security. For example, does the company know where a customer's stock certificate is?

Privacy of records is particularly salient when one thinks of records as paper surrogates for customers themselves. Consequently, care needs to be taken with these records, just as if the customer were actually present. Electronic Fund Transfers have not been the large success expected, not due to technological limitation, but due to the lack of trust customers have in the correctness of the system and the privacy they feel they will be jeopardizing.

Rational Approach for Managing the Queuing Process

The careful scheduling of client arrival and the managing of client queuing can reduce the input and task uncertainties confronting the service system (Mills and Moberg 1982). Managing the queuing process is essential since customers begin forming impressions of the service delivery system and service quality during the earliest stages of the service encounter, that is, when they first get in line or have to wait (Maister 1985). If these customers become alienated during this initial wait, the service system may never be able to catch up in its efforts to satisfy them.

Maister (1982) offers useful guidelines for managing the queuing process based on the psychology of waiting lines. For example, unoccupied time feels longer than occupied time; unexplained waits are longer than explained waits; and solo waits feel longer than group waits. Relative to keeping the waiting customer occupied, Chase (1985) suggests firms use the waiting time as a period during which to do some tactful add-on and cross-selling.

Adhering to Customer Schedules

This refers to honoring the explicit or implicit service contract to start on time and to deliver the service within the time expected or agreed on. Lens Crafters and Quick Lube are examples of organizations whose businesses are in large measure made up of meeting customer time requirements. Hart (1988) has described how such schedule adherence (and other service standards) is backed up by service guarantees. Domino's Pizza's "30 minute delivery or $3 off" is a case in point.

Shifting Capacity When Needed

The fact that services tend to be produced and consumed simultaneously makes it difficult to balance the supply and demand sides of the service operation (Sasser 1976). Simultaneity dictates that when the demand for service is present, the service must be produced. This makes staffing extremely difficult because staffing to demand (e.g., peak seasons, peak business hours) is less predictable than staffing to the pace of the assembly line (Chase 1978).

Some alternatives for shifting capacity include (1) cross-training so that when the system is delivering one service at peak capacity, employees from under-utilized areas are shifted to the busy area. When the demand shifts, the employees shift again; (2) increasing customer participation in service production and delivery; (3) using part-time employees; and (4) sharing capacity with other firms.

Materials Available When and Where Needed

Too often services are perceived as being labor intensive, assuming that as long as the employee is present, the service can be rendered. However, the bank teller also needs deposit and withdrawal slips and the health-care provider needs medicines and other tools. Nearly everyone has experienced the frustration of a reservationist saying to call back because the computer is down. In this vein, the Schneider and Bowen (1985) study of bank branches found that employees' perceptions of the branch's support systems (e.g., the adequacy of machine maintenance; the availability of neat stacks of deposit slips) were positively correlated with customer perceptions of service quality.

A useful summary perspective on the systems component is suggested by the continual improvement philosophy, a central feature of quality programs in the manufacturing sector. Virtually every manufacturer who has adopted the total quality control philosophy advocated a long-term continual improvement strategy to go with it. The basic precept is that quality goals are really moving targets and that pursuit of perfection is the ideal. Typically accompanying this philosophy is a step-by-step improvement procedure undertaken by work teams. Most major Japanese manufacturers use this approach, often as an integral part of a just-in-time production system; U.S. firms such as Hewlett-Packard and IBM employ it in a similar way. Consultants are now heavily marketing training programs in continual improvement to services, particularly banking and utilities.

Understandable Processes and Procedures

The service customer is often physically on-site and is playing a role in co-producing the service. The degree to which customers are clear about executing their role within the service delivery system will likely influence their perception of the quality of service they receive. (Bowen 1986). As Chase states, "Customers usually do some of their own routing through the system, so unless the service is the amusement park fun house, all stages of the process in which customers are directly involved should be obvious to them" (1985: p. 69).

Customer Orientation and Training

Researchers in environmental psychology (e.g., Wener 1985) argue that orientation is a compelling behavioral need of individuals on entering a setting. Any customer who has stood in the wrong line at the post office, a department of motor vehicles, checkout lines at a retail store, and so on can appreciate how disorientation, combined with time constraints, is annoying and stressful. Disorientation can also result in employees spending more time answering directional questions for customers than actually providing the service (Bowen 1986).

On-site customers require two kinds of orientation. Place orientation answers the questions, Where am I? or How do I get from here to there? Function orientation deals with the question, How does this organization work? Customers answer these questions through reliance on their past consumer experiences, the inherent legibility of the system, and orientation aids such as signage provided by the service firm. A particulary clever application of this principle is the financial institution that has given its ATM a voice to remind passing customers of its presence and convenience (Northcraft and Chase 1985).

Additionally, customers may need training to effectively perform their roles within the service delivery system. For example, where self-service alternatives are introduced, service employees may need to demonstrate the equipment and answer questions. Overall, customers require sufficient role clarity, motivation, and ability to perform well in their roles as partial employees—training can ensure they have the necessary ability (Bowen 1986).

Point of Service Marketing

Every interaction with the customer should be viewed as a marketing interaction, even if no immediate sale is expected. The authors are currently developing a set of heuristics to identify what conditions in the encounter give rise to sales opportunities. Two candidate examples include areas the customer needs to be guided through the service due to its complexity (e.g., applying for a loan allows the insurance to be sold); and instances of "boy meets girl," because customers are likely to buy more from an attractive server of the opposite sex.

Gathering Customer Feedback

Clearly, from a marketing point of view, meeting customer needs requires a thorough knowledge of the customer. Some mechanisms for gathering customer feedback have been described by Haywood-Farmer (1985). He notes that the intuition of key service executives can be a valid source of information about customer needs. However, at least one study found that bank branch managers were unable to accurately identify customer preferences (Langeard et al. 1981). An analysis of customer complaints may be useful. However, the validity of customer complaints may be limited by sampling error; the sample may even be inadvertently drawn from outside the target market segment.

A better approach is to collect information from customers in a structured, systematic way, either through routinely asking them to complete questionnaires or by conducting more detailed interviews with small groups of customers. Haywood-Farmer cautions that when data is collected, it is important to capture the complete service experience rather than focusing on only a few parts.

Customer feedback can also be gathered from frontline customer-contact personnel (Schneider and Bowen 1984). These employees, for example, bank tellers, are both physically and often psychologically close to the customer. This conclusion is supported by research that indicated bank tellers can accurately report customer perceptions of the climate for service and customers' overall evaluations of service quality (Schneider and Bowen 1985)—in stark contrast to the previously cited study in which bank branch *managers* were unable to correctly identify customer attitudes. These findings indicate the desirability of involving frontline service employees in management decisions about the design and delivery of new services. It seems desirable to implement service quality circles as a mechanism for gathering customer feedback (Bowen and Schneider 1988).

Acting on Customer Feedback

Just as employee suggestion programs need a system to ensure that appropriate action is taken, a system is required to act on customer feedback. The authors recently completed a project on service quality with a major Southern California utility in which the client conceded that although reams of data were routinely collected from the customer, this data seldom guided changes in the services mix or the service delivery system.

If the design of the service system attributes *does* reflect customer feedback, then the design will effectively incorporate both the attribute and customer satisfaction theoretical approaches to service quality. In other words, both technical system attributes and customer perceptions frame the approach to service quality.

Employee Selection

Service firms often select customer-contact personnel on a seemingly random basis or merely on the basis of their perceived ability to perform the technical requirements of the job. Interpersonal skills often are not included as selection criteria in a rigorous way, however.

One explanation for the failure to consider interpersonal skills is that few selection tests in the realm of interpersonal competence have been validated. Most selection tests that have been validated assess cognitive and motor skills (Bowen 1986). There are some encouraging signs of progress in the selection area in general, however, as Albrecht and Zemke (1985) report: At Disney, during the recruiting and selection cycle, the importance of service and the expectations are made clear. Candidates listen to a one-hour presentation on what Disney stands for, what the values are, and what working at Disney is like. Disney wants people to self-select themselves out before ever seeing a guest if they have any doubt they will like the work. At Air Atlanta, three-hour group interviews and problem-solving role-plays are held with prospective in-flight people. The airline tries to look at recruits from the customer's perspective. They also make sure interviewees enjoy the selection and interview process since people not hired are potential customers who should leave with positive impressions of Air Atlanta.

Employee Skill Training

Similarly, service businesses tend to focus on technical skills, for example, how to run the cash register, fill out quest reports, and so on, but often fail to train employees in customer service techniques (Bowen 1986). Albrecht and Zemke (1985) do report some progress in the training of customer-contact personnel, particularly the training of hospital staff in guest relations skills. Overall, though, many selection and training practices are still geared to the needs of manufacturing firms, where it is less important for firstline employees to possess interpersonal skills to perform production tasks well (Bowen 1986).

Employee Attitudes

Employee attitudes are an important element of the service climate customers encounter that, in turn, influences customer perceptions of service quality. In other words, employees' experience with their service surroundings affects the customer's service experience (Bowen and Schneider 1988). For instance, findings show that when customers report hearing employees complain about their jobs and surroundings, customers report unfavorable views of service quality. Overall, this indicates that positive employee attitudes may result in positive customer attitudes. It also suggests that the weak relationship between job satisfaction and job performance typical of manufacturing settings may be stronger in service settings.

On the other hand, manufacturers that emphasize quality at the source may offer a guide for how to direct service employee attitudes toward service quality. Quality at the source refers to the fact that each individual within the organization is a quality manager directly responsible for the quality of his or her output. The quality control department's role is correspondingly changed from quality gatekeeper to facilitator, helping the individual worker or work team achieve high quality. The direct translation of this idea is most readily seen in back-office work in which the job entails processing tangible items—forms, letters, and so on—when nothing leaves your desk until its perfect. In customer-contact jobs, this is operationalized (ideally) as "I'm the representative of my organization," and "service quality is my job." Nordstrom Department Stores exemplify this philosophy with their clerks' and managers' well-publicized efforts at keeping the customer happy (Peters 1987).

Supervisor-Employee Relations

When employees report positively on how well they are trained, supervised, career-counseled, and so on, customers favorably view the quality of service received, research indicates (Schneider and Bowen 1985). Thus, service managers should treat frontline employees as partial customers, individuals deserving the same courteous treatment management wants the firm's customers to receive (Bowen 1986). Similarly, Berry (1981) suggests that frontline employees be viewed as internal customers whose needs must be met by management before they, the employees, can be expected to meet the needs of customers. Disney embodies this philosophy by dealing with their employees as cast members, underscoring their critical role in satisfying Disney customers, referred to as guests (Albrecht and Zemke 1985).

Correct Worker-Task Assignment

High- and low-contact jobs call for different sets of tasks. In the high customer-contact front office, three elements interact: the employee, the customer, and the technology. In the low customer-contact back office only two elements interact: the employee and the technology. Given these differences, high-contact workers need interpersonal skills and knowledge of the policies under which the firm operates; low-contact workers generally deal with customer surrogates, for example, invoices, and must have production skills, such as typing (Chase and Tansik 1983).

The ability to effectively match skills to tasks in high customer-contact position is constrained by the previously mentioned scarcity of mechanisms for identifying interpersonal skills. However, Tansik (1985), building on the foundation of the customer-contact model, has developed a technique for differentiating "people people" from "paper people" by observing their ability to perceive videotaped nonverbal cues. Additionally, Hogan, Hogan, and Busch (1984) have developed a personality-based measure of service orientation that might be useful in screening high customer-contact personnel.

Correct Amount of Self-Service

An important strategic issue for service managers is determining the optimal role for customers to play in operations. Bateson (1983) has addressed this issue in his study of the characteristics of self-service customers.

A framework for determining both worker-task assignments and the correct amount of self-service is found in the service delivery matrix described by Chase and Bowen (1988). This matrix identifies six alternative service delivery options and the employee skill requirements necessary to execute them. The matrix in figure 11–2 shows the six delivery options according to degree of production efficiency (horizontal axis) and sales opportunity (vertical axis). The logic of the matrix is that as a system entails more and more customer involvement and customization, it becomes less efficient but presents an increased opportunity for sales. Along the bottom of the matrix are listed the employee requirements logically associated with each option. To elaborate, the relationships between mail contact and clerical skills, and phone contact and verbal skills, are self-evident. On-site technology (such as automatic teller machines), requires helping skills on those occasions in which the customer is unfamiliar with how the equipment works. Face-to-face tight specs frequently call for trade skills (e.g., shoemaker, draftsman, maître d', dental hygienist) to "finalize" the design of the service. Face-to-face total customization tends to call for professional diagnostic skills to ascertain client needs. The "correct" amount of self-service must be determined empirically in each situation. This entails balancing the increase in production efficiency from the customer doing the work with the possible decrease in sales that would result from decoupling the customer from the server.

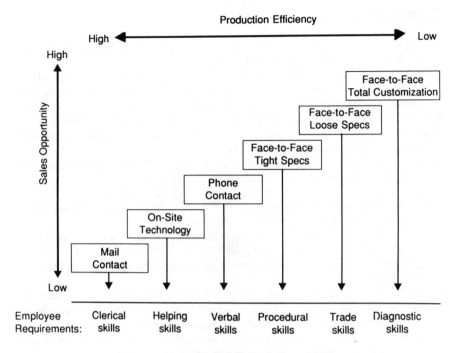

Figure 11–2. Service design matrix.

Conclusion

In this chapter a literature-driven diagnostic instrument that analyzes the effectiveness of a service delivery system has been presented. Embodied in the questionnaire are items that probe marketing, operations, and strategy effectiveness measures from the firm's perspective, as well as customer-oriented quality factors. Implicit in the questionnaire, relative to quality, is that if a firm is excelling on all operations dimensions, its service quality will be high. This, of course, is a tenuous assumption for several obvious reasons: the questionnaire may be incomplete; the customer may not perceive the beauties of the system (see the customer satisfaction theory approach); or the contact worker or technology simply did not execute their functions properly. On the other hand are the inherent problems in measuring intangible processes—developing a standard of performance and accurately perceiving the extent to which it is being met. Clearly, for all of these reasons, developing a reliable instrument is a journey rather than a destination. However, this chapter provides a useful point of departure.

References

Albrecht, K., and R. Zemke. (1985). *Service America: Doing Business in the New Economy*. Homewood, IL: Dow-Jones Irwin.

Bateson, J. E. G. (1983). "The Self-Service Consumer—Empirical Findings." In L. L. Berry, G. L. Shostack, and G. Upah (eds.), *Emerging Perspectives on Services Marketing*. Chicago: American Marketing Association.

Berry, L. (1981). "The Employee as Customer." *Journal of Retail Banking*, 3.

Blois, K. J. (1983). "The Structure of Service Firms and Their Marketing Policies." *Strategic Management Journal*, 4, 251–61.

Bowen, D. E. (1986). "Managing Customers as Human Resources in Service Organizations." *Human Resource Management*, 25, 371–84.

Bowen, D. E. and Benjamin Schneider. (1988). "Services Marketing and Management: Implications for Organizational Behavior." in *Research in Organizational Behavior*, Vol. 10, Greenwich, CT: JAI Press.

Chase, R. B. (1978). "Where Does the Customer Fit in a Service Operation?" *Harvard Business Review*, 56, 137–42.

———. (1985). "The 10 Commandments of Service Management." *Management Science Interfaces*, 15, 68–72.

Chase, R. B., and D. E. Bowen. (1988). "Linking Operations and Human Resource Management in the Service Sector." In C. Snow (ed.), *Strategy, Organization Design, and Human Resource Management*. Greenwich, CT: JAI Press.

Chase, R. B., and D. A. Tansik. (1983). "The Customer Contact Model for Organization Design." *Management Science*, 49, 1037–50.

Czepiel, J. A., M. R. Solomon, and C. Suprenant. (eds.). (1985). *The Service Encounter*. Lexington, MA: Lexington Books.

Deming, W. E. (1986). *Out of the Crisis*. Cambridge, MA: Massachusetts Institute of Technology.

Gitlow, H. S., and S. J. Gitlow. (1987). *The Deming Guide to Quality and Competitive Position*. Englewood Cliffs, NJ: Prentice-Hall.

Grönroos, C., and E. Gummesson. (eds.). (1985). *Service Marketing: Nordic Perspectives*. Stockholm: University of Stockholm, Sweden.

Hart, Chris. "The Power of Unconditional Service Guarantees." *Harvard Business Review*, Vol. 66, 54–62.

Haywood-Farmer, J. (1985). "Controlling Service Quality." *Business Quarterly*, Winter, 62–67.

Heskett, J. A. (1986). *Managing in the Service Economy*. Boston: Harvard Business School Press.

Hogan, J., R. Hogan, and C. M. Busch. (1984). "How to Measure Service Orientation." *Journal of Applied Psychology*, 69, 167–73.

Kackar, R. N. (1985). "Off-line Quality Control, Parameter Design, and the Taguchi Method." *Journal of Quality Technology*, 7, 176–88.

Katz D., and R. L. Kahn. (1978). *The Social Psychology of Organizations, rev.* New York: John Wiley.

Klaus, P. (1985). "Quality Epiphenomenon: The Conceptual Understanding of Quality in Face-to-Face Service Encounters." In J. Czepiel, M. R. Solomon, and C. F. Surprenant (eds.), *The Service Encounter*. Lexington, MA: Lexington Books.

Langeard, E. J. E. G. Bateson, C. H. Lovelock, and P. Eiglier. (1981). *Services Marketing: New Insights from Consumers and Managers*, 81–104. Cambridge, MA: Marketing Science Institute.

Levitt, T. (1972). "Production Line Approach to Services." *Harvard Business Review*, 50, 802–10.

———. (1976). "The Industrialization of Service." *Harvard Business Review*, 54, 63–74.

Lovelock, D. H. (1988). *Managing Services Marketing, Operations, and Human Resources*. Englewood Cliffs, NJ: Prentice-Hall.

Maister, D. H. (1985). "The Psychology of Waiting Lines." In J. A. Czepiel, M. R. Solomon, and C. F. Suprenant (eds.), *The Service Encounter*. Lexington, MA: Lexington Books.

Mills, P. K. (1986). *Managing Service Industries: Organizational Practices in a Post-industrial Economy*. Cambridge, MA: Ballinger

Mills, P. K., and D. J. Moberg. (1982). "Perspectives on the Technology of Service Operations." *Academy of Management Review*, 5, 255–65.

Northcraft, G. B., and R. B. Chase. (1985). "Managing Service Demand at the Point of Delivery." *Academy of Management Review*, 10, 66–75.

Oakland, J. S. (1986). "Systematic Quality Management in Banking." *Service Industry Journal*, Vol. 6, No. 2, 193–204.

Parasuraman, A., V. A. Zeithaml, and L. L. Berry. (1985). "A Conceptual Model of Service Quality and Its Implications for Future Research." *Journal of Marketing*, 49, 41–50.

———. (1986). *SERVQUAL: A Multiple-Item Scale for Measuring Consumer Perceptions of Service Quality*. Cambridge, MA: Marketing Science Institute.

Peters, T. (1987). *Quality!* Palo Alto, CA: TPG Communications.

Sasser, E. (1976). "Match Supply and Demand in Service Industries." *Harvard Business Review*, 56, 133–48.

Sasser, E., R. P. Olsen, and D. D. Wyckoff. (1978). *Management of Service Operations*. Boston: Allyn and Bacon.

Schneider, B., and D. E. Bowen. (1984). "New Services Design, Development, and Implementation and the Employee. In W. R. George and C. E. Marshall (eds.), *Developing New Services*, 82–101. Chicago: American Marketing Association.

———. (1985). "Employee and Customer Perceptions of Service in Banks: Replication and Extension." *Journal of Applied Psychology*, 70, 423–33.

Schneider, B., J. J. Parkington, and V. M. Buxton. (1980). "Employee and Customer Perceptions of Service in Banks." *Administrative Science Quarterly*, 25, 252–67.

Shamir, B. (1980). "Between Service and Servility: Role Conflict in Subordinate Service Roles." *Human Relations*, 33, 741–56.

Shostack, L. G. (1985). "Planning the Service Encounter." In J. A. Czepiel, M. R. Solomon, and C. F. Suprenant (eds.), *The Service Encounter*. Lexington, MA: Lexington Books.

Tansik, D. A. (1985). "Noverbal Communication and High-Contact Employees." In J. A. Czepiel, M. R. Solomon, and C. Suprenant (eds.), *The Service Encounter.* Lexington, MA: Lexington Books.

Thomas, D. R. E. (1978). "Strategy Is Different in Service Businesses." *Harvard Business Review*, 56, 161.

Townsend, P. L. (1986). *Commit to Quality.* Toronto: John Wiley & Sons.

Wener, R. E. (1985). "The Environmental Psychology of Service Encounters." In J. A. Czepiel, M. R. Solomon, and C. F. Suprenant (eds.), *The Service Encounter.* Lexington, MA: Lexington Books.

Wyckoff, D. D. (1985). "New Tool for Achieving Service Quality." In C. H. Lovelock (ed.), *Managing Services Marketing, Operations, and Human Resources.* Englewood Cliffs, NJ: Prentice-Hall.

Appendix 11–A
Service System Effectiveness Questionnaire

Directions: Assess the current functioning level of your organization by circling the number that most closely categorizes how you are doing in each particular characteristic.

	Good Job		Average Job		Poor Job
1. Planning the service encounter	5	4	3	2	1
2. Back-office/front-office coordination	5	4	3	2	1
3. Reliability of service	5	4	3	2	1
4. Consistency of service	5	4	3	2	1
5. Effective use of technology	5	4	3	2	1
6. Right degree of standardization	5	4	3	2	1
7. Facilities—location	5	4	3	2	1
8. Facilities—adequacy and atmosphere	5	4	3	2	1
9. Logical, consistent business hours	5	4	3	2	1
10. Handling of nonroutine customer demands	5	4	3	2	1
11. Handling of emergency situations	5	4	3	2	1
12. Provisions for customer privacy during the service encounter	5	4	3	2	1
13. Provisions for the privacy of records	5	4	3	2	1
14. Rational approach for managing the queuing process	5	4	3	2	1
15. Adhering to customer schedules	5	4	3	2	1
16. Shifting capacity when needed	5	4	3	2	1
17. Materials available when and where needed	5	4	3	2	1
18. Understandable (to customer) service process and procedures	5	4	3	2	1
19. Customer orientation and training	5	4	3	2	1
20. Point-of-service marketing	5	4	3	2	1
21. Gathering customer feedback	5	4	3	2	1
22. Acting on customer feedback	5	4	3	2	1

	Good Job		Average Job		Poor Job
23. Employee selection	5	4	3	2	1
24. Employee skill training	5	4	3	2	1
25. Employee attitudes	5	4	3	2	1
26. Supervisor-employee relations	5	4	3	2	1
27. Correct worker-task assignment	5	4	3	2	1
28. Correct amount of self-service	5	4	3	2	1

This assessment of organizational function is followed by two quality specific questions:

1. What is your estimate of how your customers rate your overall service?   5   4   3   2   1
2. How does management rate the overall service?   5   4   3   2   1

12
Implementing the Integration of Customer Expectations and Operational Capability

Robert Johnston
David Lyth

Introduction

Two main objectives of operations management are the provision of good customer service and the efficient utilization of resources in the operation's process (Wild 1977). Good customer service is the combined outcome of the quality of the products, services, and the environment in which the goods and services are provided—the quality of the service package (Voss et al. 1985). In manufacturing, quality assurance is predominantly concerned with product design and product quality conformance. This is also true in service industries since most service industries also provide goods for use within or outside the system as part of the service package. However, quality assurance in service industries is also concerned with service quality, service design, and service quality conformance. Service quality is the level of service provided by the operation (Sasser, Olsen, and Wyckoff, 1982) and is concerned with the manner in which the goods are provided and the way in which the customer is treated. It is concerned with the *how* rather than the *what*.

This chapter deals with the design, control, and implementation of service quality. From a customer perspective, the measure of service quality is usually referred to as customer satisfaction. The chapter starts by defining customer satisfaction, then considers factors that create that customer satisfaction. Implications of mismatches in these two are then discussed and strategies are proposed for ensuring that customer expectations and operational capability are closely matched when these implications and strategies are implemented.

Customer Satisfaction

Customer satisfaction is the degree of fit between customers' expectations of service quality and the quality of the service as perceived by the customer (Grönroos 1984; Johnston 1987). In most cases customer satisfaction will not be based on a single factor; it will be the result of a combination of several factors customers determine to be appropriate in the creation of satisfaction. Some factors may be more important than others. This can be represented by the equation:

$$CS = Wx * \sum_{x=1}^{n} SFx$$

Customer satisfaction with a service (CS) is the sum of the satisfactions of the various factors (SF), weighted in accordance with customers' feelings (W), for all (x) factors. It is important to note that both the weights and factors may change during the service. Initially, an airline customer may not place much weight on the safety of the transportation service; he or she may be more interested in making a connecting flight. If the airplane develops a mechanical difficulty during the flight and his or her life is in jeopardy, safety becomes paramount in service assessment. A safe landing becomes significantly more important than the missed connection. By the same token, the customer's satisfaction with the factors (SF) is a weighted average of the perception of those factors throughout the service. For example, the cleanliness of a restaurant is a function of the cleanliness of the dining area, rest room facilities, and kitchen. The weights assigned by each customer will differ resulting in a different satisfaction value for each customer.

Enhancing and Hygiene Factors

Two types of factors that provide customer satisfaction exist: enhancing and hygiene factors. Enhancing factors are those that, when in evidence, enhance a customer's satisfaction with the service. Furthermore, if they do not exist, they do not detract from a customer's feeling of satisfaction. An example of an enhancer might be a personal greeting provided by the head waiter. If it is not there, it may have little or no impact on the customer's satisfaction, but if it is provided, it will enhance the service and thus provide a feeling of satisfaction. Hygiene factors are those factors customers expect to be evident. If they are not present or fall below some expected level, they become a source of dissatisfaction. In a restaurant, for example, the time taken to answer the telephone call to make the reservation or the cleanliness of the table and cutlery are hygiene factors. They are expected and are an intrinsic part of the service. Furthermore, if the quality of that service falls below some level, it becomes a source of dissatisfaction. If a fork is dirty or the telephone is not answered for several minutes, the customer may consider that he or she has been the recipient of poor service.

Also, hygiene factors at some point may provide greater customer satisfaction if their level is beyond expectations, thus enhancing the customer's perception of satisfaction. For example, a freshly starched and ironed table cloth rather than a clean table cloth or a telephone answered within a few rings, may be beyond expectations and thus provide enhanced satisfaction with the service. The drawback here is that it may affect the customer's future expectations of the quality of service, making it more difficult for the organization to provide adequate and better than adequate satisfaction in the future. Figure 12–1 summarizes the three levels of satisfaction to be derived from hygiene factors.

To ensure that satisfaction is achieved, an organization must be aware of all factors, enhancers and hygiene, involved in a customer's perception of satisfaction. It should also understand the relative importance customers may attach to each factor and the levels of quality it can provide. Furthermore, it needs to recognize that the range of each customer's expectations are not as wide as all customers' expectations and that the server can alter the service provision to a certain degree to respond to specific customer requirements.

This chapter is limited to considering the implications of a single hygiene factor in terms of the provision and expectation of quality and the implications of a mismatch between the two. A final section proposes strategies to deal with the implementation of the service provision when such mismatches exist.

Customer Expectations of Service

The degree of service expected will be based on customers' understanding of the service that they will receive. Such understanding will be based on their understanding of the image or the operation. That image will be

Poor Quality	Adequate Quality	High Quality
(Dissatisfaction)	(Satisfaction)	(Extreme Satisfaction)

Quality Expected

Figure 12–1. Levels of expected satisfaction for hygiene factors.

created by previous experiences, the experiences of others, and the organization's marketing efforts. It is important to communicate quality to customers before the service in order to manage expectations. It is also important for the server to accurately assess customer expectations. If expectations are too high the customer will be disappointed. If they are too low the organization may attract the wrong customer.

> Communicating a promise of service through advertising requires skill in order to make the intangible tangible. Lufthansa's service starts long before the first cocktail evokes the preparation of the aircraft. "A perfect climate for body and soul", projects Club Med's vacation experience (Horowitz 1986).

Therefore, the role of marketing is to provide customers with a defined range of expectations for each quality factor. It may be necesary to undertake market research to understand customer expectations. By adequately assessing customer expectations, a customer enters the service with realistic expectations of the quality to be provided. For example, a customer at an exclusive gourmet restaurant would not expect to receive prepackaged or previously prepared food. Conversely, a customer of a fast-food restaurant would not expect a five-course gourmet meal.

A source of conflict arises if a mismatch exists between operation's and marketing's definition of the service. The role of operations is to provide a service package based on existing specifications. Marketing's role is to stimulate demand and create customer expectations that match the design and capability of the service operation. A problem occurs when the marketing-driven package and the operations-driven package do not match. Service quality is subsequently lowered when this occurs.

In a recent survey undertaken in a British National Health Service clinic (an outpatient department), patients expected to wait for treatment;

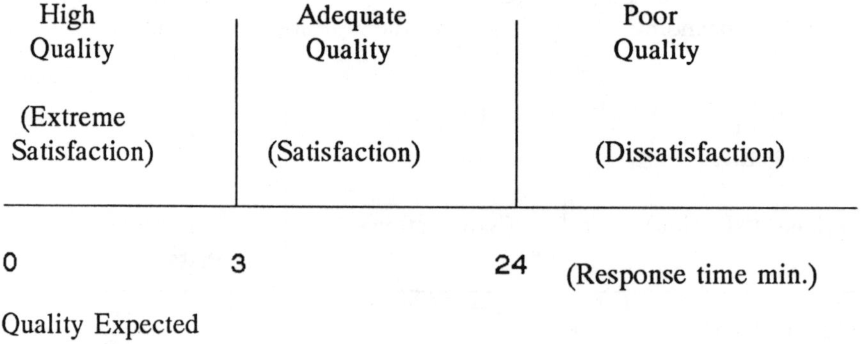

High Quality	Adequate Quality	Poor Quality
(Extreme Satisfaction)	(Satisfaction)	(Dissatisfaction)

0   3   24   (Response time min.)

Quality Expected

Figure 12–2. Defined breakpoints for waiting times.

however, patients became dissatisfied if they waited longer than twenty-four minutes. If patients were seen within three minutes, they were extremely satisfied. Thus the breakpoints for the levels of satisfaction for this hygiene factor have been determined and are identified in figure 12–2.

With a given set of operational resources and methods, and demand for services at a particular time, the operation will be able to provide the service within a particular range, with some variation due to the nature of service provision (Johnston and Morris 1985). In the case of the hospital and the waiting time factor, the actual waiting times on one particular day varied from five minutes to two hours. Figure 12–3 illustrates the service provided by the hospital department.

Implications of Customer Satisfaction

Customer satisfaction is the degree of fit between customer expectations of the service level to be provided and the actual service provided. Implications of this can be seen by combining the two prior figures showing expectations and capability as shown in figure 12–4. One should keep in mind the performance parameter used in this example. As customer waiting time increases, customer satisfaction decreases; therefore, the two variables are inversely related.

A perfect match between the two would be achieved if the boundary of the service provided spanned the boundary of service expectations. As shown in this case, no customers will receive high quality because the system is incapable of providing service with a waiting time of less than five minutes. That waiting time would need to be under three minutes in order for the customer to have classified the service to be of "high quality." Correspondingly, any customers receiving service with a waiting time of over twenty-four minutes classified the service to be of "low quality."

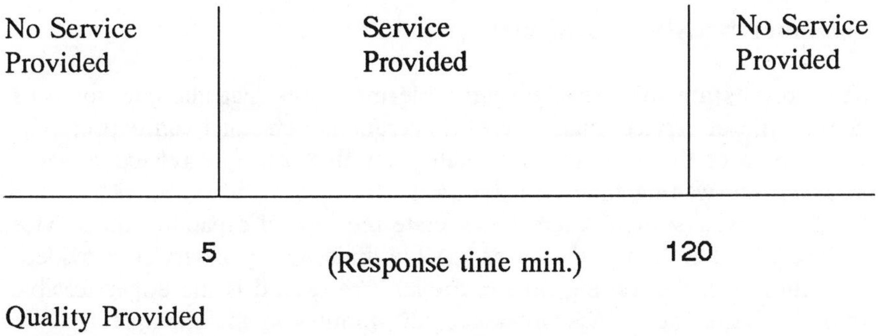

No Service Provided	Service Provided	No Service Provided

5   (Response time min.)   120

Quality Provided

Figure 12–3. Service levels provided by the hospital department.

Quality Expected

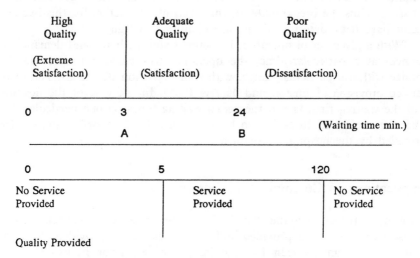

Figure 12–4. **Customer satisfaction: The match between service provided and service expected.**

This system is capable of providing satisfaction if the service provided is below 24 minutes, that is, satisfaction threshold B. Further, extremely good service is provided if the waiting time is below threshold A, three minutes or less. This system, therefore, is only capable of providing its customers with adequate ·or poor service.

Providing the scope and scale of service provided and the scope and scale of service expected are the same, and lower than the level B, customers will always be satisfied. If service is always provided between limits A and B, the quality of all customer encounters will be adequate and no service will be perceived as being poor or excellent.

Customer Satisfaction Model

These results are somewhat generalizable into cases that allow us to focus on the type of service quality results operations personnel can expect. For the purpose of this discussion, a quality variable inversely related to satisfactions, like waiting time, will be used.

Two service system parameters dictate the type of capability the service can provide. The first is the lower feasible limit (LFL) of service provided, five minutes in the waiting time example. The second is the upper feasible limit (UFL) of the service provided, 120 minutes in the example.

The remaining two parameters that dictate service quality provisions deal with customer expectations. The first parameter (A) represents the boundary between high and adequate quality, three minutes in the waiting time example. The second parameter (B) refers to the boundary between adequate and poor quality, twenty-four minutes in the example.

Plotting expectations and capability together, one is provided a way of identifying the type of quality the service can provide.

The relationship between the lower feasible limit (LFL) and high/ adequate boundary (A) allows the system designer to determine if any customers will classify the service as high or adequate. The relationship between the upper feasible limit (UFL) and the adequate/poor boundary (B) allows the system designer to determine if any customers will classify the service as adequate or poor. Figure 12–5 represents the capability/ expectation match presented in the waiting time example.

The point *x* represents the combination of the lower feasible limit (LFL) and the high/adequate boundary (A). The diagonal line identifies those points where the lower feasible limit (LFL) and high/adequate boundary (A) or the upper feasible limit (UFL) and adequate/poor boundary (B) are equal. Because the point *x* is below that diagonal line, it indicates an inability on the part of the service system to provide service deemed "high" quality. Correspondingly, the point *y* identifies the combination of the upper feasible limit (UFL) and adequate/poor boundary (B). Interpreting its position, it is possible for a customer to deem the service "poor" because it is below the diagonal line indicating equal limits.

When one looks at all possible relationships between the two sets of

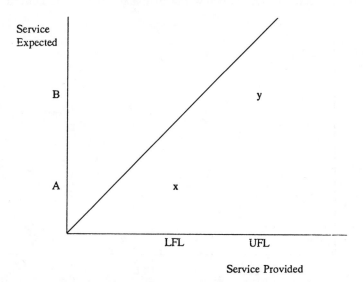

Figure 12–5. Service levels provided by hospital department.

Table 12–1
List of Possible Conditions

Condition	Possible service outcome	Point
1. LFL ≥ A	No "high" quality possible	X_1
2. LFL < A	"High" quality possible	X_2
3. UFL ≤ B	No "low" quality possible	X_3
4. UFL > B	"Low" quality possible	X_4

limits, a set of four consequences are possible, two dealing with determinations of "high" quality and two with "low" quality. They are shown in table 12–1. It is assumed that if any overlap occurs, some "adequate" quality is assured.

As was the case with the waiting time example, the quality of service increases as the measurement decreases. These four conditions are shown in figure 12–6.

Operations managers faced with the situation identified by point X_1," can expect customers to receive, at most, "adequate" quality; the system is incapable of meeting their "high" quality demands (X_1 is above the diagonal). If the combination of LFL and A correspond with point X_2, the service system is capable of providing the customer with "high" or "adequate" quality (X_2 is below the diagonal).

At the other end of the quality scale, operations managers faced with a scenario identified by point X_3 have a system that will not result in "poor" quality to the customer (X_3 is below the diagonal), but if the combination

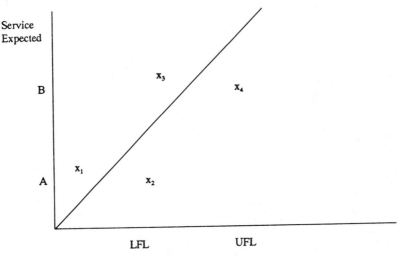

Figure 12–6. General relationships between LFL/A and UFL/B.

Table 12–2
Summary of Quality Outcomes

LFL/A Relationship	*UFL/B Relationship*	
	UFL ≤ *B*	*UFL* > *B*
LFL ≥ A	+, 0	+, 0, −
LFL < A	0	0, −

Note: + indicates the system can provide "high" quality.
   0 indicates the system can provide "adequate" quality.
   − indicates the system can provide "poor" quality.

is identified by X_4 some customers may receive "poor" quality (X_4 is below the diagonal).

At this point, one can combine the two sets of relationships between LFL/A and UFL/B to determine the set of possible outcomes of service. These are shown in table 12–2

By identifying the relationship between expectations and capability, operations personnel can identify the strategic implications associated with the implementation of the service under a given set of expectations and capabilities.

Specific strategic implications for the four situations presented above are identified in table 12–3.

Strategies for Integrating Service Expected and Service Provided

The previous sections have identified a need for a appropriate match to be made between the levels of service customers expect and the levels of service provided by the operation. To ensure a fit between the two requires close collaboration between service marketing and service operations.

Table 12–3
Implications of the Different Quality Outcomes

Service Provided	*Implications*
0, −	Loss of market share or longer term adjustment of customer expectations.
0	Cost of operations become more critical to success and no "excellent" or "poor" service provided to customer.
+, 0	Short-term competitive advantage, long-term increase in customer expectations.
+, 0, −	Total cost minimization approach balancing cost of "poor" service with cost of "excellent" service.

The marketing function is required to identify a market segment and define the acceptable range of expectations are appropriate to that segment. The operations function needs to ensure that the operation is capable of providing service at those levels (service quality design), and then that service is provided at those levels (service quality conformance).

Some organizations are able to define quite carefully their market segment and the service to cater for that market. This is common in many franchised operations. For example, a certain chain of hairstyling salons in the United States gives nicknames to its stylists, Bunny, Chip, Dolly, and so on. Each stylist has areas of specialization, and this assignment of specializations is the same in all franchised salons. If a customer goes into any one of the salons in any location, they need only ask for Bunny and they will be provided with the same style regardless of location. This reduces the range of service variability and the range of customer expectations. Marketing's role in this example is to ensure that the market is aware of the range of styles available. The operational role is to ensure that all styles are always available and to provide the first time entrant to the system with training on the choice of stylists.

There may be occasions and operations in which mismatches between service expected and service provided exist. It is the role of operations to have service quality control measures in place to identify such mismatches. These are usually carried out by questionnaires or surveys of customers; British Rail and many hotels, for example, constantly monitor how well they have served their customers. Once mismatches are identified, three basic strategies can be applied. The organization may choose to amend its marketing, change its operational capabilities, or attempt to change customer perceptions of the service provided.

Marketing

Marketing may be able to reduce the range of customer expectations by changing marketing to capture customers with the appropriate expectations for the operation, or to amend the expectations of potential customers to ensure that they are appropriate to the operational capabilities.

Operations

For some organizations it may be inappropriate or not feasible to change the expectations of customers before entry to the service system. However, once inside the service system it may be possible to explain to customers what will happen and how they will be dealt with, in order to either create appropriate expectations and/or to filter out customers who would not find the treatment satisfactory. A second strategy is for the operation to widen its quality levels to provide for a greater range of customer expectations.

Perceptions

A third type of strategy to deal with a mismatch between expected and provided service quality might be to accept that mismatches will occur. Assuming that it is inappropriate to change marketing and inappropriate or too costly to change the operation, an organization might be able to change customers' perceptions of the service quality they have received without changing the actual quality levels. One example would be the queue at a theme park where clients' perception of a long waiting time has been reduced by a careful use, location, and layout of the queue. Such queues are single lines to provide continual movement, and are usually located so that the customer can see the attraction while waiting. Airports deal with their queues and the need to have customers at the airport well in advance of the flight by providing several different types of queue and queuing areas between entering the airport and boarding the plane.

Conclusion

This chapter has considered only hygiene factors. To be in control of customer satisfaction, management must be aware of all factors involved, the acceptable ranges of service provision, and the capabilities of their operations. They also need to know the relative weightings that may be applied across the range of factors. British Rail is aware that the reliability of trains is four times more important for its passengers than the other performance factors it measures. This one, then, is given more management time and attention. Systems need to be in place to monitor operational performance against the factors identified, and mismatches, when identified, have to be dealt with. The use of one or a combination of the three basic strategies identified should be able to provide improved customer satisfaction with the service provided.

References

Grönroos, C. (1984). "A Service Quality Model and Its Marketing Implications.", *European Journal of Marketing*, Vol. 18, no. 4, 36–44.

Horowitz, J. (1986). "Squashing the Bugs That Prevent Good Service." *The Wall Street Journal*, December 30.

Johnston, R. (1987). "A Framework for Developing a Quality Strategy in a Customer Processing Operation." *International Journal of Quality and Reliability Management*, Vol. 4, No. 4, 37–46.

Johnston, R., and B. Morris. "Monitoring and Control in Service Operations." *International Journal of Operations and Production Management*, Vol. 5, No.1, 32–38.

Sasser, W. E., R. P. Olsen, and D. D. Wyckoff. (1982). *Management of Service Operations.*, Boston: Allyn and Bacon.

Voss, C. A., C. G. Armistead, R. Johnston, and B. Morris. (1985). *Operations Management in Service Industries and the Public Sector*. Chichester: Wiley.

Wild, R. (1977). *Concepts for Operations Management*. Chichester: Wiley.

13
Strategy and Organization for Service

Alan Dale
Stuart Wooler

Introduction

This chapter describes a process for working with a project group within an organization in order to identify what makes a difference to service and to assess how they are doing in relation to each such organizational element, how important each one is for them, and, consequently, which are most likely to repay effort. The methodology uses a combination of decision analytic techniques, group-decision conferencing, content derived from the experience of the group, and content derived from a scan of the relevant literature. The chapter reports preliminary work in developing both the process and content of the model, including its test within one organization. It is currently being developed into a general-purpose model capable of being tailored to meet the needs of any organization with minimal outside help.

The Issues

Enormous interest exists at present in organizations of all kinds in improving service to customers, clients, users, or whomever. Management is bombarded with a wide variety of views on how to improve service: some prescriptive and rigid, others more diagnostic and flexible. To a large extent, they rely mainly on the advice of particular consultants or follow other organizations that have already started. Some attempt to think it out for themselves, although this seems to be restricted to a few pioneers and independently minded organizations.

The authors, engaged in a wide-ranging collaborative research and development program for service with a group of seven organizations, have attempted to develop general models and processes for tackling such issues. Starting from a belief that all strategy is *contingent* (although elements within a strategy may be universal), such an approach must work from

concepts through diagnosis toward strategy development, resource allocation, and commitment. Further, it is essential that there is *corporate* understanding of and commitment to such strategies. Third, a simplistic
concentration on a few elements was avoided in favor of a *systemic* approach, emphasizing interactions and coherence.

Objectives

The authors set out to develop:

- a standard set of concepts, organized into a framework, to give organizations an overview of the elements likely to influence service performance.
- the opportunity for an organization's management to modify both the
  content and the structure of the framework to suit its situation.
- a process for handling the development and modification of the model
  within each organization.
- a process for revealing and resolving differences of viewpoint among
  members of that organization.
- the opportunity to use the model at varying degrees of detail.
- a method for assessing how well the organization is doing on each
  element and how important each element is.
- a means of ranking elements so that management can see which are
  most likely to repay attention.

Research and Development Process

The seven collaborating organizations have identified a list of priority topics
for research and development work. The first two are (1) to develop methods for producing strategies likely to lead to better service and (2) to
produce methods for monitoring actual service performance and setting
appropriate standards. The project reported here addresses the first.

Working with representatives of the seven organizations, a simple version of repertory grid technique was first used (Kelly 1955) to elicit constructs about service. Then the constructs were discussed with them as a
group in relation to the experiences they described and, over the course of
two days, were developed into a preliminary model of the organizational
elements believed to have most impact on service performance. At this
stage no attempt was made to offer the authors' beliefs or to feed in
findings from the literature. The model produced at this stage is shown in
figure 13–1; table 13–1 defines the terms used. After the preliminary

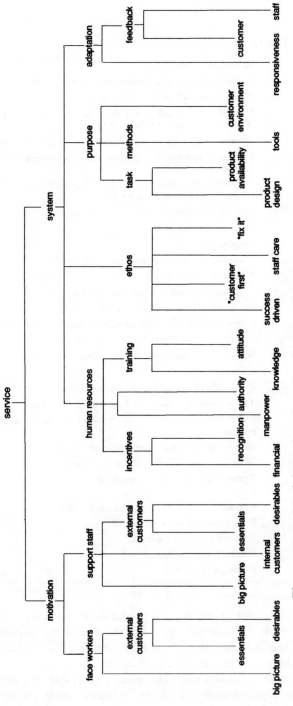

Figure 13–1. Model produced at the first workshop. See table 13–1 for definitions.

Table 13–1
Definitions for Figure 13–1

Motivation	In relation to service
Face Workers	Those employees who meet the customers/clients
Support Staff	Those who work behind the scenes
Big Picture	Employees motivated to see what they do as part of the total effort to serve the customer/client
External Customers	External customers or clients: the final recipients of the service
Essentials	Employees motivated to provide customers/clients with what is essential for them
Desirables	Employees motivated to provide customers/clients with desirable "extras": more than is called for
Internal Customers	Internal "customers": other departments
System	The organization as a whole
Human Resources	Employees
Financial	Financial incentives/rewards for good service
Recognition	Nonfinancial incentives/rewards for good service
Manpower	Sufficient employees to provide good service
Authority	To do what is necessary for good services
Knowledge	Employees have requisite knowledge to give good service
Attitude	Employees have the right attitudes for service
Ethos	Shared beliefs and values about service
"Customer First"	A specific value
Success Driven	A practice of spreading success, not blame
Staff Care	The organization takes good care of its employees
"Fix It"	Employees encouraged to fix problems themselves whenever possible
Product Design	Product designs that meet customers' needs
Product Availability	Products available when and where needed
Methods/Tools	Technologies, systems, procedures
Customer Environment	Customer environment appropriate to their needs
Adaptation	By organization as a whole
Responsiveness	Responsiveness to feedback
Customer	Feedback from customers
Staff	Feedback from staff

model was produced, each of the seven representatives rated their organization's performance on each element, and further, scored the importance of each. This was then fed back to each as their own implicit ranking of the elements most likely to repay management effort.

The general process worked well. However, it was clear that the experience of the seven representatives, while an invaluable basis for the model (and more particularly for increasing their own understanding and commitment), was not an adequate one. There were some obvious omissions and also some muddled conceptualization. The authors therefore proceeded to a further stage of development.

A preliminary scan of the literature on service quickly revealed many elements missing from the model, which were added. At the same time, some confusion and redundancy was removed from the first version, and the entire framework was arranged within a *systemic* view of organizing under the broad headings of task; technology/systems; structure; culture; employees; management; and physical environment. This increased both the width and depth of the model, making it large and unwieldy. The authors persisted at this point, in the belief that it was important to enrich the approach before refining it into a more elegant form. It is perhaps sufficient to note for the moment that the revised model was more than four times as large as the original one.

This revision was presented at another one-day meeting of the collaborative group, and almost the entire meeting was devoted to reaching a common understanding of terms. There was no substantial disagreement about the content of the model, but one or two omissions were noted and subsequently corrected. Essentially, this stage checked the comprehensiveness, clarity, and usability of the model.

After this second meeting some further slight revisions were made, and one of the seven organizations (a life insurance company) agreed to conduct an intensive field test. It set up a project group consisting of managers drawn from different levels and functions within the organization: all with some responsibility for service improvement. The authors met with this group for three separate full-day meetings. The general approach was the decision conferencing method developed by Philips and his colleagues (Philips 1984). The principle of this approach is to use a variety of decision aids with a *management* group to help them reach the necessary understanding and make strategic decisions for improving service in their organization. The analysts not only provide decision-making tools but also deal with the process of the group itself and attempt to develop a true understanding and commitment to strategies. The approach on each of the three days was as follows:

Day 1

Detailed discussion of concepts to develop a common language and to clarify and correct inappropriate or missing aspects of the model. (This did prove necessary in some limited respects. Computer-assisted technology allowed it to be done on-line). After the meeting, the model was tidied a bit more.

Day 2

The general objective for this day was for the group to discuss each of the bottom-line (the most detailed) elements until they were able to allocate a performance score to each, with a rating of its importance in their particular organization. They were doubtful of the feasibility of this objective, believing that they were likely to get into deep disputes. In fact, this happened in only one or two cases. This is typical in groups in which appropriate process and content models are used to aid their work. Apparent and perceived disputes are dissolved by focusing debate and removing ignorance of one another's positions. In the few instances in which a real dispute remains, further techniques can be used to assess their impact (that is, whether a decision one way or another would have much effect on the overall *set* of decisions).

In this case, the software used provides, among other facilities, the ability to:

> combine the group's judgments of their organization's performance on each element in the model with their rating of its strategic importance for improving service

> in the light of these judgments, provide them immediately with a list of the critical organizational weaknesses they must address

> test, using sensitivity analysis, whether any disputed judgments affect this order of priorities

Day 3

The process of scoring the model continued for part of the third day, during which the group explored the process of "zooming" up and down to deal with elements in more or less detail. This proved to be a fruitful approach that enabled the group to get through more quickly without sacrificing any more than necessary. The group members were well able to cope with the zooming process, and the software allows one to go into more or less detail at will. The resultant model for this particular group was about half the size of the previous general version. A portion of it is given in figure 13–2 and table 13–2. It differs substantially from the previous version in that some aspects are omitted, others redefined, and still others treated in less depth. The computed ranking of items that the group believes will have most impact on service in their organization is given in table 13–3.

The field testing of the general model allowed removal of certain redundant aspects. It became clear afterward that some included aspects had

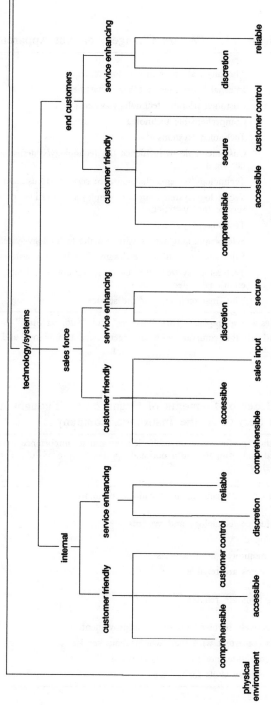

Figure 13-2. Part of model for an insurance company.

Table 13–2
Definitions for Figure 13–2 (Where Changed, or Not Apparent)

Physical Environment	The physical environment for customers
Internal	Internal "customers": other departments
Customer Friendly	Customer-friendly technology/systems
Comprehensible	Comprehensible technology/systems
Accessible	Technology/systems
Customer Control	Customer able to influence the technology/systems: procedures not rigid
Service Enhancing	Technology/systems that enhance service to customer
Discretion	Technology/systems support employee discretion to "tailor" service for customer
Reliable	Technology/systems
Sales Force	Salespeople and agents who use the technology/systems
Sales Input	Sales staff can influence design of technology/systems
Secure	Technology/systems for the customer are technically, socially, emotionally (feels) secure
End Customers	The final recipients of the service

1. "Internal" and "Sales Force" replace "Face Workers" and "Support Staff"
2. A recent merger had left this company with an urgent need to integrate and improve its technology and systems.

Table 13–3
Computed Rank Order of Elements of Organization Thought Most Likely to Improve Service in the Insurance Company

The group's scores of their performance on each element and its importance for their company were combined and compared to a notional "perfect" score of 100. The top 10 (out of 41) are given below.

	Sum vs. 100
*1. Management's strategy for changing the organization towards service	6.60
†2. Sales staff can influence technology and systems	11.47
3. Service ethos developed	16.23
*4. Quality of service monitored in all aspects	20.03
†5. Technology and systems are reliable (for end customers)	23.82
†6. Technology and systems are reliable (for sales force)	27.61
*7. Top management actively involved in service improvement	31.24
8. Management deeds consistent with their words about service	33.71
9. Service seen as a corporate, not functional, responsibility	36.16
10. Employees have necessary skills for service	38.02

* Not shown in figure 13–2

† These items are obviously interrelated. Taken together, they are easily the top priority.

nothing to do with *organizing* for service but with defining the service levels actually achieved. They were removed as well (to be pursued in a separate project). The resultant new general model is now in a form believed to be widely applicable, given in figure 13–3 and table 13–4. Naturally, it will be further improved in the light of experience and increased understanding. It is not finished, complete or "bug-free," but it is powerful and useful. In outline, this is achieved by means of:

A general model of manageable size (figure 13–3 and table 13–4)

Subsidiary models ("submenus") that enable the user to "zoom down" into more detail under the headings given (see figure 13–4 for an example)

The facility for the user to delete, amend, or add categories under any heading

The facility to score each element (in whatever detail is chosen) and combine the scores into an overall set of priorities for action.

Discussion

In developing this model, the authors aimed to provide a "service on service," working with client organizations to produce models that are both general-purpose yet capable of being tailored for use in a particular setting.

The process used for development has a number of unusual features:

Content and process modeling proceeds simultaneously.

Content is developed iteratively, taking the emergent categories from the client organization(s) and comparing them with the "imported" (predetermined, theoretical) categories drawn from the literature (Spencer and Dale 1979).

Likewise, the definition of meaning is a collaborative process between researchers and clients (Spencer and Dale 1979).

The content of the model can also be easily amended by an individual user. It has both universal and situational aspects (Spencer and Dale 1979).

The model produced may be used in different degrees of detail (depth) according to the interest of the users.

Although analysis proceeds element-by-element, the elements are linked in a *systemic* framework and the scoring procedures explicitly require users to consider them in relation to one another.

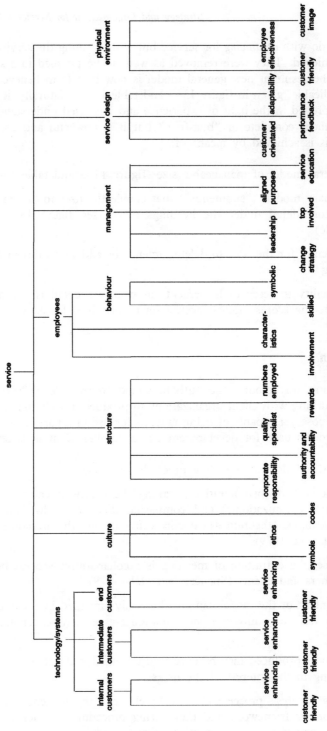

Figure 13-3. The current general-purpose version of the model. See table 13-4 for definitions.

Table 13–4
Definitions for Figure 13–4

Technology/Systems	Hardware, software, forms, procedures, etc.
Internal Customers	Other departments
Intermediate Customers	Brokers, agents, distributors, wholesalers, franchisees, etc.
End Customers	The final recipients of the service
Customer Friendly	Technology/systems/physical environment that are accessible, comprehensible, secure, etc., for the customer
Service Enhancing	Technology/systems that enhance service to customers
Culture	Collective values, beliefs, norms, symbols, etc., that apply to all staff
Symbols	Logos or other artifacts that communicate and focus attention on key values
Ethos	Shared values and beliefs
Codes	Written or unwritten, conscious or unconscious, codes of practice, standards, etc.
Structure	The organization structure
Corporate Responsibility	Service is accepted as a corporate (not merely functional) responsibility by the top executive group
Authority and Accountability	Staff have the authority needed to give good service, and are held accountable for it
Numbers Employed	Sufficient for good service
Quality Specialist	A high-level employee is accountable for specialist support to managers to improve service quality
Rewards	Appropriate incentives for and reinforcement of a service performance
Employees	Those involved in giving service
Involvement	Employee motivation, involvement, orientation toward service
Characteristics	Individual characteristics appropriate for service-giving
Behavior	In relation to service
Skilled	Behavior for the service given
Symbolic	Behavior for the service given (appropriate dress, demeanor, etc.)
Management Change Strategy	Management's strategy for bringing about service orientation and performance
Leadership	Managers initiate, envision, direct, and otherwise emphasize service
Top Involved	Chief executive or similar roles involved, as well as other managers
Aligned Purposes	Values, missions, strategies, plans, actions are all in line and focused on service
Service Education	Managers educated about service

(continued)

Table 13–4 (Continued)

Service Design	The way in which the service is produced, delivered, and adjusted to meet customer needs
Customer Orientated	Designs are focused on customer needs
Performance Feedback	There are mechanisms for getting feedback on service from customers and staff
Adaptability	The organization responds to such feedback by taking appropriate action
Physical Environment	Layouts, signage, physical conditions, etc. that have an effect on service
Customer-Friendly	The physical environment is welcoming, comprehensible, secure, etc. for the customer
Employee Effectiveness	The physical environment helps employees give good service
Customer Image	Physical environment communicates a service image to the customer

Taken together, these features make up a distinctive approach that generates sound theory, user understanding, and commitment; and which is itself of practical service to the user by leading naturally to action.

Current effort is now focused on developing the model further in a variety of formats from pencil and paper to on-line computer-aided. The tools thus developed should be capable of use with little or no additional external support, enabling organizations to develop practical strategies for service improvement.

This process needs to be continued. Each new organization that uses the general model may not only modify it to suit its own situation but may also find ways of further improving it for general use. Ideally, the results of their experience with the model should be fed back. Parallel to this, further published material or the author's continuing research may also lead to amendments. This process should lead to publication of a second version in due course. Indeed the authors see no end to this process. The model cannot and should not ever be "finished." Instead, it will evolve as understanding improves. Thus, version two will lead inexorably to version *n*, although of course revisions will be less frequent as refinement proceeds.

It remains to be seen just how general this model will prove to be. Will significant differences be needed in publicly owned service organizations (health, welfare, education, etc.)? The authors hope to find out soon by working with a group of such organizations. Will the model be influenced by the external environment of the organization (the local culture, laws, economy, etc.)? The authors would welcome opportunities for testing it in a

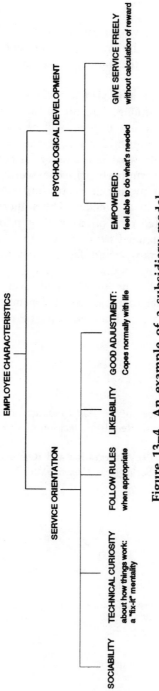

Figure 13–4. An example of a subsidiary model.

variety of environments. Certainly, comparative research is essential to improve the theoretical basis of the model. At present it is not known whether it adequately describes the variety of conditions in organizations concerned with service.

A potential weakness of the approach is the relative lack of attention given to systemic interactions among elements in the model. Clearly, many instances exist when attention to one element will be useless unless another is also tackled. (For example, training for service may be useless unless job holders have the authority to do what is necessary for good service and are surrounded by a culture that supports it). The scoring procedure takes account of this to some extent by linking scores horizontally across the set of elements on any given line of the model. The authors also assume that when a group sees the computed rank ordering of its priorities, it is usually able to spot the need for interrelated *sets* of actions to be taken. However, it could be that a particular group would fail to spot them. Perhaps they could be prompted for likely interactions by building in a "standard" (i.e., theoretically based) set of relations to the model, or at least explicitly asking them to *consider* whether each element is dependent on any other. It may be that relational data-base techniques could be used to achieve such an objective.*

References

Kelly, G. A. (1955). *The Psychology of Personal Constructs*. New York: Norton.
Philips, L. D. (1984). "A Theory of Requisite Decision Models." *Acta Psychologica*, 56.
Spencer, L., and A. J. Dale. (1979). "Integration and Regulation in Organizations: A Contextualist Approach." *Sociological Review*, Vol. 27, No. 4.

---

*We are grateful to our colleague, John Øvretveit, for this suggestion, and for other comments on this chapter.

14
Empowering Consumers within Public Human Services:
The Case for Civil Democracy

Richard B. Saltmann
Casten von Otter

Although economic issues of cost containment and service productivity continue to dominate the European debate about human services, important political and normative issues remain on the agenda. Consequently, the application of service management theory within public human services should reflect key politically generated values, in particular, the importance of consumer empowerment within public human service design and delivery. This chapter explores the broader questions of democratic control over welfare-state–supplied human services and the principles that should guide the organization of human- and health-related services generally. The chapter concludes that the concept of civil democracy can provide a useful policy model in political and normative, as well as economic, terms.

Introduction

The rigidities of public service delivery reflect deeply rooted patterns of institutional authority and organizational behavior within the public human service sector generally (Weale 1985). The reliance on an allocative rather than an innovative planning methodology, the centrality of use value rather than exchange value in service design, the focus on input measures rather than output and/or outcome measures, and the inherent potential for an imperfect fit between services supplied and services desired by individuals can be observed in varying degrees in the education, day-care, and social-service (home-care) sectors of most existing public systems (Saltmann and von Otter 1987).

This observation should not be construed as dismissing the unique advantages to be gained from planned public human services. On the contrary, the above critique addresses crucial limitations that prevent the welfare state from achieving its intended goals and objectives.

As the pervasiveness of the issue suggests, a variety of broadly conceived efforts have attempted to reorient the administrative framework within which the human service sector has operated. In this chapter, brief descriptions of prior efforts and proposals to improve the quality of public service delivery are provided. Subsequently, the authors reconceptualize the core assumptions that underlie two major reform paradigms—one based in administrative theory; the other following service management theory—as a prelude to presenting an alternative theoretical analysis on which to ground organizational and administrative change in the public sector.

The main argument can be broadly conceptualized as a challenge to further develop the central definition of democracy within the welfare state. In Sweden as elsewhere in Northern Europe, democratic theory has involved increasing opportunities for formalized participatory influence over three major aspects of social and political life: (1) over political institutions—via elections, party consultation with organized interest groups, and so on, (2) over social institutions—particularly pensions and social insurances against disability, unemployment, and so on, and (3) over economic institutions—via industrial unions and worker codetermination. What welfare state democracy as presently practiced still does not include is formal participatory influence (4) over civil institutions—namely residence-related human services such as health care, education, and child care. Although labor unions and left-of-center political parties have placed major emphasis on the transformation of political, social, and economic life, they have traditionally viewed changes that increase the direct influence of the individual as a consumer of human services with considerable trepidation (Martin 1982). Reflecting this hesitation, the modern welfare state continues to allow individuals little effective influence over the residence-based institutions that in the twentieth century compose an increasingly important segment of what nineteenth century idealist philosophers referred to as civil society."

In a pragmatic sense, the central notion underlying this argument is quite straightforward. Within private organizations, the importance placed on attaining particular goals, and the interests served by the goals selected, reflect an intricate pattern of internal and external decision-making power. (Crozier 1964). Within publicly controlled organizations, despite formal structures of electoral accountability, this pattern of organizational power and self-interest takes on an indirect yet central role. (Long 1949). In market-driven organizations, where profitability defines viability, management is obligated to supply products that maximize exchange-value to the producer rather than use-value to the consumer (Saltmann and von Otter 1987). Whether publicly accountable or market-driven, large organizations contain inherent pressures to pursue internal objectives and self-interest in lieu of meeting what are diverse and often diffuse consumer needs. Civil democracy, as will be argued, becomes a necessary mechanism to empower individuals, enabling them to redress the decision-making balance within public human services.

Efforts at Participatory Reform

A variety of reform measures has been proposed and/or undertaken to reshape the face of public-sector human-service administration in Sweden. While these efforts reflect the differing concerns of their proponents, the intended objective has been to make the existing administrative apparatus more responsive to the public being served. This section concentrates on two proposed reforms that suggest not only the nature of the debate but also the conceptual dimensions of previously developed administrative alternatives within the Swedish public system.

Political Administration

In Sweden, an effort to increase citizen involvement in the design and delivery of community-based services was developed by the social democratic party during its years in opposition (1976 to 1982) and has since become official government policy. The party's central assumptions about the public sector—developed during forty years of uninterrupted social democractic government—were reassessed, and, as outsiders, it was easier to adopt a more skeptical view of intrabureaucractic life. In 1983, on recapturing control of the government, a new Ministry for Public Administration (Civildepartementet) was established to promote policies that would, in the words of Prime Minister Palme, "protect the citizen against the bureaucrat." The concept is much the same as that of its more radical predecessor movements (Saltmann and von Otter 1989): to excite local interest and participation in issues surrounding the design and delivery of municipal and regional (county) services. To accomplish this goal, the Ministry proposed to restructure local government and the lines of program responsibility inside the existing administrative apparatus (Regeringens Skrivelse 1984/85). The tight legislative grip was to be eased, allowing district boards to integrate public sector services horizontally at the same level at which services were delivered, thus replacing what had previously been a vertically structured organization on a separate program basis (Eklund and Kronvall 1988).

The underlying objective has been to shift local decision-making responsibility within the existing administrative apparatus to a new participatory body, reflecting an explicit concern with reinvigorating public interest and participation in the daily administrative life of the Swedish public sector. Attracted by more radical models that conceptualized the population as "citizens" to be incorporated in a participatory local-government structure, becoming both empowered individuals and involved co-producers, the official party response is somewhat less dramatic. It nonetheless seeks to invigorate local politics and the political party apparatus by empowering citizens as laypeople at the expense of appointed official and professional experts.

Service Management

Although recent Swedish reforms have emphasized the political and administrative aspects of public sector decision making, they have also sought to incorporate key elements of service management theory. The importance of process management in the selection and motivation of employees and in work design has received considerable attention within a variety of national, county, and municipal agencies (Normann 1984; Grönroos 1983). Indeed, in certain instances these notions may have been adopted too uncritically, without sufficient consideration of the intrinsic distinctions that separate public human-service delivery from customer satisfaction activities in the airline, restaurant, and hotel industries.

Viewed analytically, these and other recent Swedish proposals can be interpreted as efforts to increase popular participation within the existing governmental administrative apparatus (Saltmann and von Otter 1989). Particularly for community-resident–related human services like health, education, and day-care, the proposals seek to supplement the representative democratic power of regular elections with the participatory democratic power of direct local activity within the decision-making apparatus. This attempt to shift from the distributionist notion of substantive democracy traditionally propounded by the Swedish Social Democratic Party (Pincus 1986) to a more directly process-oriented participatory concept of democratic decision making has important conceptual implications for the character of the Swedish welfare state. Before exploring these implications, it may be useful to explore the underlying theoretical premises on which these reform proposals are based.

On the Limitations of Voice

In terms of Hirschman's notions of exit, voice, and loyalty (Hirschman 1970), the proposals for change previously described rely in their essential components on what he termed *voice*—disagreeing with organizational policy from inside, as a member of the system. As a call for reform from within, voice has fundamentally different characteristics from the other active responses Hirschman posited: that of withdrawal from the organization or *exit*. Most importantly, voice involves a commitment to remain within the organization even if ultimately it does not change—hence

Hirschman's notion of *loyalty*, which becomes an important threshold to the use of exit (Stryjan 1987).

Evaluated as expressions of voice, the official policy proposals have strengths and weaknesses typical of this approach to organizational reform. Positively, voice-oriented reforms preserve organizational continuity and coherence, guaranteeing the continued importance of the existing decision-making apparatus in future allocations of authority and responsibility. Moreover, by retaining the existing organizational structure, voice can be seen to be consistent with the solidarity and universality essential to the social democratic concept of equity within distributionist welfare-state programs. It encourages the individual to see his or her own needs and wants in a broader social perspective, and, if dissatisfied, to pursue not solely his or her own personal advantage but rather changes that would benefit all those in the same predicament. In Sweden, these characteristics have been viewed as instrumental in creating social cohesion and solidarity, a degree of classlessness, and the attainment of certain collective goods (LO 1986).

Negatively, however, one can point to a number of class-tied resources that are necessary if voice is to be exercised successfully. Those with better education, better self-presentation, and better rhetorical and organizational skills are more likely to find voice an effective option (Miller 1988). Further, the individual requires unencumbered time to participate, and thus, apart from issues of social class, the individual's ability to exercise voice properly is directly inverse to the number of arenas in which his or her voice is necessary. Perhaps most damaging, voice alone can lead to passivity and/or fear of punishment if the effort at reform fails, a result Barry (1974) terms *silent non-exit*. Kavanagh (1972) notes that this pattern of withdrawal from politics is both cumulative and selective.

The alternative Hirschman posits—exit—has traditionally been rejected by welfare state proponents as being in fundamental conflict with the central public character of the modern welfare state (LO 1986). In the context of public-sector human services, exit has been viewed as directly associated with expensive private-sector providers, thus placing the exit option beyond the reach of less-well-off individuals. As Swedish reform proposals imply, suitable models of change are seen as those that reinforce rather than dismantle the existing universal and solidaristic character of welfare-state services.

Yet, quite unintentionally, this exclusive emphasis on voice has served to validate exit as the only effective alternative, and thus legitimate Hirschman's conceptualization of organizational change. Recent Swedish proposals, consistent with Social Democratic ideology, do not consider the utility of what could be termed *lateral reentry*—that is, the notion of partial withdrawal followed by reentry elsewhere within the boundaries of the public-service sector. By presuming that an option to leave one's immediate service provider is tantamount to leaving the entire public system, these reform proposals essentially close off alternatives beyond voice that fall short of complete exit. This insistence on centripetal cohesion ironically has introduced inexorable pressures for the centrifugal dissolution of the public human-service sphere of the Swedish welfare state.

On Choice and Civil Democracy

The above analysis of prior Swedish reform proposals suggests that the present definition of welfare-state democracy—in Sweden and elsewhere—needs to be broadened. Although past expansion from a predominantly political understanding of democracy has generated increased opportunity for formalized participatory influence over several major areas of modern postindustrial society, an important conceptual gap remains with regard to publicly provided human services.

First and foremost, democracy as formally defined involves direct public control over *political institutions*, via elections, party consultation with organized interest groups, and the various official instruments of public-policy formation (Lively 1975). The social democratic vision of democracy, however, has traditionally extended beyond formal participation in political activities to providing guarantees that ensure the equality of individuals in the formal control and distribution of key economic resources. Hence the practice of democracy within the Swedish welfare state has also included direct public influence over *economic institutions*—via industrial unions and worker codetermination (also, the controversial issue of wage-earner funds); over *social institutions*—particularly pensions and social insurances against disability, unemployment, and so on; and over *private commodities*. With minimal exception, what welfare-state democracy as presently practiced does not include is the direct participatory influence of individuals over residence-related human services such as health care, education, and child care. In the current system, no equivalent act of individual validation for human services exists that parallels voting in elections, accepting entitlement disbursements, joining a union, or purchasing a consumer durable (see figure 14–1). The dilemma of civil democracy within the Swedish welfare state reflects the fact that one has been empowered as a citizen in political life and as a recipient of entitlements in social life; one is at least struggling to be empowered as a worker in economic life and as a consumer of private-sector commodities; yet one remains all but powerless as a community resident with regard to publicly provided human services.

Some proponents of the existing model of human-service delivery defend this lack of direct individual influence on both theoretical and political grounds. Drawing on a broad body of writings on substantive or content democracy and the importance of "public good" and "public commons" arguments, traditional social democratic theorists argue that a mandated

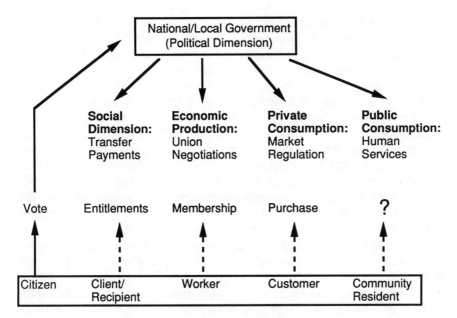

Figure 14–1. **Constituent Components of Welfare Democracy: A Process Model.**

framework of equal conditions for human service like health and education is necessary to ensure the proper development of a just society (Korpi 1978; Castles 1978) Criticism of the level of individual influence is deflected by pointing to the multiple opportunities within the centrally administered structure to exercise voice from inside the system. On more practical grounds, proponents point to the obvious achievements of the existing system in raising overall living standards and to the enormous difference between the situation of the "children of the welfare state" and that of children in the preceding generations (Eriksson and Åberg 1987).

The distinction between content and process forms of democracy can be viewed as reflecting different concepts of freedom. From this perspective, content democracy can be logically associated with what could be termed *freedom-through*: that is, the German idealist notion that the individual obtains the central elements of freedom in and through the social group—in and through society. Process democracy, on the other hand, can be taken as implying *freedom-from*: that is, the Lockean notion that the individual gains freedom in separation from and often in opposition to the demands of other individuals.

In the present-day welfare-state context, the appropriateness of continuing to maintain a predominantly content rather than process model of decision making for publicly provided human services can be questioned on pragmatic economic and political grounds, as well as on theoretical and/or ideological grounds. One economic argument consists of the contrast between the minimal nature of individual influence over publicly provided services on the one hand, and the mechanisms available on the private sector side of personal consumption on the other.

In most industralized societies, private commodities are subject to indirect individual influence in the form of general governmental regulation concerning quality, labeling, and safety. This influence is exercised through the electoral system. Yet in the case of private commodities, this highly indirect form of political influence is supplemented by a direct, individually wielded instrument: the choice of the individual to buy a particular product from a particular manufacturer. As a consequence, the specific production decisions of the private sector and the assumptions about individual needs and preferences that influence those decisions are subsequently subjected to an explicit process of individual validation, or, if one prefers a more cynical view of supplier-dominated market behavior, at least serial ratification.

Given the (occasionally incorrect) presumption of a real market with multiple independent suppliers of qualitatively different products, individual validation serves to ensure that an adequate fit between actual production and personal consumption decisions. It is not necessary to adopt the notions of radical-right economists (Friedman and Friedman 1981) or accept their trivialization of "public needs" and "use value" as only illegitimate forms of "individual wants" and "exchange value," to recognize the fundamentally different level of individual impact on the internal behavior of the private as against the public sector.

A second economic criticism of the substantive rather than the participatory view of the individual's relationship to publicly provided human services concerns the shift in the type of services—in the economic products—that the modern welfare state produces. Certain areas of state production continue to involve collective consumption much the same as they have since the Lockean "nightwatchman state" of the eighteenth century, for example, public safety and external defense, or, as in the early days of the emerging welfare state, services directly related to the bare necessities of life. Yet human services provided by the modern welfare state involve the production of individually consumed services that cannot be as readily standardized (OECD 1987). Public services now touch on life-style–related values difficult to derive from democratic or general welfare-related social theories, but founded instead in individual preferences, experiences, and resources (von Otter 1988). This major shift in the nature of public production reinforces the importance of reconsidering the mechanisms of individual influence on service content and delivery.

The Case for Choice

The political questions that can be raised concerning substantive democratic notions of human-service provision revolve around the differences between choice or lateral reentry on the one hand and voice on the other. As previously noted, choice among alternative public-sector human services has been rejected by welfare-state proponents as tantamount to exit and thus politically unacceptable. Yet in the present context, a strong argument exists that the most effective mechanism for enhancing individual influence over the array of residence-tied human services—for generating civil democracy—is that of lateral reentry within the existing publicly operated service system.

Choice within the public-rather than the private-sector is only minimally dependent on an individual's personal (class-tied) resources. One need not argue or organize others persuasively; find sufficient time and/or prioritize among competing participatory arenas; or fear that sitting authorities will dismiss one's service preferences as secondary to other intraorganizational and/or political imperatives. Most importantly, one need not practice "silent nonexit" out of concern for subsequent bureaucratic retribution. Instead, relying on one's right of lateral reentry, one can simply take one's custom elsewhere in the public sector.

Viewed from the present Swedish perspective, with its highly articulated human-services structure, publicly delimited choice would be a more egalitarian mechanism of individual influence than voice. Indeed, in seemingly logical contradiction, precisely the realistic opportunity to exercise choice in the form of conveniently accessible lateral reentry, would serve to empower and democratize voice. Once individuals had the option to change public providers—particularly if public budgeting for service units reflected such changes contemporaneously—human service organizations would undoubtedly become more responsive to the expressed concerns of their client population.

Similarly, resident and/or client association concerned about quality of service questions would find themselves taken more seriously than they are at present in an exclusively voice-oriented environment. Adding choice to voice would create precisely the structural pressure to ensure responsiveness from the elected politicians and appointed officials who administer human services in the welfare state.

A more general argument about the educational advantages in creating a learning environment that facilitates as much choice as possible within society is possible. Numerous social commentators have observed that individual and/or associational decision making increases the overall knowledge, confidence, and ability of the citizenry. Mills (1944) aptly summarized this notion: "the most important point of excellence which any form of government can possess is to promote the virtue and intelligence of the people themselves."

Conclusion

Viewed conceptually, the exercise of public sector choice would add the validating aspects of process democracy to the existing elements of content democracy. By combining a substantial measure of civil democracy with present opportunities to exercise political, social, and economic democracy, adding public sector choice for community-tied human services would expand the existing framework of democratic life within the welfare state.

A public competition model that could facilitate the development of civil democracy has recently been proposed for the Swedish health care system (Saltmann and von Otter 1987). Grounded on the concept of public market share, this model empowers the community resident by linking individual choice among (public) health providers directly to the short-term operating budget of service delivery units. Combined with additional incentives for internal efficiency, this confluence of patient choice and flexible budgeting can create a new administrative and managerial environment within which would remain a publicly operated health care system.

The adoption of this public competition approach to other publicly operated human services could provide a suitable means to pursue civil democracy within the context of the welfare state generally. Armed with the ability to exercise individual preferences reflecting service quality, convenience, and effectiveness, and reinforced by budgetary consequences for service providers contingent on the exercise of these individual preferences, the consumer would become truly empowered within the public sector delivery apparatus. Indeed, safe within the protective cocoon of a politically accountable public delivery system, individuals could exercise considerably greater power in terms of achieving desired outcomes within this public market than they can typically exert within a traditional caveat emptor private marketplace. Viewed pragmatically, public competition can provide an appropriate vehicle through which to adapt the basic principles of service management theory to the unique circumstances surrounding the delivery of public human services in the welfare state.

References

Barry, B. (1974). "Exit, Voice and Loyalty: A Review Article." *British Journal of Political Science, 4,* 79–107.

Castles, F. G. (1978). *The Social Democratic Image of Society: A Study of the*

Achievements and Origins of Scandinavian Social Democracy in Comparative Perspective. London: Routledge and Kegan Paul.

Crozier, M. (1964). *The Bureaucratic Phenomenon*. Chicago: University of Chicago Press.

Eklund, L. K., and K. F. Kronvall. (1988). *Responsiveness, Decentralization and Implications for the Roles of the Employees*. Paper for the O.E.C.D./I.U.L.A. Workshop on Urban Services and Consumer Needs, Amsterdam, April 22–25. Stockholm: Center for Working Life.

Eriksson, R., and R. Åberg (eds.) (1987). *Welfare in Transition: A Survey of Living Conditions in Sweden 1968–1981*. Oxford: Clarendon Press.

Friedman, M., and R. Friedman. (1981). *Free to Choose*. New York: Harcourt Brace, Jovanovich.

Grönroos, C. (1983). *Strategic Management and Marketing in the Service Sector*. Boston: Marketing Science Institute.

Heclo, H., and H. Madsen. (1987). *Policy and Politics in Sweden: Principled Pragmatism*. Philadelphia: Temple University Press.

Hirschman, A. (1970). *Exit, Voice and Loyalty*. Cambridge: Harvard University Press.

Kavanagh, D. (1972). "Political Behaviors and Political Participation." In G. Parry (ed), *Participation in Politics*. Manchester: Manchester University Press.

Korpi, Walter. (1978). *The Working Class in Welfare Capitalism: Work, Unions, and Politics in Sweden*. London: Routledge and Kegan Paul.

LO (Landsorganisation). (1986). *Fackföreningsrörelsen och välfärdsstaten*. Stockholm: Landsorganisation.

Lively, J. (1975). *Democracy*. Oxford: Basil Blackwell.

Long, N. (1949). "Power and Administration." *Public Administration Review*, 9, 257–64.

Martin, A. cited in de Faramond, G. M., Harrington, and A. Martin. (1982). "Sweden Seen from the Outside." In B. Ryden and V. Bergström (eds.), *Sweden: Choices for Economic and Social Policy in the 1980's*. London: George, Allen, and Unwin.

Miller, T. (1988). *Consulting Citizens in Sweden: Planning Participation in Context*. Stockholm: Swedish Council for Building Research; D10.

Mills, J. S. (1944). "Representative Government." In *Utilitarianism, Liberty and Representative Government* (Everyman ed.), 193.

Normann, R. (1984) *Service Management: Strategy and Leadership in Service Business*. New York: J. Wiley & Sons.

OECD. (1987). *Administration as Service: The Public as Client*. Paris: OECD.

Pincus, Ingrid. (1986). *Demokratiseringsintentionerna i Den Nya Hälso och Sjukvårdslagen*. Örebro: Institutionen för Politik med Förvaltning.

Regeringens skrivelse. (1984/85). *Den offentliga sektorns fönyelse*, 202. Stockholm.

Saltmann, R. B., and C. von Otter. (1987). "Revitalizing Public Health Care Systems: A Proposal for Public Competition in Sweden." *Health Policy*, 7, 21–40.

———. (1989). "Voice, Choice and the Question of Civil Democracy in the Swedish Welfare State." *Economics and Industrial Democracy*, 10 (forthcoming).

Serner, U. (1980). "Swedish Health Legislation: Milestones in Reorganization Since

1945." In A. J. Heidenheimer and N. J. Elvander, *The Making of the Swedish Health Care System.* New York: St. Martin's

SOU. (1985). Aktivt folkstyre i kommuner och landsting. Betänkande från *1983 års demokratiberedning.* Stockholm.

Stryjan, Y. (1987). *Impossible Organizations: On Self Management and Organizational Reproduction.* Uppsala, Sweden: Uppsala University.

von Otter, Casten. (1988). *The Rationalities of the Welfare State.* Address delivered at the OECD Workshop on Urban Services and Consumer Needs, Asterdam, April 22–25. Stockholm: Swedish Center for Working Life.

Weale, A. (1985). "Why Are We Waiting? The problem of Unresponsiveness in the Public Social Services." In R. Klein and M. O'Higgins (eds), *The Future of Welfare.* Oxford: Basil Blackwell.

15
Development of a Personnel Selection System for Service Jobs

Benjamin Schneider
Daniel Schechter

Introduction

Research and theory about service have focused on services marketing and/ or the management of service organizations. The literature has been characterized by the development of models for understanding how services differ from goods and, thus, how service organizations may need to be organized and/or managed differently than goods-producing organizations to achieve effectiveness (Bowen and Schneider 1988; Parasuraman, Zeithaml, and Berry 1985).

Services marketing scholars and practitioners have made some impressive progress in identifying some specific issues consumers consider in the evaluation of service quality (Parasuraman, Zeithaml, and Berry 1986). In contrast, specification of the management and organizational design issues requiring attention to facilitate the delivery of excellent service quality has lagged. Thus, although a number of books exist detailing some broad categories of issues that organizations must attend to in managing the service encounter (Czepiel, Solomon, and Suprenant 1985; Lovelock 1988; Normann 1984), little practical help is provided with respect to the actual steps required to make changes happen.

Obviously, any one of a number of organizational issues might serve as a focus of organizational change. For example, organizations might focus on appraisal and reward systems (Kerr 1988), on training programs (Goldstein 1986), on the creation of climate or culture (Schein 1985; Schneider 1987a), or any of the issues conceptually related to ultimate service effectiveness. One or all of these topics would make for an interesting chapter. This chapter, however, focuses on a topic almost nonexistent in the literature on service and service organizations—personnel selection.

We appreciate the people in the organization who helped us carry out this project. In addition, we thank Paul Hanges for his assistance in analyzing the data reported here. Finally, we express our appreciation to the Computer Science Center of the University of Maryland, College Park, for supporting the data analyses we did.

Personnel Selection and Services Marketing

Much literature on services marketing and the design of service organizations emphasizes the importance of the quality of the people delivering service (e.g., Berry, Parasuraman, and Zeithaml 1988). These literatures include ideas about the basic service inclination of employees and the importance of basic competencies. Service inclinations refer to individuals' interests in doing service-related work; the term *competencies* refers to the various skills and knowledge necessary to be effective in this type of work.

Exactly how or when employees acquire the inclinations and competencies is usually unspecified. Indeed, it is sometimes assumed that all employees have these inclinations (often through self-selection into these jobs) and that it is inhibitive managerial practices that keep employees from providing excellent service (Schneider and Bowen, 1985).

While the majority of service organization employees may have this service inclination, some employees clearly have more than others. This has been demonstrated by Hogan, Hogan, and Busch (1984) who showed that service effectiveness is correlated with having service-oriented personality characteristics (e. g., helpfulness, thoughtfulness, etc.). Perhaps most interesting in the Hogan, Hogan, and Busch research was the fact that the people studied were all applicants for a service job at the same organization. It is safe to conclude, then, that not all applicants for a service job are equally inclined toward providing excellent service.

Beyond the issue of inclination to provide service is the question of service competencies. As with service inclinations, it seems clear that people are differentially competent in their ability to deliver, or in their ability to learn to deliver, excellent service. In a typical applicant pool for a service position, one might expect even *more* variability in service-related skills than inclinations or interests in doing service work.

Parasuraman, Zeithaml, and Berry (1986) have clearly shown that service quality is multidimensional in nature; it follows that the delivery of excellent service requires people who are multidimensional in their service inclinations and competencies. Thus, because service quality is perceived by customers along many dimensions (e.g., courtesy, reliability, responsiveness, and so forth), service providers must demonstrate inclinations toward and competencies in these areas to be effective in meeting customer expectations.

The present chapter is about selecting employees who are service oriented both in terms of their inclinations and their competencies. The chapter is based on a number of premises:

1. An organization can be only as effective as the typical people in it; this is especially true in organizations that require interdependent behavior

for achieving organizational goals (Bass 1982). This is so because individual excellence cannot compensate for poor performers when it takes a team effort to achieve success. Most service organizations, especially consumer service organizations, require interdependent behavior for effectiveness, as evidenced in Albrecht and Zemke's (1985) service "cycle" diagnostic model. Furthermore, given the highly interactive nature of service "production," often no *opportunity* exists to compensate for poor service.

2. An organization's climate or culture is a function of the kind of people who predominate there (Schneider 1987b). Therefore, it will be difficult to find an organization that is service-oriented if the modal interests of workers are not in service-related work (i.e., the predominant interests are in isolated work or the predominating competencies are in analytic or mathematical areas). Indeed, service-related inclinations and competencies, like other inclinations and competencies, appear to be relatively stable individual attributes. The dramatic, stable effects of collective employee attributes have some depressing potential consequences for those interested in effecting organizational change. It suggests that some organizations may find it extremely difficult, if not impossible, to create a (service) climate without radically changing the composition of their work force.

3. The best predictor of future behavior is past behavior—this principle argues for the selection of people based on information about, and optimally observation of, behaviors essential to the provision of quality service.

These are the fundamental premises that have led to emphasis on the role of selection in achieving organizational effectiveness (Schneider 1987b; Schneider and Schmitt 1986). Selection is *not* the only crucial issue for organizational effectiveness. However, when an organization makes initial staffing decisions that yield people with the appropriate competencies and service inclinations, the goal of service excellence will be more easily achieved. People are likely to learn more quickly and effectively, to function more on their own (important in consumer service facilities because of the interactive "real-time" nature of service production and service delivery), to stay longer in the service position, and to contribute to the kind of climate important for service excellence (Schneider and Bowen 1985).

Designing a Service-Oriented Selection Process

Six steps comprise the design of any selection process:

1. Task analysis—identifying the specific tasks accomplished by job incumbents.

2. Personal attributes analysis—identifying the inclinations and competencies required to do and enjoy the tasks *and* identify which must be present when the person is hired (as compared with those for which people can be trained).

3. Selection system design strategy—selecting existing and/or building new selection procedures to assess the inclinations and competencies required on day one of the new hire's tenure. The eventual procedures are chosen based on their anticipated contribution to the achievement of the selection program's objectives.

Optimally, multiple procedures relevant to each objective are included to increase the reliability of the selection process. Where this is the case, a multiple hurdle approach in which early stages screen out the candidates with the least potential for success is often effective.

Legally and practically, the selection procedures chosen or built must focus heavily on the most important skills and inclinations—the ones shown in the job analysis to be critical for job performance.

4. Train people to use the selection processes and pilot them—this step provides for uniformity in administration of each selection procedure (e.g., interview or job simulation). It also is an opportunity to assess the logistical feasibility of the procedures.

5. Assess systems logistics and political feasibility—this should occur throughout the development of the selection process, for a new selection process is, in fact, a major organizational intervention. This assessment involves the consideration of any practical implementation constraints, including politically sensitive areas that may need high levels of internal support before implementation. Examples might include a legal department's obvious concern over the use of paper and pencil tests, employee fears that job analysis is really designed to eliminate jobs, identification of those who will monitor and manage the selection process, or geographical dispersion of the units for which hiring decisions need to be made.

6. Make the system operational and begin tracking results—this step is called validation and evaluates how well the selection system performs against important criteria of effectiveness. In the present case these criteria include effective job performance and retention on the job for at least one year. The logic for job performance is straightforward but an explanation of retention as an important issue may be useful.

Research (Schneider and Bowen 1985) suggests that organizations in which employee turnover is low are also organizations in which customers report they receive superior service. In fact, Schneider and Bowen demonstrated that where employee turnover intentions are high *customer* account retention intentions are low. It is extremely important for service organizations to have relatively low turnover rates, especially when compared to potential competitors.

A brief overview of each of these steps for a telephone sales and service job follows. The job is typically filled by young people or returning home-makers who possess few marketable skills (e. g., computer programming) or knowledge (e. g., legal or accounting knowledge).

Task Analysis

The following steps isolate task components of jobs:

1. Choose random samples of incumbents in groups of four to six people and hold a meeting to discuss (1) the goals of the job and (2) the tasks that need to be accomplished for the goals to be met. Incumbents are used based on a finding by job analysts that if one wants to know what gets done on a job, the people who do it should be asked. Several first-line supervisory groups are also interviewed to provide a broader view of the important goals and tasks.

2. Observe the work being done to gather any tasks that may have been missed and to gain increased understanding of the job and job context.

3. Prepare a task survey for all incumbents to complete. This will be used to gather quantitative job information; incumbents report on the criticality/importance of each task and the relative amount of time they spend at each task.

Table 15–1 shows excerpts of some specific tasks included in the survey. The tasks listed in table 15–1 were the twenty most critical tasks as rated by job incumbents. Those twenty tasks were statistically analyzed to reveal their underlying dimensions. This statistical procedure, technically called principal components factor analysis, yielded the four factors identified in Table 15–1.

These factors are called Attention to Detail (Detail), Sensitivity, Informing Customers (Informs), and Courtesy. These same twenty task statements were used in the present study as the basis for the measure of effectiveness. Thus, supervisors were asked, approximately one year after the new employees were hired, to complete the appraisal of how effectively the newcomers were performing these twenty critical tasks. Obviously, the challenge for the selection procedure is to predict these ratings (and retention, as mentioned earlier).

Personal Attributes Analysis

The compiled task analysis results are used as input to help discover the kinds of personal attributes the job requires. The following steps are taken to identify these attributes:

Table 15–1
Critical Tasks for the Job Identified in the Task Analysis

Task	I	II	III	IV
		Factor		
1. Guides customer through questions.	.39	.36	.58	.33
2. Compiles information to prepare cost quotations.	.66*	.25	.45	.22
3. Determines present situation.	.49	.39	.56	.24
4. Obtains supervisor authorization.	.68	.27	−.06	.44
5. Uses appropriate sources for cost quotes.	.74*	.30	.28	.09
6. Explains contract to applicant.	.30	.48	.60	.29
7. Identifies customers' needs.	.35	.67*	.39	.28
8. Solves service problems.	.38	.77*	.25	.22
9. Calms distressed callers.	.31	.81*	.27	.16
10. Completes documents while on phone.	.71*	.25	.26	.12
11. Adjusts language to customer.	.29	.67*	.30	.35
12. Gives own name and thanks customer.	.18	.30	.23	.82*
13. Uses customers' name.	.10	.23	.36	.80*
14. Gives complete information.	.52	.36	.50	.30
15. Reviews own paperwork.	.69*	.15	.38	.07
16. Explains contract and assists customer.	.32	.29	.72*	.19
17. Informs customers to check and complete application in mail.	.34	.22	.62*	.37
18. Establishes customer rapport.	.24	.61	.42	.41
19. Answers customer questions.	.30	.42	.68*	.22
20. Reviews memos on changes and updates.	.70*	.31	.32	.08

NOTE: Factor I = Detail; Factor II = Sensitivity; Factor III = Informs; Factor IV = Courtesy. Factor loadings with an asterisk (*) were scored as that factor in later analyses as the performance data. Sample size for this analysis was $N = 531$.

1. In group meetings (ranging in size from six to twelve participants), supervisors and managers are asked to review the important job tasks and report the kinds of attributes incumbents must have to do these tasks.

2. An inventory of the attributes emerging from these sessions is created and supervisors make a series of ratings for each. These ratings include:

- the importance of possessing each attribute for effective job performance

- the degree to which possession of the competency is required the first day on the job

- how difficult it is to acquire the competency if it is not present the first day on the job

These ratings, in combination, provide the data required to identify which attributes need to be focused on at selection—versus those more efficiently or effectively gained through training, for example.

Table 15–2 presents examples of some categories of the important competencies identified as being necessary for effective task performance.

Although only competencies are listed in table 15–2, in actuality the measurement of work-related inclinations follows closely from the critical skills identified and used on the job. Thus, in the service selection research, the authors operationally define service inclination as interest in carrying out activities using the skills and abilities required by the tasks of the job. More detail about how these inclinations and competencies are assessed is provided in the next section.

Choosing and Designing Procedures

The choice and design of selection procedures is where the selection researcher really gets to assess his or her skills as a psychologist, playwright, and director! The challenge is to choose and/or create a series of procedures that permit an assessment of the degree to which job candidates possess the attributes required by the job. The procedures must not only assess the attributes identified, but must also be such that some group or groups in the organization (e. g., supervisors or managers) can be trained to adminis-

Table 15–2
Examples of Competencies Required for a Sales and Service Job

1. *Persuasion*—Ability to influence the opinions and actions of others through skillful use of information

2. *Comprehension and memory*—Ability to understand the written and spoken language of others; skilled at listening; ability to learn, understand, and remember large amounts of facts, rules and procedures, and codes.

3. *Reasoning*—Ability to apply learned rules and procedures, use judgment, combine pieces of information, and make decisions.

4. *Social sensitivity*—Ability to act enthusiastically in interpersonal situations. Involves skillful adjusting of behavior to fit demands of a call and requires figuring out how others are likely to act or react. Involves the skillful use of control and assertion.

5. *Understandability*—Ability to express oneself through written and/or spoken language so that others will understand.

6. *Clerical speed and accuracy*—Ability to quickly and accurately look up, write down, and/or key in facts, codes, data, numbers, and so forth that are heard, looked up, or already in memory.

7. *Dealing with pressure*—Ability to act and react without losing effectiveness given the very strong requirements on rapid, efficient, and courteous sales and service.

ter the procedures. Also, the total selection process should appear to candidates to be relevant for the job.

Fortunately, all of these considerations are served when selection procedures are chosen that mirror the important characteristics of the job. Thus, interactive selection procedures are most appropriate for positions in which effectiveness is heavily dependent on interaction with others. Aptitude testing is appropriate when the job requires the ability to learn highly technical information and/or procedures related to the aptitude.

Perhaps the most useful way to demonstrate the process is to describe some of the procedures selected and designed for the sales and service job.

Basic Competencies

Basic reading and arithmetic competencies were assessed with two paper and pencil tests that matched the level of requirements in the job. This match was accomplished by careful review of numerous off-the-shelf tests for a fit to the job. In particular, the arithmetic test was such that applicants had to respond to verbal problems similar to those actually encountered on the job and requiring competency at arriving at solutions (as in Reasoning) and being able to pick up details (as in Clerical Speed and Accuracy).

Choosing tests like these is complicated by the fact that so many are available on the market. The authors required the tests to have demonstrated validity for similar jobs in similar circumstances and to be a significant predictor of performance on the job simulation designed. The latter requirement was established because the paper and pencil tests were to be used as a screening process to get to the more time-consuming interview and job-simulation procedures.

In fact, the two tests eventually chosen were two of five tests actually piloted; the two dropped were discarded based on evidence of weaker correlations with performance on the job simulation as well as appearing less job relevant for the context. An additional consideration in choosing the tests concerned adverse impact. Thus, the two tests that were dropped revealed more adverse impact against protected minority groups than the tests that were retained.

The Interview

The selection process was designed so that people who qualified on the paper and pencil tests then appeared for an interview. The interview process attempted to measure the level of an applicant's inclinations to do the kind of work offered in the kind of environment in which it exists. Although many companies employ interviews for the assessment of skills, the evidence indicates that skill assessment is problematic in an interview—

except for the assessment of verbal skills (Schneider and Schmitt 1986).

This interview process emphasizes assessment of the following issues:

1. To what extent has the applicant worked in or otherwise encountered (through school or hobbies) conditions and job activities similar to those connected with this job? To what extent has she or he enjoyed and/or felt comfortable with these kinds of activities?

Detailed probing into the applicant's work and educational history, as well as reactions to a realistic description of the current job and work setting, provides much of the evidence needed to assess the applicant's appropriateness for the position.

2. Often applicants for these kinds of service jobs are young and without much prior work history. Where no similar work experiences exist, the interview focuses more on candidate reactions to a realistic job preview (RJP) of the specific job and job environment (Wanous 1980) and to the interest inventory described next.

3. A basis for one part of the interview process is an interest inventory built around the attributes required for the job. This inventory requires applicants to indicate the degree of interest they have in using the kinds of skills required for effective performance of a particular task. High and low interest areas identified by the inventory are probed in the interview. The result of this probing is data on the job-related inclinations of applicant.[1]

The interview is a structured interview in that interviewers must obtain responses to specific questions even though they may not ask all of the questions. Interviewers take notes during the interview (the format of the interview leaves space for note-taking regarding each question), and then make a series of ratings at the end of the interview that helps them make the final decision on applicants. These rating items are built around the particular skills, tasks, and context issues found to be important for effective job performance.

Interviewers are trained (for two and one-half days) in interviewing skills, most of the time allotted to structured practice opportunities. This practice includes the use of real candidates who may have recently accepted job offers for the job in question. The interview takes approximately eighty minutes to administer (from scoring the interest inventory through making the ratings). The interview yields a rich picture of the applicant's prior work history, likes and dislikes, and inclinations vis à vis the skills and tasks required to do the job.

The Work Simulation

Because this procedure may be the newest to readers of the present chapter, a bit more detail about the process, including a brief history of the use of simulations in selection, is now presented.

The use of simulations for selection is quite old, but they were primarily used for hiring people for relatively simple physical tasks until the mid-1950s. At that time a major breakthrough in selection was demonstrated by psychologists at AT&T (Bray and Grant 1966). These psychologists built on procedures developed by the British and the Germans for selecting spies during World War II and applied them to the selection of managers in the work setting. They showed that performance by applicants for manager jobs on a three-day series of exercises revealed considerable accuracy in predicting their accomplishments (promotion and salary level relative to their peers) up to eight years after hiring.

In the United States in particular, but now throughout the world, the use of what have come to be called assessment centers for the selection of managers has become commonplace. More recently, industrial and organizational psychologists have been using a broader concept of job simulation for hiring workers in positions as diverse as clerical, sales, police, firefighters, high school principals, equipment repair persons, and so on (Schneider and Schmitt 1986).

Simulation means something special. A simulation is a series of exercises that parallel the demands of a job and thus assess the skills and competencies needed to do a job without requiring the candidate to have the knowledge required by the job. The latter point is important because at the time of selection, candidates for many jobs do not have the knowledge required to do them. Simulations must then be designed to capture skills and competencies in the raw. Industrial and organizational pychologists speak of the necessity to capture the psychological fidelity of the job rather than duplicating the job's physical characteristics or capturing its physical fidelity. Essentially, the goal is to create simulated situations that are psychologically close enough to the real job situation to cause the candidate to duplicate the mental processes and behavior she or he would display on the job. Then the effectiveness of those behaviors can be assessed.

Some feel for the simulation may be gained from a brief description of the instructions and exercises built to assess the attributes required for effective job performance. For each exercise, the competencies most tapped by the exercise are highlighted.

Candidates learn what they are supposed to do in different situations by reading and studying an instruction manual describing rules and guidelines for their job. The manual is written in language at the same level of complexity as materials used on the job and in training; time for reading the manual is precisely monitored and controlled by the assessors. Because the job is a telephone sales and service job, the simulation is administered entirely by telephone.

Exercise one for the simulation is a simple sales call in which the candidate must persuade callers to purchase more than they initially ask for (persuasion) and to accurately complete a series of forms summarizing the sale (clerical speed and accuracy).

Exercise two is a person who is unqualified, uncooperative, and eventually abusive calling to make a purchase. This call offers a number of opportunities to assess how sensitive the candidate can be (social sensitivity) as well as how he or she can handle interpersonal pressure (*dealing with pressure*). In addition, because paperwork is completed for this call, an additional assessment of *clerical speed and accuracy* is possible.

Exercise three is a service call and requires the candidate to resolve a dispute over a late payment fee. The caller is an established customer who moved and received his or her statement late, eventually causing a bill for a late payment fee. The customer argues it was not his or her fault, and the candidate needs to handle the issue. One part of the exercise requires the candidate to write a memo to his/her supervisor about the incident.

Obviously, this exercise has many components that can be assessed: *understandability* of the memo and the telephone conversation, *comprehension and memory* regarding the candidate's ability to understand the problem and his or her memory for what the manual says about these kinds of problems, *sensitivity* to the caller's problem and ability to reason out a useful solution for both the caller and the company.

Table 15–3 shows the checklists used by the assessor to identify the effective behaviors of the candidate in response to the problems confronted in exercise three. As shown in Table 15–3, a paperwork checklist is used to evaluate the memo to the supervisor, and a series of checklist items rates how the call is handled.

Note that the particular competency being assessed is identified next to the item. This is done so that at the end of the exercises a simple sum of the candidate performance on each dimension can be obtained. These totals are, in turn, compared with the total possible scores as a basis for judging the candidate's overall level of competence. It should also be noted that space is left for notes next to the checklist item. This allows for raters to note issues not covered by the checklist. The rule here is that no matter how comprehensive the attempt, all issues are never included.

The point of this description is that the assessment of candidates through this simulation procedure is based on the observation of behavior psychologically similar to the competencies required on the actual sales/ service job. People are playing out roles like those required by incumbents, and they are confronting situations requiring responses that have psychological fidelity to the job.

Furthermore, candidates are not just casually observed; they are observed for the display of quite specific competencies enumerated in behavior checklists for each exercise. Unlike an interview where only words are available, or paper and pencil tests that only require marking an answer

Table 15-3
Sample Behavior Checklists—Exercise Three

Paperwork Checklist			*Notes*
CompMem	(	)	Candidate completes exception form.
Persuas	(	)	Candidate indicates to supervisor that exception should be granted to maintain customer good will.
CompMem	(	)	Memo written by candidate reflects a correct understanding of the customer's particular circumstances.
UnderStand	(	)	Memo written by candidate is understandable and free from distracting grammatical or spelling errors. (Note: Minor errors that don't cloud the meaning are not distracting.)

Telephone Contact Checklist			
SocialSensi	(	)	Candidate answers call politely.
Reason	(	)	Candidate recognizes that this is a billing-related service call and responds appropriately.
UnderStand	(	)	Candidate explains clearly that a late payment penalty is due when the fee is not received (rather than mailed) by the due date.
CompMem	(	)	Candidate correctly indicates the amount of the penalty (i.e., 1/3 of 1% for each day late).
Reason	(	)	Candidate indicates that an exception may be made no later in the call than immediately after the point when the caller indicates that the company does have his or her new address.
Reason	(	)	Regardless of when he or she does so, candidate indicates that an exception to the policy may be called for.
SocialSensi	(	)	Candidate indicates understanding of the caller's situation without criticizing the late payment policy.

sheet, simulations permit the development of realistic scenarios that require the display of job-relevant competencies. This behavioral orientation reduces the possibility of bias and hunch as a basis for decisions and enhances the probability that decisions will be based on what candidates can actually do (Latham and Wexley 1981).

Training and Piloting the Process

Supervisors and managers of the job in question are trained to conduct the interviews and to administer the simulation. In the latter case, this includes playing the roles required, as well as completing all checklists and arriving at a pass-fail decision.

It was decided that supervisors and managers should play an active role in the selection process based on the idea that full participation in the choice of new employees breeds commitment to ensuring the success of those employees. In many selection situations supervisors are not involved in the selection of their own subordinates, yielding, perhaps, less commitment to the people hired.

The training program lasts four and one-half days and consists of the following steps:

1. An introduction to the task and attribution analysis results combined with the reasons for the particular selection strategy and system design.
2. A walk through the exercises (or interview) and rating systems followed by a series of paper candidates the trainees must rate.
3. Monitored practice with one another.
4. The final and longest stage of training is to work with real candidates.

Steps 2, 3, and 4 are conducted for both the interview and the simulation.

This brief description of the training illustrates that it is extensive, intensive, and focused on both efficiency and accuracy. Interviewers must be able to ask the appropriate questions and follow-up probes in order to gather all the relevant information and learn to use that information to rate the candidates' inclinations to stick with the job. Assessors must be thoroughly familiar with the exercises for them to flow smoothly and for the candidate to have a full chance to demonstrate his or her competencies. They must also become familiar with and proficient at using the checklist rating systems if valid ratings are to be an outcome of the simulation process. At the end of training, two assessors can process one candidate per hour through the entire simulation, including the ratings and a final decision.

Logistical and Political Feasibility

While all the technical issues are moving forward, several political and logistical issues must be monitored and attended to. For example, how well will the personnel department accept the new procedures, who will monitor the actual day-to-day use of the process, who will be trained to use the process, will new staff be required because of the procedures? In addition, considerations (as noted later) of the consequences of a selection procedure need to be identified. For example, in the present project, new training procedures as well as new procedures for training the *supervisors* of the new people were necessary as a result of the implementation of the selection program described.

230 • *Service Quality*

Validation

Selection researchers are gluttons for punishment; they attempt to evaluate the effectiveness of the procedures they introduce. As noted in the introduction to the chapter, the purpose of the present effort was to facilitate, through employee selection, increased levels of performance and retention. Performance was operationalized by supervisors' ratings of new employees with respect to effectiveness in carrying out the twenty tasks shown in table 15–1. As noted earlier, these twenty tasks were rated as the most important tasks in the task analysis inventory.

Retention was operationalized as the requirement to be employed one year after hiring. This period of time was chosen as reasonable by the organization given the level of the job and the investments it made in recruiting, hiring, and training. It is also a fairly typical retention criterion in selection research for a job at this level (Schneider and Schmitt 1986).

A problem in assessing the effectiveness of selection procedures is that the selection procedures themselves are frequently used to make selection decisions, as was true in the present case. This produces what is called the restriction of range problem (Aitken 1934; Alliger and Alexander 1984). Restriction of range is a problem because any correlations calculated between selection data and performance contains only a portion of the information for both the predictors and the criteria; the information missing is the information for the people *not* hired.

Fortunately, some techniques have been developed for correcting for restriction of range. These techniques take into account existing information on the predictors for those (hired versus not hired), the performance of those hired and the observed relationships among the predictors, and job performance to make a statistically educated guess about the relationship without any range restriction. The correction has been shown to be inherently conservative (Linn, Harnisch, and Dunbar, 1981), so the results to be presented can be accepted as reliable.

A second issue in conducting selection validation is that the effectiveness of people hired can be measured only within an organizational context that affects the display of individual competencies and inclinations. Thus, actual success in selection is always something less than 100 percent accurate in predicting employee effectiveness or employee retention. In effect, personnel selection provides only the raw material for effectiveness, not the finished product. By analogy, auto manufacturers do not evaluate the utility of their steel acquisition procedures by how well the car that is produced sells or how well it runs; the steel is the raw material but everything else that happens to the steel also determines the eventual product. It is the selection process that should provide the raw human resources who possess the potential to be effective and stay on the job. It is the organizational context that constrains or facilitates the development of this potential.

The multiple correlations, R, (corrected for range restriction) of the selection system against the four performance criteria were:

- Detail $R = .07$
- Sensitivity $R = .17$
- Informs $R = .19$
- Courtesy $R = .12$

These relationships are modest and may be interpreted as indicating that, with respect to Informs, for example, the selection system is accounting for 19 percent of what a perfectly valid selection system would accomplish. A perfectly valid selection system here would be one that predicts with 100 percent accuracy each employee's ratings.

In predicting the retention of new hires for a minimum of one year, the selection system was more successful, yielding a multiple correlation, R (corrected for range restriction), of .30.

Internal analyses of the various components of the selection system revealed that the paper and pencil tests contributed more to the prediction of retention than did the job simulation, with the interview contributing an intermediate amount. This may be due to the fact that the paper and pencil tests were selected specifically because they correlated with the simulation, yielding a somewhat duplicate measurement. The interview, however, was not significantly correlated with either the paper and pencil tests or the simulation, permitting it to account for a proportion of variance in retention unaccounted for by the tests or the simulation. For this particular effort, the interview was also the strongest correlate of the various performance criteria. This is an unusual finding in that performance is usually more effectively predicted by competency assessments than by interviews. It may be that for service jobs like the one studied here, so much of the job involves interpersonal issues that interviewers are picking up enough information to make a somewhat accurate prediction. This issue requires attention in subsequent efforts.

It may be informative to note some of the other positive organizational consequences that the implementation of this selection system has triggered (Schneider, 1990). First, the trainers of the newly hired employees noted how much quicker the new hires caught on to the training. Subsequently, the training has been redesigned and made more efficient as a result of the improved competencies of the new hires. The task analysis information provided the foundation for the training redesign effort. Second, the service focus of the new employees has highlighted some of the weaknesses of the supervisory staff. This has caused the supervisors of the job in question to undergo training in an attempt to increase their competencies and service focus to keep pace with the competencies and needs of this somewhat different employee.

Finally, to take advantage of the increased competencies and tenure of the new job incumbents, the organization has designed ways for employees to stick with this job without suffering financially. Thus, in the past, the best job incumbents would post out of this job to obtain a raise; now the job has been given additional steps and incentives so that employee effectiveness can be capitalized on by retaining the best performers. Together, and over time, these systems side effects are profoundly impacting the climate for service of the organization (Schneider, 1990).

A result of this stream of changes has been a significant decrease in turnover. So even though the selection system only accounted for a portion of the prediction of turnover, turnover has, in fact, been cut by nearly one-third as the result of the *stream* of efforts instituted. These data support the raw materials metaphor presented earlier and emphasize the fact that personnel selection alone cannot be expected to achieve dramatic results; it often takes a system of organizational efforts to produce the desired performance and retention.

Conclusion

This chapter outlines the logic and procedures underlying a system for selecting employees with service inclinations and competencies who will remain on the job. The different phases used to do this have been presented. These have included some examples of how jobs, inclinations, and competencies are described so that procedures can be built that have psychological fidelity to the actual job.

The purpose was to clarify for a services marketing and service management audience some of the conceptual and practical realities of actually doing something about selecting service workers. Prior to concluding this description, however, it is important to comment on the time and money the company invested in the design of the system.

The costs to the company for designing the simulation included:

- hiring a consulting firm to carry out the task and competency analyses and to design the system.
- partial salaries for the three company persons who worked closely with the consulting firm to facilitate access to the various persons required to carry out the different phases.
- expenses involved in traveling around the United States to train supervisors and managers to use the simulation process; salaries and lost productivity for the supervisors and managers while in training.

Why would a company invest so much money in enhancing its selection system? Because organizations can be no more effective than the people in them. In other words, this company made the decision to build its service climate from the ground up based on the hypothesis that the people who interact with the customer are critical for service effectiveness. Of course, excellent evidence in the literature now shows the quite dramatic payoffs companies of all kinds can obtain from investments in selection systems (Hunter and Schmidt 1982).

This particular company had an extremely broad definition of service effectiveness. Its definition was that everything had to be done correctly, that the goal of the company was to make it easy for customers to conduct business, and that it required more than a smile to be effective. The company became convinced that an essentially one-time, up-front, commitment of resources would yield an acceptable return on investment within less than two years and that profits would grow as a function of the improved competencies of the people controlling the service encounter.

One of the critical support features necessary for the success of the intervention described was an organizational focus on longer term gains. The organization knew that changes in an organization through selection is a slow process because new people are added to veterans slowly. Thus, the effectiveness of a selection intervention may be felt only after a significant portion of the incumbents in a job have been hired through that process. Perhaps it is when the newcomers hired through the new process become old-timers that the effects are fully realized.

Indeed, subsequent to the implementation of the service simulation described here, the company has developed four more selection systems for other jobs and designed a simulation to provide data for the promotion of the supervisors of the employees in the sales/service job. This information is presented to show how an organization can promote a service climate through more than words spouting how important service is. This organization is literally putting its money where its mouth is by investing in the people who are the conveyers of that climate to the customer world.

Two messages channel through. First, delivering excellent service is as difficult as any business task can be because it requires appropriately directed compulsive attention to so many details, and this requires people with appropriate inclinations and competencies. Second, there *is* something companies can do about service excellence besides talk about it but, like service itself, the something that can be done requires compulsive attention to the details—like personnel selection.

Notes

1. The first version of the interest inventory used in this project actually asked people to report on their skills. However, this version was subsequently changed to

interests. We are unable to tease apart the impact of the different forms for the present project but we are working on this for a future effort. Our opinion is that the appropriate issue for the interview is interests (inclinations).

References

Albrecht, K., and R. Zemke. (1985). *Service America: Doing Business in the New Economy.* Homewood, IL: Dow-Jones Irwin.

Alliger, G. M. and R. A. Alexander. (1984). "Correcting for Multivariate Range Restriction: Two Computer Programs." *Educational and Psychological Measurement*, Vol. 44, 677-678.

Bass, B. M. (1982). "Individual Capability, Team Performance, and Team Productivity. " In M. D. Dunnette and E. A. Fleishman (eds.), *Human Performance and Productivity: Human Capability Assessment.* Hillsdale, NJ: Erlbaum.

Berry, L. L., A. Parasuraman, and V. A. Zeithaml. (1988). "The Service-Quality Puzzle." *Business Horizons*, Sept–Oct., 35–43.

Bray, D. W., and D. L. Grant. (1966). "The Assessment Center in the Measurement of Potential for Business Management."*Psychological Monographs*, 80, Whole No. 625.

Bowen, D. E., and B. Schneider. (1988). "Services Marketing and Management: Implications for Organizational Behavior." In B. M. Staw and L. L. Cummings (eds.), *Rearch in Organizational Behavior* (Vol. 10). Greenwich, CT: JAI Press.

Czepiel, J. A., M. R. Solomon and C. Suprenant. (eds.). (1985). *The Service Encounter.* Lexington, MA: Lexington Books.

Goldstein, I.L. (1986). *Training in Organizations: Needs Assessment, Development, and Evaluation.* (2nd Ed.) Monterey, CA: Brooks/Cole.

Goldstein, I. L., and M. J. Gessner. (1988). "Training and Development in Work Organizations." In C. L. Cooper and I. Robertson (eds.), *International Review of Industrial and Organizational Psychology.* London: Wiley.

Hogan, J., R. Hogan, and C. M. Busch. (1984). "How to Measure Service Orientation." *Journal of Applied Psychology*, 69, 167—73.

Hunter, J. E., and F. L. Schmidt. (1982). "Fitting People to Jobs: The Impact of Personal Selection on National Productivity." In M. D. Dunnette and E. A. Fleishman (eds.), *Human Performance and Productivity: Human Capability Assessment.* Hillsdale, NJ: Erlbaum.

Kerr, S. (1988). "Some Characteristics and Consequences of Organizational Reward." In F. D. Schoorman and B. Schneider (eds.), *Facilitating Work Effectiveness.* Lexington, MA: Lexington Books.

Linn, R. L., D. Harnisch and S. B. Dunbar. (1981). "Corrections for Range Restriction: An Empirical Investigation of Conditions Resulting in Conservative Corrections." *Journal of Applied Psychology*, Vol. 66, 655–663.

Lovelock, C. H. (ed.). (1988). *Managing Services: Marketing, Operations, and Human Resources.* Englewood Cliffs, NJ: Prentice-Hall.

Normann, R. (1984). *Service Management: Strategy and Leadership in Service Business.* New York: Wiley.

Parasuraman, A., V. A. Zeithaml, and L. L. Berry. (1985). "A Conceptual Model of Service Quality and Its Implications for Future Research." *Journal of Marketing*, 49, 41–50.

Parasuraman, A., V. A. Zeithaml, and L. L. Berry. (1986). *Servqual: A Multiple-Item Scale for Measuring Consumer Perceptions of Service Quality.* Cambridge MA: Marketing Science Institute.

Schein, E. A. (1985). *Organizational Culture and Leadership.* San Francisco: Jossey-Bass.

Scheider, B. (1986). "Notes on Climate and Culture." In C. Marshall, D. Schmalansee, and V. Venatesan (eds.), *Creativity in Service Marketing.* Chicago: American Marketing Association.

―――. (1987a). "Imperatives for the Design of Service Organizations." In C. Suprenant (ed.), *Add Value to Your Service.* Chicago: American Marketing Association.

―――. (1987b). "The People Make the Place." *Personnel Psychology,* 40, 437–53.

―――. (1990). Alternative Strategies for Creating Service-Oriented Organizations." In D. Bowen and T. Cummings (eds.), *Service Management Effectiveness.* San Francisco: Jossey-Bass.

Schneider, B., and D. E. Bowen. (1985). "Employee and Customer Perceptions of Service in Banks: Replication and Extension." *Journal of Applied Psychology,* 70, 423–33.

Schneider, B., and N. Schmitt. (1986). *Staffing Organizations.* 2d ed. Glenview, IL: Scott, Foresman.

Wanous, J. P. (1980). *Organizational Entry.* Reading MA: Addison-Wesley.

16
An Evolution of Research on Professional Service Quality

Teresa A. Swartz
Stephen W. Brown

Professional services represent a huge sector of the economy that is newly awakening to client challenges, competition, and many of the realities of the business world. Long-standing canons of professional ethics are being challenged as professionals like attorneys and physicians overtly and sometimes even aggressively pursue new clients. Even existing clients are noticing changes, such as increased sensitivity to their needs and new innovations (e.g., client newsletters, evening and weekend availability). As competition intensifies, client sensitivity increases, and professional malpractice suits become more frequent, a greater need for understanding the professional service encounter has emerged.

An insight into the socialization process associated with professional-client interactions is important to understanding the nature of professional service encounters. An individual's socialization relative to professionals begins at an early age and is likely to start with a visit to a physician or dentist. From these early encounters and throughout one's life, many people tend to place professionals on a pedestal. Because of the professional's years of training, special expertise, and an often favorable demand-supply situation, most clients (especially at the consumer level) have a tendency to perceive professionals high in both the social and competence hierarchies.

Because of distinctions such as those previously noted, one can appropriately argue that professional service encounters are somewhat different from their counterparts in other sectors of the service economy. As a result, the professional-client relationship offers a somewhat unique service experience that may require special evaluation considerations.

Many individuals, along with the First Interstate Center for Services Marketing at Arizona State University, have contributed to the stream of research highlighted in this chapter. We wish to acknowledge the contributions of A. Parasuraman, Texas A & M University; Bruce Walker, University of Missouri; Goutam Challagalla, University of Texas at Austin; and Larry Crosby, Michael Hutt, Michael Mokwa, and Nancy Stephens, all of Arizona State University, Tempe.

Assessing quality, whether for goods or services, has never been easy. In a professional setting, the assessment of service quality is even more difficult and complex. Generally, the clients of professionals do not have the luxury of going to a retail outlet to examine various "brands" before selecting a professional to provide services. Even if such an option were available, many consumers would find it difficult to compare the quality of one professional's services with that of others. Consider, for example, how difficult it is for the consumer to compare one lawyer's ability and skill with another's. Because a major part of what the client is buying is the expertise and knowledge she or he lacks, the evaluation of service quality is difficult indeed.

Even though difficult, clients *will* and *do* evaluate professional service quality. Although it is known that an evaluation happens, what is lacking is a clear understanding of how this assessment occurs and the importance of various components of the service encounter to the analysis.

Despite professional services' uniquenesses and importance, little scholarly work has focused on evaluating this type of service encounter and on professional service quality. Most of the work done in professional services is general and descriptive in nature (Bloom 1984; Kotler and Bloom 1984; Brown, Morley, Bronkesh, and Wood 1989; Brown and Morley 1986; Gummesson 1978, 1981; Quelch and Ash 1981; and Stiff and Gleason 1981). Some of the more current writing has featured the identification of marketing challenges facing professionals and the appropriate strategies for dealing with these challenges. One key challenge identified for professionals is buyer uncertainty, including the difficulties associated with the selection and evaluation of professional services (Bloom 1984). Related to this evaluation is the concept of service quality, its perception, determinants, and measurement (Lehtinen and Lehtinen 1982; Lehtinen 1983: Berry, Zeithaml, and Parasuraman 1985; Parasuraman, Zeithaml, and Berry 1985).

This chapter reports on a stream of professional services research that the authors conducted during the 1980s. A unique feature of this research is its focus on the evaluation of service quality and satisfaction for the perspectives of *both* the client and the provider.

The first study focused on a specific professional service problem, namely consumer medical complaint behavior. Using consumer dissatisfaction and complaint behavior literature as a base, various aspects of the medical malpractice problem were examined from the perspectives of both consumers and physicians. Discriminants of medical complaint behavior, expressed through malpractice suit inclinations, were isolated, and various alternatives to litigation were proposed.

Although the first study was in part stimulated by interest in medical complaint behavior, the data from that study also contributed to a second and broader article on consumer and provider expectations and experiences associated with professional service quality. Quality and the service encounter were viewed from both the provider and client perspective.

The third study represented an extension of the prior research in terms of instrument design and the fact that the participating consumers and providers had actual professional-client relationships. Using a modified "gap analysis," physicians and their patients' perceptions of service quality were measured.

Each of the three studies is summarized in the following sections. After this review, future research opportunities are presented.

Consumer Medical Complaint Behavior Study

A major stimulus that helped initiate work in professional service quality was the medical malpractice problem in the United States. The number of medical malpractice suits, the size of settlements, and the legal fees associated with these suits are matters of concern to insurance companies, attorneys, physicians, government leaders, and the public as a whole. Also intertwined with this elaborate medical-legal-insurance process is the actual physical and mental suffering of patients and their families, along with the medical professionals caring for them.

In the initial research, dissatisfaction and complaint behavior constructs were used to provide valuable insights into the medical complaint process, and viable alternatives to litigation were then examined. Dissatisfaction is based on the discrepancy between one's expectations and the outcomes (i.e., a dissatisfied consumer does not have his or her expectations met on consumption of the good or service). Many dissatisfied customers of professional services often refrain from taking any action because of a feeling of helplessness. This feeling results from the nature of the service provider (his or her expertise and competence) and the perception that oftentimes dissatisfaction cannot be corrected because no tangible product is involved. Nevertheless, research suggests that consumers are more likely to take action when *severely* dissatisfied with services than when discontented with goods. Furthermore, the intensity of the complaint is likely to be greater because of the high level of dissatisfaction.

In the medical arena, the outcome of services often extends beyond the individual directly involved to include the patient's family and friends. Because of these features and the intimacy and high level of involvement often found in the medical exchange process, extraordinary possibilities exist for extremely high satisfaction or dissatisfaction to occur.

When dissatisfaction occurs consumers may take public or private action. Public action includes seeking redress directly from the professional, taking legal action, or complaining to business, private, or government agencies. Private actions are usually confined to stopping purchase/payment or warning friends about the service.

It should be noted that dissatisfaction alone is often insufficient to result in action. The three categories of factors that also influence complaints are marketing channels factors, situational factors, and consumer variables. Consumer variables are the focus of this chapter because they appeared to offer the greatest initial insight into medical complaint behavior, while at the same time providing opportunity to explore potential alternatives to malpractice litigation.

Methods

Consumer variables associated with medical complaint behavior include health care/service usage experiences, sociodemographic factors, interpersonal influences, internal characteristics (e.g., perceived risk, assertiveness, life satisfaction), and consumer attitudes toward the profession. Two surveys, one sampling consumers and the other physicians, were administered to measure attitudes and behavior toward health care, physicians, medical malpractice, and alternatives to malpractice litigation.

A random consumer sample of 993 usable respondents represented a cross-section of a Western state's population, with all adult age groups, family sizes, income levels, and geographic areas included. The consumer questionnaire measured physician usage information, opinions on general statements concerning health care, physicians, medical malpractice suits *and* their causes, as well as possible solutions.

Two scenarios were also presented to respondents, who were asked to indicate how likely they would be to initiate legal action in each situation. The first scenario involved the respondent, his or her own physician, and a medical problem in which the respondent believed that the physician might be at fault. The second scenario involved the death of the respondent's spouse or parent. In this case the respondent believed that the spouse or parent's physician might be at fault.

Completed questionnaires were received from 576 physicians selected randomly from the membership roster of the state's medical association. The questionnaire measured physicians' views on various consumer complaint alternatives to medical malpractice litigation.

From the consumers' sample, two major groups emerged. One group represented those who were likely to sue for malpractice when dissatisfaction occurs, and the other group represented those who were unlikely to sue when dissatisfied. Step-wise discriminant analysis was used to determine any differences between these two groups.

Results

The scenario results reveal that those individuals likely to sue were younger and more apt to believe that doctors were generally responsible in malpractice situations. Women were less likely to sue than men. Also, when considering the first scenario, respondents who are likely to sue felt that doctors charged too much, while respondents unlikely to sue were more neutral. When studying the second scenario results, two key factors emerged in segregating those likely to litigate from those not likely to do so: (1) patient-physician communications and (2) the possibility of having physicians spend more time explaining potential problems associated with treatment. Those likely to sue believed that physicians tend to do a poor job explaining health problems and wished they had more or better information available. Thirty and 39 percent of the respondents said they were likely to sue when presented with the first and second scenarios respectively.

In an effort to identify viable alternatives to litigation consumers and physicians were presented with five possible solution or modifications to existing procedures:

1. an upper dollar limit on malpractice claims
2. improved communication between physician and patient
3. submitting medical disputes to arbitration
4. limiting the attorney's percentage of the financial settlement
5. submitting disputes to a panel of experts prior to going to court.

Support was exhibited for all the solutions proposed. This may be indicative of a desire by both consumers and physicians to consider alternatives to litigation. Furthermore, a majority of the respondents who indicated that they were likely to sue expressed support for each of these five potential solutions. These results may indicate that consumers sue due to lack of appropriate alternatives to litigation.

Discussion

The results suggest that one way to lessen both the likelihood of dissatisfaction with the service rendered and the potential for litigation is to improve both the quality and quantity of time spent in communicating with the patient and others involved in the situation. The more informed consumers are, the less likely they will form unrealistic expectations, often the cause for extreme dissatisfaction.

Malpractice or litigation prevention programs, paralleling product liability programs, could be designed to encourage extensive dialogue between the parties involved throughout the exchange process. The purpose of this dialogue would be to ensure that both the professional and the consumer have a clear understanding of what services are being purchased and the possible outcomes of these services.

Improved communications and information exchanges cannot eliminate lawsuits. Other complaint alternatives also need to be considered, along with various restrictions on claims. Five modifications received respondent support and should be studied further:

1. Upper financial limit for general, and even specific, medical damages could be established by state legislatures. (This proposal received mixed support from the respondents.)
2. Actual liability settlements could be extended over a greater number of years to lessen the immediacy and magnitude of an award's impact on insurance company expenses, malpractice insurance rates, and ultimately on the fees consumers absorb for physician services.
3. Legislation could more clearly address the existence of multiparty liability.
4. Imposing limits on attorney's contingency fees or percentages could help make the pursuit of these suits less attractive to these professionals.
5. A panel of expert and impartial physicians could review all disputes or claims before they go to court and/or act as an arbitrator between the contending parties.

A useful feature of this chapter is that the implications can be extended to other professional services (eg., dental, legal, accounting).

Consumer and Provider Expectations and Experiences Study

The database from the previously discussed research also provided insights to a broader study on professional service quality. Scholars and executives are increasingly recognizing the importance of quality in the success or failure of services.

Two factors that research in this area focuses on are (1) *what* the result of the services performed is (referred to as outcome, technical, or physical quality) and (2) *how* the service is performed (referred to as process, functional, or interactive quality). The evaluation of outcome quality occurs after service performance, and the assessment of process quality occurs during service performance. Both quality dimensions are situational in nature and are often assessed on a per incident basis. This quality evaluation results in degrees of one or two outcomes: satisfaction or dissatisfaction.

As previously mentioned, customers of services are unlikely to complain unless extremely dissatisfied with the service. As a result, service providers are generally unaware of "normal" consumer complaints, so the provider may be under the false impression that consumer needs are being satisfactorily met. This pseudosecurity is enhanced by the professional's perceptions of his or her own expertise and authority.

Research suggests that assessing the perceptions of *both* providers and clients/consumers enhances understanding of service quality. To gain insights into medical service quality, the perceptions of physicians and consumers/patients were studied regarding three areas relating to performance and thus affecting quality. The areas of professional competence, professional credibility, and communications were selected because of their direct impact on the consumer's evaluation of the service provider and ultimately the service encounter. An analysis was performed to identify discrepancies between providers' and consumers' perceptions of the three areas mentioned.

Methods

The same consumer and physician samples used in the first study were presented with a series of statements concerning physicians, health care, and the public's view of each. Respondents were asked to indicate their level of agreement or disagreement with each statement using a five-point scale ranging from "strongly agree" to "strongly disagree."

Up to four items were used to measure physicians' and consumers' perceptions relating to each of the areas of professional competence, professional credibility, and communications. An analysis of the items suggested construct validity. Bonferroni's t-tests were performed with significant differences observed between providers' and consumers' perceptions.

Results

Differences exist in how consumers actually view physicians and how providers/physicians *believe* they are perceived by the public. In general, physicians believe that the public has a lower opinion of them than actually exists. However, physicians attribute consumers with having a more active interest in health and health-care topics than the results indicate. Physicians also overestimated consumers' interest in and use of health-care information. These can have serious consequences because providers may neglect to educate/inform consumers assuming the patients are already well informed.

Comparisons between providers' perceptions of their profession and the providers' perceptions of consumers' beliefs resulted in discrepancies of one-half to one scale interval. Consumers' actual perceptions fell between providers' own perceptions of the service and the providers' *belief* of consumers' perceptions. The implication is that if providers develop and design their practice's marketing mix based on where *they* perceive their current and potential consumers to be, they will clearly miss the mark.

Discussion

Because consumer and provider perceptions differ, a closer examination of service quality evaluation is needed to identify ways in which perceived quality can be managed. For both parties, the assessment of quality seems to be a function of both expectations (X) and experiences (Ec). Furthermore, the individual's perception of his or her experiences is a result of the process (Ps) *and* outcome (Os) experienced. In addition, expectations (X) seem to result from an individual's past experience (Ep) and *also any* communications (C) he or she has received related to the professional service. Analytically,

$$Qp = f (X, Ec)$$
$$Ec = f (Ps, Os)$$
$$X = f (Ep, C)$$

where Qp is the perception of service quality.

The study reveals discrepancies between providers' and consumers' perceptions. Using those results and the aforementioned analytical statements, four major perceptual gaps were revealed:

Intra—Client Gap between:
• client expectations versus client experiences.

Gaps Between Client and Professional:
• client expectations versus provider perceptions of client expectations

• client experiences versus provider perceptions of client experiences

Intra—Provider Gap Between:
• provider expected service versus provider perceptions of client expectations.

In view of these findings, the following thesis has been formulated:

If client and professional provider perceptions differ because of greater consumer expectations and/or less favorable consumer interpretations of experiences (process and outcomes), then the probability of lower quality service ratings occurring is greater than when both groups' perceptions are identical.

Dyadic Evaluation of Professional Service Quality

Building directly on the previously discussed research, the third study addressed service quality and its evaluation by examining the perspectives of clients *and* the actual professionals with whom they have a relationship. To this point, no research had focused on this topic area using a dyadic approach. Such an approach enables a richer identification and analysis of the perceptual gaps that exist between the two parties.

This study benefited from the advances in gap analysis research by Parasuraman, Zeithaml, and Berry (1985). Their model, however, is too extensive for initial work in the professional services arena. A more basic framework that focuses on the two key parties, the professional and the client, of the service exchange is necessary. After all, professional perceptions affect the design and delivery of services offered, and clients' perceptions more directly determine evaluation of the services consumed. In addition, as previously identified, potential gaps that relate to service quality represent both sides of the service exchange (intraclient gaps and client-professional gaps).

Because this study represented the first of its kind, the focus was on only one service (medical) and specifically physician-patient encounters. Thirteen physicians agreed to participate in the study and allowed a sample of their patients to be contacted. All the physicians who participated are involved in primary care, specializing in the areas of internal medicine or family practice.

Methods

Patients received a mail questionnaire along with an individualized cover letter from their physicians requesting cooperation with the study. Of the 2,416 patients contacted, 1,128 responded and represented the final sample. Physicians received a questionnaire identical to their corresponding patients, except for some necessary changes in classification questions. In order to allow for a direct comparison between clients' perceptions and professionals' perceptions of their clients' views, the physicians were asked to respond to the items the way they believed their patients would respond.

Items on the questionnaire were generated by reviewing past research and consulting with medical professionals. Furthermore, the measures corresponded with the determinants of service quality proposed by Parasuraman, Zeithaml, and Berry (1985). Specifically, sixty-five statements related to aspects of the service encounter and one statement evaluated the overall experience.

Results

Three specific gaps were examined. Gap A represented the difference between a patient's expectations and experiences (intraclient gap). Gaps B and C related to differences between an individual patient and his or her physician, with B relating to expectations and C experiences (client-professional gaps). In other words, Gap B represented differences between a patient's expectation and his or her physician's perception. Gap C referred to the difference between a patient's experiences and his or her physician's perceptions of these experiences.

For each of the items measured, gap scores were computed by taking the above noted differences. These scores were then related back to an overall measure of satisfaction. The results indicated that items representing A and C directly related to the level of satisfaction reported. Clear support for a relationship between Gap B items and satisfaction was not evident. However, this lack of support may have been a function of the weakness of the Gap B measures as opposed to a true lack of relationship.

In addition, stepwise regression analysis was used to explore how individual gap measures corresponded in determining overall evaluation. Results from the final model revealed that the most significant independent regression variable was physician interactions, a Gap C variable. This suggests that the interactions with the primary service provider may be the most important in assessing professional service quality. However, it is important to note that factors from the other gaps are also in the model, supporting the multidimensionality concept of service evaluation. The entire service encounter affects the overall evaluation, not just the time spent with the primary professional provider.

Discussion

This research shows a significant relationship between perceptual gaps and the evaluation of professional services. Since customers are often reluctant to complain when negative service encounters occur, management must take a proactive approach in monitoring service quality. One approach to this is gap analysis.

Through gap analysis professionals can clearly identify when and where client expectations and experiences are inconsistent and likely to lead to dissatisfaction (Gap A). Areas where client expectations exceed the professional's perceptions of such expectations also need to be identified (Gap B) because they can affect design and delivery of the service.

Gaps occurring between client experiences and the professional's perceptions of such experiences (Gap C) can also affect the overall service evaluation. The magnitude and direction of the inconsistencies will determine customer reactions.

More consistent expectations and experience perceptions can be achieved by (1) altering service providers behaviors and expectations and (2) altering client expectations and experiences. The professional obviously has more control over his or her behaviors and perceptions. Two strategies they should consider are the following: (1) becoming more aware of factors consumers use to evaluate service quality and their professional provider, or (2) assuming a broader and more user-sensitive view in relating to clients.

On the other hand, strategies for altering clients' expectations and experiences include (1) providing candid educational and/or promotional communications, and (2) involving the client more in his or her own case or treatment. Although these strategies may seem basic for many marketers, for many professionals these ideas represent a new dimension of thinking.

Future Opportunities

Despite the progress that researchers have made, additional research is needed in the area of professional service quality. Data from these studies of one profession cannot provide conclusive results on medical services encounters, let alone all professional services. The research stream does provide, however, tests of the value of gap analysis and its applicability to professional services, and a foundation on which to build further research. As such, future research needs to be undertaken to answer some of the following questions:

1. How can professional service expectations and experiences be effectively measured? A weakness of studies to date is the lack of a one-to-one correspondence between expectation and experience measures. Measurement scales for each of these need to be developed and refined. Care must be taken, however, to ensure that the relevant evaluation factors are measured for each service investigated. These evaluation factors may vary significantly from professional service to professional service.

2. What is the impact of the various dimensions of service quality on the overall evaluation of service? Much of the previous service quality research has focused on identifying its various dimensions (e.g., Lehtinen and Lehtinen 1982; Grönroos 1983; Berry, Zeithaml, and Parasuraman 1985), yet empirical work assessing the impact of each dimension is lacking. By way of example, subquestions such as the following are worthy of investigation: Does process quality play a greater role than outcome quality in the overall professional service evaluation? How important is the image of the service provider in quality evaluation?

3. How do the multiple, interpersonal contacts with a number of individuals within both the provider and client organizations affect the service evaluation process? The focus of research to date is on the dyadic interaction between a single professional and a single client. Yet, often the client's time is spent interacting with support staff and/or multiple professionals. Furthermore, the professional practice may interact with a number of people within the client firm or household. With greater understanding of the basic professional-client interaction, research needs to explore the impact of the multiplicity of contacts on the service evaluation process.

4. How can additional dyadic work be encouraged in services marketing research? Additional interpersonal, provider-client research is needed in a variety of settings. Using this stream of research and other paradigms as frameworks, contributions are needed in other professional service settings, as well as in financial, telecommunications, transportation, and other service environments.

Conclusions

The overriding theme of the foregoing research is that the discrepancies between perceptions of expectations and experiences contribute to a degree of satisfaction or dissatisfaction among professional service clients. From a professional provider's perspective, the challenge is to manage these expectations and experiences, which ultimately lead to satisfaction or dissatisfaction.

The provider's task is to identify and understand inconsistencies in expectations and performance outcomes and then take appropriate actions. Proactively, this could involve assuming a genuine client orientation, including altering client expectations through realistic communications, and/or altering the professional(s)' behavior. By bridging the service quality gaps and providing client-consistent service, a professional can lay the foundation for long-term relationships with his or her clients.

References

Berry, Leonard L., Valerie A. Zeithaml, and A. Parasuraman. (1985). "Quality Counts in Services, Too." *Business Horizons*, 28 (May/June), 44–52.

Bloom, Paul N. (1984). "Effective Marketing for Professional Services." *Harvard Business Review*, 62 (October), 102–10.

Brown, Stephen W. and Andrew P. Morley, Jr. (1986). *Marketing Strategies for Physicians*, Oradell, NJ: Medical Economics Books.

Brown, Stephen W., Andrew P. Morley, Jr., Sheryl J. Bronkesh, and Steven D. Wood. (1989). *Promoting Your Medical Practice: Marketing Communications for Physicians.* Oradell, N.J.: Medical Economics Company, Inc.

Brown, Stephen W. and Teresa A. Swartz. (1984). "Consumer Medical Complaint Behavior: Determinents of and Alternatives to Malpractice Litigation." *Journal of Public Policy & Marketing,* Vol. 3, 85–98.

———. (1989). "A Gap Analysis of Professional Service Quality." *Journal of Marketing,* April 92–98.

Grönroos, Christian. (1983). *Strategic Management and Marketing in the Service Sector.* Boston: Marketing Science Institute.

Gummesson, Evert. (1978). "Towards a Theory of Professional Service Marketing." *Industrial Marketing Management,* 7, 89–95.

———. (1981). "The Marketing of Professional Services—25 Propositions." In James H. Donnelly and William R. George (eds.), *Marketing of Services.* Chicago: American Marketing Association, 108–12.

Kotler, Philip, and Paul N. Bloom. (1984). *Marketing Professional Services,* Englewood Cliffs, NJ: Prentice-Hall.

Lehtinen, Jarmo R., and Uolevi Lehtinen. (1982). "Service Quality: A Study of Quality Dimensions." Unpublished working paper, Helsinki: Service Management Institute.

———. (1983). "How to Measure Customer Expectations and Perceptions Regarding Service Quality." Unpublished working paper, Helsinki: Service Management Institute.

Parasuraman, A., Valerie A. Zeithaml, and Leonard L. Berry. (1985). "A Conceptual Model of Service Quality and Its Implications for Future Research." *Journal of Marketing,* Fall, 41–50.

Quelch, John A., and Stephen B. Ash. (1981). "Consumer Satisfaction with Professional Services." In James H. Donnelly and William R. George (eds.), *Marketing of Services.* Chicago: American Marketing Association, 82–85.

Stiff, Ronald, and Sandra E. Gleason. (1981). "The Effects of Marketing Activities on the Quality of Professional Services." In James H. Donnelly and William R. George (eds.), *Marketing of Services.* Chicago: American Marketing Association, 7881.

Swartz, Teresa A., and Stephen W. Brown. (1989). "Consumer and Provider Expectations and Experiences in Evaluating Professional Service Quality." *Journal of Academy for Marketing Science,* Spring, 189–95.

Part IV
How to Assess
Service Quality

Assessing the quality of the offering is an important part of service quality. The development and implementation of a quality program requires an understanding of service quality issues, and how these issues affect both the customer and provider. However, as illustrated in this section, many facets of quality need to be measured to ensure a comprehensive and accurate assessment of service quality. This section presents a selection of alternative methods of assessment.

One of the most extensive and well-known streams of research in service quality is that of A. Parasuraman, Leonard Berry, and Valarie Zeithaml. Their lead chapter in this section reports three phases of their systematic study of service quality. The authors begin with an overview of an exploratory investigation that led to the development of a conceptual model of service quality (phase one). Phase two had the dual objectives of 1) developing a measurement instrument for consumers' perceptions of service quality, and 2) gaining an increased understanding of the causes of quality problems. Phase three is discussed as a validation of the relationships implied in the extended model of service quality. The development and testing of the service quality conceptual model is presented along with the resulting SERVQUAL instrument.

Quality assessments are concerned with developing extended relationships with customers. Lawrence Crosby's chapter addresses managerial issues related to after-sale interactions and communications between buyers and sellers. A value-added framework is used to examine the impact of various types of follow-up communications on satisfaction and the impact thereof on customer retention. The importance of relationship development in service industries is discussed, along with the implications of consumer satisfaction on relationship marketing strategy.

Franklin Allen and Gerald Faulhaber's chapter follows with the contention that service firms will stand or fall according to their abilities to assure quality. They maintain that customers will indeed pay a premium price for the services of firms with reputations for providing high quality. Service offerings require inputs and produce outputs, but because customers are unable to observe the quality of the inputs, they must infer service quality from observed outputs. Given this point, an economic model is presented in which firms purchase inputs with either good or poor quality, and the output is monitored for two output periods. The reputation model presented demonstrates that economic equilibrium is drastically altered when quality "noise" is added to the production process.

Kiyoshi Kobayashi, David Batten, and Åke Andersson's chapter offers an analytical framework to investigate the economic structure of service markets with free entry. A comparative analysis is made to evaluate the impacts of shared knowledge on market structure, and the quality of the services supplied in local markets. The authors present an analytical foundation for investigating relationships among market structure, service quality, and research and development intensity. The impact on both market structure and service quality from R&D knowledge spillover from one firm to another is also discussed.

Lastly, a process-oriented, holistic, and multidimensional model for assessing service quality in organizations is presented by Bo Edvardsson and BengtOve Gustavsson. Following the elaboration of a theoretical framework, the concept of service quality is critically reviewed in terms of a management-oriented model for quality assessment. A contingency approach to operationalizing the model is presented, in addition to a brief discussion of the advantages and shortcomings of the model.

17
Understanding, Measuring, and Improving Service Quality
Findings from a Multiphase Research Program

A. Parasuraman
Leonard L. Berry
Valarie Zeithaml

Introduction

Increasing deregulation, escalating competition, and more demanding consumers have propelled product quality to the forefront in many industries. In the service industry in particular, delivering high quality has been recognized as the most effective means of ensuring that a company's offerings stand out from a crowd of look-alike competitive offerings. Research has also demonstrated the strategic benefits of superior quality in contributing to market share and profits (Buzzell and Gale 1987).

Despite the growing importance of quality in the service sector, efforts at defining and measuring quality have come largely from the goods sector (Crosby 1979; Garvin 1983). However, knowledge about goods quality is insufficient to understand service quality because of three distinguishing characteristics of services: *intangibility, heterogeneity, and inseparability* (Parasuraman, Zeithaml, and Berry 1985). The intangibility of services implies that precise manufacturing specifications concerning uniform quality can rarely be set for services as they can for goods. This difficulty is compounded by the fact that services, especially those with a high labor content, are heterogeneous: their performance often varies from producer to producer, from customer to customer, and from day to day. As a result, uniform quality is difficult to ensure. Finally, the inseparability of production and consumption of services implies that quality cannot be engineered and evaluated at the manufacturing plant prior to delivery to consumers. Clearly, goods-quality principles are not directly pertinent to services.

Service quality has been discussed in only a handful of writings (Grönroos 1982; Lehtinen and Lehtinen 1982; Lewis and Booms 1983;

Sasser, Olsen, and Wyckoff 1978). Examination of these writings and other literature on services suggests three underlying themes:

1. Service quality is more difficult for the consumer to evaluate than goods quality.
2. Service quality perceptions result from a comparison of consumer expectations with actual service performance.
3. Quality evaluations are not made solely on the outcome of a service; they also involve evaluations of the process of service delivery.

Although these themes are insightful, they are not rich enough to provide a sound conceptual foundation for investigating and improving service quality. Therefore, the authors began a systematic study of service quality in 1983 with encouragement and financial support from the Marketing Science Institute (MSI) in Cambridge, Massachusetts. The research program on service quality under MSI sponsorship is ongoing, but three major phases of research have been completed. The purpose of this chapter is to briefly describe these phases and summarize the results and implications stemming from each.

Phase I (1983–1984)

The first phase of research was exploratory and involved a series of focus group interviews with consumers and in-depth interviews with executives to develop a conceptual model of service quality. These interviews were conducted with respondents from four different service industries—retail banking, credit card, securities brokerage, and product repair and maintenance—to ensure that the conceptual insights generated would be applicable to a broad cross-section of industries.

Focus Group Interviews

A total of twelve focus group interviews were conducted, three for each of the four selected services. The focus groups were formed in accordance with guidelines traditionally followed in the marketing research field (Bellenger, Bernhardt, and Goldstucker 1976). Respondents were also screened to ensure that they were current or recent users of the service in question. The group discussion centered on consumer experiences and perceptions relating to the service in general, and covered such topics as reasons for satisfaction and dissatisfaction with the service, what the service should ideally look like, the meaning of service quality, and factors important in evaluating service quality.

Responses from the focus group participants revealed several common patterns or underlying themes across groups and across services. Positive and negative experiences with various services described by the focus group participants implied that consumers had certain expectations—that is, what a service provider *should* offer—against which they compared the actual service performance in evaluating the quality of the service rendered. Therefore, service quality as perceived by consumers results from a comparison of *perceived service* with *expected service*.

The focus groups also revealed that regardless of service category consumers used similar criteria in evaluating service quality. These criteria fall into ten key categories or dimensions, several of which may be interrelated. The ten dimensions and brief descriptions of what they represent are listed below:

- *Tangibles* include the physical evidence of the service such as appearance of the service facilities and personnel.
- *Reliability* involves consistency of performance and dependability. It means that the firm performs the service right the first time. It also means that the firm honors its promises.
- *Responsiveness* concerns the willingness or readiness of employees to provide service. It involves timeliness of service.
- *Competence* means possession of the required skills and knowledge to perform the service.
- *Courtesy* involves politeness, respect, consideration, and friendliness of contact personnel (including receptionists, telephone operators, and so forth).
- *Credibility* involves trustworthiness, believability, honesty. It involves having the customer's best interests at heart.
- *Security* is the freedom from danger, risk, or doubt.
- *Access* involves approachability and ease of contact.
- *Communication* means keeping customers informed in language they can understand. It also means listening to customers.
- *Understanding the consumer* involves making the effort to understand the customer's needs.

Another finding from the focus groups concerns factors that may influence the types and levels of expectations consumers have along the various dimensions. Specifically, the focus group discussions suggested that consumers' expectations are shaped by word-of-mouth communications (i.e., what they hear from other consumers), personal needs of individual consumers, their experience with the service, and communications they receive from the service provider (e.g., advertisements).

Executive Interviews

To obtain insights about what constitutes service quality from the marketer's standpoint and what gets in the way of superior service delivery, in-depth personal interviews were conducted with three or four senior executives in each of four nationally recognized service companies (one from each of the four industries studied). A total of fourteen in-depth interviews were conducted with executives who held titles such as president, senior vice president, director of customer relations, and manager of consumer market research.

As in the focus group interviews, consistent patterns and common themes emerged from the four sets of executive interviews. These commonalities suggested four key discrepancies or gaps regarding executive perceptions of service quality and the tasks associated with service delivery to consumers. These gaps are briefly described.

Gap 1: Consumer expectation–management perception gap. While managers seemed to have a good understanding of consumer expectations, in each set of interviews ample evidence indicated that executives were either totally unaware of certain critical consumer expectations or were misreading the importance of those expectations to consumers. For instance, privacy or confidentiality during transactions emerged as a pivotal quality attribute in every banking and securities brokerage focus group. Rarely was this consideration mentioned by executives when asked what they felt were key expectations of consumers.

Gap 2: Management perception–service quality specification gap. The executive interviews revealed that even in instances in which management was aware of critical consumer expectations (e.g., executives in the appliance repair and maintenance firm were fully aware that prompt response to appliance breakdowns was a key determinant of service quality), a variety of factors— resource constraints, market conditions, and/or management indifference might prevent them from setting specifications to meet those expectations.

Gap 3: Service quality specifications–service delivery gap. It was clear from the executive interviews that even when formal specifications were in place for performing services well, the performance of the service frequently fell short of those specifications. When asked the causes of service quality problems, executives consistently mentioned the critical role of contact personnel and the wide variability in their performance, and the consequent difficulty in maintaining uniform, standardized quality.

Gap 4: Service delivery–external communications gap. A potential reason for poor perceptions of service quality by consumers is that their expectations are boosted by media advertising, sales presentations, and other communications to levels beyond a company's capabilities. Insights from the executive interviews confirmed such an elevation of consumer expectations by a company's external communications. The executive interviews also suggested that companies may sometimes fail to inform consumers of special efforts to assure quality that are not apparent to consumers. Such failures are missed opportunities for enhancing consumers' *perceptions* of the delivered service. In short, the gap between service delivery and external communications about it—in the form of exaggerated promises and/or the absence of information about service delivery aspects intended to serve consumers well—can influence consumer perceptions of service quality.

Conceptual Model of Service Quality

A key finding from the focus groups was that service quality as defined by consumers can be characterized as the discrepancy or gap between their perceptions and expectations. The executive interviews revealed that this service quality gap (Gap 5) on the consumer's side is a function of the organizational gaps (Gaps 1 through 4) on the marketer's side. The exploratory research findings collectively suggest a conceptual model of service quality linking the consumer's and marketer's sides of the service quality equation. This model is shown in figure 17–1 and can serve as a foundation for understanding, measuring, and improving service quality. More detailed discussions of the findings from the first phase of research can be found elsewhere (Parasuraman, Zeithaml, and Berry 1985; Berry, Zeithaml, and Parasuraman 1985).

Phase II (1984–1986)

The second phase of research had two main objectives: (1) to develop an instrument for measuring consumers' perceptions of service quality (i.e., Gap 5 in figure 17–1), and (2) to develop a more in-depth understanding of the causes of service quality problems (i.e., Gaps 1 through 4 in figure 17–1). The first objective was accomplished through a series of consumer surveys culminating in a parsimonious instrument called SERVQUAL. Accomplishing the second objective involved a thorough search of the organi-

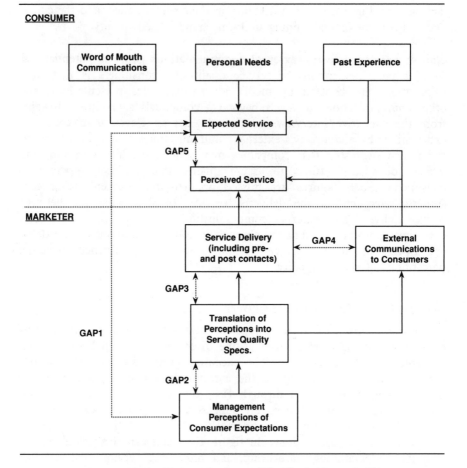

Figure 17–1. Conceptual model of service quality.

zational behavior and marketing literatures, an in-depth case study of a large retail bank, and a group interview with senior executives from several large service firms. The two components of Phase II are described in greater detail.

Development and Testing of SERVQUAL

The process used to develop SERVQUAL was in accordance with guidelines recommended by Churchill (1979). The process began with the conceptual definition of service quality (i.e., the difference between perceptions and expectations represented by Gap 5) and the ten dimensions that play a role in service quality assessment. Specifically, the notion of discrepancies between perceptions and expectations along the various dimensions was operationalized as the following describes.

Items representing various facets of the ten service-quality dimensions were generated to form the initial item pool for the SERVQUAL instrument. This process resulted in the generation of ninety-seven items (approximately ten items per dimension). Each item was recast into two statements—one to measure expectations about firms in general within the service category being investigated and the other to measure perceptions about the particular firm whose service quality was being assessed. A seven-point scale ranging from "Strongly Disagree" (1) to "Strongly Agree" (7), with no verbal labels for scale points 2 through 6, accompanied each statement. The expectation statements were grouped together and formed the first half of the instrument. The corresponding perception statements formed the second half.

The ninety-seven-item instrument was then subjected to two stages of data collection and refinement. The first stage focused on (1) condensing the instrument by retaining only those items capable of effectively discriminating across respondents having differing quality perceptions about firms in several service categories, and (2) examining the dimensionality of the scale and establishing the reliabilities of its components. The second stage was primarily "confirmatory" in nature and involved reevaluating the condensed scale's dimensionality and reliability by analyzing fresh data from four independent samples.

Data for initial refinement of the ninety-seven-item instrument were gathered from a quota sample of two hundred adult respondents recruited by a marketing research firm in a shopping mall in a large metropolitan area. The sample was close to equally divided between males and females and was spread across five different service categories: appliance repair and maintenance, retail banking, long-distance telephone, securities brokerage, and credit cards. For each service category, a quota of forty recent users of the service was established. To qualify for the study, respondents had to have used the service in question during the previous three months.

For the expectations section of the questionnaire, respondents were instructed to indicate the level of service that should be offered by firms within the service category in question. For the perceptions section, respondents were first asked to name a firm (within the service category) that they had used and with which they were most familiar. Respondents were then instructed to express their perceptions about the firm. An illustrative statement from the expectations section and the corresponding statement from the perceptions section follows:

	Strongly Disagree						Strongly Agree
Expectation statement (E):							
When these firms promise to do something by a certain time, they should do so.	1	2	3	4	5	6	7
Perception statement (P): When XYZ promises to do something by a certain time, it does so.	1	2	3	4	5	6	7

The data obtained from the survey were converted into P-E gap scores, which were subjected to an iterative sequence of item-to-total correlation analyses (within each of the ten dimensions) followed by a series of factor analyses. These analyses resulted in the elimination of approximately two-thirds of the statement pairs and the consolidation of the remaining statement pairs into seven dimensions with acceptable reliability values (i.e., coefficient alphas).

To further evaluate the condensed scale and to confirm its psychometric properties, data were collected pertaining to the service quality of four nationally known firms: a bank, a credit-card company, a firm offering appliance repair and maintenance services, and a long-distance telephone company. For each firm, an independent shopping-mall sample of two hundred customers was recruited by a marketing research firm. To qualify for the study, respondents had to have used the services of the firm in question within the previous three months.

The P-E gap scores obtained from the four samples were analyzed separately to examine the robustness of the scale. The analyses once again involved an iterative sequence of computing item-to-total correlations and coefficient alphas, followed by factor analyses to examine the dimensionality of the scale. The pattern of results from these analyses were extremely consistent across the four samples and suggested the deletion of several more items-and further consolidation of the seven scale dimensions. The deletions and consolidation resulted in a refined SERVQUAL scale with good reliability and validity and containing twenty-two items (i.e., statement pairs) spread among five dimensions. Three of the original ten dimensions—tangibles, reliability, and responsiveness—remained intact throughout the iterative scale refinement and consolidation process, while the remaining seven dimensions melded into two new dimensions labeled *assurance* (capturing the original dimensions of competence, courtesy, credibility, and security) and *empathy* (capturing the original dimensions of access, communication, and understanding the consumer).

An examination of the content of the final items making up each of SERVQUAL's five dimensions (three original and two combined dimensions) suggested the following concise definitions for the dimensions:

Tangibles:	Physical facilities, equipment, and appearance of personnel
Reliability:	Ability to perform the promised service dependably and accurately
Responsiveness:	Willingness to help customers and provide prompt service
Assurance:	Knowledge and courtesy of employees and their ability to convey trust and confidence
Empathy:	Caring, individualized attention the firm provides its customers

The twenty-two-item SERVQUAL instrument, having been developed and refined with data from a variety of industries, is suitable for use across a broad spectrum of services. As such, it provides a basic skeleton through its expectations/perceptions format, encompassing statements for each of the five service quality dimensions. When necessary, the skeleton can be adapted or supplemented to fit the characteristics or specific research needs of a particular organization.

What has been presented here so far about SERVQUAL is merely an overview of the development of the scale. A much more elaborate discussion of the scale-development process, particularly the statistical details pertaining to SERVQUAL's reliability and validity, can be found in Parasuraman, Zeithaml, and Berry (1988). This reference also discusses several potential uses of SERVQUAL and contains a listing of the scale items. A discussion of the relative importance customers attach to the five dimensions can be found in Berry, Parasuraman, and Zeithaml (1988).

An Extended Model of Service Quality

The second component of Phase II focused on gaining a better understanding of the causes underlying the four gaps on the marketer's side of the conceptual model of service quality. The purpose was to identify a reasonably exhaustive set of factors potentially affecting the magnitude and direction of the four gaps. To accomplish this purpose, insights from a review of relevant literature in the organizational behavior and marketing fields were combined with findings from the executive interviews in Phase I, a comprehensive case study of a nationally known bank, and a systematic group interview with eleven senior executives of six nationally known service firms (two full-service banks, two national insurance companies, and two national phone companies).

The bank case study involved three of the bank's regions, each of which had at least twelve branches. Managers and employees at various levels of the bank were interviewed individually or in focus groups. Managers responded to open-ended questions about their perceptions of consumer expectations of service quality (Gap 1), service quality standards set in the organization to deliver quality (Gap 2), and differences between standards set by management and the level of service actually delivered (Gap 3). Also, managers associated with the bank's external communications (both bank and advertising agency executives) were interviewed to identify the factors responsible for Gap 4—the differences between the delivered service and communicated service. Finally, a total of seven focus gap interviews with tellers, customer service representatives, lending personnel, and branch managers from within the three regions were held to identify factors contributing to Gaps 3 and 4.

The systematic group interview with managers was intended to verify and generalize the findings from the bank case study and other relevant research. In the group interview, the conceptual model was presented, the four gaps explained, and managers were questioned about factors responsible for the gaps in their firms. Lists of factors (i.e., potential causes of the gaps) identified from earlier stages were presented and discussed. The managers augmented the lists and evaluated the factors on the basis of experience in their industries and organizations.

The following paragraphs briefly describe the key factors hypothesized to influence each of the four gaps.

Factors Influencing Gap 1. Investigation suggested that three factors or constructs are potential determinants of the size and direction of Gap 1, the discrepancy between consumer expectations and management perceptions of those expectations.

1. *Marketing Research Orientation* (-)*—the extent to which management conducts and uses marketing research and the degree to which such research focuses on service quality issues. This factor also involves the extent to which managers interact directly with consumers.
2. *Upward Communication* (-)—the extent to which management interacts with customer contact personnel and seeks inputs from them.
3. *Levels of Management* (+)—the number of supervisory or managerial levels separating senior managers from customer contact personnel.

Factors Influencing Gap 2. Even when managers have a good understanding of what consumers expect, management may still fail to set service

---

*In the presentation of these constructs, a minus sign indicates that a factor's presence should decrease the gap, a plus sign indicates that the factor should increase the gap.

specifications to meet consumer expectations. The gap between management's understanding of consumer expectations and the translation of those expectations into service quality specifications depends on the following factors:

1. *Management Commitment to Service Quality (-)*—the extent to which top management allocates resources (money and people) to service quality, has in place internal initiatives for improving quality, and rewards employees who provide superior service.

2. *Goal Setting (-)*—existence of a formal mechanism for setting quality of service goals.

3. *Task Standardization (-)*—the extent to which service roles in the firm are standardized and routinized, thus facilitating the setting of standards.

4. *Perception of Feasibility (-)*—the extent to which managers believe that consumer expectations can be met economically.

Factors Influencing Gap 3. Gap 3 is the discrepancy between the specifications for the service and the actual delivery of the service. This service performance gap occurs when service providers are unable and/or unwilling to perform the service at the specified level. The following factors influence the service performance gap:

1. *Teamwork (-)*—the extent to which employees feel management cares about them, experience cooperation with other employees, and feel personally involved and committed in the service role.

2. *Employee-Job Fit (-)*—the extent to which employees hired to perform service roles have the requisite skills and qualifications.

3. *Technology-Job Fit (-)*—the appropriateness and adequacy of the tools or technology employees use to perform their service roles.

4. *Perceived Control (-)*—the extent to which employees perceive they are in control of their jobs and have the needed flexibility to serve their customers.

5. *Supervisory Control Systems (-)*—the extent to which employees are evaluated on what they do (behaviors) rather than solely on output quantity.

6. *Role Conflict (+)*—the extent to which employees feel pressure due to competing or conflicting demands made on them by customers, supervisors, and top managers.

7. *Role Ambiguity (+)*—the extent to which employees are unsure of what supervisors or managers expect of them, how to satisfy those expectations, and how their performance will be evaluated and rewarded.

Factors Influencing Gap 4. The discrepancy between the actual service delivered and what is communicated to consumers about the service can result from one or both of the following factors:

1. *Horizontal Communication* (-)—the extent to which effective two-way communication exists between service providers and those in charge of advertising/selling the services; also the extent to which similarity of procedures exist across departments and branches within the firm.
2. *Propensity to Overpromise* (+)—the extent to which executives feel pressure to generate new business, believe that competitors are overpromising, and believe they have no choice but to make strong promises as well.

Figure 17–2 presents an extended model of service quality that summarizes the various factors influencing Gaps 1 through 4, the SERVQUAL dimensions representing Gap 5, and the relationships among the gaps. The extended model provides a foundation for conducting empirical research into the causes of the various gaps and the impact of Gaps 1 through 4 on Gap 5. The theoretical underpinnings of the extended model are discussed in greater detail in Zeithaml, Berry, and Parasuraman (1988), and its practical implications are discussed in Berry, Parasuraman, and Zeithaml (1988).

Phase III (1986–1989)

The primary objective of the third phase of the research program was to verify empirically the relationships implied in the extended model of service quality. As such, this phase focused on the following two questions:

1. To what extent are the factors hypothesized to influence each gap actually associated with that gap? In other words, what are the key drivers of each gap?
2. What is the degree of association between the gaps on the marketer's side and service quality as perceived by consumers (i.e., Gap 5)?

The first question can be examined by obtaining data from a cross-section of employees from a single service organization. Specifically, respondents' perceptions about the extent to which a certain gap exists within their organization can be regressed on their perceptions about the extent to which the corresponding factors are present in the organization. The results of such an analysis will indicate the key drivers of each gap.

Examining the second question, however, requires data from a cross-section of *organizations*, rather than a cross-section of respondents within an organization. This requirement stems from the fact that the question calls

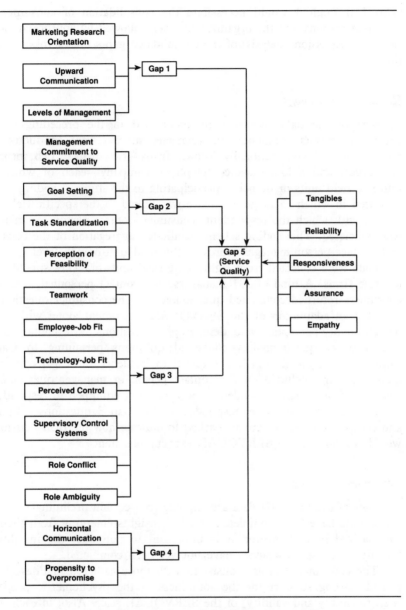

Figure 17–2. Extended model of service quality.

for an examination of an organization's service quality as perceived by consumers (i.e., Gap 5, the dependent variable) vis-à-vis internal gaps as perceived by *employees* (i.e., Gaps 1 through 4, the independent variables). Therefore, empirical examination of the association between Gap 5 and

Gaps 1 through 4 would necessitate the consolidation of consumer and employee responses at the organization level, followed by appropriate analysis (e.g., regression analysis) of the consolidated gap scores across organizations.

Research Methodology

In view of the data requirements mentioned in the preceding section, consumer, contact personnel, and manager surveys were conducted in a cross-section of five nationally known firms—two banks, two insurance companies, and a long-distance telephone company—each of which had multiple field units or branches participating in the study. A coding scheme was used in which each questionnaire was linked to the specific field unit/ branch with which the respondent (consumer, contact person, or manager) was associated. This coding scheme facilitated aggregation of the consumer and contact person/manager scores at the field unit/branch level.

Data were collected from eighty-nine field units/branches spread across the five firms. A total of 231 managers, 728 contact personnel, and 1,936 consumers returned completed questionnaires. The consumer questionnaire included an adaptation of the SERVQUAL instrument along with several overall-quality-perception and demographic questions. The contact person and manager questionnaires contained questions pertaining to Gaps 1 through 4 and the factors hypothesized to influence those gaps. The gap questions were included on the contact person or manager questionnaires were based on which respondent group was best equipped to respond. For example, contact personnel responded to the Gap 3 questions. Managers and contact employees were also asked to indicate how the firm's customers would respond to the SERVQUAL expectations items.

Preliminary Findings

Analyses of the Phase III data are ongoing, but certain preliminary analyses of the data have been completed and key insights emerging from them are summarized here. However, it is important to note that the insights are tentative because all analysis have not yet been completed.

The consumer data are consistent with those gathered in Phase II and provide strong support for the soundness of the psychometric properties (i.e., reliability and validity) of the SERVQUAL scale. Also, in each of the five consumer samples, reliability, responsiveness, and tangibles consistently emerge as the most important, second most important, and least important dimensions of service quality, respectively. The firms' gap scores (i.e., P-E scores) are worst for the reliability dimension and best (in fact slightly positive for all companies companies) for the tangibles dimension, indicating that the sample firms are performing least effectively in the area of greatest importance to customers.

The consumer data also suggest that the gap scores overall are least negative when consumers have had no recent service problem with the firm and are most negative when consumers have had a problem that was not resolved to their satisfaction. Moreover, the data reveal a strong positive association between consumers' perceptions of a firm's service quality and their inclination to recommend that firm to others needing the service.

The contact personnel and manager data pertaining to the gaps and their hypothesized causes are still being analyzed. A more complete discussion of Phase III of the research, along with additional analyses and implications will be forthcoming as a monograph to be published by the Marketing Science Institute (Parasuraman, Zeithaml, and Berry 1990).

Conclusion

The purpose of this chapter was to provide an overview of a stream of research on service quality that began in 1983 and is still ongoing. Concepts and conclusions emerging from the first two phases of this research stream and preliminary insights from a third phase were reviewed. Due to space constraints, it was not possible to provide more than a brief discussion of the research phases and their findings. More comprehensive discussions of the research and findings can be found in articles included in the references.

References

Bellenger, Danny N., Kenneth L. Bernhardt, and Jac L. Goldstucker. (1976). *Qualitative Research in Marketing*. Chicago: American Marketing Association.

Berry, Leonard L., A. Parasuraman, and Valarie A. Zeithaml. (1988). "The Service-Quality Puzzle." *Business Horizons*, September–October, 35–43.

Berry, Leonard L., Valarie A. Zeithaml, and A. Parasuraman. (1985). "Quality Counts in Services, Too." *Business Horizons*, May–June, 44–52.

Buzzell, Robert D., and Bradley T. Gale. (1987). *The PIMS Principles*, New York: The Free Press.

Churchill, Gilbert A., Jr. (1979). "A Paradigm for Developing Better Measures of Marketing Constructs." *Journal of Marketing Research*, 16 February, 64–73.

Crosby, Philip B. (1979). *Quality Is Free: The Art of Making Quality Certain*, New York: New American Library.

Garvin, David A. (1983). "Quality on the Line." *Harvard Business Review*, 61 September–October, 65–73.

Grönroos, Christian. (1982). *Strategic Management and Marketing in the Service Sector*, Helsingfors: Swedish School of Economics and Business Administration.

Lehtinen, Uolevi, and Jarmo R. Lehtinen. (1982). "Service Quality: A Study of Quality Dimensions." Helsinki: Service Management Institute, Finland OY, Unpublished working paper.

Lewis, Robert C., and Bernard H. Booms. (1983). "The Marketing Aspects of Service Quality." In L. Berry, G. Shostack, and G. Upah (eds.), *Emerging Perspectives on Service Marketing*. Chicago: American Marketing Association, 99–107.

Parasuraman, A., Valarie A. Zeithaml, and Leonard L. Berry. (1985). "A Conceptual Model of Service Quality and Its Implications for Future Research." *Journal of Marketing*, 49 Fall, 41–50.

Parasuraman, A., Valarie A. Zeithaml, and Leonard L. Berry. (1988). "SERVQUAL: A Multiple-Item Scale for Measuring Consumer Perceptions of Service Quality." *Journal of Retailing*, 64 Spring, 12–40.

Parasuraman, A., Valarie A. Zeithaml, and Leonard L. Berry. (1990). "A Test of the Extended Model of Service Quality." *Marketing Science Institute Monograph* (forthcoming).

Sasser, in. Earl, Jr., R. Paul Olsen, and D. Daryl Wyckoff. (1978). *Management of Science Operations: Text and Cases*. Boston: Allyn & Bacon.

Zeithaml, Valarie A., Leonard L. Berry, and A. Parasuraman. (1988). "Communication and Control Processes in the Delivery of Service Quality." *Journal of Marketing*, 52 April, 35–48.

18
Building and Maintaining Quality in the Service Relationship

Lawrence A. Crosby

Introduction

A recent article reported efforts to test competing models describing the impact of after-sale interaction and communication on the strength of the buyer-seller relationship (Crosby and Stephens 1987). The research was conducted in a life insurance marketing context with primary attention to the *public policy* implications of the findings. This chapter reexamines that data from a *managerial* standpoint. The analysis addresses additional research questions within an integrated value-added framework: for example, what is the reinforcement value of various types of follow-up communication versus core service upgrading? To what extent does media advertising affect postpurchase evaluations? Does satisfaction predict retention? What are the implications regarding relationship marketing strategy?

Emphasis on Service Relationships

Service providers in a variety of industries are working to establish stronger and more enduring bonds with their customers. Among the hoped-for gains of relationship marketing is improved customer retention. Attracting a new customer is approximately five times more expensive than retaining a current one. The need for relationship marketing is particularly apparent given the increasing levels of competition in services (Berry 1983). Insurance providers in the United States, for example, face expanded competition from banks and other financial institutions.

This study was conducted under grants from The National Association of Life Underwriters, Washington, D.C., The Life Office Management Association, Atlanta, GA., and The First Interstate Center for Services Marketing, Arizona State University, Tempe, Arizona, U.S.A.

Nature of Relationship Marketing

The basic concept of relationship marketing is to transform transaction customers into relationship customers (Jackson 1985). Rather than conducting business as a series of discrete transactions, customers are encouraged to make an indefinite commitment to the seller for satisfaction of their requirements in a given area (e.g., banking needs). Normally, customers are willing to do this only if the seller makes a reciprocal investment in the relationship (e.g., designation of a personal banker). While relationship marketing concepts have been most widely discussed in the channels and industrial marketing literatures (e.g., Dwyer, Schurr, and Oh 1987), they can also be applied to services (e.g., Berry 1983).

There is a positive incentive to *enter* a relationship when expected relationship benefits exceed costs (Kelley and Thibaut 1978). Potential returns from a close buyer-seller relationship include reduced uncertainty, lower transaction and search costs, and better information and suggestions (Hakansson 1982). Potential relationship costs include the investment of time, money, and effort required to enter the relationship as well as foregone benefits that might have been obtained elsewhere (opportunity costs). The parties have an incentive to *stay* in the relationship when the costs of switching (e.g., risk exposure) exceed the net benefits of switching (i.e., returns available from best alternative minus returns provided by current relationship).

Complementing these explanations of *why* relationships are formed and maintained are IMP Group theories regarding the *process* of relationship development (Hakansson 1982). According to the IMP Interaction Model, marketing relationships build over time with the accumulation of short-term interaction episodes that link buyer and seller. Interaction episodes involving product, financial, information, and social exchange give rise to relationship benefits and costs, and, eventually, commitment (as the parties adapt and roles become institutionalized). According to the IMP Model, product and financial exchange are facilitated by information and social exchange.

A Value-Added Interpretation

Based on these considerations, it appears that one major approach to relationship marketing is customer value enhancement (i.e., to reduce or eliminate net switching benefits). It seems likely too that customers' perceptions of value will depend considerably on the interactions and communications they have with the service provider. This realization coincides with recent calls for a "value-added" approach to services marketing (Grönroos 1987).

Although many examples can be cited of how services marketers have augmented their core products or adjusted pricing to deliver more benefits to relationship customers (e.g., airline frequent flyer programs, bank all-in-one accounts), less consideration has been given to the influence of follow-up communication and personal interaction in helping cement a stronger bond. There is reason to believe these factors are of critical importance in services marketing (Solomon et al. 1985).

Dependent Variables

The criterion of ultimate interest is the strength of the buyer-seller relationship. Technically, relationship strength is a dyadic concept that involves the dispositions of both parties, the structure of their interaction, and the atmosphere in which they interact. However, in a buyer's market where competition is particularly strong (life insurance), it is probably sufficient to concentrate on the buyer because he or she is more likely than the seller to terminate the relationship. In this light, customer satisfaction has previously been identified as one indicator of the buyer's psychological commitment to the relationship (Dwyer, Schurr, and Oh 1987). It was the dependent variable of primary concern in this study. Relationship satisfaction was conceived as having three dimensions: satisfaction with the contact person (agent), with the core service (policy), and with the institution (insurance company).

According to Wilson (1977), the relationship of dyadic partners can be measured through the attribute sets that link them. These sets pertain to the salesperson, product, and company. More recently, Jackson (1985) refers to the objects of the customer's commitment as including the salesperson, product, and company. Theories of service quality draw a parallel distinction between the functional/interactive, technical, and institutional elements of quality (Grönroos 1986; Lehtinen 1985). Assuming that service quality is a prerequisite for relationship quality, these elements may also serve as anchor points for the customer's commitment.

Independent Variables

The study included eight independent variables, representing different categories of customer postpurchase experiences, that were anticipated to influence relationship strength (satisfaction). The predictors included those that add value to the relationship (rewards), those that add cost, and those that increase the attractiveness of alternate relationships.

Value Enhancers

The value-enhancing variables included core service upgrading, personal follow-up contact, direct company communication, and company advertising exposure. All are controllable from a marketing standpoint and primarily communications related, with the exception of core service upgrading.

Core Service Upgrading. Service augmentation has been identified as a fundamental component of effective relationship marketing (Berry 1983). Augmentation involves building "extras" into the service to reward loyalty. Berry comments that "the 'extras' can be anything so long as they are valued by the target market and not easily matched by competitors" (p. 27). It is possible, however, to distinguish between enhancements in technical quality (outcomes) versus the quality of service delivery (process). Core service upgrading refers to the former; the other value-enhancing variables deal with the latter.

From 1983 to 1984, an exceptionally high proportion of whole life policies were discontinued by insurance customers. Many were so-called baby policies purchased twenty to thirty years earlier by parents for their children. High market interest rates driven by double digit inflation seriously eroded the value of older policies during the 1980s. In an effort to stem the loss of customers (and their assets), many companies instituted voluntary programs to upgrade existing policies. Typically, this involved increasing the amount of coverage for a given premium or reducing the premium for a given amount of coverage.

Personal Contact. Service augmentation can also be achieved through enhanced interaction and communication with customers. Most U.S. life insurance companies depend on field agents to maintain an appropriate level of personal contact. Personal contact can add value to the service relationship in the following areas:

Social Reinforcement. Refers to satisfaction of the buyer's esteem and affiliation needs—for example, when the agent sends the policyholder something personal such as a birthday card or holiday gift.

Reassurance. Refers to the seller providing evidence of trustworthiness, reliability, commitment, and concern (reduces uncertainty)—for example, when the agent contacts policyholders to stay in touch and make sure they are still satisfied.

Benefit Reinforcement. Involves calling attention to evidence of service performance (reduces uncertainty)—for example, when the agent explains why it is a good idea to keep a policy in-force.

Problem Solving. Refers to providing expert counseling on the customer's present and future needs (reduces search and evaluation costs)—for example, when the agent (re)assesses the policyholder's needs and provides information on new services.

Customization. Refers to adapting the service and/or payment procedures to fit the individual customers' needs (overlaps somewhat with problem solving)—for example, when the agent makes changes in the insurance policy or program to better serve the customer's needs.

Labor Substitution. Refers to performing activities on behalf of customers to increase their convenience (reduces transaction costs)—for example, when the agent files paperwork to modify the policy such as changing beneficiaries.

Direct Company Communication. Direct media may provide additional opportunities to augment the service with enhanced customer communication. American Express maintains high frequency in its direct communication with customers to extend the perceived benefits of the service relationship. Likewise, some U.S. life insurance companies specializing in term insurance rely exclusively on direct marketing techniques to both acquire and retain customers. In general, service providers worldwide are making increased use of direct mail and telemarketing. The basic requirement is a solid customer list, which naturally exists if customers have a membership relationship with the service organization. Despite increasing popularity, the usefulness of direct communication for customer retention has yet to be demonstrated in different service contexts. Direct communication might logically be expected to add value to the service relationship in the following areas:

Social Reinforcement. For example, sending personalized letters that foster a sense of belonging among customers and make them feel "special" or part of an elite group.

Reassurance. For example, sending policyholders copies of the company's annual report as evidence of financial stability.

Benefit Reinforcement. For example, sending periodic statements to customers indicating their cash value accumulation, paid-up insurance, reasons for keeping the policy in-force.

Problem Solving. For example, sending customers information about the company's related services such as mutual funds and annuities.

Company Media Advertising. In theory, the value of the service can also be enhanced through the company's media advertising. Formally known as *agenda setting* (Sutherland and Galloway 1981), it is suggested that advertising media weight has a significant influence on the perceived prominence of a brand and that prominence connotes popularity. In general, people gain satisfaction from knowing they are engaged in socially approved behavior (*social reinforcement*). The company's media advertising can also add value to the service by providing additional *reassurance* ("You're in good hands with All-State."). The customer gains confidence from being represented by a strong and well-established company, an image fostered by frequent appearance in major national media.

These arguments notwithstanding, a case can also be made that media advertising has a limited role to play in relationship marketing. Some feel that broadcast media have a reduced role because of their "abstracting qualities which only compound the already abstract nature of services" (Liechty and Churchill 1979, p. 510). Another problem is the lack of message tailoring. With personal contact and direct communication, the agent or company can "talk" to the customer as an individual rather than just a member of a segment. This is said to be a hallmark of relationship marketing (Berry 1583). This opportunity does not exist with mass media advertising.

Cost Penalizers

From a managerial perspective, other types of buyer-seller interactions are dangerous since they have the potential to push the relationship apart (rather than to pull it together). This occurs when the customer intiates contact, seeking help in the handling of a request, problem, or complaint. Customers uniformally expect their requests to be dealt with effectively and efficiently. The *failure* to do so detracts from the relationship by adding transaction costs. Specifically, customers must invest time and effort in resolving the problem and must deal with the psychological tension and frustration of being in a conflict situation. On the other hand, the successful handling of requests seldom evokes buyer's positive feelings as it is considered a minimum requirement of the service (Brandt 1987). The two controllable variables investigated in this category were agent service failure and corporate service failure.

Doubt Creators

The uncontrollable exposure of customers to negative product information via mass media or word-of-mouth (W-O-M) sources can raise doubts about the existing relationship. The information calls attention to the fact that other alternatives have desirable attributes (opportunity costs). This tends to pull the relationship apart by making the net benefits of switching appear more favorable relative to the costs of switching. Negative product information via W-O-M sources also contains an element of social disapproval. Customers want to be perceived by others as making intelligent service choices and may consider switching when their decisions are called into question (negative W-0-M adds social cost to staying in the existing relationship).

With regard to the relative impact of these two sources of negative information, it is claimed that consumers favor W-O-M communication to determine the type and quality of service (Liechty and Churchill 1979). Yet, mass media editorial sources are also known to be highly influential in molding people's attitudes and opinions (Hovland 1972).

The Survey

To better understand how after-sale interaction and communication can add value (or costs) to the service relationship, a longitudinal study was conducted among owners of whole life insurance. The research took the form of a correlational study using a panel design (for more details see Crosby and Stephens 1987). In 1982, twenty thousand heads of households, twenty-five to forty-four years old, were selected from a U.S. consumer panel. Of these, 5,398 were qualified as owners of whole life insurance. The wave one questionnaire was mailed to a 90 percent subsample. The 2,311 returned and usable questionnaires represented a 48 percent response rate. Demographic comparisons revealed only minor differences between the final sample and the study population. The items of measurement in wave one dealt with customer satisfaction and recent insurance experiences. Approximately thirteen months later, the wave two questionnaire was mailed to 1,671 respondents who participated in wave one and were still panel members. Of this group, 983 completions were obtained for a 59 percent response rate. The wave two measures included most of the items in wave one. In addition, respondents were asked about changes in the status of their policies since wave one. About 16 percent of the whole life policies were discontinued between waves one and two.

Measures of Dependent Variables

Satisfaction with the agent, policy, company, and overall relationship were each globally measured by averaging responses to three, seven-point semantic differential scales: Satisfied—Dissatisfied, Pleased—Displeased, Favorable—Unfavorable. The resulting indices were found to have extremely high reliabilities in both waves (alphas > .97). In wave one only, a specific method of measurement was also used to assess satisfaction with the agent, policy, and company. This involved having respondents rate their satisfaction on a series of attributes pertinent to each dimension using seven-point Satisfied—Dissatisfied scales. For example, satisfaction with the policy included such attributes as affordability of premiums, rate of cash value growth, policy flexibility, and so on. A specific index was constructed for each relationship dimension by summing the detailed attribute evaluations. Reliabilities of the specific indices were also extremely high (alphas > .88). A multitrait/multimethod analysis was performed to assess the convergent and discriminant validity of the global and specific approaches to satisfaction measurement. The results confirmed three distinct but moderately correlated dimensions of relationship satisfaction.

Measures of Independent Variables

The eight predictors measured the frequency of various categories of customer experiences based on self-reports, that is, core service upgrade, personal contact, direct communication, advertising exposure, personal service failure, corporate service failure, negative mass media, negative W-O-M (for more details see Appendix in Crosby and Stephens 1987). The span of recall was two years in wave one and approximately one year in wave two. The eight variables corresponded to different factors that emerged when the raw questionnaire items were factor analyzed. The core service upgrade variable was coded 1 = policy was upgraded, 0 = otherwise (18 percent were upgraded in the two years prior to wave one, 27 percent in the thirteen months between waves one and two). The seven other variables were multiitem, additive scales with acceptable levels of reliability (alphas > .60 and most > .80). The advertising recall variable was validated using company data on advertising expenditures. Examination of the predictors revealed minimal multicollinearity. Only four of twenty-eight intercorrletations exceeded .30 in wave one; the largest was .48 (between negative mass media and negative W-O-M). Only three of twenty-eight intercorrelations exceeded .30 in wave two; the largest was .38 (between direct company communication and personal contact).

Results

Regression Analysis

Each dependent variable was regressed on the set of eight independent variables. To provide an indication of the stability of the results, separate regression estimates were obtained for wave one and wave two. The results are reported in table 18–1. In general, a better fit was obtained (adjusted r^2 criterion) in wave one than wave two. This might be explained by the longer recall period in wave one, which allowed the independent variables to capture a greater number of significant postpurchase events. As an aid to interpretation, variable relationships found to be large (beta $> \pm .10$) and statistically significant ($p < .01$) in both waves were surrounded by a box.

Core service upgrading had a minimal or nonsignificant impact on the satisfaction variables although the effects were somewhat more pronounced in wave two than wave one (consistent with the higher rate of policy upgrading reported by respondents). Policyholders who were contacted more frequently by the agent and/or for a broader range of purposes tended to be more satisfied with the agent, policy, company, and the relationship overall. Limited evidence existed to show that the frequency/extent of either direct company communication or company advertising exposure affected customer satisfaction. Closer examination of the results revealed the same pattern of association for these two independent variables, that is, a significant linkage to policy, company, and overall satisfaction in wave one only. The findings indicated that policyholders who had experienced problems with their agent's handling of requests were notably less satisfied with their agent. Policyholders who had experienced problems in dealing directly with the company were less satisfied with the company. A clear linkage was also found between exposure to unfavorable mass media information and satisfaction with the policy, company, and overall relationship. Contrary to expectations, the influence of unfavorable W-0-M communciation was negligible and mainly affected satisfaction with the policy (wave one only). Overall satisfaction was found to be a function of satisfaction with the agent, policy, and company in both waves ($R^2 = .70 - .78$, no table).

Clarifying Advertising Effects

The limited association between advertising recall and satisfaction was considered important in light of the substantial resources some firms devote to this promotional activity. The range of consumer advertising expenditures by U.S. life insurance companies in 1983 was between $0 and $30 million. Undoubtedly, many large advertisers include the objective of reinforcing customer loyalty as one of the aims of their promotional program.

Customers may make rather limited inferences about the company based on (their recall of) its advertising frequency. Theory suggests that frequency connotes prominence/popularity only, but company image is obviously much broader than this. To provide a more refined criterion for examining the effects of advertising, the twelve specific attributes of company satisfaction were subjected to a factor analysis with varimax rotation.

Table 18-1
Regressions of Customer Satisfaction Variables on Relationship Communications Variables[1]

	Beta Weights for							
	Value Enhancers				Cost Penalizers		Doubt Creators	
Dependent Variables	Core Service Upgrade	Personal Contact	Direct Co. Comm.	Co. Adv. Exposure	Service Failure (Personal)	Service Failure (Corporate)	Negative Mass Media	Negative W-O-M
Overall Satisfaction								
Wave 1 (R^2=.29)	.06	.23	.14	.12	-.15	-.06*	-.28	-.11
Wave 2 (R^2=.20)	.14	.29	.02*	.02*	-.12*	-.03*	-.23	-.06*
Satisfaction With Agent								
Wave 1 (R^2=.30)	.03*	.38	.03*	.05*	--.28	-.04*	-.14	-.07*
Wave 2 (R^2=.24)	.14	.39	.03*	.00*	-.18	-.06*	-.10*	-.06*
Satisfaction With Policy								
Wave 1 (R^2=.23)	.07	.18	.13	.12	-.09	-.02*	-.28	-.14
Wave 2 (R^2=.16)	.16	.19	.01*	.07*	-.08*	-.08*	-.27	-.05*
Satisfaction With Company								
Wave 1 (R^2=.26)	.05*	.21	.14	.13	-.12	-.15	-.21	-.09
Wave 2 (R^2=.16)	.14	.23	.02*	.05*	-.00*	-.13	-.22	-.08*
Mkt. Presence** (R^2=.16)	.02*	.09	.15	.30 →	-.05*	-.02*	-.08	-.03*
Cons. Orient.** (R^2=.29)	.03*	.29 ←	.12	.12	-.15	-.17	-.18	-.05*

* Association not significant at p < .01

** Measured in wave one only

[1] Regressions employed listwise deletion of missing data (by wave). Wave one cases n = 1,359; Wave two cases n = 529.

Table 18–2
Factor Analysis of Specific Attributes Pertaining to Company Satisfaction

Satisfaction with These Attributes	Factor Loadings*	
	Factor 1	Factor 2
Image: "Consumer Orientation"		
Value of communications	.74	
Accessibility and responsiveness	.71	
Friendly, courteous home office	.68	
Quality of agents	.58	
Image: "Market Presence"		
Strength of reputation		.92
Size and amount of assets		.89
Is established and stable		.88
Extent of geographic coverage		.65

* After Varimax rotation

As shown in table 18–2, two distinct factors emerged. The first factor, labeled *consumer orientation*, seemed to capture the interactive aspects of company image. The second factor, *market presence*, appeared to tap the company's image of being large and well-established. Additive indices representating these subdimensions were formed by summing the attributes (wave one only) having their highest loading on each factor.

The consumer orientation and market presence indices were then regressed on the eight postpurchase experience variables, with results as reported at the bottom of table 18–1. The predictors explained more of the variance in consumer orientation satisfaction (adj. R^2 = .29) than market presence satisfaction (adj. R^2 = .16). Examination of the beta weights revealed that company advertising exposure was the variable most strongly associated with market presence satisfaction (beta = .30). All the other predictors had a nonsignificant or weak linkage with market presence satisfaction. In contrast, personal contact with the agent was the most important predictor of satisfaction with the company's consumer orientation. Further analysis revealed that consumer orientation and market presence satisfaction combined accounted for a substantial portion of the variance in overall company satisfaction (adj. R^2 = .67). The beta coefficients for the predictors were both rather large: market presence = .59, consumer orientation = .53.

Retention Outcomes

The study was also concerned with one of the purported consequences of effective relationship marketing, namely customer retention. Theory and research in services marketing have often assumed that loyalty is a direct consequence of customer satisfaction, yet this association has seldom if ever been empirically examined.

Permanent forms of insurance such as whole life are devices by which insurance companies can capture customer assets for investment. Much like a bank, the insurance company wants to pay as little as possible for these funds and invest them at a higher rate of return. Policyholders can, at any time, recall their assets by surrendering their policies. Approximately two-thirds of surrendered whole life policies are replaced with a different policy. From an insurance company perspective, replacement may be desirable if it is "internal," that is, from one of the company's policies to another. This way the company retains the customer's assets. Internal replacement is especially desirable if it is to a much larger policy (typically the case). Therefore, internal replacement represents an opportunity to capture an even larger share of the customer's assets.

As the results in table 18-3 indicate, relationship satisfaction was indeed related to retention of the customer's assets. This table compares the wave one satisfaction levels of four groups defined on the basis of what happened to their policies between waves one and two. The few customers who internally replaced their policies (group three) displayed the highest satisfaction in wave one across all dimensions. Those who kept the policy in-force were typically the next most satisfied (group one).

Discussion

The findings specifically apply to whole life customers across the spectrum of companies within the U.S. life insurance industry. Scmewhat different

Table 18–3
Relationship between Satisfaction Measures and Service Persistency Behavior

Perdictor Variables From Wave I	Means for Wave Two Outcome Groups*				One-Way Anova Results			
	Still In-Force (Group 1)	Policy Discontinued						
		Not Replaced (Group 2)	Internal Replacement (Group 3)	External Replacement (Group 4)	df	F	Prob.	Significant Contrast @ p < .05
	(N = 848)	(N = 52)	(N = 18)	(N = 65)				
Satisfaction:								
Overall	5.29	4.79	5.94	4.99	3,798	4.82	.0025	1,2,4<3 2<1
Agent	5.54	5.45	6.21	5.22	3,539	1.80	NS	4<3
Policy	5.20	4.78	5.69	5.01	3,796	3.00	.0300	2,4<3 2<1
Company	5.47	4.96	6.02	5.23	3,797	4.00	.0077	2,4<3 2<1

* 7 = extremely satisfied, 1 = extremely dissatisfied

results may apply within specific market segments or for other forms of insurance. Caution must also be taken in attempting to generalize the findings from life insurance to other service contexts. However, this concern is mitigated somewhat if the generalization is to other services in the same category, that is, doubly intangible services (Lovelock 1983). Doubly intangible services involve intangible actions directed at people's intangible assets, for example, financial planning, trusts, limited partnerships, and so on.

The results confirm the need for a carefully crafted relationship marketing strategy. Directly at stake is the retention of existing customers and the opportunity to do more business with them. In making the initial sale, a foundation for relationship development is established. However, these early ties may be weak and are subject to erosion, internal sabotage, and external attack—typical problems in the marketing of most any doubly intangible service.

Preventing Erosion

Erosion refers to the learning process of *extinction* in which the bond between buyer and seller is gradually diminished by a lack of postpurchase contact and reinforcement. Without contact, the seller again becomes a remote and unfamiliar entity to the buyer. Without reinforcement, the buyer is prone to forget why the service was originally purchased. Given a relationship weakened by inattention or one that has never fully crystalized, the stage is set for competition to make inroads. Erosion may be a special problem for doubly intangible services given their characteristics, for example, little visible evidence of service quality, complexity, uncertainty surrounding future benefits, limited customer participation, and so on. It follows that positive steps should be taken to fill this postpurchase reinforcement vacuum. Of course, the question is how.

Core Service Upgrading versus Communication. The findings of this study were that adjustments in insurance coverage/pricing did little if anything to foster relationship satisfaction. This may indicate that the average magnitude of these rewards was insufficient for customers to perceive much value. Alternatively, the problem may be the complexity of the service itself. Complicated calculations are required to determine the true value (price vs. quality) of whole life insurance. Even with an upgrade, customers may remain uncertain as to whether they have a competitive policy. This finding does not diminish the long-run need for sellers to maintain a competitive offering. However, it does suggest that greater leverage can sometimes be obtained with existing customers by applying the interactive resources of the firm.

Enhanced interaction and communication did appear effective in fostering stronger bonds with customers. This confirms speculation that communication plays a central role in the service quality evaluation process (Parasuraman, Zeithaml, and Berry 1985) and in strategies to retain customers (Levitt 1981). In particular, personal follow-up appeared to be the locomotive driving satisfaction with whole life insurance. This adds to a growing body of literature suggesting that a continuous dialogue between the customer and contact person helps ensure satisfaction with complex services (e.g., Day and Bodur 1977; Solomon et al. 1985).

Personal Contact. The importance of personal relationship building for doubly intangible services can probably not be overstated. Due to the long time horizon of service delivery, customers must have considerable faith that providers will keep their promises (high need for reassurance). It is probably easier to trust a person encountered face-to-face than a large, impersonal corporation. However, without adequate opportunities for social exchange and information disclosure, trust cannot develop (Crosby, Evans, and Cowles 1988; Swinth 1967).

Given a complex service and a complex set of needs, customers may become highly dependent on the contact person for technical advice and counseling assistance. Information disclosed face-to-face enables the seller to discriminate the buyer's unique characteristics and needs (Miller and Steinberg 1975). The buyer is no longer a customer but rather a client (Berry 1983). Armed with this idiosyncratic information, the contact person is effectively positioned to identify appropriate service solutions for the client (*ongoing* process of problem solving and customization). Relational communication may also contribute to the contact person being perceived as expert and credible in the buyer's eyes (reassurance and reinforcement). Relationship marketing, the antithesis of mass marketing, gives contact personnel a key role in rewarding customers with social acceptance (social reinforcement) and finding creative ways to build extra performances into the service (labor substitution). Managers of service organizations should examine their compensation systems to determine whether sales and/or service staffs have sufficient incentive to perform follow-up activities and maintain adequate contact with customers (generally not the case in insurance).

Impersonal versus Personal Communication. Personal follow-up was found to contribute more to relationship satisfaction than either direct communication or advertising. While the nature of the communication may partially explain this difference (see following), reciprocity and relationship equity factors may also be involved. Buyers expect their own investment in a relationship to be matched by a similar investment on the seller's part. To be meaningful, the investment should be nontransferable to other relationships. Time spent by the contact person interacting with the customer is, clearly, a nontransferable investment. Advertising and (to a lesser extent) direct communication, may not be perceived as relationship-specific.

Direct Communication. Even with skillful copy design and research, it is doubtful that direct communication from the company can fully compensate for a lack of face-to-face interaction in the context of complex services. Although a minority of sophisticated customers may be able to monitor their own needs and appraise service performance from company-supplied data, the majority lack this expertise. Therefore, information that should technically reassure and reinforce customers about core service benefits is often too difficult to process.

The lack of interactivity in direct media may also be an obstacle to providing adequate customization and problem solving. While direct communication messages can be targeted to individual customers, the flow of information is not instantaneously two-way. however, even the new interactive communications technologies (e.g., videotext) do not appear to have the level of "personalness" many customers seem to require (Cowles 1987). Noninterpersonal sources may be acceptable for market surveillance purposes, but interpersonal communication is desired for affective and behavioral guidance in complex decisions.

Company Advertising. The limited effects of company advertising on policyholder satisfaction also deserve scrutiny. Satisfaction with the institution's market presence was a function of the salience of the company's advertising. Apparently, customers do find it rewarding to own a policy from a company perceived to be large, well established, and preferred by many other customers. In insurance, size connotes that the organization has staying power and will be there to deliver on promises (reassurance). Largeness also implies that many other customers have made the same purchase choice (social reinforcement).

However, it does not appear that advertising is strongly effective in convincing customers the company is consumer oriented. This finding may be attributable to the primary communication role of advertising, namely, to set expectations. These expectations are promises of what the organization *will* deliver in the area of customer service. They are unfilled promises until such time that action is taken, whether that be a response to a customer-initiated request or a follow-up call by the contact person. In other words, customers probably do not see advertising as delivering service *outcomes*.

Avoiding Sabotage

The findings also suggest that personal contact can potentially be quite harmful if handled improperly. This is most likely to occur when the interaction is initiated by the customer who has a particular problem, request, or complaint (e.g., a billing dispute). The avoidance learning that results from ineffective and/or inefficient personal service can be exceedingly difficult for the service organization to extinguish. Subsequent efforts by the marketer to overcome the service weakness may go unnoticed by the customer, who is now attempting to avoid the service and its personnel.

Companies must carefully analyze the reasons for customer service breakdowns. Too often contact personnel cannot or will not take responsibility for solving customer problems. Potential remedies include changes in employee hiring practices, job socialization, and organizational culture. It is also important to empower employees to be problem solvers and to recognize their service achievements. Also, internal marketing is needed to obtain employee input on the formulation of customer service policies, to gain acceptance of the policies once developed, and to seek adoption of appropriate customer service attitudes and behaviors. An information system that tracks the processing of requests/problems/complaints is critically important to effective customer service, as is the availablity of adequate time and people resources to handle the volume of customer contacts (Rosenberg and Czepiel 1983).

Repelling Attack

Perhaps as the result of high source credibility, exposure to negative product information via mass media was found to have a substantial (adverse) impact on satisfaction. This reflects a trend whereby it is becoming increasingly difficult to maintain lasting relationships in the highly competitive financial services sector of the U.S. economy. The media report a steady stream of new products that contravene the customer's prior decisions and give competitive sellers a ready-made premise for their sales approach. This was certainly the case with whole life, the traditional form of permanent insurance, which was challenged by the introduction of universal life policies and by attacks from the Federal Trade Commission (Lynch and Mackay 1985). Faced with this type of external pressure, companies have two basic choices to preserve their customer base. One is to continually innovate and, as needed, move customers into the newer versions of the service. The other alternative is to attempt to fight the trend and convince customers that their original decision remains valid. An opportunity exists to leverage personal contact by attempting to inoculate customers with counterarguments that stress the merits of service loyalty. For example, the uncertainties of switching can be pointed out, customers can be urged to recall their motives for originally buying the service, and they can be encouraged to take a long-term view of what is in their own best interest.

Perhaps the one finding most indicative of a need for theory refinement is that the frequency of exposure to negative W-O-M communication was virtually unrelated to relationship satisfaction. It is particularly anomalous in light of growing evidence regarding the influence of W-O-M sources in service contexts (Reingen et al. 1984). It is possible that outside personal influence only becomes important as the customer moves closer to a decision to switch. This would be consistent with the tendency for consumers to rely on personal sources for behavioral guidance and referrals.

Conclusion

Although attractive from a cost standpoint, the results of the study were not encouraging for the use of an impersonal ("high-tech") relationship strategy for doubly intangible services such as whole life insurance. Given close proximity to the customer and consequent opportunities for relational communication, the contact person (e.g., a life insurance agent) is uniquely positioned to offer added value to the service, control the quality of customer service, and monitor/defend against uncontrollable external influences. Value can be added by providing social reinforcement, reassurance, benefit reinforcement, problem-solving assistance, customization, and labor substitution. Given service complexity, these approaches to strengthening the service relationship appear more effective than gradual improvements in the core service. Although product and technological advances will continue to be important to customer retention, their main application may be in helping contact personnel be more effective as relationship managers.

References

Berry, Leonard L. (1983). "Relationship Marketing." In L. L. Berry, G. L. Shostack, and G. D. Upah (eds.), *Emerging Perspectives on Service Marketing*. Chicago: American Marketing Association, 25–28.

Brandt, Randall D. (1987). "A Procedure for Idenitfying Value-Enhancing Service Components." Paper presented at the 6th Annual Services Marketing Conference, American Marketing Association, September 27–30, San Diego, California.

Cowles, Deborah L. (1987). "Determinants of Consumer Acceptance of Interactive Information/Communication Technologies." Tempe, Arizona: College of Business, Arizona State University, unpublished Ph.D. dissertation.

Crosby, Lawrence A., Kenneth R. Evans, and Deborah L. Cowles. (1988). "Relationship Quality in Services Selling: An Interpersonal Influence Perspective." Paper presented at the 15th International Research Seminar in Marketing, La-Londe-Les-Maures, France.

Crosby, Lawrence A., and Nancy Stephens. (1987). "Effects of Relationship Marketing on Satisfaction, Retention, and Prices in the Life Insurance Industry." *Journal of Marketing Research*, 24 (November), 404–11.

Day, Ralph L., and Muzaffer Bodur. (1977). "Consumer Response to Dissatisfaction with Services and Intangibles." In Ralph L. Day (ed.), *Consumer Satisfaction and Complaining Behavior*. Bloomington, IN: University of Indiana Press.

Dwyer, F. Robert, Paul H. Schurr, and Sejo Oh. (1987). "Developing Buyer-Seller Relationships." *Journal of Marketing*, 51 (2), 11–27.

Grönroos, Christian. (1986). "Developing Service Quality: Some Managerial Implications." Swedish School of Economics, Helsinki, Finland, unpublished working paper.

———. (1987). "Developing the Service Offering—A Source of Competitive Advantdge." Swedish School of Economics, Helsinki, Finland, unpublished working paper.

Hakansson, Hakan. (1982). *International Marketing and Purchasing of Industrial Goods*. New York: John Wiley and Sons.

Hovland, Carl I. (1972). "Effects of the Mass Media of Communication." In Charles S. Steinberg (ed.), *Mass Media and Communication*. New York: Hastings House Publisher, 498–540.

Jackson, Barbara B. (1985). *Winning and Keeping Industrial Customers: The Dynamics of Customer Relationships*. Lexington, MA.: Lexington Books.

Kelley, Harold H., and John W. Thibaut. (1978). *Interpersonal Relations: A Theory of Interdependence*. New York: John Wiley and Sons.

Lehtinen, Jarmo. (1985). *Quality Oriented Services Marketing*. Helsinki: Service Management Institute.

Levitt, Theodore. (1981). "Marketing Intangible Products and Product Intangibles." *Harvard Business Review*, 59 (May–June), 95–102.

Liechty, Margaret G., and Gilbert A. Churchill, Jr. (1979). "Conceptual Insights into Consumer Satisfaction with Services." In Neil Beckwith et al. (eds.), *Educators' Conference Proceedings*. Chicago: American Marketing Association, 509–15.

Lovelock, Christopher H. (1983). "Classifying Services to Gain Strategic Marketing Insights." *Journal of Marketing*, 47 (Summer), 9–20.

Lynch, Michael P., and Robert J. Mackay. (1985). *Life Insurance Products and Consumer Information*. FTC Staff Report by the Bureau of Economics, Washington, DC: U.S. Government Printing Office.

Miller, George R., and Mark Steinberg. (1975). *Between People: An Analysis of Interpersonal Communication*. Chicago: SRA.

Parasuraman, A., Valarie A. Zeithaml, and Leonard L. Berry. (1985). "A Conceptual Model of Service Quality and Its Implications for Future Research." *Journal of Marketing*, 49 (Fall), 41–50.

Reingen, Peter H., Brian Foster, Jacqueline Johnson Brown, and Stephen B. Seidman. (1984). "Brand Congruence in Interpersonal Relations: A Social Network Analysis." *Journal of Consumer Research*, 11 (December), 771–783.

Rosenberg, Larry J., and John A. Czepiel. (1983). "A Marketing Approach for Customer Retention." *Journal of Consumer Marketing*, 1 (2), 45–51.

Solomon, Michael R., Carol Surprenant, John A. Czepiel, and Evelyn G. Gutman. (1985). "A Role Theory Perspective on Dyadic Interactions: The Service Encounter." *Journal of Marketing*, 49 (Winter), 99–111.

Sutherland, Max, and John Galloway. (1981). "Role of Advertising: Persuasion or Agenda Setting." *Journal of Advertising Research*, 21 (October), 25–29.

Swinth, R. L. (1967). "The Establishment of the Trust Relationship." *Journal of Conflict Resolution*, 11 (September), 335–44.

Wilson, David T. (1977). "Dyadic Interactions." In Arch G. Woodside, Jagdish N. Sheth, and Peter D. Bennett (eds.), *Consumer and Industrial Buying Behavior*, New York: Elsevier North-Holland, 355–65.

19

Quality Control in the Service Firm and Consumer Learning

Franklin Allen
Gerald R. Faulhaber

Introduction

Quality control in the management of service firms has been discussed extensively, but subjected to little formal modeling. Several authors have stressed the unique importance of quality for the service firm. For example, Normann (1984, p. 105) states that "the cost of inconsistent quality and the value of . . . consistent quality are . . . of burning interest in the world of management today;" and Shaw (1978, p. 6) notes that "lasting competitive success . . . lies in . . . deliver[ing] quality services."

In virtually every industry, quality matters to customers, and their choice among vendors depends on an assessment of quality, even (perhaps especially!) in the absence of the ability to make prepurchase observations. The intangibility of the service purchase puts the service customer at risk in every transaction, placing a special burden on the marketing strategy of service firms to reduce that risk, to make it easier for the customer to buy its service rather than that of its competitors. This might explain why service firm managers seem to be obsessed with quality control; in many industries, the customers' belief that a particular firm will deliver high-quality service is the principal competitive advantage the firm possesses. The service firm's market strategy will stand or fall on its ability to assure quality *and its customers' beliefs about that quality.*

A service firm's ability to command a premium price in its markets may depend critically on the beliefs that its potential customers hold regarding its ability and willingness to provide consistent quality. How can the firm help shape those beliefs? Clearly, advertising can play a role in informing the market of the intentions of the firm. But ultimately, only one way exists for a firm to convince customers it provides high quality, it must establish a high-quality track record with that customer and with those to whom he or she talks. In other words, the firm's *reputation* in the minds of customers depends on the firm's past performance.

It is useful to view the reputation of a firm as an asset, just as the more traditional manufacturing firm views its plant and equipment. Because reputation is intangible, its value does not show up on the balance sheet. But in economic terms, it may be far more important than the physical assets of the service firm, likely to be minimal. Like any asset, reputation must be carefully maintained; for the service firm, stringent quality control is the long-run investment needed to maintain the firm's quality reputation.

Nelson (1970) referred to goods consumers must actually use to assess their quality, like services, as *experience* goods. Recently, a number of articles have appeared in the economics literature on reputation. In the context of rational choice models, customers will pay a premium for firms with reputations for producing high quality, and the fear of losing future profits from this premium price may dissuade firms from cheating on quality (see, for example, Klein and Leffler (1981), Shapiro (1982, 1983), Dybvig and Spatt (1983), Rogerson (1983), and Allen (1984)).

However, this literature presumes that the quality of the firm's delivered service is perfectly correlated with its input choices. In other words, if a firm has good people, trains them well, and buys the best equipment, then it produces high quality service 100 percent of the time. In fact, even the best-run service firms produce lemons from time to time, and even poorly run firms can have moments of glory. Quality control is never perfect, no matter how much effort is devoted to it. Adding noise to a reputation model would seem to be a trivial generalization. At first blush, it would be expected that the product of a firm delivering high quality only 90 percent of the time to be worth roughly 90 percent of the value of the product of a firm that had perfect quality control, and it could overcome its disadvantage by reducing its price.

In Allen and Faulhaber (1988) a model was investigated with a monopoly firm that was not able to perfectly control its quality. This chapter extends the model to consider competitive markets in which firms likewise cannot perfectly control their quality. The market for high quality may not be sustainable in the presence of such noise. Because customers cannot observe the quality of a firm's inputs, such as human capital (assumed to be fixed and sunk), they must infer this quality from observed outputs. In market equilibrium, customers' initial beliefs about the quality of the firm's inputs are determined by what they (correctly) predict to be the firm's strategy; observations of the output lead them to revise these beliefs, according to Bayes' law.

In keeping with modern microeconomic theory, the model assumes fully rational customers and firms, in which each type of agent maximizes value by making use of all information available, including their knowledge of the structure of the model. The model is characterized by information asymmetry; customers do not know the quality of the firm's inputs although the firm does. Of course, all firms would be willing to claim their inputs are good, but customers do not find "cheap talk" credible. In this model, advertising does not pay. Customers base their beliefs about firms on experience via Bayesian learning. Buyers can predict the strategies that the firm will adopt to maximize profit, and the firm can predict the beliefs of customers, conditional on the firm's output quality, and therefore customers' willingness to pay. The model might best describe markets for business services in which both buyers and sellers are sophisticated market players.

In the second section, the analysis is extended in Allen and Faulhaber (1988) and shown that for competitive market structures, the market for high quality may collapse with even a small amount of noise. Because consumers cannot observe the quality of firms' inputs, they must infer this quality from observed outputs. Thus are firms' reputations established. If input quality is perfectly correlated with output quality, then a single observation suffices for consumers to deduce input quality. However, with quality noise, the consumers' decision problem is Bayesian. The authors require consumers to have consistent conjectures, so that in equilibrium their prior distribution of input quality is correct.

In brief, this result follows from the fact that if consumers are sure that firms will produce high quality, then it pays for the firms to "cheat" and produce low quality because Bayesian learning will be slow (or zero). Consumers know that optimistic beliefs invite deception. Hence, the only consistent conjecture is that all firms will produce low quality. This offers a possible explanation for the emphasis placed by firm managers on the quality control issue and may also explain the puzzling absence of markets for high quality good in situations where both the demand and the potential for market supply seem to be present.[1]

To clarify the exposition, a model is presented in which firms purchase an input (a machine or an education) with one of two quality levels (good or bad); a good machine costs more than a bad machine. The input is sunk for two periods, and in each period will produce either high- or low-quality output, with high-quality output more highly valued by consumers than low-quality output. Good machines produce high-quality output with higher probability than bad machines. The analysis presented in this chapter is limited to two input quality levels, two output quality levels, and two periods. However, it is important to note all results are obtained in a model with a continuum of input quality levels, a continuum of output quality levels, and any number of periods. The generalizations are straightforward (though lengthy) and are omitted from the chapter.

In the third section, the model is extended to include firms' imperfectly choosing inputs, either because the choice process is subject to error or because of quality noise in the upstream production of machines. This extension softens the stark results of the second section, but leads to the paradoxical result that the fewer incompetent firms there are, the more likely it is that a given level of quality noise in production will lead to high-quality market collapse. The fourth section contains concluding remarks.

The Model

First considered are firms that each purchase a machine that will produce output (normalized to one unit) in each of two subsequent periods, at zero marginal cost. A firm can choose either a good machine at a cost c_G or a bad machine at a cost of c_B, with $c_G > c_B$. Both good and bad machines can produce high-quality output, but good machines yield high quality with probability π_G, and bad machines yield high quality with probability π_B with $\pi_G > \pi_B$. Firms are risk neutral and maximize expected profits, discounting second period receipts by the factor δ.

Consumers are (homogeneous) price-takers and expected utility maximizers; they value high quality output at v_H, and low quality output at v_L, with $v_H > v_L$. They know both π_G and π_B, so they are willing to pay

$$w_i = \pi_i v_H + (1-\pi_i)v_L \qquad (1)$$

for the output of a machine they know to be of type i.

It is Pareto optimal for the firm to buy a good machine if the total value of a good machine exceeds both zero and the total value of the bad machine; that is,

$$(1+\delta) \, w_G - c_G > 0, \qquad (2)$$

$$(1+\delta) \, (w_G - w_B) > c_G - c_B. \qquad (3)$$

It is assumed throughout that these inequalities are satisfied.

In general, consumers may not know the firm's machine type, but they do know the level of quality noise: $1 \geqslant \pi_G > \pi_B \geqslant 0$. If these inequalities are strict, consumers cannot tell for sure whether the firm's machine is good or bad, even after observing the first period's output.[2] Consumers have a prior probability r_0 that the firm's machine is good. Using Bayes' rule, consumers' posterior probability that the machine is good, having observed a high quality output, can be expressed as:

$$r_H = \frac{r_0\pi_G}{r_0\pi_G+(1-r_{0)}\pi_B}, \qquad (4)$$

and the probability that the machine is good, having observed a low quality output,[3] as:

$$r_L = \frac{r_0(1-\pi_G)}{r_0(1-\pi_G+(1-r_0)(1-\pi_B)}. \tag{5}$$

Consumers' willingness to pay for the output of a machine in the first period ($j = 0$), or the second period, given that outcome $j = H,L$ was observed, is

$$W_j(r_0) = r_j w_G + (1-r_j)w_B, \qquad j = 0,H,L. \tag{6}$$

Rational expectations are assumed: consumers and firms both know the structure of the model. In equilibrium their expectations must be correct given this knowledge.

The authors assume that firms as well as consumers are price-takers. Each firm buys one (and only one) machine, so supply changes occur through entry/exit, not expansion of existing firms. Because firms are capacity constrained, price can exceed marginal cost in equilibrium. Firms enter or exit if expected profits at market prices are positive or negative, respectively; so in equilibrium, expected profits are zero. Machines (and hence firms) last two periods; previous market growth ensures that in any period new firms coexist with firms with high-quality and low-quality records. In equilibrium, relative prices must be such that consumers are indifferent among these three types of firms. Denoting first period price as p, and second period price, conditional on the outcome $j = H,L$ of the first period's production, as p_j, relative prices must satisfy

$$W(r_0) - p = W_H(r) - p_H = W_L(r) - p_L, \tag{7}$$

so that relative prices depend on consumers' beliefs about firms' quality r_0.

Expected profits for the firm from a machine of type i are

$$EZ_i(r_0) = p(r_0) + \delta\{\pi_i p_H(r_0) + (1-\pi_i)p_L(r_0)\} - c_i. \tag{8}$$

Equation (8) is written to show the explicit dependence of expected profits on the consumers' prior r_0.

The zero profit competitive equilibrium condition is

$$\max_{i=G,B} EZ_i(r_0) = 0. \tag{9}$$

The equilibrium prices are determined from equations (7) and (9) as functions of r_0.

Firms will install a good machine if and only if

$$\Delta EZ(r_0) = EZ_G - EZ_B > 0 . \tag{10}$$

Clearly, the choice of machine affects profits only insofar as it affects the likelihood of a high quality output in the first period, and thus a higher price in the second period.

Three cases are considered.

1. Firms' machine types are observable, that is, the baseline case of complete information.
2. Firms' machine types are not observable, and $\pi_B = 0$, $\pi_G = 1$, that is, information asymmetry but no quality noise.
3. Firms' machine types are not observable, and $0 < \pi_B < \pi_G < 1$, that is, information asymmetry and quality noise.

In case 1, the firm can control r_0 because its machine type can be observed by the consumer. Thus, r_0 is either zero or one, depending on whether the firm installs a good or bad machine. From (4) and (5), it can be seen that $r_H = r_L = r_0$, so that the consumer has no need of further information. In this case, condition (10) is identical to (3), and the firm will always install a good machine: the first-best outcome is always achieved.

In case 2, it is noted from (4) and (5) that $r_H = r_L = 0$ independent of r_0,[4] which expresses the "no noise" assumption that a single observation of output suffices to establish quality. Hence, second period prices p_H and p_L are also independent of the consumers' prior r_0, and therefore so is condition (9). Both consumers as well as firms will know whether or not (9) obtains; good machnes are either profitable or not. Therefore, the only two possible consistent consumer priors are $r_0 = 0$ and $r_0 = 1$. Without consumer observability of the firm's machine type, the firm cannot affect consumers' priors; in evaluating (9), the firm takes r_0 as independent of its choice of machine type. In this case, the firm installs a good machine if and only if

$$\Delta EZ = \delta(v_H - v_L) - (c_G - c_B) \geq 0 \tag{11}$$

(assuming that if the firm is indifferent, it chooses a good machine). If this incentive compatibility condition obtains, the first-best outcome is achieved. However, if it is not met, then the firm will not install a good machine because a bad machine is more profitable. Thus, the firm will install a bad machine if it is profitable to do so $((1+\delta)v_L > c_B)$, and otherwise will install no machine. The result here is similar to Allen (1984), in which information asymmetries may or may not lead to an inefficiency, in contrast to Shapiro (1983), in which asymmetries always lead to an inefficiency.

In the most general situation, case 3, both consumers and firms know whether or not condition (10) obtains for any given r_0, and therefore whether the firm will install a good or bad machine. Again, the only consistent consumers' priors are $r_0 = 1$ and $r_0 = 0$. Evaluating condition (10) at these points, we have

$$\Delta EZ(0) = \Delta EZ(1) = -(c_G - c_B) < 0 . \tag{12}$$

If consumers have the optimistic prior of $r_0 = 1$, then it is more profitable for the firm to install a bad machine, and hence this prior is not consistent. The only consistent prior is $r_0 = 0$.[5]

These results can be summarized as follows:

Proposition 1:

In a free-entry, zero-profit competitive market,

1. if machine types are observable, then firms always install good machines (case 1).
2. if machine types are not observable and if $\pi_B = 0$ and $\pi_G = 1$, then firms install good machines if and only if $\delta(v_H - v_L) > c_G - c_B$; otherwise, the firm installs a bad machine if profitable at a competitive $p \leq w_B$, and no machine if not (case 2).
3. if $0 < \pi_B < \pi_G < 1$, then firms never install good machines; they install bad machines if profitable at a competitive $p \leq w_B$, and no machine if not (case 3).

A comparison of parts 1, 2, and 3 of Proposition 1 shows the sharp discontinuity in the equilibrium outcome as a result of introducing even the smallest amount of quality noise. This rather surprising collapse of high quality equilibria with less than perfect quality control is suggestive of a moral hazard version of Akerlof's (1970) lemons market. The reason for the part 3 result is that consumers' ability to deduce from the model firms' optimal behavior leads them to have these extreme priors, which in turn leads them to ignore learning. No track record could be so poor as to discourage the optimistic consumer, and no track record could be so outstanding as to impress the jaded skeptic. Consumers know, as do firms, that optimism invites deception. They thus choose the skeptic's role, and firms find it optimal to fulfill their expectations. Because all real production processes involved some measure of quality noise, this result suggests that this "optimism invites deception" problem may be at the base of managers' concerns about quality control, quoted in the introduction.

This discontinuity result seems too strong. Though the concerns of managers regarding quality consistency suggest strong forces at work, intuition says that high-quality producers do exist in many markets. The next section introduces yet more randomness into the model, softening the strong discontinuity result and still explaining potential market failures and real firms' concern for quality control.

Imperfect Input Selection

The analysis of the previous section assumed that all firms are identical, have access to the same technology, and are able to choose which type of machine to install. Once installed, the machines are subject to quality noise; but firms are assumed to make their input choice faultlessly. Clearly, this assumption is neither realistic nor in keeping with the spirit of this chapter. This section introduces noise into the input selection process and analyzes the effects on the equilibrium outcomes. Several possible sources of input selection noise exist.

1. There may be quality noise in the upstream production of machines; even if the firm buys its machine from a reputable machine firm, it may still be a "lemon."
2. The internal process by which firms choose machines may be inherently noisy.

In either case, it is assumed that the fraction λ of firms intending to buy a good machine will end up with a good machine, $0 < \lambda < 1$,[6] and the fraction $1 - \lambda$ of such firms will end up with a bad machine. Both firms and consumers know λ.

A firm's expected profits from installing what it hopes is a good machine are

$$EZ_{\lambda G} = p + \delta\lambda\{\pi_G p_H + (1 - \pi_G)p_L\} + \delta(1 - \lambda)\{\pi_B p_H + (1 - \pi_B)p_L\} - c_G \quad (13)$$

and expected profits from installing a bad (for sure) machine are

$$EZ_{\lambda B} = p + \delta\{\pi_B p_H + (1 - \pi_B)p_L\} . \quad (14)$$

The zero profit condition is

$$\max_{i=G,B} EZ_{\lambda i}(r_0) = 0 , \quad (15)$$

which, combined with (7) determine equilibrium prices.

Subtracting (14) from (13), and using (6) and (7), to obtain

$$\Delta EZ_{\lambda}(r_0) = \delta\lambda(\pi_G - \pi_B)(r_H - r_L)(w_G - w_B) - (c_G - c_B) . \quad (16)$$

As before, if r_0 is zero or one, then $p_H = p_L$, and the expected difference in profits from installing a good machine is the negative of the cost difference of the two machine types, as in (12). However, interest now turns to the behavior of $\Delta EZ_{\lambda}(r_0)$ between these two extremes. Using (7) and (9) it can be shown that $d^2\Delta EZ_{\lambda}/dr_0^2 < 0$, so that $\Delta EZ_{\lambda}(r_0)$ is a concave function of r_0. The example in figure 19–1 shows a situation in which $\Delta EZ_{\lambda} < 0$ for $r^* < r_0 < r^{**}$. It is also possible that for all r_0, $\Delta EZ_{\lambda} < 0$.

Because consumers as well as firms know λ, the only consistent priors are $r_0 = 0$ (if consumers believe firms will choose a bad machine) and $r_0 = \lambda$ (if consumers believe firms will try to install a good machine and will be successful with probability λ). Because $\Delta EZ_{\lambda}(0) < 0$ for all λ a consistent equilibrium always exists in which the firm installs a bad machine if profitable and no machine if not. If $\Delta EZ_{\lambda}(\lambda) < 0$, no other equilibrium exists. However, if $\Delta EZ_{\lambda}(\lambda) \geq 0$, then λ is a consistent prior, and an equilibrium exists in which the firm intends to install good machines and is successful with probability λ. This good machine equilibrium Pareto dominates the bad machine equilibrium because (1) consumers prefer the case in which firms attempt to buy good machines (generalizing (3) to $(1+\delta)\lambda(w_G - w_B) > c_G - c_B$), and (2) firms are indifferent because they earn zero profits in either equilibrium.

These results can be summarized as follows.

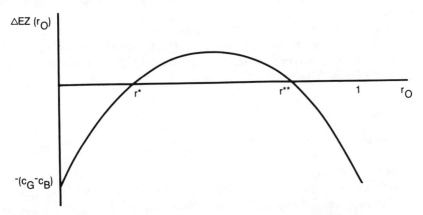

Figure 19–1. Expected profits for a good machine conditional on consumers' expectations.

Proposition 2:

In a free entry zero profit competitive market, if firms who intend to install good machines are successful with probability λ, then

1. an equilibrium exists in which no firm intends to install good machines.
2. an equilibrium exists in which all firms intend to install good machines, if and only if $\Delta EZ_\lambda(\lambda) \geq 0$. This equilibrium Pareto dominates the equilibrium of part 1.

Comparing Propositions 1 and 2 reveals that accounting for noise in the input selection process allows the possibility of a high quality equilibrium, even with quality noise in the production process. Introducing an additional source of noise has reestablished the good machine equilibrium. However, Proposition 2 is a paradoxical result: only if enough bad machines are chosen will a high quality equilibrium be sustainable in the presence of quality noise. Only the possibility of enough bad machines will ensure that there will be any good machines!

The intuition behind this result comes from the nature of the "optimism invites deception" result; if consumers are too optimistic ($r_0 = 1$), they know that firms will take advantage of that optimism and install bad machines. However, if consumers expect a certain number of firms to have bad machines (or equivalently, they expect that the monopoly firm will have a bad machine with a certain nonzero probability). Consumers are then sufficiently skeptical, so they do not fall into the "optimism invites deception" trap. Their prior is not so strong that they ignore the data, and thus they reward high quality in the first period with higher prices in the second period. It is this rational skepticism that permits high quality to be sustained.

A high quality equilibrium obtains under Proposition 2 if and only if $\lambda \in [r^*, r^{**}]$. It can be shown that higher π_G (better quality control) leads to higher r^{**}, and it is therefore more likely that the good machine equilibrium will obtain. This leads to

Proposition 3:

Given some exogenous $\lambda < 1$, a critical π_G exists such that $r^{**} = \lambda$; for $\pi_G < \pi_G$, the bad machine obtains, and for $\pi_G \geq \pi_G$, the good machine equilibrium obtains.

Profit consequences for the monopoly firm are shown in figure 19–2. Profits change discontinuously at the critical π_G, which suggests a reason for the concern of managers for quality consistency. A small change in the quality control level may lead to a large change in profits.

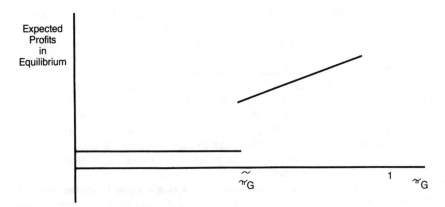

Figure 19–2. Expected profits as a function of quality control results.

Conclusion

Adding quality noise to the production process can drastically alter the nature of the equilibrium, as shown in the context of a simple reputation model. If every firm can choose without error the type of machine to install, then no good machine equilibria exist in the presence of any quality noise. A good machine equlibrium exists only if firms make imperfect input choices so that consumers are sufficiently skeptical for their priors to adjust rapidly in the light of firms' performance.

The results suggest that not all industries need be successful at sustaining a high-quality equilibrium. Examples were cited of markets in which both demand and supply conditions would appear to be ripe for a high-quality market, but none can be sustained.

Even those industries successful at sustaining a high-quality equilibrium have no guarantee of its permanence. An exogenous shift in either quality control or in input selection noise may destroy an existing high-quality (more profitable) equilibrium. The profit penalty from even small changes may be quite severe.

This chapter has illustrated the "optimism invites deception" result in the context of a simple model. However, it seems clear from the nature of the argument that the result is applicable in many other rational expectations models with learning.

Notes

1. One hundred percent of the authors' unscientific sample of two-career families with young children agree on the uniformly low quality of private for-hire day-

care services, although non-profit day care, or day care bundled as part of employment, is reported to be superior. A more exotic, and more tragic, example is given in Rashid (1988). He describes the adulteration of milk, and consumers' correct expectations of adulteration, in Dacca, Bangladesh. Newspapers regularly publish photographs of farmers diluting milk with filthy canal water on their way to market, so consumers are well aware of the problem. However, no market for unadulterated (high quality) milk seems to be sustainable.

2. Another interpretation of this model is possible: the "noise" may be in consumers' ability to perceive the quality of output rather than in the firms' quality control. For example, a doctor with a high-quality education (a good "machine") may always deliver high-quality output to patients, but patients may make errors in judging the quality they receive.

3. It is assumed that each consumer sees a single draw from the Bernoulli distribution in the first period. This would be true if all units produced by the machine in a single period were of the same quality. A more realistic model would have each consumer experiencing a separate draw from the distribution and consumers sharing information, so that the first period would generate a sample size of $n > 1$. All the results would obtain for this model as well; we use the simpler approach to avoid unnecessary complexity.

4. This follows directly for $0 < r_0 < 1$. At $r_0 = 0$, equation (4) is of the form "0/0" and is undefined. However, taking the limit as $r_0 -> 0$, we have that $r_H ->$ 1. Similarly, at $r_0 = 1$, equation (5) is undefined, but as $r_0 -> 1$, $r_L ->0$.

5. There may exist other consistent priors; suppose that if good machines and bad machines are equally profitable firms choose a good machine with probability α, and suppose further that at $r_0 = \alpha$ good machines and bad machines actually are equally profitable; then $r_0 = \alpha$ is a consistent prior, and a mixed strategy equilibrium exists. In this chapter as in Allen and Faulhaber (1988) we focus on pure strategy equilibria.

6. If quality noise π^*_G in the upstream production process caused this selection error, then $\lambda = \pi^*_G$.

References

Akerlof, G. (1970). "The Market for Lemons." *The Quarterly Journal of Economics*, 84, 488–500.

Allen, F. (1984). "Reputation and Product Quality." *The RAND Journal of Economics*, 15, 311–27.

Allen, F., and G. Faulhaber. (1988). "Optimism Invites Deception." *The Quarterly Journal of Economics*, CIII, 397–407.

Dybvig, P., and C. Spatt. (1983). "Does It Pay to Maintain a Reputation? Consumer Information and Product Quality." Mimeo, New Haven, CT: Yale University.

Klein, B., and K. Leffler. (1981). "The Role of Market Forces in Assuring Contractual Performance." *Journal of Political Economy*, 89, 615–41.

Nelson, P. (1970). "Information and Consumer Behavior." *Journal of Political Economy*, 78 (March/April), 311–29.

Normann, R. (1984). *Service Management*. New York: Wiley.

Rashid, S. (1988). "Quality in Contestable Markets: A Historical Problem?" *The Quarterly Journal of Economics*, CIII, 245–49.

Rogerson, W. (1983). "Reputation and Product Quality." *The Bell Journal of Economics*, 14, 508–16.

Shapiro, C. (1982). "Consumer Information, Product Quality and Seller Reputation." *The Bell Journal of Economics*, 13, 20–35.

_____. (1983). "Premiums for High Quality As Returns to Reputations." *The Quarterly Journal of Economics*, 98, 659–80.

Shaw, J. (1978). *The Quality-Productivity Connection*. New York: Van Nostrand.

20

Service Quality and Knowledge Production

Kiyoshi Kobayashi
David F. Batten
Åke E. Andersson

This chapter develops an analytical framework to investigate the structure of local service markets with free entry. Market structure and service quality are determined endogenously and simultaneously. A simple comparative analysis is made to evaluate the impacts of knowledge spillover on market structure and the quality of services supplied in local markets. Improvements to network efficiency and hence accessibility are found to increase the degree of concentration and the R&D intensity of firms.

Introduction

Service sectors in most nations occupy a large part of the economy and are undergoing gradual but major qualitative changes. Although most consumers still have relatively few basic service needs—such as transportation, education, health, and the like—myriads of changes are occurring at the intermediate stages of production or distribution, as well as among the individual choice processes of households. Regardless of whether intermediate services or final services are considered, advancing sophistication and technological evolution consist mainly of substituting new means of consumer satisfaction for old ones. The basic needs do not undergo radical changes, but the detailed ways and means of satisfying them may alter markedly (Batten and Johansson 1987).

Since the pioneering work of Schumpeter (1947), much research attention has been paid to the relation between the pace of inventive and innovative activity and the structure of markets. A substantial part of the recent industrial organization literature appears to have interpreted tests of the Schumpeterian hypothesis in different ways. Many empirical studies exist that investigate various aspects of R&D activities and relate them to the structure of the markets in which such activities are undertaken. Most of this research has been directed at the behavior of a single industrial firm engaged in R&D in the midst of an exogenously given environment.

To understand the structure of local service markets undergoing technological innovation, it is necessary to move beyond the analysis of a single firm engaged in R&D and consider a set of interacting firms. Recently, Dasgupta and Stiglitz (1980) provided an analytical framework relating the market structure under oligopolistic competition to the nature of inventive activities. They argued that except in the short run, both market structure and the nature of inventive activities are endogenous—both depend on more basic ingredients, such as the technology of R&D, demand conditions, the nature of capital markets, and so on. Although they succeeded in paving the way to investigate the relationship between market structure and R&D intensity, some important aspects of R&D are excluded from their discussions. Their interests are confined to process R&D (i.e., R&D designed to reduce the cost of production) in the industrial sector. Knowledge is supposed to be monoplized by a firm; R&D activity is undertaken exclusively by that firm. These assumptions seem less applicable in the investigation of the structure of local service markets, in which R&D activity may be expected to contribute to the enhancement of service quality.

This chapter offers an analytical foundation to investigate the relations between market structure, service quality, and R&D intensity in local service markets. In this framework, R&D activity can contribute not only to a reduction in the costs of producing services, but also to the improvement of service quality. Diffusion of knowledge among firms forms an essential ingredient of the external economy in service production. Thus, earlier work must be modified in an investigation of market structure and R&D activity in the service sectors. Focus is on the relationship between the degree of concentration and the R&D intensity of service activities. The authors also discuss the attributes of knowledge—the final outputs of R&D—as a public good; knowledge can be shared by all firms. This property of knowledge has important consequences not only for market structure but also for service quality.

First, the analytical framework in which some basic properties of local service markets are characterized is described. The third section proposes a basic model for the behavior of service-producing firms who undertake their knowledge production (R&D) exclusively and then discusses the long-term structure of local service markets with free entry. In the fourth section the model is extended to consider knowledge diffusion among other firms. The impacts of knowledge spillover both on market structure and on service quality are discussed.

Local Service Markets and Knowledge Production

The Role of Knowledge in Service Production

Knowledge production (Machlup 1980) can contribute to not only a reduction in the costs of producing a service but also an enhancement of service quality. Some difficulties in assessing the role of knowledge in service production exist. For most service production, knowledge cannot be distinguished from measurements of inputs and outputs. Regardless of whether knowledge production contributes to cost reduction or quality improvement, still lacking are the means to evaluate the knowledge component in most service activities. Although this treatment remains far from comprehensive, at least some of the intrinsic features of knowledge are explicitly taken into account.

Knowledge stocks are treated as endogenous public goods. Rather than being used up in the process of production, knowledge is expanded and enhanced by way of exchange processes on a human network in a local service market (Batten, Kobayashi, and Andersson 1989). The emphasis here will be on the spillover effects of knowledge in service production, derived from the exchange process of knowledge among individuals interacting on local networks. The exchange quality of this human network is crucial in knowledge diffusion. The various stocks of knowledge resources are also important determinants. Knowledge infrastructure (which facilitates all kinds of knowledge diffusion) plays an essential role in shaping the external economy for service production.

The following section develops an analytical foundation for the economic analysis of service production. To cater to the public goods character of knowledge, the assumption is made that the production of knowledge designed to increase service quality is separable from that designed for cost reduction. A production function for knowledge stocks in each firm is derived in terms of the size of its knowledge-handling work force (hereafter called K-workers) and the aggregate level of accessibility to knowledge stocks in all firms in the local service market. The optimal R&D policy for each firm in an oligopolistic market is formulated as a profit-maximization problem in which the level of service quality is included as an endogenous variable.

Outputs of service production and service quality are influenced by the preferred characteristics of that service, the demand elasticity for service quality, the chosen knowledge production technology, and the level of knowledge accessibility in the region. Such overall properties of a regional economy determine market structure and the R&D intensity of local service sectors. Given a regional environment of service markets, each firm will choose the optimal level of service quality and of quantity supplied. The market structure and the R&D intensity of identical subcategories of service sectors may vary in different regions. To some extent, these variations reflect differences between regional environments. A given region's environment can be characterized by (1) service production technology, (2) knowledge production technology, (3) demand for service quality and quantity, (4) stocks of knowledge resources, and (5) quality of contact networks. The aim here is to identify a set of characteristics within a regional environment that strongly influence each firm's R&D strategy, to wit, how much should be spent on R&D and what kind of research strategy should be pursued. Each of these decisions has important consequences not only for market structure but also for service quality.

Description of Local Service Markets

In this section, an analytical framework is developed relating the market structure for services to the nature of R&D in the private service sectors. The purpose is to show that both market structure and R&D activities are endogenously determined within the regional environment (as discussed in the previous section). The objectives of this section are to formalize the local service market as an oligopolistic market with free entry and to formulate a model within which the trade-off between production efficiency and service quality can be discussed.

The essential character of a local service market can be described by the following factors: (1) the level of service quality provided, (2) the price of services, (3) the quantity of service supplied by each firm, and (4) the number of firms in the market. Suppose that all services supplied by local firms are homogeneous; that the service market is symmetric (i.e., firms behave identically); and that firms possess the same production technology. Consideration of heterogeneous service markets—which depend on other analytical strands—is postponed for the present. Suppose in addition that the local market structure is endogenous. There is free entry into the market. Let n be the number of service-producing firms in the local market; let $q_i(>0)$ $(i=1,—,n)$ denote the outputs of each firm i; q_i can be measured by the number of contracts or service transactions. Then it follows that a local service market can be characterized by

$$\Omega[n;(p_1,v_1,q_1),—,(p_n,v_n,q_n)], \tag{1}$$

where p_i is the price and v_i the quality level of service supplied by firm i. Let $\hat{q_i}(i=1,...,n)$ denote the quantity of services supplied by all firms other than the i-th firm. Under the assumption of a symmetric market and homogeneity of services, we have $p_1 = --- = p_n = p$, $q_1 = --- = q_n = q$, $q_i = (n-1)q$ and $v_1 = --- = v_n = v$. In our local market, the customers spend their money on services offered by firms in the local market. The demand schedule that firm i faces can be described by

$$Q = D\{p,v\} \tag{2}$$

The Local Service Market with Free Entry

Knowledge and Service Production

Both types of activities—producing knowledge and producing services—complement each other in the supply of services. The production of knowledge denotes activities designed to increase the quality of services. This can be achieved by creating new knowledge and/or by acquiring the relevant knowledge from elsewhere to enhance service quality. Activities contributing to the increase of service quality are referred to as product R&D. Production of services means activities that contribute to the technical production of services. Some customer services require technical endeavor. For example, the improvement of service production technology may raise the level of service productivity. Such activities are not necessarily intended to increase the quality of services, but rather to capitalize on knowledge accumulated from past experiences and from recent new ideas. Such activities will be termed *process R&D*.

Consider a firm facing the demand schedule (2). Suppose that product R&D technology is strongly separable from process R&D technology. Two types of production function can then be introduced: a knowledge production function and a service production function, and its associated division of the labor force—"knowledge-handling worker (K-workers)" and "service-handling workers (S-workers)." The category of K-workers includes any persons who are literally engaged in producing knowledge. Researchers, scholars, artists, planners, and so on are included in this category. The category of S-workers contains a broader class of workers mainly concerned with refining or providing the service itself. Besides secretaries, clerks, executives, and office workers, all workers engaged in physical activity will be in the S-category.

Our typical firm is supposed to produce services with inputs of K-workers, S-workers, and capital goods. The rate of quantitative outputs is regulated by the input levels of S-workers, K-workers, and capital goods. K-workers contribute to knowledge usage in service production, for example, the adaptation of new knowledge for service production. The quantitative technological relationship between the rate of the final outputs q_i and the required levels of inputs can be summarized by a service production function. Suppose that a large amount of capital goods is not required in product R&D in our local markets. Accessibility to accumulated knowledge in the region is then rather crucial. The relation between the rate of qualitative outputs v_i, the inputs of K-workers, and the level of accessibility to regional knowledge resources can be expressed by a knowledge production function. The service levels of knowledge infrastructure should also be included as a variable in the knowledge production function.

As discussed so far, the rate of quantitative outputs is regulated by a service production function. Suppose that process R&D technology (e.g., adaptation of new technology) is separable from the classical part of a service production function. The service production function takes the following weakly separable form:

$$q_i = \Phi \{f(K_i, X_i), g(s_i, c_i)\} , \qquad (3)$$

where K_1 is the number of K-workers, X_i is the accessibility to regional knowledge resources, s_i is the number of S-workers, and c_i is the amount of capital goods. Suppose that the function g retains the properties of a neoclassical production function with constant returns to scale; f and Φ are twice continuously differentiable and quasiconcave.

A product R&D function explains the relation between the levels of inputs and the rate of qualitative outputs (represented by a shift parameter v_i in the demand schedule). Suppose that a product R&D function is assumed to take the following general form:

$$v_i = h(G_i, Z_i) , \qquad (4)$$

where G_i is the number of K-workers, and Z_i is the accessibility to knowledge resources in the region; h is also twice continuously differentiable and quasiconcave.

The Microeconomic Behavior of a Service-Producing Firm

Consider the inverse demand function of equation (2), expressing the price of services as a function of the quantity supplied q_i and the service quality v_i:

$$p_i = p(q_i + \hat{q_i}; v_i) , \qquad (5)$$

Given the output levels of all firms other than i-th firms, $(\hat{q_i}, \hat{v_i})$, the problem of firm i is given by

$$\text{Max}_{K_i, G_i, s_i, c_i} \{p(q_i + \hat{q_i}, v_i)q_i - \omega_1(K_i + G_i) - \omega_2 s_i - \omega_3 c_i\} \qquad (6)$$

subject to

$$q_i = \Phi\{f(K_i,X_i), g(s_i,c_i)\} \text{ , and}$$
$$v_i = h(G_i,Z_i) \text{ ,} \tag{7}$$

where ω_1, ω_2 and ω_3 are the factor prices. Under the assumption of constant returns to scale in g, the following cost function is obtained:

$$C_i = C(K_i;\omega_2, \omega_3)q_i \text{ .} \tag{8}$$

For simplicity, let ω_1 be a numeraire. Then the problem can be transformed to

$$\text{Max}_{q_i,K_i,G_i} \{[p(q_i + q_i^{\hat{}}; h(G_i,Z_i)) - C(K_i,X_i)]q_i - G_i - K_i\} \text{ .} \tag{9}$$

Suppose for the moment that R&D activity is exclusively undertaken in the service sector. In other words, knowledge is monopolized by a firm when it pays for it. This assumption is relaxed in the next section. Firms are assumed to behave in a Cournot fashion (i.e., each firm chooses its own R&D expenditures and production levels to maximize profits in a noncooperative manner). The basic model without knowledge spillover is then

$$\text{Max}_{q_i,K_i,G_i} \{[p(q_i + q_i;h(G_i)) - C(K_i)]q_i - G_i - K_i\} \text{ .} \tag{10}$$

The first-order optimality conditions are

$$p(Q,v) \{1 - q_i/\varepsilon(q_i,v)Q\} = C(K_i) \tag{11}$$

$$(\partial p/\partial G_i)q_i = 1 \tag{12}$$

$$(\partial C/\partial K_i)q_i = -1, \tag{13}$$

where $\varepsilon(Q,v) = -(p/Q)(\partial Q/\partial p(Q,v))$, which is the elasticity of demand for services. Equation (11) equates the marginal revenue of services to the marginal cost of service production. From equation (12), we understand that the marginal revenue of product R&D is equal to its marginal cost. It is also clear from equation (13) that the marginal cost reduction obtained by process R&D is equal to the marginal cost of process R&D.

Market Equilibrium Condition in The Long Run

Suppose that market structure is endogenous and free entry into a local market exists. Let n^* be the equilibrium number of firms in the region. Denote the market equilibrium Ω^* by $\{n^*,p^*,v^*;(q^*_i,G^*_i,K^*_i)i=1,\text{---}$

,n*}, which can be characterized by the following conditions:

$$\sum_{i=1}^{n} \{p^*(Q^*,v^*) - C(K^*_i)\}q^*_i - \sum_{i=1}^{n^*} (G^*_i + K^*_i) > 0, \tag{14}$$

and

$$\sum_{i=1}^{n} \{p^{**}(Q^{**},v^{**}) - C(K^*_i)\}q^*_i - \sum_{i=1}^{n^*} (G^*_i + K^*_i) +$$

$$\{p^{**}(Q^{**},v^{**}) - C(K^*_{n^*+1})\}q^*_{n^*+1} - G^*_{n^*+1} - K^*_{n^*+1} < 0, \tag{15}$$

where $Q^* = \sum_{i=1}^{n^*} q^*_1$, and $Q^{**} = \sum_{i=1}^{n^{**}} q^*_i$. Conditions (14) and (15) must be satisfied if there are no barriers to entry. It is then impossible for a new firm to enter and to earn positive profits, if the i-th firm in the market $(i=1,—,n^*)$ chooses to produce at the level (q^*,G^*,K^*).

The characteristics of this equilibrium with free entry are greatly simplified, if p^*,q^*,G^*,K^*, and n^* characterize a symmetric equilibrium with free entry, and if the number of firms is large enough to assume that free entry results in firms earning negligible profits. Conditions (14) and (15) can then be simplified to the following conditon:

$$\{p^*(Q^*,v^*) - C(K^*)\}Q^* = n^*H^* , \tag{16}$$

where the total outputs at equilibrium are $Q^* = n^*q^*$, and $H^* = G^* + K^*$ are the firms' total expenditures on R&D. The first-order optimality conditions can be simplified to

$$p^*(Q^*,v^*)\{1 - 1/n^*\varepsilon(Q^*,v^*)\} = C(K^*), \tag{17}$$

$$\phi^*Q^*/n^* = 1, \tag{18}$$

$$\psi^*Q^*/n^* = -1, \tag{19}$$

where $\phi^* = (\partial p/\partial G)_{p^*,G^*}$, $\psi^* = (\partial C/\partial K)_{K^*}$. Then, n^*, Q^*, K^*, and G^* are obtained from equations (16) and (17), (18), and (19).

The authors now proceed to analyze the market equilibrium conditions in detail. From equations (16) and (17), the following can derived:

$$\frac{1}{n^*} = \varepsilon \, \frac{n^*H^*}{p^*Q^*} = \varepsilon R^*, \tag{20}$$

where $R* = n*H*/p*Q*$ is the fraction of industry sales that is spent on R&D; an obvious index for the R&D intensity of local industries. The LHS of equation (20) can be regarded as an index of the degree of concentration. Thus equation (20) defines the relation between the degree of concentration and the degree of R&D intensity in local industries. If ε is constant in the cross-section study of different regions, the degree of concentration is proportional to $R*$. It shows that if R&D intensity increases, the degree of concentration will increase.

In deriving equation (20), equations (18) and (19) were ignored. R&D intensity does not depend on firms choosing their R&D strategies with a view to profit maximization. It depends instead on R&D technology itself. From equations (18) and (19), comes

$$\phi* = -\psi*, \tag{21}$$

Let us define $\alpha = (\partial p/\partial G)/(P*/G*)_{q*G*}$, $\beta = -(\partial C/\partial K)/(C*/K*)_{K*}$, ($\alpha > 0$, $\beta > 0$), which are the price elasticity with respect to knowledge inputs and the cost elasticity with respect to knowledge resources, respectively. Equations (18) and (19) lead to

$$\frac{n*G*}{p*Q*} = \phi*G*/p* = \alpha, \tag{22}$$

and

$$\frac{n*K*}{p*Q*} = -\psi*K*/p* = \beta C*/p*. \tag{23}$$

From equation (16), it is known that

$$R* = (p* - C*)/p*, \tag{24}$$

which is identical to the definition of Lerner's index of monopolistic power. From equations (22), (23), and (24), the following is derived:

$$R* = (\alpha + \beta)/(1 + \beta). \tag{25}$$

The definition of R leads to $1 \geqslant R \geqslant 0$. If $1 \geqslant \alpha \geqslant 0$, $\beta \geqslant 0$, R can be properly defined.

Condition (21) helps in understanding each firm's R&D strategy. The optimal R&D share between process and product R&D is given by

$$\frac{K^*}{G^*} = \frac{\beta(1 - \alpha)}{\alpha(1 + \beta).} \tag{26}$$

Considering equation (25), the following results:

$$\frac{n^*G^*}{p^*Q^*} = \alpha, \tag{27}$$

$$\frac{n^*K^*}{p^*Q^*} = \frac{\beta(1 - \alpha)}{1 + \beta}. \tag{28}$$

The terms on the LHS of equations (27) and (28) define the relative intensity of product and process R&D, respectively.

Thus, R&D intensity and the expenditure-share between process and product R&D are endogenously determined depending on the elasticity of prices with respect to knowledge inputs and that of cost reduction with respect to knowledge inputs. Then, the degree of concentration can be characterized by R&D technology. From equations (20) and (24), one obtains the equilibrium number of firms as

$$n^* = \frac{1 + \beta}{\varepsilon \, (\alpha + \beta).} \tag{29}$$

Equations (25) and (29) reveal that the larger the elasticity of demand ε, the smaller the number of firms. For any given number of firms, service activities with a smaller demand elasticity can be characterized by a higher value of R&D intensity. The higher degree of price elasticity with respect to knowledge inputs results in a higher degree of R&D intensity; the higher elasticity of cost reduction also leads firms to a higher R&D intensity.

If each firm chooses decision (q^*, G^*K^*), which satisfies the conditions (27), (28), and (29), each will have maximized its profits given the choice of others. Two extreme cases are investigated here: (1) $\alpha \to 0$, $\beta \to 0$, and (2) $\varepsilon \to 0$, . Assume that α, β, and ε are constants. If $\alpha \to 0$, $\beta \to 0$ for given $\varepsilon > 0$, we have $R^* \to 0$. From equation (24), $C^*/p^* \to 1$. Equation (31) shows that $n^* \to \infty$ as $\alpha \to 0$ and $\beta \to 0$. In the limit as $\alpha \to 0$, $\beta \to 0$, our service market approaches a perfectly competitive market. However, if $\varepsilon \to 0$ for certain values of $\alpha(\alpha > 0)$ and $\beta(\beta > 0)$—that is, each firm's demand is highly inelastic—the local service market can sustain a large number of service activities although firms possess some monopolistic power. Lerner's index (24) can then take positive values. In this model, a firm's decisions (q^*, G^*, K^*) are endogenously determined under the given

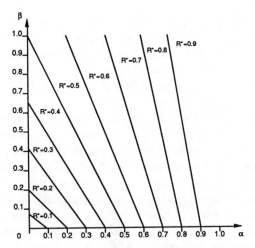

Figure 20–1. Relations among R*, α, and β.

local environment characterized by α, β, and ε. Figures 20–1 and 20–2 summarize the individual firm's optimal R&D policy.

Market Equilibrium with Knowledge Spillover

External Economy in Service Production

The emphasis in this section will be on the spillover effects on market structure of knowledge among firms from the process of knowledge ex-

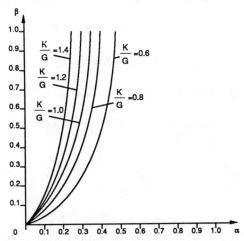

FIgure 20–2. Relations among $\frac{K}{G}$, α, and β.

change across human networks. The level of accessibility to knowledge resources represents a significant factor in service production. The tenet is that knowledge ought to be considered as a public good, endogenously produced by R&D efforts among all firms in the region. Knowledge infrastructure can foster this public good by catalyzing knowledge exchanges among individuals in the region.

Suppose that knowledge stocks are accessible to all firms in the region. Knowledge diffusion occurs by way of exchange processes across local human networks. The psychological and physical characteristics of accessibility to knowledge are important factors determining the levels of availability of knowledge stocks. Suppose that accessibility to knowledge is dependent on the quality of human networks and the knowledge stocks in the region. The total stock of knowledge can be determined from all firms' R&D activities in the region. Let $\bar{G}_i$ and $\bar{K}_i$ denote the amounts of knowledge stocks for product and process R&D, respectively. Suppose that $\bar{G}_i = \Sigma_{j \neq i} G_j$, and $\bar{K}_i = \Sigma_{j \neq i} K_j$. Denote by Z_1 and X_i the accessibility to knowledge stocks for product and process R&D, respectively defined as follows:

$$Z_i = M(G_i, \bar{G}_i; \rho), \text{ and} \tag{30}$$

$$X_i = N(K_i, \bar{K}_i; \rho), \tag{31}$$

where M and N are twice continuosuly differentiable functions and ρ is a parameter representing the quality of human networks in the region.

Market Equilibrium with Knowledge Spillover

The first-order optimality conditions can be summarized as

$$p(Q, v)\{1 - 1/n\epsilon(Q, v)\} = C(K_i, X_i), \tag{32}$$

$$\{(\partial p/\partial G_i) + (\partial p/\partial Z_i)(\partial Z_i/\partial G_i)\}q_i = 1, \tag{33}$$

$$\{(\partial C/\partial K_i) + (\partial C/\partial X_i)(\partial X_i/\partial K_i)\}q_i = -1. \tag{34}$$

Let n^* be the equilibrium number of firms in the local market, and assume symmetry of firms such that:

$$p_i^* = p^*, q_i = q^*, G_i^* = G^*, K_i^* = K^*,$$
$$\bar{G}_i^* = (n^* - 1)G^*, \text{ and } \bar{K}_i^* = (n^* - 1)K^*.$$

Definitions: Let $\alpha^* = (\partial p \partial G)/(p/G)_{q^*, G^*, Z^*}, \beta^* = -(\partial C/\partial K)/(C/K)_{K^*, X^*}$, denote the elasticity of prices and costs with respect to the pertinent knowledge inputs. Further let $\eta^* = (\partial p = \partial Z)/(p/Z)_{q^*, G^*, Z^*}, \xi^* = -(\partial C/\partial X)/(C/$

K)$_{K^*,X^*}$, denote the electicity of prices and costs in terms of accessibility to the pertinent knowledge stocks. Further, $\theta^* = (\partial Z/\partial G)/(Z/G)_{G^*}$, $\tau^* = (\partial X/\partial K)/(X/K)_{K^*}$ is defined to be the elasticity of accessibility to product and process R&D knowledge with respect to the pertinent knowledge inputs, respectively. Then the market equilibrium is characterized by

$$p (1 - 1/n^*\varepsilon^*) = C^* , \tag{35}$$

$$(\alpha^* + \eta^*\theta^*) = n^*G^*/p^*Q^* , \tag{36}$$

$$(\beta^* + \xi^*\tau^*)C^*/p^* = n^*K^*/p^*Q^* , \tag{37}$$

$$(p^* - C^*)Q^* = n^*H^* , \tag{38}$$

where $p^* = p(Q^*,v^*)$, $v^* = h(G^*,Z^*)$, $C^* = C(K^*,X^*)$, $Q^* = n^*q^*$, and $H^* = G^* + K^*$.

From equations (35) and (38), the market structure condition can be derived:

$$\frac{1}{n^*} = \varepsilon R^* , \tag{39}$$

which is identical to equation (20). The optional R&D policy with knowledge spillover effects can then be derived from equations (36), (37), and (41). Taking equation (24) into account,

$$R^* = (\alpha^* + \beta^* + \eta^*\theta^* + \xi^*\tau^*)/(1 + \beta^* + \xi^*\tau^*) . \tag{40}$$

R^* can be properly defined if $1 > \alpha^* + \eta^*\theta^* > 0$. Equations (33) and (34) lead to

$$\frac{K^*}{G^*} = \frac{(\beta^* + \xi^*\tau^*) (1 - \alpha^* - \eta^*\theta^*)}{(\alpha^* + \eta^*\theta^*) (1 + \beta^* - \xi^*\tau^*)} , \tag{41}$$

$$\frac{G^*}{p^*q^*} = \alpha^* + \eta^*\theta^* , \tag{42}$$

$$\frac{K^*}{p^*q^*} = \frac{(\beta^* + \xi^*\tau^*) (1 - \alpha^* - \eta^* \theta^*)}{(1 + \beta^* + \xi^*\tau^*)} . \tag{43}$$

Suppose that $\alpha(>0), \eta(>0)$ are constants for q^*,G^*,Z^*; that $\beta(>0),\xi(>0)$ are also constants for K^*,X^*. Denoting as R_0 and R_1 as the

R&D intensity without and with knowledge spillover effects, the difference between R_0 and R_1 is given by

$$R_1 - R_0 = \frac{(1 + \beta^*)\eta^*\theta^* + (1 - \alpha^*)\xi^*\tau^*}{(1 + \beta^*)(1 + \beta^* + \xi^*\tau^*)} . \quad (44)$$

Because $1 > \alpha > 0$, it is known that $R_1 > R_0$. For a given Q, it is also known that $n_1^* < n_0^*$, where n_1^* and n_0^* are the equilibrium number of firms in the market with and without knowledge spillover effects, respectively. Moreover, if $1 > \alpha^* + \eta^*\theta^* > 0$, from equation (42) is obtained

$$\frac{\partial R}{\partial \theta} = \frac{\eta^*}{(1 + \beta^* + \xi^*\tau^*)} > 0 \quad (45)$$

and

$$\frac{\partial R}{\partial \tau} = \frac{\xi^* (1 - \alpha^* - \eta^*\theta^*)}{(1 + \beta^* + \xi^*\tau^*)^2} > 0 , \quad (46)$$

These conditions imply that if the elasticity of accessibility with respect to knowledge input θ^* and τ^* increases, both the degree of concentration and the R&D intensity will also increase. Improvements to the efficiency of local networks can increase the level of accessibility. The following section investigates the impacts of network improvements on market structure and R&D intensity.

Quality of Networks and Market Structure

First, the properties of the elasticity measures θ^* and τ^* are investigated. From earlier definitions of accessibility (equations (30) and (31)), the pertinent elasticity measures can be described as follows:

$$\theta = (\frac{\partial M}{\partial G_i} + \frac{\partial M}{\partial \bar{G}_i} \frac{\partial \bar{G}_i}{\partial G_i})/(z_i/G_i) , \quad (47)$$

$$\tau = (\frac{\partial N}{\partial K_i} + \frac{\partial N}{\partial \bar{K}_i} \frac{\partial \bar{K}_i}{\partial K_i})/(x_i/K_i) , \quad (48)$$

where $\partial \bar{G}_i/\partial G_i$ and $\partial \bar{K}_i/\partial K_i$ are conjectural R&D intensity variations. Each of these represents firm i's suppositions about how other firms will modify their R&D activities in response to firm i's own level of R&D intensity.

Conjectures are formed by various factors that characterize the psychological, historical, and social conditions of the local market. Specific assumptions about these conjectures lead to specific measures of the elasticity of accessibility. Under the assumptions of symmetrical firms,

$$(\partial \bar{G}_i / \partial G_i)_{G^*} = G^* \partial (n^* - 1) / \partial G_i + (n^* - 1) \partial G^* / \partial G_i,$$
$$(\partial \bar{K}_i / \partial K_i)_{K^*} = K^* \partial (n^* - 1) / \partial K_i + (n^* - 1) \partial K^* / \partial K_i.$$

Suppose that $\partial (n^* - 1) / \partial G_i = 0$ and $\partial (n^* - 1) / \partial K_i = 0$.
Then, $\partial \bar{G}_i / \partial G_i = (n^* - 1) \mu$ and $\partial \bar{K}_i / \partial K_i = (n^* - 1) \nu$,
where $\mu = \partial G^* / \partial G_i$ and $\nu = \partial K^* / \partial K_i$.

In order to closely investigate the properties of the elasticity measures, certain forms of the accessibility measures are specified. Suppose that accessibility measures can be defined in terms of the synergistic effects that are generated by knowledge exchanges between the K-workers of firm i and other firms. This accessibility measures may be defined as follows:

$$Z_i = \gamma_i G_i^{\gamma_2} G_i^{\gamma_3} \text{, and}$$
$$X_i = \delta_1 K_i^{\delta_2} K_i^{\delta_3} \text{,} \tag{49}$$

where γ_k and δ_k $(k = 2,3)$ are parameters representing the quality of networks in the region. Then the sought elasticity measures are given by

$$\theta = \gamma_2 + \gamma_3 \mu \text{, and}$$
$$\tau = \delta_2 + \delta_3 \nu \text{.} \tag{50}$$

The improvement of network technology can contribute to the increase of parameter values γ_k and δ_k $(k = 1,2,3)$. It can be assumed that $\partial \gamma_k / \partial \rho > 0$ and $\partial \delta_k / \partial p > 0$ $(k = 2,3)$, where ρ is the quality of network technology. From equation (42) and the assumption of constant elasticity of α, β, η, and ξ, marginal changes in R&D intensity with respect to the improvement of the quality of network technology in the region can be evaluated:

$$\frac{dR}{d\rho} = \frac{(1 - \alpha - \eta\theta)\xi d\theta/d\rho + (1 + \beta + \xi\tau)\eta d\tau/d\rho}{(1 + \beta + \xi\tau)^2}. \tag{51}$$

It is known from equations (50) that $d\theta/d\rho > 0$ and $d\tau/d\rho > 0$. Therefore $dR/d\rho > 0$. The implication is clear. Any improvement in the network technology stimulates an increase in R&D intensity in the local market.

Conclusion

In this chapter the authors attempted to develop an analytical foundation for probing the relations between market structure and R&D intensity in a local market. The role of R&D activity in service production and its impacts on market structure has also been analyzed. In this framework, market structure and R&D intensity are determined endogenously and depend on certain characteristics of local markets, such as technology, knowledge resources, demand for services, and contact networks. Emphasis here has been on the knowledge spillover effects in service production. The impacts of qualitative improvements to local networks on market structure and R&D intensity have also been discussed. However, it must be stressed that this is not a complete study of interdependencies between structure and R&D intensity in the service sector. The analytical results presented in this chapter require substantiation with the aid of empirical data. The suggested approaches may be most instrumental in stimulating further debates concerning the role of knowledge infrastructure in the revitalization of local service sectors.

References

Batten, D., and B. Johansson. (1987). "Dynamics of Product Substitution." In Å. E. Andersson, D. F. Batten, B. Johansson, and P. Nijkamp (eds.), *Advances in Spatial Theory and Dynamics*. Amsterdam: North-Holland.

Batten, D., K. Kobayashi, and Å. E. Andersson. (1989). "Knowledge Nodes and Networks." In Å. E. Andersson, D. Batten, and C. Karlsson (eds.), *Knowledge and Industrial Organization*. Berlin: Springer-Verlag.

Dasgupata, P., and J. Stiglitz. (1980). "Industrial Structure and the Nature of Innovative Activity." *The Economic Journal*, 90, 266–93.

Lerner, A. P. (1933–1934). "The Concept of Monopoly and the Measurement of Monopoly Power." *The Review of Economic Studies*, 1, Nos. 1–3, 157–75.

Machlup, F. (1980). *Knowledge and Knowledge Production*. Princeton, NJ: Princeton University Press.

Schumpeter, J. (1947). *Capitalism, Socialism and Democracy*. (2d ed.). London: Allen and Unwin.

21

Quality in Services and Quality in Service Organizations
A Model for Quality Assessment

Bo Edvardsson
BengtOve Gustavsson

Introduction

In this chapter a model for quality assessment in service organizations is presented and discussed.

After a background and definition of aims, the second section elaborates the theoretical framework that forms the basis of the analytical model. This model is described in the following section in which the emphasis is placed on a number of key concepts that should be used when examining quality in service organizations. The fourth section considers how the key concepts—analytical tools—may be operationalized, using a contingency approach. The chapter concludes with a brief discussion of the advantages of the model as well as its shortcomings as well as some areas for further research.

Background

In recent years, both practitioners and researchers in the management field have paid special attention to services and service-producing organizations. Management principles that are valid for the production of goods cannot be applied in the same form in service industries. Thus, a new body of knowledge, based on the unique characteristics of services and service organizations, is now being developed (Grönroos (1982); Normann (1984); Albrecht and Zemke (1985); Carlsson (1985); Heskett (1986); Gummesson (1987); Edvardsson and Gummesson (1988)).

Successful service companies, such as Scandinavian Airlines System, Citibank, and Paul Revere Insurance Company, have developed a service-based management system. What is it, then, that is unique about service management as compared to goods management?

The following are some of the important features that have fundamental implications for management:

The production system for services is less easy to control.

It is generally important for the customer to be involved in the service production system, which is normally not the case with goods.

Quality control is often more easy to handle in the production of goods than in service production.

The production of goods is person-machine–oriented and the production of services is person-person–oriented. Social competence, that is, the ability to relate to and interact with the customer on a personal basis, is therefore of the greatest importance.

Services are often produced and consumed at the same time so that it is normally not possible to store services.

It is not as easy for a customer to test a service for quality before purchasing it as it is for him or her to test goods.

During the last few decades greater emphasis has been placed on quality, particularly in manufacturing. This interest in quality can be traced to the United States in the 1920s and to Japan in the 1930s where there was an urgent need to develop the production process for goods. However, it was only in the 1970s that service quality came to be seen as a special field for study for a number of reasons. Hart and Casserly (1985) mention the following:

Consumerism: the consumer-rights movement has led today's consumers to believe they have a right to receive products and services that work.

Media attention: publicity about the high quality of Japanese products has made consumers sensitive to the issue of quality.

Increased advertising and promotional attention: in response to consumers' interest in quality, companies have made an attempt to focus on quality in their marketing efforts.

Continual technical progress: companies have improved their ability to produce high-quality products.

Although many models have been presented, researchers have not come very far in understanding what service quality is or how quality is affected, positively or negatively, by different circumstances. Much remains to be done before quality management and quality development in service organizations can be placed on a solid foundation.

So far, much of the service quality research has focused on the service encounter (the moment of truth) in a dyadic producer-consumer perspective. However, there now seems to be a tendency to go beyond customer contacts and the service encounter to take the support or back-up organization into account (King, 1987a). Thus, terms like internal customer and internal services have been introduced. Service production is now viewed more as a process that includes a number of interactive producer-customer relationships, starting within the service company and terminating with the external customer, a consumer, or another company/organization. A number of microprocesses take place before the end-customer experiences the service.

In these processes company goals and objectives are interpreted by the company's personnel and, in some instances, by customers as well. These interpretations determine how people view their role in the service-production process. Furthermore, they provide a basis for thinking, decision making, and action, that is, for the implementation of company policies and strategies. This illustrates how important it is, when discussing service quality, to make a much clearer distinction between quality in objective terms and quality as a subjective/experienced phenomenon than has been the case so far (Parasuraman, Zeithaml, and Berry 1986).

Moreover, in many of the attempts to define the concept service quality, too much importance has been attached to general criteria (see, for instance, Grönroos (1983); Lehtinen (1983); Berry, Zeithaml, and Parasuraman (1985)). Like Lindqvist (1987) and others, the authors feel that a distinction must be made between general and specific quality dimensions, and, in this chapter, attempt to show that notions of what service quality is are largely culture-relative; that is, they are dependent on both the culture in which the service is produced and the culture that forms the customer/ user's frame of reference. This also means that it is important to develop a less rigid approach to the factors that color the customer/user's views and experiences than previous research on service quality has achieved.

Aim

The aims of this chapter may be defined as follows:

to show that quality in services is best understood by examining quality in service organizations

to develop a process-oriented, holistic, and multidimensional model capable of explaining the conditions in a service-producing organization that affect, either directly or indirectly, the quality of the services produced;

to show the ways in which this management-oriented model may be made operational in order to measure/assess the quality of the service produced.

Theoretical Framework

This section presents the theoretical framework that forms the basis of the analytical model discussed in the following sections. Initially, the authors intend to give a general account of the theoretical premises for the approach and argumentation and then discuss some of the concepts central to understanding how the model is constructed. Interest is concentrated on the concept of service quality but also considered are other closely related aspects, such as how different customers/users experience the consumption of a service and what it is that causes them to experience it in a certain way. This leads into a discussion of the importance of the cultural context for attitudes to service quality. The section concludes with a brief consideration of some epistemological and methodological questions essential to the goal of constructing a model for analyzing the quality aspect of service processes in service organizations.

General Theoretical Premises

The model for analyzing a service company presented in the following chapter is based partly on experiences gained from empirical studies of service-producing companies and organizations (see, for instance, Edvardsson (1986); Edvardsson (1988); Gustavsson and Lindgren (1987)) and partly on a theoretical frame of reference originating in general social and behavioral theory with special emphasis on organizational theory, social psychology theory, and theories of service management.

The following is a presentation of factors taken from these various sources considered relevant to the issue at hand.

The Concept of Service Quality: A Critical Review

Of concern here is service quality in terms of developing a management-oriented model for quality assessment. A comprehensive overview of the various definitions of quality or service quality models is not intended; for a survey of the literature on product quality, see Garvin (1984), and on service quality, King (1987b).

The discussion is based on the authors' perception of the limitations in present research and quality concepts; a process-oriented, holistic, multidimensional approach would be more appropriate. In spite of the difficulties this would entail, such an approach is essential to achieve a deeper understanding of service quality and quality management.

In the literature, a number of definitions of the quality concept have been suggested. Some researchers make a distinction between technical or output quality, on the one hand, and functional or process quality, on the other (see, for instance, Grönroos (1983) and Lehtinen (1983)). Others also distinguish between subjective and objective quality (see Holbrook and Corfman (1985); Dodds and More (1985); Jacoby and Olsson (1985); Zeithaml (1986)). Most of the definitions are based on empirical observations rather than on theoretical discussion.

These definitions have, of course, influenced empirical research and the design of theoretical models. Most of the research focuses on delimited aspects of the complex and intertwined area of service quality. Among marketers, for example, customer evaluation of services dominates; quality is a question of identifying customer requirements and meeting expectations. The basis for evaluating service from the customer's viewpoint is the comparison between expected service and perceived service.

Our overall criticism of service management research at present is that it rests too heavily on delimited and aspect-oriented studies and frames of reference; the unit of analysis is, for instance, restricted to service quality as perceived by the customer. An extremely important area, but, at the same time, it is only a small part of a process that starts within the service company and often includes a number of internal service encounters that are affected by different company conditions. In order to gain an understanding of what service quality is, it is essential to consider the service processes not only in the service encounter but also within the company. In this context, the concepts of internal services and internal customers would seem extremely useful, and high quality in internal service processes is a precondition for high and even external quality as perceived by the customer, often in long-term interactive customer relationships.

Also, the analyses of the customer's perception of service quality is insufficiently deep. In most cases, the only aspect or unit of analysis considered is a comparison between the service expected and that perceived by *end customers*; it is assumed that expectations are only influenced by the customer's earlier experiences of the service in question. No consideration is given to the various references the customer might have for judging quality in general or in certain more specific categories of service. The knowledge and theories on consumer perception developed in social psychology have a contribution to make to the understanding of how the customer perceives quality. Therefore, this body of knowledge is included in this model for quality assessment.

In most instances, more or less general quality determinants have been presented (see, for example, Berry, Zeithaml, and Parasuraman (1985) and Grönroos (1982); an exception is Lindqvist (1987), who makes a distinction between general and specific quality determinants. It is insufficient when dealing with service quality from a management perspective to merely establish general quality determinants that would be valid for various kinds of services and in various situations. Instead, a situation-specific approach is required, in which general or, rather, basic quality determinants would be of great value in the attempt to understand the situation-specific quality factors.

A fourth criticism has to do with the neglect of the cost and price aspects of service quality (see, for instance, Grönroos (1982); Parasuraman, Zeithaml, and Berry (1985); Swartz and Brown (1987)). The relationship between cost and errors in both internal and external service production should be taken into account when assessing quality. The authors do not share Crosby's (1979) opinion that quality is always free but agree with him when he says that nonquality or quality errors are always associated with costs. Mistakes in internal services do not always affect the end-customer but may be hard to detect and much time and effort may be required to solve the internal problems created. Internal nonquality will, however, often lead to quality problems for the customer, that is, to low external service quality. It can be costly to deal with critical incidents and satisfy or compensate the customer. Poor service quality may lead to weakened or even broken customer relationships and have a negative effect on the company's image. Thus, a service-production process with few or no mistakes will produce favorable results, not only from the quality viewpoint but also from a cost and profitability angle. It should also be emphasized that raising the level of quality by offering auxiliary or back-up services might be a profitable investment. This does, of course, entail higher costs but may help to strengthen customer loyalty, attract new customers, raise the level of service quality as perceived by the customer, and improve profitability, as a result. Cost aspects should then be taken into account when analyzing service quality from a management perspective and should be examined in much greater detail than is often the case.

When judging quality—perceived service in relation to expected service—the price of the service is too often ignored. This is completely unrealistic and underlines the fact that quality is multidimensional and must be analyzed in a given context.

Despite the shortcomings of present research, some useful work is being done, thus reflecting the current interest in service quality. The gap-analysis approach developed by Parasuraman, Zeithaml, and Berry (1985) is perhaps the most useful for obtaining a wider understanding or quality in service processes. It takes into account not only the gap (or potential gap) between the customer's expectations and his or her perception of a services, but also gaps in service processes within the service-producing process. A more dialectic relationship between the various components/dimensions in a service-producing organization exists.

The Perception of Quality in a Sociocultural Context

In most attempts to define service quality, some discussion occurs on how the customer/user perceives/experiences the service provided. It seems, however, that this aspect of quality is dealt with in a superficial manner in most cases. Grönroos, Gummesson, and Berry, for instance, assume that the customer/user's perception is determined by his or her expectations before the service is provided and how well the service actually meets these expectations. Other authors comment on the factors influencing such expectations; Parasuraman, Zeithaml, and Berry (1985) name word-of-mouth communication, personal needs, and past experience as such factors.

However, much can be gained by using the theories and concepts of social psychology to describe this situation; it is especially important to widen the frame of reference determining the customer/user's expectations by introducing variables relating him or her to a concrete cultural and sociomaterial structure. Expectations are not formed in a vacuum but are the direct result of previous experiences in similar situations and of other frames of reference with which all individuals are provided by their social affiliation, and so forth.

One way of achieving a wider frame of reference is to use the concept of aspiration level. The following simple model attempts to show how an individual's level of aspiration is formed in relation to various concrete phenomena. At the most fundamental level is a need structure common to all individuals (see, for instance, Maslow (1943). However, it may be noted that, in a given concrete situation, these needs always exist in relation to one or more goals. The goal is to satisfy the need but for the concept to be useful, it must be formulated in concrete terms. What is it, then, that leads the individual to choose one of a series of goals? Many factors are at work but, in the final analysis, the choice of goal is determined by the opportunities provided by the society in which the individual lives, by its structure and culture. However, in this process a more direct influence is exerted on the individual by his or her reference groups. The groups one strives to emulate are important both for the type of goal one strives to attain and for the level at which this goal should be set. A further aspect of this influence is that an individual's reference groups play a large part in determining the importance or value of attaining different goals.

Naturally, an individual's previous experience in similar situations is of major importance, especially when it comes to his or her assessment of the chances of attaining the goal. This includes relating his or her aspirations to his or her own material possibilities, which means that his or her aspirations are adapted to current economic realities and are not just unrealistic wishes.

In conclusion, then, it may be said that an individual's social environment—society and reference groups—determines the value, and his or her experience determines his or her perception of the possibilities. The result is that the individual establishes a certain level of aspiration in relation to different concrete objects and situations (see figure 21–1).

As regards quality in service production, both in society as a whole and in specific groups within different societies, norms define good quality. Therefore, it is vitally important for the individual service producer to offer a service that fulfills the quality norms the individual customer/user brings to the service encounter.

Meanwhile, these different sets of norms interact at the society level. The internal norms for good quality found within the service-producing organization have developed within the same society in approximately the same manner as for each individual (see Berger and Luckman 1967). Reference groups at the individual level may be said to be equivalent to various professional and trade organizations at the organization level, providing points of reference for the service-producing organization. Certain implicit assumptions regarding the significance of these internally oriented norms are to be found in, for instance, Brown and Morley (1986) and Swartz and Brown (1987), but this aspect must be highlighted much more boldly. Figure 21–2 illustrates this argument.

In a more long-term perspective numerous opportunities for mutual influence and feedback between the various components/levels exist. However, they are not considered here.

Service Quality and Organizational Culture

In the last section cultural aspects of service quality were discussed. The role played by the cultural values both of society in general and of the reference groups to which the customer relates were considered. The importance of society and industry-specific cultures for determining quality in a given context were stressed. The point is that quality analysis must take

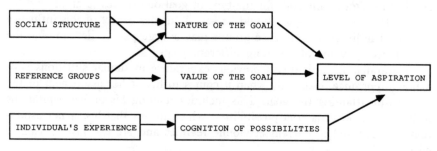

Figure 21–1. Determinants for level of aspiration.

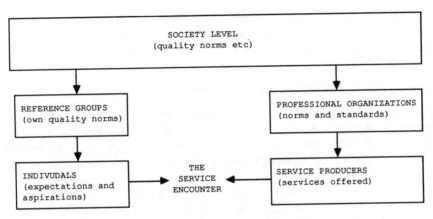

Figure 21-2. Quality in sociocultural context.

into account not only the customer's cultural context but also that in which the service organization operates.

Schein (1987) discusses the concept *organizational culture* and criticizes the definitions presented by other authors, such as Goffman (1967): "observed behavioral regularities when people interact, such as the language used and the rituals around defence and demeanor"; Deal and Kennedy (1982): "the dominant values espoused by an organization, such as product quality or price leadership"; and Pascale and Athos (1981): "the philosophy that guides an organization's policy toward employees and/or customers." Schein argues that although these definitions do reflect the organization's culture, "none of them is the essence of culture." He continues: "I will argue that the term *culture* should be reserved for the deeper level of basic assumptions and beliefs that are shared by members of an organization, that operate unconsciously and that define in a basic *taken-for-granted* fashion an organization's view of itself and its environment" (p.6). Our view of organizational culture is in accord with that put forward by Schein.

The culture and value structure of target customer groups must be taken into consideration when the service company develops its managerial system. Quality development should be based on a quality-oriented organizational culture. Quality culture is a powerful tool in service production, especially when it comes to high-contact/face-to-face services. This view is consistent with that propagated by Riddle (1986), who argues that customer satisfaction demands that service delivery systems be modified to fit the key values of the culture and the customer. The important point is that company culture and customer culture match and that the quality culture of the service company is not rigid but *embodies* the ability to adapt to changes in customer culture and values.

The quality of soft technology, that is, the skill training provided for employees, is one way to build and develop an organizational quality culture; others are recruitment policy and style of leadership.

Epistemological and Methodological Premises

As stated, the aim is to develop a model for the analysis of quality in service-producing organizations on the basis of a general theoretical frame of reference. The model, as pointed out, has its origin partly in various empirical studies of service-producing companies and organizations and partly in a critical analysis of existing theories on service quality.

What can be achieved is a theoretically based model with a number of well-defined concepts systematically organized in relation to one another. The model does not claim to provide a general, all-embracing definition of service quality but given its structure, it should be possible to use it as a general analytical model for the discussion and evaluation, in qualitative terms, of service production in each specific case (company/organization).

This belief rests on the authors' theoretically based view of service quality and on a methodological approach that requires the final operationalization of the model be carried out in a concrete situation, that is, on an actual case. This concurs, then, with the methodological tradition emphasizing understanding on the basis of theoretical concepts and models generated from the empirical data being analyzed (see, for instance, Glaser and Strauss (1967); Lindholm (1979); Eneroth (1984)).

In the following sections, therefore, the model is presented in two forms: first as a theoretical model with concepts generally adaptable to various situations, and second in the form of a discussion of possible operationalizations in various types of service companies/organizations. In the latter context, a "toolbox" approach is used, that is, a discussion of various techniques available in different situations and how they can be used. As previously noted, however, it is not possible at this level to work in general terms; the model must be operationalized in close contact and cooperation with the service-producing organization being studied.

A Theoretical Model for the Analysis of Quality in Service Organizations

Before presenting a detailed model for the analysis of service quality, several general premises are presented for argumentation, most based on the discussion in the second section. First, a summary of the authors' view of service quality and then a number of criteria/restrictions resulting from this view are considered. Thereafter, the model is outlined and its various components examined.

General Premises

In summarizing the previous section, the authors present their definition of service quality, which takes into consideration all various points raised. Service quality should be defined as the sum of the demands placed on a service in order that it may meet the expectations and aspirations of society in general, of specific groups, and of individuals. In certain contexts, the concept may be given a more objective or intersubjective import, and in others, it will have a more individual/subjective tenor. At the same time, a dialectic relationship will always exist between objective and subjective dimensions.

This, then, is the general and theoretical import of the concept, but for it to be operationally applicable, it is necessary for it to be placed in (1) a sociocultural context, that is, related to a concrete societal and cultural reality—service quality differs from one culture to another, (2) an organizational context, that is, related to the specific organizational/corporate culture within which the service is produced; and (3) an individual context, that is, related to the specific customer/users who will consume the service in question.

Based on this definition, a number of more concrete criteria/restrictions that will function as premises for the construction of the analytical model can be established. The following would seem to be valid:

1. An analysis of quality in a service company must be based on a holistic view of the company and its operational logic.
2. The analysis must be multidimensional, for instance, not merely in terms of customer perception.
3. The model must be operationalized in the form of a dialogue with representatives of the company being analyzed—each service company is unique.
4. The range and depth of the analysis ultimately determines the tools and technique to be used.

The Main Features of the Model

The model is based on two of the central dimensions in an organization. First is the disparity that always exists between the organization as such and the actors/individuals within the organization:

formal ....individual
objective   subjective

Second is the basic disparity present in all social systems between idea and action, or, as it is formulated in the model, between goal and outcome:

goal .... outcome

At the same time, this dimension has a scale of *permanency*; that is, the conditions on the left of the continuum may be said to be the most permanent.

The model's main fields of analysis are obtained by allowing the two dimensions to intersect at right angles, as shown in figure 21–3.

The four fields of analysis thus formed may be described as follows:

1. *Formal goals:* In this field the emphasis is on an examination of the goals formulated at a formal/official level within the organization.

2. *Subjective goals:* Here the analysis concentrates on reflecting how the various actors within the organization perceive/experience the organization's goals.

3. *Formal outcome:* The analysis in this field is aimed at gaining insight into the organization's activities as revealed by various formal documents, that is, documents that, at a formal level, indicate the results of decisions reached, measures taken, and soon.

4. *Subjective outcome:* Here the focus is on the relationship between the

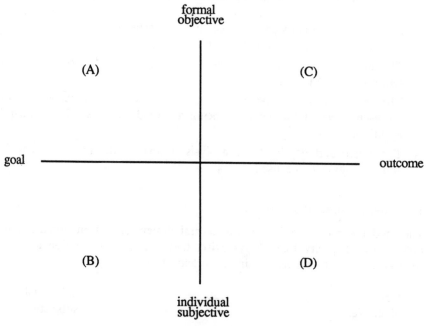

Figure 21–3. Main fields of analysis.

organization and its customers/users, that is, on analysing how the latter experience/perceive the quality of the service offered/delivered.

Auxiliary Concepts Used in the Analysis

In each of the fields, analysis can be based on a set of central concepts that attempt to capture the essential nature of the service-producing company/ organization. Normann's (1984) model of a service-management system with a number of main components has influenced this analysis. After some reworking, this provided a set of useful auxiliary concepts for analyses:

1. Market segment/target group: the specific customer/user group for whom the whole service system has been developed.

2. The service concept: the offer made to the customer/user. This usually consists of complex combinations of values, some more concrete while others lie on the psychological or emotional plane. Some are of greater importance and may be designated as the core service; others are more peripheral in character.

3. The production system: in a service company, this also includes the system for conveying the service to the customer/user. This system includes such components as personnel, customers, and the physical environment/technology.

4. Image and profiling: the image of the company/organization held by the individuals and groups involved, and measures the organization has taken to alter its image.

5. Culture context: the often tacit assumptions within the company/ organization that form the environment in which all the decisions controlling the individual's actions within the organization are taken. This applies to the cultural context of the customers as well.

Consistency Analysis

An important feature of the entire model is the comprehensive analysis carried out when each of the four fields has been considered. This analysis is called a consistency analysis, implying that the most significant step here is to discover whether any inconsistencies exist within and between the fields of analysis examined. In other words, the differences between the various pictures one gets of the service company's activities from an analysis of the four fields indicate problem areas that, in one way or another, may have a negative effect on service quality. This type of analysis may, then, be termed problem-identification, that is, its main function is to identify areas within the company/organization that ought to be the object of particular interest or of special measures if one wishes to improve the quality of service production.

At the same time, analyzing the patterns that emerge from each of the four fields is important. Even these can be of value for understanding different forms of imbalance in the system/organization.

The Theoretical Model: A Summary

This presentation may be summarized as follows:

1. The analytical model is based on an approach to service quality that emphasizes the cultural, multidimensional, and dialectic aspects of the concept.

2. The model is constructed on two main dimensions (goal—outcome; formal/objective—individual/subjective), thus providing four fields of analysis for the study or a company/organization.

3. A number of auxiliary concepts is indicated for each field, which may be of use in forming a picture of the organization and its service production.

4. The various concepts must be operationalized in direct connection with the activities to be analyzed—each service company is unique, and service quality in a concrete sense is specific to each individual case.

5. By means of what the authors term consistency analysis, the analysis leads to identification of problem areas, which should be dealt with if service quality is to be improved.

Possible Ways of Operationalizing the Model

This section begins with a description of the different steps to be taken when using the model. In the second section, the analytical concepts used in the model are operationalized. This is followed by a presentation of some useful techniques for collecting data, and, in the final section, an outline of how the data may be analyzed and the outcome/results communicated.

Routines

When using this model for analyzing the quality aspect of a service organization, the following steps are necessary:

1. discussions with company representatives to determine the purpose and focus of the assessment

2. the operationalization of the analytical concepts used. The operationalizations suggested in the next section form a basis for discussions with representatives of the organization
3. the choice of suitable data collection technique
4. the assessment, using a company-adjusted/tailored model
5. the analysis of the data, in cooperation with organization representatives
6. feedback to company representatives during the assessment and the communication of the results

The Operationalization of Auxiliary Concepts

This section is concerned with possible operationalizations of the five analytical concepts presented in the model.

Market Segment/Target Group. Here it is often useful to distinguish between primary and secondary customer/user groups, and, in the primary group, to consider key customers individually. A division into consumers and businesses is also helpful (see figure 21–4).

The analysis can be extended to include previous and/or potential customers, which makes a study of change in the customer/user groups possible.

The Service Concept. Of concern here is the description of the concept(s) the company in question wishes to offer to customers, in particular those offered to primary customers. The service offered is described in detail, as is the correlation between the service concept and the customer needs to be satisfied. In this context, it may be meaningful to make a distinction, on the one hand, between core service and peripheral service, and, on the other, between primary and secondary customer needs (see, for instance, Edvardsson (1986)). The hypothetical model sketched in figure 21–5 might be useful in some cases.

Peripheral services in connection with air travel might include, for

	Consumers	Businesses
Primary Customers		
Secondary Customers		

Figure 21–4. Possible consumer/user groups.

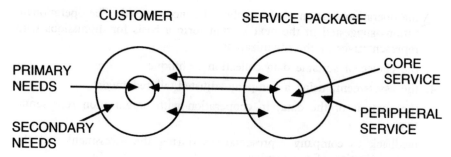

Figure 21–5. Customer needs and service offerings.

example, ground transport to and from the airport, hotel reservations, the availability of telefax apparatus at the airport. These would add to the attractiveness of the core service, the flight. The following situation illustrates secondary customer needs: a person traveling from one place to another might find it necessary to be accessible by telephone, telefax, or other means. A suitably designed peripheral service would meet these so-called secondary needs, which arise when the primary need is to be satisfied.

Service Production System. In this third concept, the following components can be usefully identified:

personnel: for instance, education, experience, and motivation

accessibility: for instance, the location of premises, office hours, telephone, telefax

technolgy: for instance, equipment, technical aids, various systems utilized in service production such as the information system, payments system, decision procedure, and control system

customers: for instance, the extent to which customers participate in the production of the service, interaction customer—customer, customer—personnel and customer—technical aids, and systems the service company use

organizational structure: for instance, the formal organization, the distribution of responsibility and authority, the system of rewards

Image and Profiling. Image is the view customers actually hold of the service company and individual services. Profile, on the other hand, is the view or attitude the company management wants the market and, in the first place, the customers to have of the company and its services, its distinctive character in relation to competitors. *Profiling* is the term used for the various measures and steps that the company takes to alter/improve its image.

Cultural Context. Cultural context is the final analytical concept. Within the service company, it refers to the basic attitudes or values that distinguish the organization. They may have been formally decided on but are often part of the informal organization without being documented. The organizational culture may often be usefully described with the aid of the following components:

basic beliefs and norms

leadership and decision-making style

cultural codes such as dress and behavior requirements

These components may also be used to analyze the cultural context of the customers. An important additional aspect is the understanding of multicultural interaction.

Techniques for Collecting Data

The third section showed that the analytical model consisted of four different fields that form the areas in which the concrete empirical analysis will be carried out. This section outlines various possible techniques for collecting data in these fields.

It is possible to distinguish five major techniques; the fifth—experimental design—is really a combination of the others, but used in a different way.

Content Analyses. Content analysis is a method for analyzing the various official documents available, particularly those referring to the service company being studied. These documents include articles of association, action programs, strategic plans, annual reports, instructions, and manuals. Different forms of content analysis of this type of document provide much valuable information, especially about the formal/objective level within the organization.

When making content analyses, one should concentrate primarily on qualitative rather than strictly quantitative methods.

Available Data. *Available data* is the term used to refer to the various empirical studies of the organization in question and of employees and customers originally carried out for purposes other than the present analysis of service quality. For example, data is collected on a continuous basis for the company's accounting system. Much of this information contains details of value for the analysis of service quality. The main use of these techniques is to collect material for the analysis of *formal outcome*.

Survey Techniques. The term *survey technique* is here used to cover various types of interviews, polls and questionnaires. It seems this form of data collection has so far played a dominant role in empirical studies of service quality. By no means are these techniques rejected—even in this model they remain one of the most important means of collecting data—but their limitations indicate the need to complement them with other techniques. It is primarily the individual/subjective dimension of service quality that is measured by survey techniques, but even in the case of the formal/objective level they can sometimes be useful for obtaining information from key individuals who represent this level in the organization/company.

Observational Techniques. This term is used to describe all the methods of collecting data in which researchers obtain information about the object inquiry by personal observation of developments in the particular social system. This can be achieved by direct participation, or by passive or even hidden participation. This type of technique will not be particularly common in analyses of service quality, but situations may arise where the method might be preferable, for example, if one suspects that survey techniques would give consistently distorted data as a result of uncontrollable interview effects, and so on.

One technique used in recent years to study service companies is the so-called critical incident technique. Nyquist, Bitner, and Booms (1985) describe it as an indirect observational technique in which in-depth interviews with the relevant parties (customers and employees) are used to gain an understanding of effective and ineffective behavior in a given situation. This form of indirect observation may be extremely useful at certain stages in the analysis proposed here.

Experimental Design. As previously indicated, this is not really another type of data collection technique; in an experimental design it is possible to make use of several of the aforementioned techniques. Nevertheless, this approach should be distinguished from the other techniques in order to point to the possibility of using an experimental construct to carry out, for example, an advance test on a service that a company plans to launch on the market.

Compilation, Analysis, and Communication of Results

As regards compilation and analysis, it is difficult to provide general instructions about methods and techniques. The compilation of the data depends on the choice of collection technique of course.

However, it may be stated as a general rule that the data should be compiled in such a way as to enable a comparison of the results of the variables in each of the four fields. This consistency of analysis is important, that is, of finding out whether the different variables get the same values in the different dimensions represented by the fields of analysis.

From a technical viewpoint, this comparison may be difficult to achieve because the data from the various fields may differ considerably in character. Therefore, as a first step in the analysis, an effort should be made to transform the data into comparable categories. This will no doubt have negative effects on reliability and validity, but it must be done all the same.

A further general point is that the analysis should be primarily geared to identifying problems, that is, searching for inconsistencies in and between fields in order to be able to establish the areas/factors in the company in which there is imbalance. Inconsistencies between fields suggest problems within the organization that should be attended to. Consistency between the fields is not the same as high quality, yet such consistency is a precondition for high quality. In the same way, inconsistencies reduce the likelihood of high service quality in an organization.

The areas that reveal inconsistencies can then be studied in greater detail both by making closer analyses of the data and by collecting further data. In this respect, the model may be said to be iterative, that is, a number of data collections and analyses may be necessary before an acceptable level of understanding is attained.

Turning to the communication of the results of the analysis, the main aim should be to create greater understanding. The results should be communicated in such a way that the commissioning organization and others whom the latter considers to be important are able to participate actively in the process of interpretation and comprehension. One way of achieving this is to communicate the results in the form of a dialogue in which the company concerned participates directly in the later stages of analysis and interpretation.

One question that arises here is whether result communication should be formulated as an ongoing feedback process. This is not always necessary but it has advantages. Continual feedback may be preferable if the aim of the quality analysis is to bring about long-term, permanent changes in service production. There are, however, situations in which continual feedback should be avoided, for instance when evaluating a specific program, new working method, or specific part of a company's operations. Drawing attention to certain preliminary results during the process of evaluation may make it difficult to reach a decision at a later stage on those aspects the evaluation originally concerned.

Conclusion

The model developed in this chapter is tentative in that it has not, as yet, been tested to any significant degree. It has, however, been applied in two empirical studies, where it proved useful both as a frame of reference for data collection and as a tool for detecting inconsistencies and quality problems.

The development of the model is part of an ongoing research process focusing on quality in service production. The next phase is to test the model in empirical studies/assessments of different service organizations and in different cultural contexts. The authors also want to elaborate the cultural aspects and take the cultural context of the customer more into account than has been the case so far. Another goal is to make the model more dynamic and process-oriented as regards the consistency analysis.

References

Albrecht, A., and R. Zemke. (1985). *Service America! Doing Business in the New Economy.* Homewood, IL: Dow-Jones Irwin.

Berger, P. L., T. Luckman. (1967). *The Social Construction of Reality.* New York: Anchor Books.

Berry, L. L., V. Zeithaml, and A. Parasuraman. (1985). "Quality Counts in Services Too." *Business Horizons,* May/June.

Brown, S. W., and A. P. Morley. (1986). *Marketing Strategies for Physicians—A Guide to Practice Growth.* Oradell, NJ: Medical Economics Books.

Brown, S. W., and T. A. Swartz. (1987). *A Dyadic Evaluation of the Professional Services Encounter.* Tempe: First Interstate Center for Services Marketing, Arizona State University, Working Paper No. 8.

Carlsson, J. (1985). *Riv pyramiderna.* Stockholm: Bonnier.

Crosby, P. (1979). *Quality is Free.* New York: McGraw-Hill.

Deal, T. E., and A. A. Kennedy. (1982). *Corporate Cultures.* MA. Addison-Wesley.

Dodds, W. B., and K. B. More. (1985). "The Effects of Brand and Price Information on Subjective Product Evaluations." In E. Hirschman and M. Holbrook (ed.), *Advances in Consumer Research, Vol. 12.* Provo: Association for Consumer Research.

Edvardsson, B. (1986). *Tjäster som konkurrensmedel i industriell marknadsfouming.* Karlstad: Service Research Centre, University of Karlstad, Research Report 86:1.

———. (1988). "Service Quality in Customer Relationships—A Study of Critical Incidents in Mechanical Engineering Companies." *The Service Industries Journal.* Vol. 8, No. 4.

Edvardsson, B., and E. Gummesson. (eds.). (1988). *Management i tjänstesamhället.* Lund: Liber.

Eneroth, B. (1984). *Hur mäter man "vackert."* Stockholm: Akademilitteratur.

Garvin, D. (1984). "What Does 'Product Quality' Really Mean?" *Sloan Management Review,* Autumn.

Glaser, B., and A. Strauss. (1967). *The Discovery of Grounded Theory: Strategies for Qualitative Research.* Chicago: Aldine.

Goffman, E. (1967). *Interaction Ritual.* New York: Aldine.

Grönroos, C. (1982). *Strategic Management and Marketing in the Service Sector.* Helsingfors: Swedish Commercial Institute for Advanced Studies, Research Report No. 8.

————. (1983). *Marknadsföring i tjänsteföretag.* Lund: Liber.

Gummesson, E. (1987). *Quality—The Ericsson Approach.* Stockholm: Ericsson.

Gustavsson, B. O. and A. M. Lindgren. (1987). *Från motion till friskvård.* Karlstad: Service Research Centre, University of Karlstad, Research Report 87:2.

Hart, C., and G. D. Casserly. (1985). "Quality: A Brand-new, Time-tested Strategy." *The Cornell H.R.A. Quarterly,* November.

Heskett, J. L. (1986). *Managing in the New Service Economy.* Boston: Harvard Business School Press.

Holbrook, M. B., and K. P. Corfman. (1985). "Quality and Value in the Consumption Experience: Phaedrus Rides Again." In J. Jacoby and J. Olsson (eds.), *Perceived Quality.* Lexington, MA: Lexington Books.

Jacoby, J., and J. Olsson (eds.). (1985). *Perceived Quality.* Lexington, MA: Lexington Books.

King, C. A. (1987a). "A Framework for a Service Quality Assurance System." *Quality Progress,* September.

————. (1987b). *Service Quality—Where Are We Now?* Paper presented at the World Hospitality Congress Ill, Boston.

Lehtinen, J. (1983). "Customer Oriented Service System." Service Management Institute: Helsingfors, unpublished working paper.

Lindholm, S. (1979). *Vetenskap, verklighet och paradigm.* Stockholm: Almqvist & Wiksell.

Lindqvist, J-L. (1987). *Kvalitet och tjänstekonsumtion.* Paper presented at the Third Nordic Meeting for Service Management, Karlstad.

Maslow, A. H. (1943). "A Theory of Human Motivation." *Psychology Review,* Vol. 50.

Normann, R. (1984). *Service Management.* London: Wiley.

Nyquist, J. D., M. J. Bitner, B. H. Booms. (1985). "Identifying Communication Difficulties in the Service Encounter: A Critical Incident Approach" In J. A. Czepiel, M. R. Solomon, and C. F. Surprenant (eds.), *The Service Encounter—Managing Employee/Customer Interaction in Service Business.* Lexington, MA: Lexington Books.

Parasuraman, A., V. Zeithaml, L. L. Berry. (1985). "A Conceptual Model of Service Quality and Its Implications for Future Research." *Journal of Marketing,* Vol. 49 (Fall).

————. (1986). *SERVQUAL: A Multiple-Item Scale for Measuring Customer Perceptions of Service Quality.* Cambridge: Marketing Science Institute, Report No. 86–108.

Pascale, R. T., and A. G. Athos. (1981). *The Art of Japanese Management.* New York: Simon & Schuster.

Riddle, D. I. (1986). *Innovative Management of the Customer-Employee Relationship in International Service Firms.* Proceedings of the annual meeting of the Decision Sciences Institute, Honolulu.

340 • *Service Quality*

Schein, E. H. (1987). *Organizational Culture and Leadership*. San Francisco: Jossey-Bass.

Swartz, T. A., and S. W. Brown. (1987). *Consumer and Provider Expectations, and Experiences in Evaluating Professional Service Quality*. Tempe: First Interstate Center for Services Marketing, Arizona State University, Working Paper No. 4.

Zeithaml. V. (1986). *Defining and Relating Price, Perceived Quality, and Perceived Value*. Durham, NC: Duke University, working Paper.

Index

List of Contributors

Gary Akehurst, Department of Hospitality Management, Dorset Institute, Poole, Dorset, United Kingdom.

Franklin Allen, The Wharton School, University of Pennsylvania, Philadelphia, United States.

Åke E. Andersson, Institute for Futurological Studies, Stockholm, Sweden.

David F. Batten, Department of Economics, Umeå University, Sweden.

Leonard L. Berry, Center for Retailing Studies, College of Business Administration, Texas A&M University, College Station, United States.

Mary Jo Bitner, First Interstate Center for Services Marketing, Department of Marketing, Arizona State University, Tempe, United States.

Lennart Blomquist, Service Research Center, University of Karlstad, Sweden.

David E. Bowen, Business Programs, Arizona State University-West Campus, Tempe, United States.

Stephen W. Brown, First Interstate Center for Services Marketing, Department of Marketing, Arizona State University, Tempe, United States.

Richard B. Chase, School of Business Administration, Center for Operations Management, Education, and Research, University of Southern California, Los Angeles, United States.

David A. Collier, Faculty of Management Sciences, College of Business, The Ohio State University, Columbus, United States.

Lawrence A. Crosby, First Interstate Center for Services Marketing, Department of Marketing, Arizona State University, Tempe, United States.

Alan Dale, Institute of Organization and Social Studies, Brunel University, Uxbridge, United Kingdom.

Bo Edvardsson, Service Research Center, University of Karlstad, Sweden.

Gerald R. Faulhaber, The Wharton School, University of Pennsylvania, Philadelphia, United States.

Jean-Paul Flipo, Groupe Ecole Supérieure de Commerce, Lyon, France.

William R. George, Department of Marketing, Villanova University, Villanova, Pennsylvania, United States.

Orio Giarini, Graduate Institute of European Studies, Geneva, Switzerland.

Barbara E. Gibson, Richmond Metropolitan Blood Bank, Richmond, Virginia, United States.

Evert Gummesson, Service Research Center, University of Karlstad, Sweden.

BengtOve Gustavsson, Service Research Center, University of Karlstad, Sweden.

Friedhart Hegner, Institute for Social Planning and Management, Berlin, Federal Republic of Germany.

Benny Hjern, Service Research Center, University of Karlstad, Sweden.

Kiyoshi Kobayashi, Department of Social Systems Engineering, Tottori, University, Tottori, Japan.

Robert Johnston, Service Operations Management, University of Warwick, Coventry, United Kingdom.

Jarmo Lehtinen, SMG Enterprises, Helsinki, Finland.

David Lyth, Industrial Engineering Department, Western Michigan University, Kalamazoo, United States.

Casten von Otter, Swedish Center for Working Life, Stockholm, Sweden.

A. Parasuraman, Department of Marketing, Texas A&M University, College Station, United States.

Richard B. Saltmann, University of Massachusetts, Amherst, United States.

Daniel Schechter, Department of Psychology, University of Maryland, College Park, United States.

Benjamin Schneider, Department of Psychology, University of Maryland, College Park, United States.

Martin Senior, Department of Hospitality Management, Dorset Institute, Poole, Dorset, United Kingdom.

Teresa A. Swartz, First Interstate Center for Services Marketing, Department of Marketing, Arizona State University, Tempe, United States.

Stuart Wooler, London School of Economics, London, United Kingdom.

Valarie A. Zeithaml, Fuqua School of Business, Duke University, Durham, North Carolina, United States.

About the Editors

Stephen W. Brown, Ph.D., is Professor of Marketing and Executive Director of the First Interstate Center for Services Marketing at Arizona State University. He is also a recent president of the American Marketing Association. His capabilities have been recognized with various prestigious national and university awards, and he is the co-author of six books and over one hundred articles on various marketing topics. Dr. Brown serves as an adviser and board member for a number of respected firms in services industries/professions. His current research interests lie in the areas of service quality, internal marketing exchange, professional services, and medical marketing.

Evert Gummesson is professor of service management at the Service Research Center—CTF, University of Karlstad, Sweden, and is also on the faculties of the Universities of Stockholm and Gothenburg, Sweden, and the Swedish School of Economics and Business Administration, Helsinki, Finland. Dr. Gummesson is a senior consultant and director of Cicero, a major Scandinavian management consulting firm. His consultancy is directed toward corporate and marketing strategy and quality management. He is the author of nine books on marketing, corporate strategy, quality management, and scientific methodology, among them the first book on services marketing to be published in Scandinavia.

Bo Edvardsson holds a Ph.D. in business management from Uppsala University, Sweden, and is director of the Service Research Center (CTF) at the University of Karlstad, Sweden. He has published a number of research reports and two books. His current research interests lie in the field of quality in services with the emphasis on assessment problems.

BengtOve Gustavsson holds a Ph.D. in sociology from Gothenburg University, Sweden, and is Vice-President and Director of Research at the University of Karlstad. He has published a number of research reports and other works and has co-edited a major international publication. His current research interests concern the quality of services, in particular evaluation and assessment.